Physics Alive

Peter Warren

Co-ordinator of Science
Acton High School

John Murray

©Peter Warren 1982
Reprinted 1982, 1985, 1988

All rights reserved. No part of this publication may be
reproduced, stored in a retrieval system, or transmitted,
in any form or by any means, electronic, mechanical,
photocopying, recording or otherwise, without the prior
permission of John Murray (Publishers) Ltd,
50 Albemarle Street, London W1X 4BD

Set in Great Britain by The Yale Press Limited

Printed and Bound by
Colorcraft Ltd., Hong Kong.

British Library Cataloguing in Publication Data

Warren, Peter
Physics Alive
1. Physics
I. Title
530   QC23

ISBN 0-7195-3782-7

Preface

This book is designed for use throughout a two or three year course leading to a limited grade GCSE examination in physics.

Traditionally, physics courses have been designed for the future specialist. Today, increasing numbers study the subject either because it forms a useful basis for future occupations, or simply to gain a wider understanding of the natural and man-made environment. For these reasons, material is designed to be both active and attractive to use. Each new idea is introduced carefully, words amplified by illustrations, and investigated by simple experiments. Possible outcomes of observations are included for those who are not able to do, or observe, all the experimental work. Active involvement with equipment and learning from first-hand experience are, however, implicit in the presentation. Summaries of important findings appear at the bottom of almost every page, identifying a body of knowledge for examination purposes.

Large numbers of short structured questions are included. Each can be answered in a few words and serves to check understanding. At intervals there are further banks of examination-type questions covering a range of topics.

The order of presentation represents one logical route through the material. However the breakdown of topics will permit a wide variety of different teaching routes. The text is concise and self-contained, so it can be used effectively for revision. Examination and revision hints are included to help students in organizing and consolidating the essential information.

Many find language a barrier to understanding and the level of language used here has been most carefully monitored. Diagrams, photographs and cartoons complement the words, conveying their information in a more immediate way. The pictures also show physics as a human – and so humorous – involvement with the (sometimes) puzzling and unexpected. The book aims to help its users enjoy grappling with scientific ideas, so that the physics they learn will stay alive as part of their experience.

I am very grateful to Pat Lowry for his advice on language usage and other 'readability' factors. I must also thank the colleagues and pupils who have been a great influence in the preparation of this book.

Peter Warren

Contents

Section	Chapter		Page
		Hints on studying and revision	1
Energy	1	Energy	4
Light energy	2	Light and shadows	12
	3	Pinhole camera	14
	4	Mirror images	16
	5	Curved mirrors	19
	6	Refraction of light	22
	7	The image formed by a lens	27
	8	Lenses and rays	29
	9	Optical instruments	33
	10	Colour	43
Wave and sound energy	11	Waves	50
	12	Vibrations we can hear	54
	13	Sound waves	56
	14	Resonance	62
Heat energy	15	Heat at work	66
	16	Heat and change of state	71
	17	Boiling and freezing	76
	18	The expansion of solids	83
	19	Expansion and convection	87
	20	Conduction of heat	91
	21	Radiation	93
	22	Temperature	98
	23	Heat and temperature	100
Force, matter and motion	24	Measuring matter	106
	25	Measuring motion	113
	26	Forces	116
	27	Force and motion	122
	28	Work	127
	29	Power	129
	30	The turning effect of forces	131
	31	Machines	134
	32	Pressure	139

Electricity
- 33 Electric circuits 152
- 34 Conductors and insulators 156
- 35 Electric heating 161
- 36 Cells and voltage 163
- 37 Measuring resistance 167
- 38 Measuring electrical energy 170
- 39 Magnets 174
- 40 Magnetic fields 177
- 41 Uses of solenoids 179
- 42 When an electric current crosses a magnetic field 184
- 43 Making electricity 190
- 44 Making electricity again 196
- 45 Electricity in the home 202
- 46 Electric charge 210
- 47 Electrons in space 218

Invisible radiations and electronics
- 48 X-rays 226
- 49 Radioactivity 227
- 50 The electromagnetic spectrum 233
- 51 Radio waves 234
- 52 Electronics 237

Examination hints 243

Answers 244

Index 245

Hints on studying and revision

It is important to learn how to study. Here are a few ideas that may help you.

Where?

Find a quiet place on your own if you can. Get a table for your books and a good light. Studying should be active, so have a pencil and paper ready for making notes and testing yourself.

When?

Study when you are not too tired, and for short periods at a time. Plan to work in short bursts (say half-an-hour sessions) with a break in between.

How?

You should organize your work in the way that suits you best, but here is one way you can study with this book.

Make a revision notebook (or revision cards)

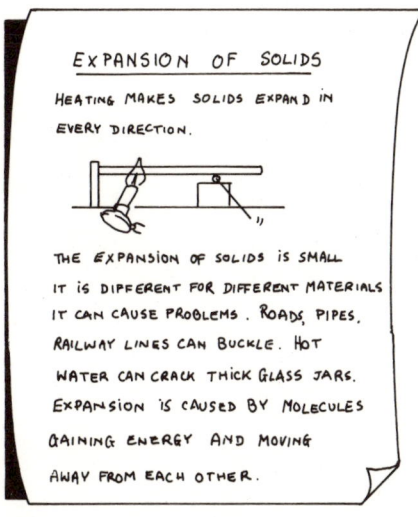

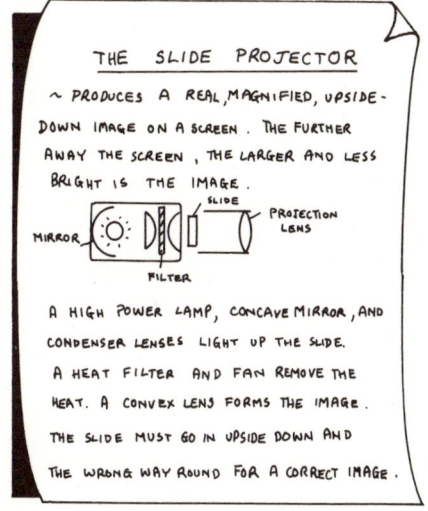

1. Turn to a page and write down the topic title.
2. Copy the summary of the topic that is indicated by an orange square at the bottom of most pages.
3. Draw a diagram of apparatus used to study that topic.
4. Read the page and write a list of facts about the topic. Most of the topics can be summarized in this way, allowing you to build up a revision notebook and to learn at the same time. You should then go through these notes a number of times until you can remember them.

Acknowledgements

The author would like to thank the following who have kindly permitted the reproduction of copyright photographs:

Ardea p.39 (left); Barnaby's Picture Library pp.11,18,39 (right), 60,65,90 (left), 105,227,234; BBC Television p.72 (bottom); Biophoto Associates p.225; British Airways p.67; British Rail Hovercraft Ltd p.120; British Railways Board p.114; Central Electricity Generating Board p.200; Bruce Coleman p.80; Ealing Beck Ltd. p.42; Fire Research Station p.96; Professor R. Fletcher p.37; (from PSSC Physics) reproduced by permission of D.C. Heath and Co., copyright 1965, Educational Development Center p.72 (top); Ilford Ltd p.15; Howard Jay pp.90 (right), 152,153,237; Popperfoto p.130; The Post Office pp.19,53; J.A.L. Cooke, Oxford Scientific Films p.151; Chris Smith p.3; St Mary's Hospital p.226; United Kingdom Atomic Energy Authority p.232; Joe Whitlock Blundell p.49.

petrol engine   69-70
photograms   15
photographic paper, chemistry
    of   15
photographing the image   14
pinhole camera   14-15
poles, magnetic   174
potential difference   163
power   129-30
    electrical   170
    equation   129
pressure   139-49
    atmospheric   141
    equation   139
    through liquids   146
projector
    home-made   28
    slide   35
proton   230
pulleys
    for lifting   137
    gears and   136
pump, air   143

radiation (heat)   93-7
    absorbers of   94
    emitters of   94
radiation (nuclear)
    background   228
    effects of   232
radiators
    car   96
    house   96
radioactivity   227-32
radio waves   52, 233, 234-6
rainbow   44
rays, lenses and   29-32
real and apparent depth   23
real image   14, 30
rectification   195
reed switches   180
reflection
    of sound waves   58
    of water waves   51
reflection of light
    at curved mirrors   19-21
    at plane mirrors   17
    law of   17
    total internal   24
refraction of light   22-6
    by a glass block   22
refraction of water waves   51
refrigerators   80

relay
    electromagnetic   181
    reed   181
    use in a car   181
resistance   158
    and temperature   169
    measuring   167-9
resistors   158
resonance   62-4
    examples of   63
right-hand rule   191
rocket engines   68

scattered light, seeing by   18
series circuits   153, 160
shadows   12
short
    circuit   162
    sight   38
solenoids   178
    uses of   179-83, 196
sonar
    active   58
    passive   58
sound
    frequency   55
    loudness of   60
    speed of   57
    waves   56-61
sound energy   5, 50-64
spark counter   227
specific
    heat capacity   101
    latent heat of fusion   103
    latent heat of vaporization   103
spectrum
    electromagnetic   233
    white light   43
speed   114
spring force   118
stability and balance   132-3
static electricity   212
steam turbines   67
strain energy   4
studying and revision, hints on   1
switches   154-5

telescope   41
televison, colour   44
temperature   98-9
    heat and   100-4
thermometers   98
    bimetal   86
    clinical   99

thermostats   85-6
ticker-timer   113
timers   113
total internal reflection   24
    by a prism   25
transformer   198-200
transistor(s)   237
    amplifier   238
    as a switch   239
transverse wave   50
tuning fork   54
turbines, steam   67
turning effects of forces   131-3

ultra-violet radiation   52, 233
umbra   13

vacuum flask   95
van de Graaff generator   213
velocity ratio   135
vibrations   54-5
virtual images   16, 31
vision
    binocular   39
    defects   38
    persistence of   40
volt   163
voltage   163
    and current   168
    cells and   163-6
voltmeter   163
volume   106

water system, hot and cold   88
watt   129
wavelength   50, 59
waves   50-3
    electromagnetic   12, 52, 233
    longitudinal   56
    diffraction of   51
    radio   52, 233, 234-6
    sound   56-61
    reflection of   51
    refraction of   51
    transverse   50
weight   117
wheel and axle machines   135
work   127-8
    equation   127

X-rays   52, 226, 233

Energy

1 Energy

Look at the pictures on this page. They show things that are moving and have a supply of **energy**. Energy is needed to get things moving so that jobs can be done.

Forms of energy

There are many ways of getting things moving. We can use our muscles. This shows that our bodies have energy. (We call this **chemical energy,** since the chemicals in our muscles change when we use them.) Or we could use a petrol engine. This shows that petrol has energy. This energy is also chemical energy since the chemicals of the petrol change when it is used.

Chemical energy getting bikes moving

Movement can come from rolling downhill. A skier or trolley at the top of a hill has energy. This energy can be used to move downhill at speed. Things that are high up have what is called **gravitational energy**. This is energy that is there ready to be used because of the pull of gravity.

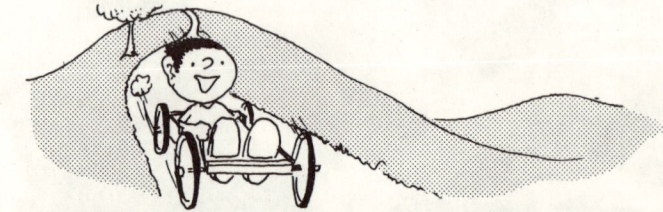
Gravitational energy getting a trolley moving

Movement can come from stretched elastic or springs. The energy is stored in the stretched elastic and can be used to move a stone. This is called **strain energy**.

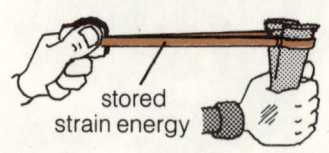 
Strain energy getting a stone moving

Potential energy

Chemical, gravitational and strain energies can be stored by things; the energy is held by them, waiting to be used. Energy that can be held in readiness is called **potential energy**. Chemical, gravitational and strain energies are all potential energies.

1   Give an example of something that has (a) gravitational energy due to its high position, (b) strain energy because it is stretched, (c) chemical energy. In each case explain how the energy can be used to produce movement.

■ Energy that can be stored is called potential energy.

Kinetic energy

Objects that are moving can make other things move. The energy of a moving body is called **kinetic energy** (kinetic means 'moving').

We have seen how the three forms of potential energy can make things move. That is, they change into kinetic energy. The following experiments show energy changing between kinetic and potential forms.

Forms of potential energy

Experiments

Make a pendulum by tying a nut onto a string and clamping the top end of the string between two wooden blocks. Raise the nut by pulling it to one side (this supplies it with gravitational energy), then let go. The nut will swing down, changing its gravitational energy into kinetic energy. Then, as it swings up, the kinetic energy changes back into gravitational energy. This goes on and the pendulum vibrates from side to side.

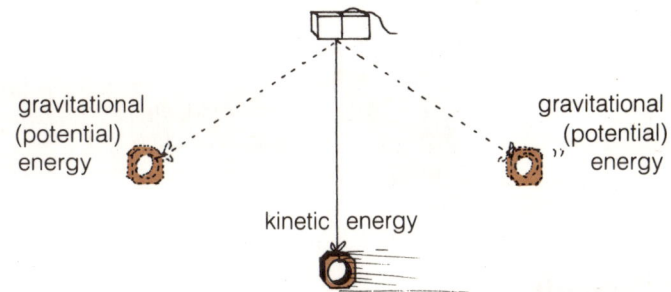
Energy changing between kinetic and gravitational forms

Build another vibrating system by connecting a trolley to two springs as shown. Provide energy by stretching and compressing the springs, then let go. Here the strain energy in the springs and the kinetic energy of the trolley interchange.

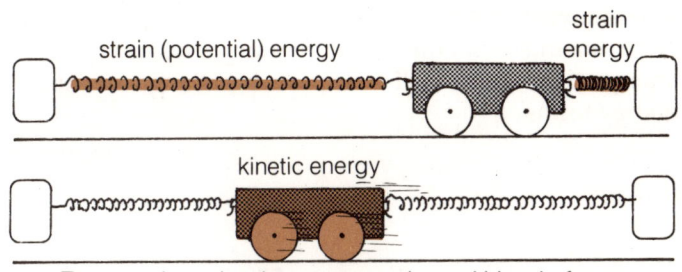
Energy changing between strain and kinetic forms

Other forms of energy

Heat, light and **sound** are forms of energy that move from place to place. Heat carries energy from things that are hot to things that are not so hot; light carries energy away from lamps or the Sun; sound carries energy away from the vibrations of a noisy object.

Electrical energy is used to bring energy into our homes and work places, where we change it into the forms we want.

2 Write a list of the forms of energy mentioned on pages 4 and 5. There are eight.

3 Give an example of an effect caused by each form of energy.

4 What forms of energy are needed to:
(a) clean your teeth;
(b) make a tape recorder work;
(c) toast a slice of bread;
(d) make water run out of a tap?

5 What form(s) of energy do the following have: a live match; a gallon of petrol; wind; waves; food; a chimney pot on top of a house; water at the top of a waterfall; an air gun?

- Energy has a number of forms.
- Chemical energy, gravitational energy and strain energy are forms that can be stored (they are all potential energies).
- A moving object has kinetic energy. Heat, light and sound are forms energy takes when it transfers from place to place.
- Electrical energy can also move from place to place and can be readily changed into other forms.

More energy changes

Think about the energy changes that take place during these events.

1 Throwing a dart
Chemical energy in the muscles changes into kinetic energy of the arm and dart. The muscles warm up slightly showing that heat energy has passed into them.

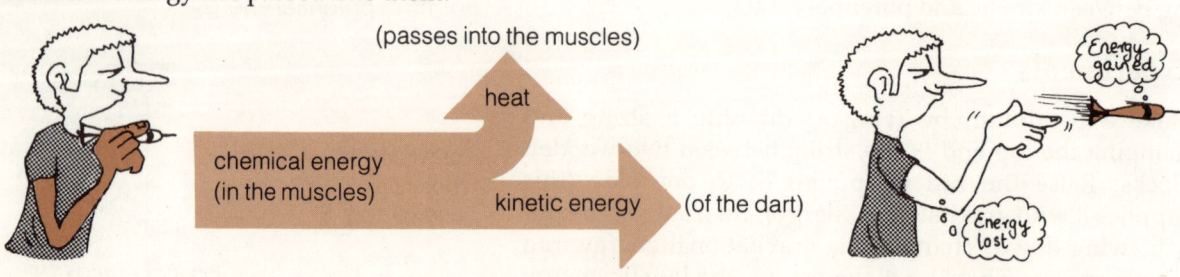

2 Catapult
Most of the energy stored in the stretched elastic changes into kinetic energy of the trolley. The wheels warm up a little showing that heat energy has passed into them. Note that this is not the end of the story. The kinetic energy of the trolley will most probably change into other energy forms.

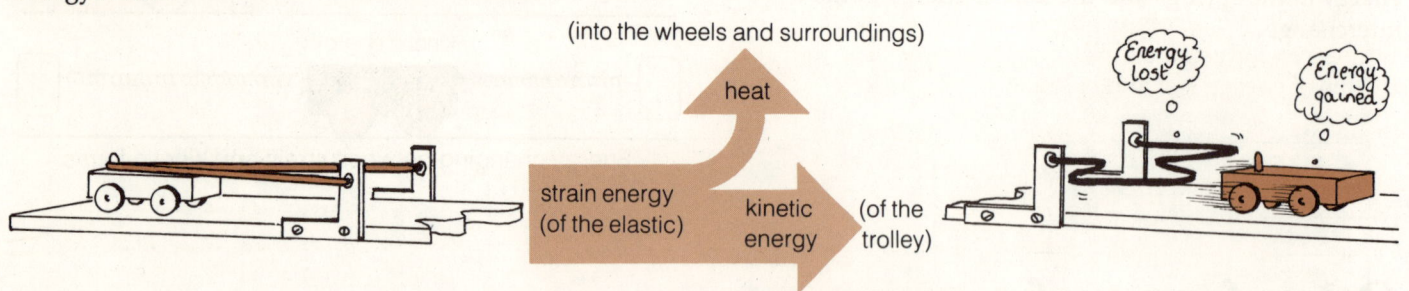

3 High diver
The diver has energy because of her height above the water. Nearly all this energy changes into kinetic energy as she falls. The air is disturbed and warms up a little showing that some of the gravitational energy has changed into heat.

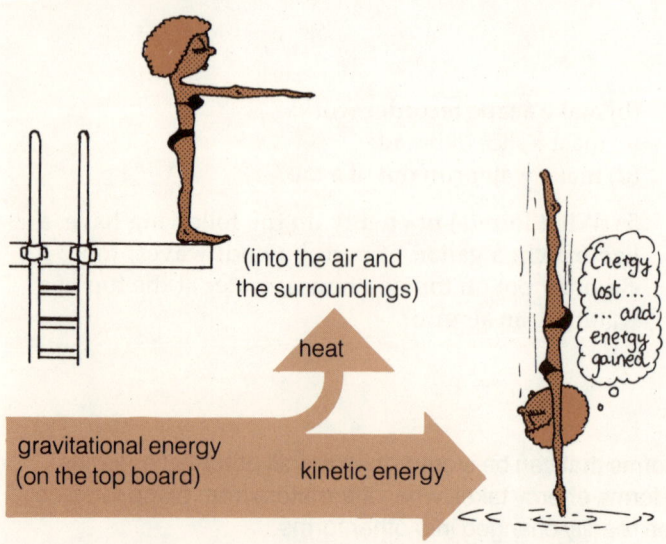

4 Electric motor
Chemical energy in the battery provides electrical energy that makes the motor go round. The weight is lifted off the ground and gains gravitational energy. Chemical energy changes into gravitational energy but passes through electrical energy on the way.

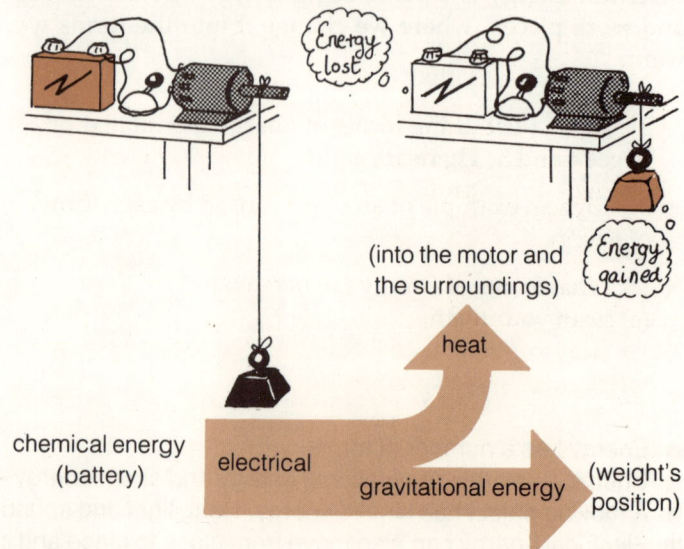

5 Spring-board diver

In this case the beginning and the end of the story are missing. The spring-board diver must have gained his kinetic energy from another form and the energy stored in the bent spring-board will not stay there long before shooting the diver upwards again.

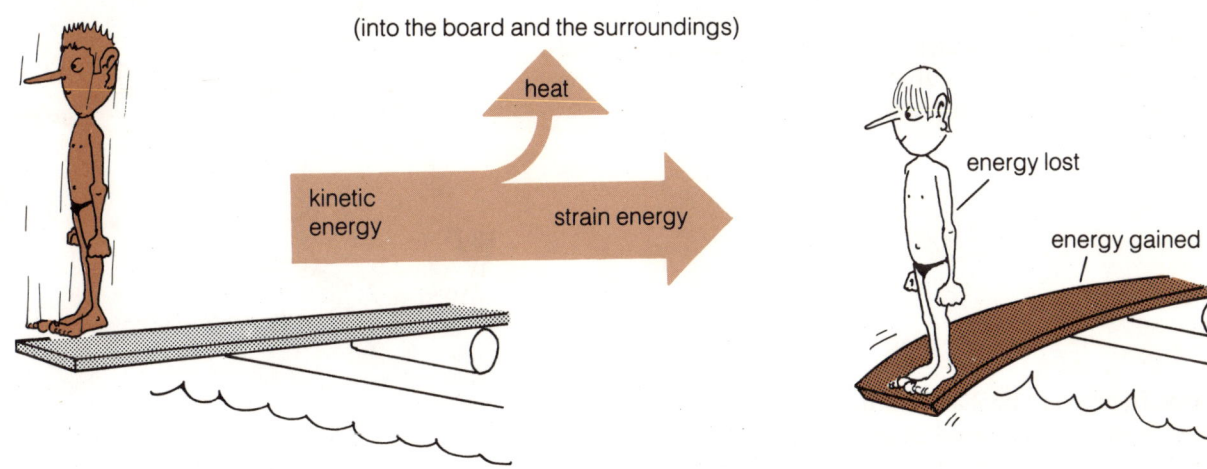

6 At the end of the transfer of energy in the five examples above, objects have lost and gained energy. Copy and complete the table showing the type of energy lost and gained.

Objects	Type of energy	Lost or gained
The muscles of the dart player		
The dart		
The elastic		
The trolley		
The diver on the high board		
The diver entering the water		
The battery		
The weight		
The spring-board diver		
The spring-board		

7 In all of these examples one other form of energy always appears that is not mentioned in your list above. What form is that?

8 Draw energy diagrams that show the energy changes of the processes that take place in
(a) a radio,
(b) a torch,
(c) a television set (all on),
(d) a fully wound watch.
In each case write a sentence that describes the energy changes that take place.

■ Energy can change freely from one form to another, but when it does some of the energy always changes into heat.
■ There is never as much energy in the new form as in the old form; some of the energy is used to warm up materials and the air.

Where does energy come from?

Sunlight provides us with almost all of the energy we use. Heat from the sun keeps us warm. It also generates wind and rain. Light energy from the sun provides essential energy for the growth of most plants. This day-to-day energy provides humans and animals with the food they need but it cannot work many of man's machines. Most machines use fuels such as petrol, coal and natural gas, fuels that have been formed in the ground over millions of years.

The sun's day-to-day energy helps provide humans and animals with the food they need

These fuels were probably formed from trees, plants and small animals that used energy from the sun to grow. They died and were buried and compressed in the ground, eventually forming coal, oil and gas. These ancient fuels took a long time to form and cannot be replaced.

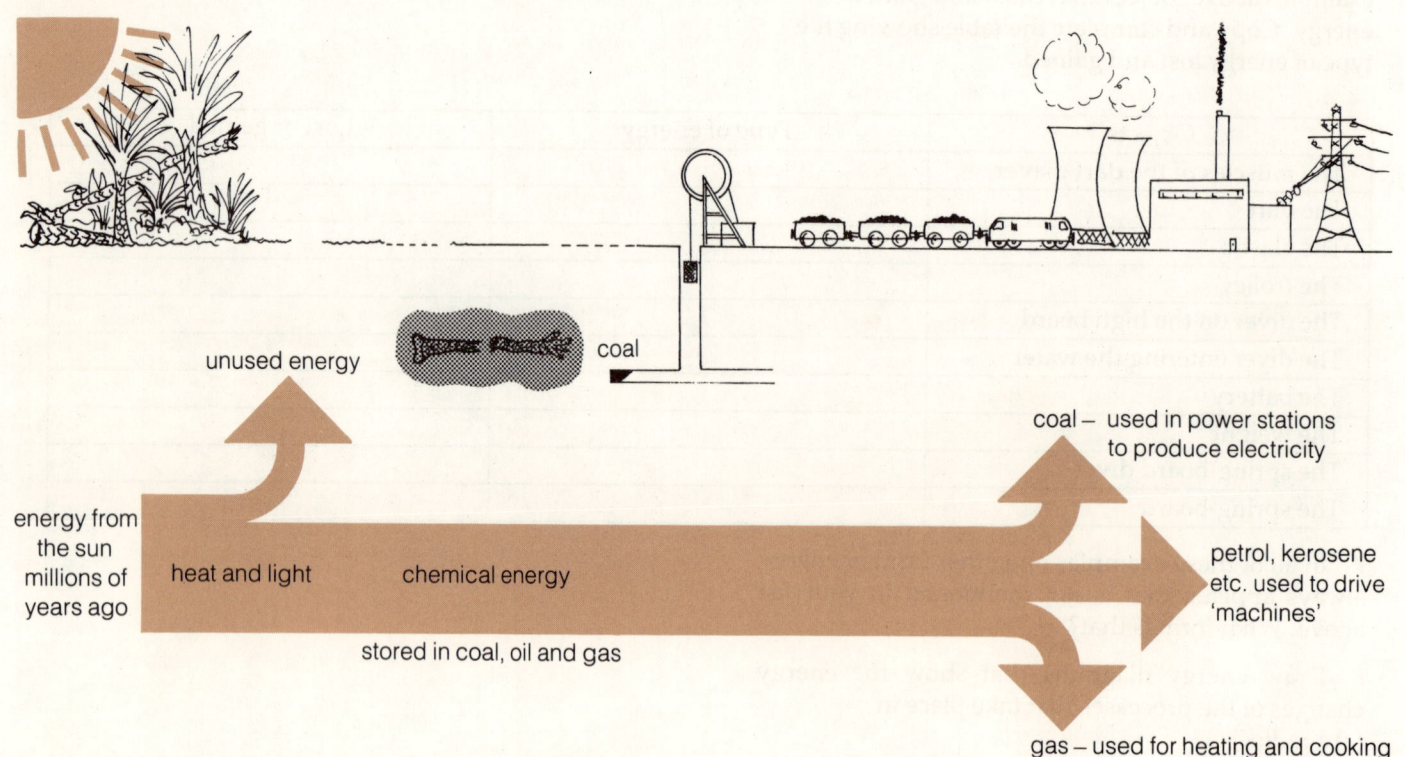

Coal, oil and gas were probably formed from ancient plants and animals that took energy from the Sun

9 Explain the two chief ways in which the sun has provided the earth with energy.

10 Describe how the sun provides energy to make
(a) a car move,
(b) a sailing boat travel along.

The conservation of energy

Think about a wound-up spring that is accelerating a clockwork toy. Strain energy changes into kinetic energy and heat (the heat energy passes into the toy and makes it slightly warmer). The total amount of kinetic energy and heat energy produced equals the amount of strain energy that disappears.

Energy can be measured, and the unit used to measure all forms of energy is the JOULE (page 127). If the spring loses 20 joules of strain energy, then 20 joules of energy must appear in other forms – kinetic and heat in this case. There can be no overall loss of energy. Energy cannot be destroyed.

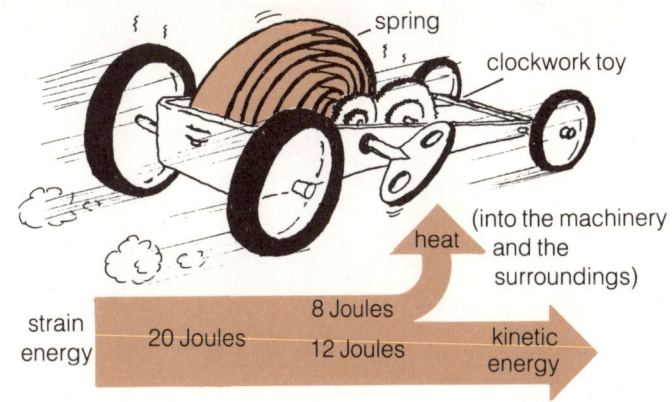

Strain energy changes into kinetic energy and heat. No energy is lost

Energy chains

The beginning and ending of this energy story are missing. The 20 joules of energy stored in the spring came from the person who wound it up. He got it from the food he ate, which got it from the sun. The clockwork toy then dashes across the floor, changing its kinetic energy into heat, warming up itself and the air around. In this way the 20 joules of energy finish up as warmth in the air. Very often, energy chains like this begin with the sun's energy and end up as warmth in the air. But through all the changes no energy is destroyed.

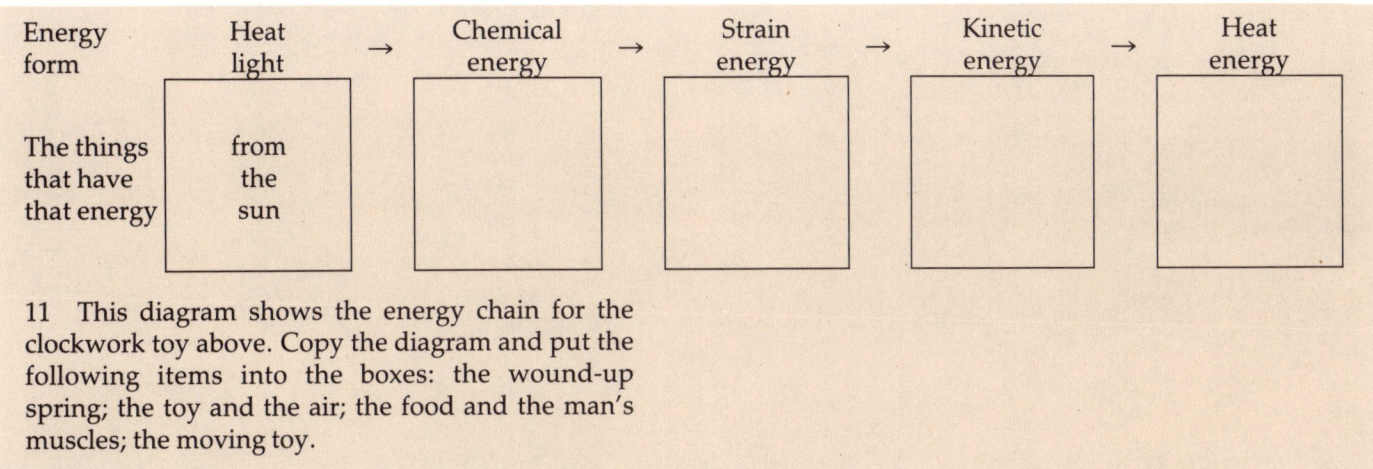

11 This diagram shows the energy chain for the clockwork toy above. Copy the diagram and put the following items into the boxes: the wound-up spring; the toy and the air; the food and the man's muscles; the moving toy.

The idea that energy cannot be destroyed and can only change into another form, is called the principle of conservation of energy.

Summary of energy

- Energy can be recognized by its ability .... to make things happen.
- Some forms of energy are .... chemical, gravitational, strain, kinetic, heat, light, sound, electrical.
- Most of the energy we use comes from .... the sun.
- The principle of conservation of energy states that .... energy cannot be destroyed.

Light energy

2 Light and shadows

Light is energy that has the remarkable ability of allowing our eyes to work. Without light, life as we know it would not be possible. We see some things by the light they send out. The Sun, electric lamps and television pictures are examples of these things. Anything that sends out light is called **luminous**. Most things are not luminous. We see them by the light they reflect into our eyes. Light carries energy from a luminous source to our eyes in the form known as **electromagnetic** (p. 52). It does this at the incredible speed of 300 000 km/s. Nothing in the Universe travels faster than light.

Luminous and non-luminous objects

Light rays

A thin beam of light is often called a **ray**. Use a ray box or lamp and slit to produce a long fine ray of light. Experiment with the light by shining it at a mirror, a sheet of glass, a prism etc. You can assume that rays always travel in straight lines, even over long distances.

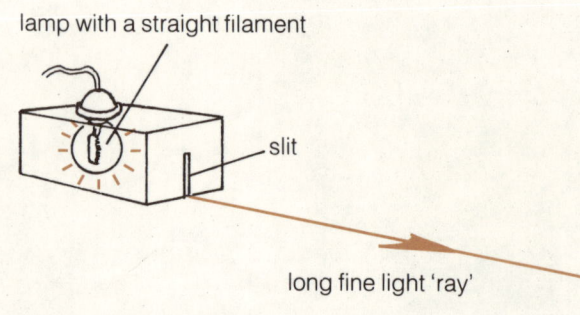

A ray box sending out a light 'ray'

Shadows

When light shines on an object some of the light is stopped while other rays pass straight on. A shadow is formed where light rays cannot reach. A small lamp (or a larger one further away) will throw sharp shadows. A large source of light such as a fluorescent tube light gives much softer shadows with very blurred edges. Try the experiments shown in the diagrams.

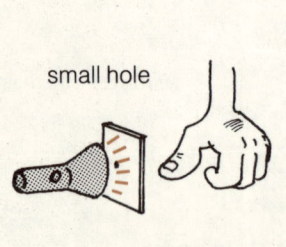

Making a large sharp shadow

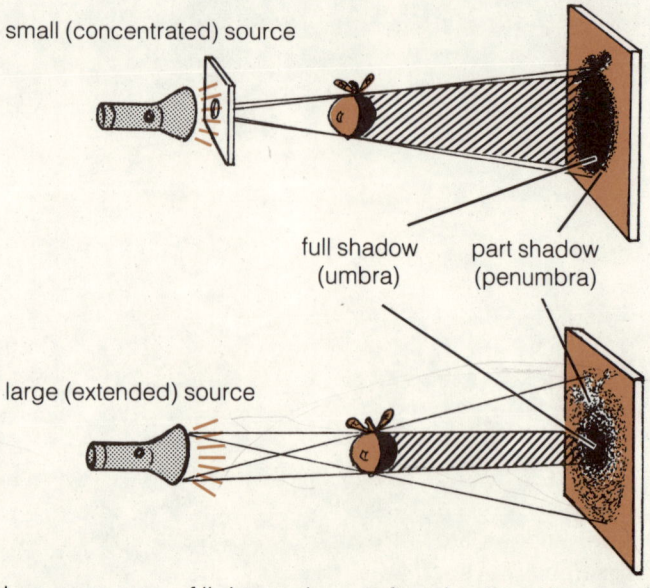

Large sources of light produce softer shadows than small sources of light

1 Is it better to use a large or small source of light to illuminate the table where you are working?

2 Describe the difference between shadows formed on an overcast day and those formed on a sunny day.

3 Describe how the shadow of a man changes as he walks away from a street lamp on a dark night.

4 Are small or large sources of light best for floodlighting a football stadium? Describe the lights that are usually used and the shadows they produce.

It is best to keep work surfaces free from sharp shadows

Eclipse of the Sun

The Moon and the Sun appear to be very nearly the same size in the sky. When they are in line, the disc of the Moon neatly covers the Sun. The shadow of the Moon just reaches the Earth and anyone standing in that shadow would experience darkness during the day.

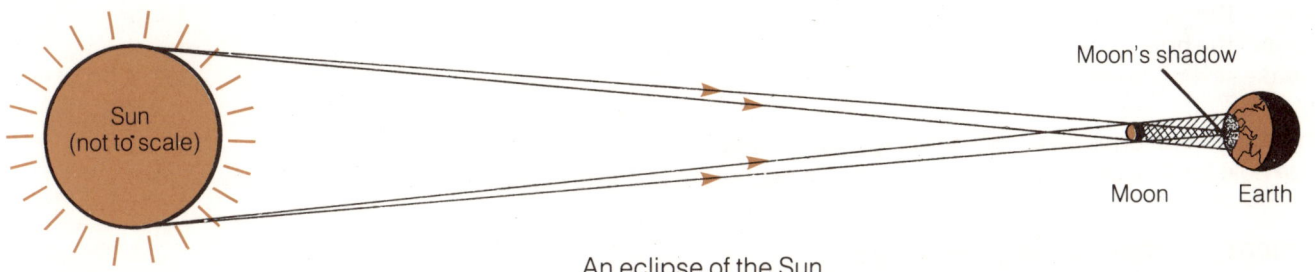

An eclipse of the Sun

5 **Eclipse** means 'to overshadow'. Does the diagram above show an eclipse of the Moon or an eclipse of the Sun?

6 An eclipse of the **Moon** occurs when the Moon passes into the Earth's shadow as shown in the diagram below. Would you see an eclipse of the Moon during the day or during the night? Explain your answer.

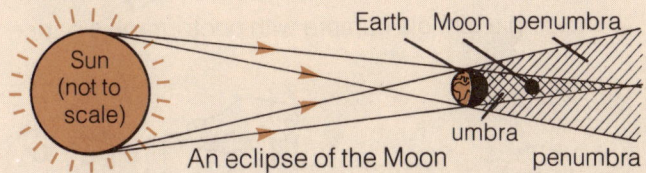

An eclipse of the Moon

7 Why do you have to be at a special place on Earth to see the Sun completely covered by the Moon during an eclipse. (Look at the size of the Moon's full shadow above).

8 Copy and complete this table.

Positions	Type of eclipse that can occur (Sun or Moon)
Sun-Moon-Earth	
Sun-Earth-Moon	

Summary of light and shadows

- An object that gives out light is called... luminous.
- Light travels in .... straight lines.
- Sharp shadows are formed when the light source is .... small.
- Soft shadows are formed when the light source is......................... large.
- An area of full shadow is called .... umbra.
- An area of part shadow is called .... penumbra.
- For an eclipse of the Sun, the Moon must be between the............. Sun and the Earth.

3 The pinhole camera

Light can be formed into an image

A pinhole camera is simply a black box with a tissue screen at one end and a pinhole at the other. The small hole can form the light from a lamp into an **image** on the screen. An image is a likeness of the lamp, not an exact copy. Look at this image and you will notice that it differs from the lamp in four ways. It is upside down, reversed (left to right), less bright and (usually) a different size to the lamp. The image is, however, the same shape and colour as the lamp. The rays of light cross over as they travel in straight lines through the pinhole. This is why the image is upside down and reversed. An image formed on a screen like this is called a **real** image.

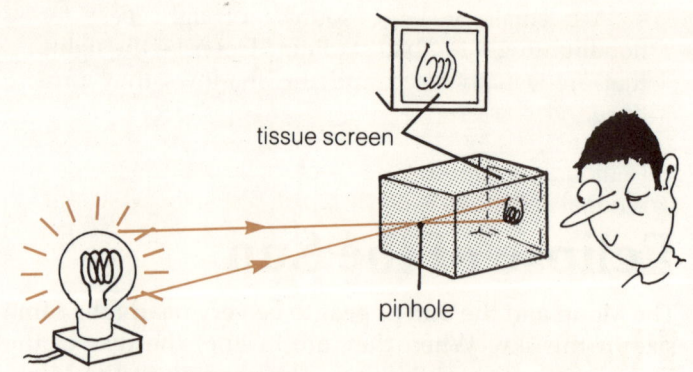

A pinhole camera forming an image on a screen

Experiment. Looking at the image

Find out by experiment what happens to the image if:
(a) you move the camera closer to the lamp,
(b) you make the hole larger,
(c) you make several holes.

■ A pinhole camera forms an upside down, reversed image.
■ A large hole forms a brighter image than a small hole, but the image is not so sharp.

Experiment. Photographing the image

Light is energy and can affect photographic paper as well as our eyes.

To take a photograph with your pinhole camera you must replace the tissue screen with a well-fitting back.

Then:
(a) Place photographic paper in the back of the camera under red 'safe' light. Cover the hole with your finger to stop white light falling on the photographic paper.

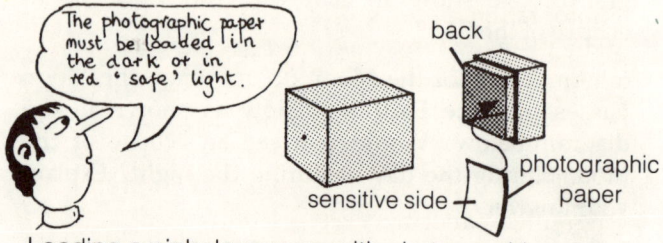

Loading a pinhole camera with photographic paper

(b) Place the camera on a firm support pointing at the lamp or an interesting view. Let the light fall on the paper by removing your finger for a time. (15 seconds for a lamp, 1 minute for an outside scene.)

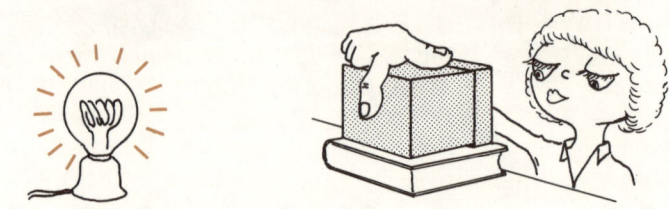

(c) Place the paper in developer until the picture appears. Wash, 'fix' for 5 minutes, then wash again for 20 minutes.

WHY NOT . . .
1. take pictures of the lamp from different distances,
2. take a picture using a larger hole,
3. take a picture using two or three holes,
. . . while your photo is washing?

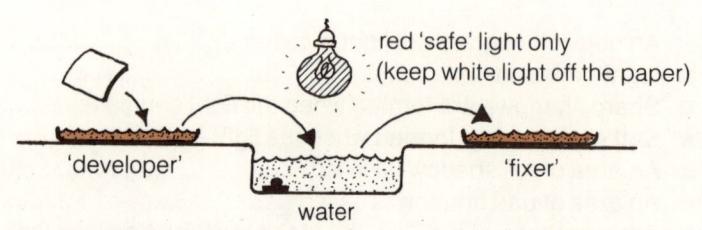

1 What part of the lamp forms a visible image?

2 Why do you think this happens?

3 Which two of these answers are correct when the hole is made larger:
(a) the image is larger,
(b) the image is brighter,
(c) the image is more blurred,
(d) the image is sharper?

4 Why could a pinhole camera photograph be called a *negative* picture?

5 A photograph of a black spiral is placed on top of a fresh piece of photographic paper. Bright light is shone through the photograph to the photographic paper beneath. This paper is then developed and fixed in the usual way. Describe the picture you would expect to get.

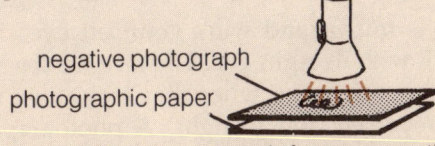

Making a positive photograph from a negative

■ Photographic paper goes black in the places where light fell.
■ A negative picture is one in which black and white are reversed.

Photograms

How does photographic paper work?

Experiment. Making a shadow photograph or photogram

1. Under red light, place an object on photographic paper.
2. Shine white light on the paper for 10 seconds.
3. Put the paper into developer until the shadow picture appears.
4. Wash.
5. Put into 'fixer' for 5 minutes, then wash again in fresh water.

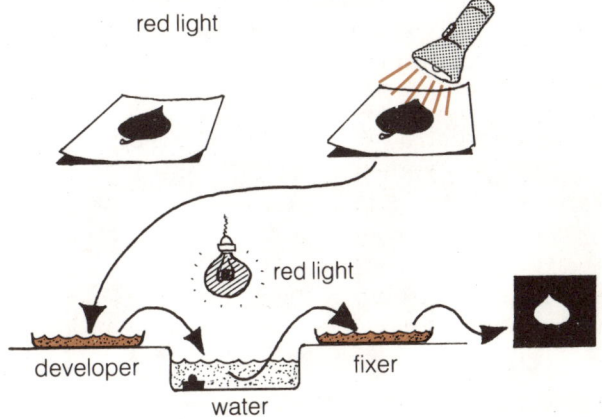

6 Copy and complete this sentence:
'Photographic paper goes _____ (after developing) in the places where white light falls. Where no light falls it _____ _____.

The chemistry of photographic paper

Photographic paper is covered with a layer of jelly that contains millions of tiny crystals of a substance called silver bromide. When light hits one of these crystals a small part of it turns into silver. The developer changes the rest of the crystal into silver. Nothing happens to the crystals that were not hit by light. The fixer removes the crystals that have not been turned into silver. Tiny grains of silver are left where the light fell. These grains are so small and there are so many that they look black from a distance.

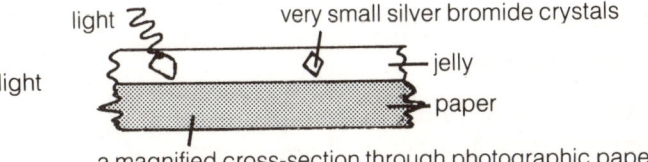

a magnified cross-section through photographic paper

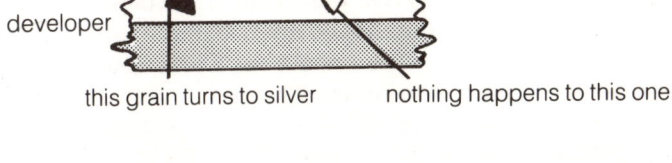

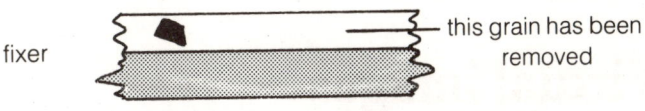

How developing and fixing photographic paper give a silver image

7 Why can a photograph be called a 'silver image'?

8 Explain how small grains of silver can form a picture that has areas of black, grey and white.

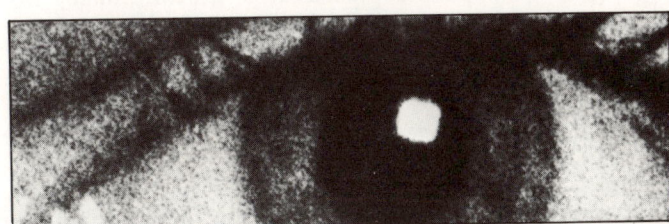

■ Photographs are made up of very fine grains of silver.

4 Mirror images

Look into a mirror and wink your left eye. The image winks back with its right eye. The face we see in a mirror is not the face others see when they look at us. The mirror image is reversed, left to right. A photograph, film or television picture show us as we really are.

Your mirror image is not the same as your photograph

1 (a) One of these photographs was printed the wrong way round. How could you make one photograph look like the other? Is the photograph that is printed the wrong way round the same as the mirror image of the person?

(b) How do you think the two photographs below were made? Are they of the same person?

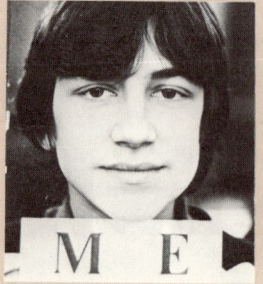 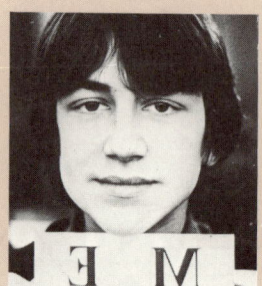 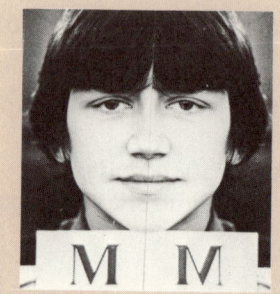 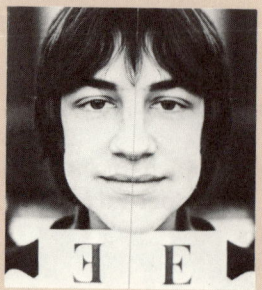

Experiment. Finding the mirror image of a candle flame

Place a lighted candle in front of a sheet of glass. Look into the glass and you will see an image of the bright flame. The glass is acting like a mirror. Find the image by moving an unlit candle on the other side of the mirror. Position this candle so that the image of the flame sits on its wick. The unlit candle must now be in the same place as the image. What do you notice about the distances of the two candles from the mirror?

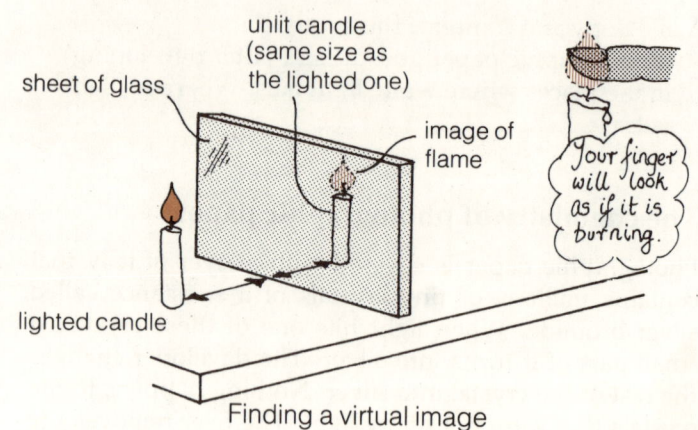

Finding a virtual image

Virtual images

We have seen how a pinhole camera forms a real image on a screen and that this image can be photographed. If photographic paper is placed at a mirror image, no photograph is formed. A mirror image can be seen by the eye but does not give a picture on film or on a screen placed where the image is formed. Such an image is called **virtual**.

■ A mirror image is: reversed left to right, as far behind the mirror as the object is in front, virtual.

2 Why is the sign on the front of an ambulance sometimes written as shown below? Would it be sensible to write the sign on the back of the vehicle like this?

ƎƆИAJUᗺMA

3 How could you arrange a candle, a sheet of glass and a beaker of water to give the illusion of a candle burning in a beaker of water?

4 Explain how this shop window trick works.

5 If you walk towards a mirror at 1 m/s, how fast do you approach your image?

6 A sheet of glass forms two images of a candle flame that are close together. Explain how the glass does this.

Experiment. The reflection of light by a mirror

Draw two lines at **equal** angles to a plane (flat) mirror and shine a ray of light along one of the lines. You will see that the mirror reflects the ray along the other line. The ray and its reflection always make the same angle with the mirror. This is the law of reflection.

A line at right angles to the mirror at the point where the ray strikes is called the **normal**.

The angles between the rays and the normal are called the **angle of incidence** and **angle of reflection**. The law of reflection can be written:

angle of incidence = angle of reflection

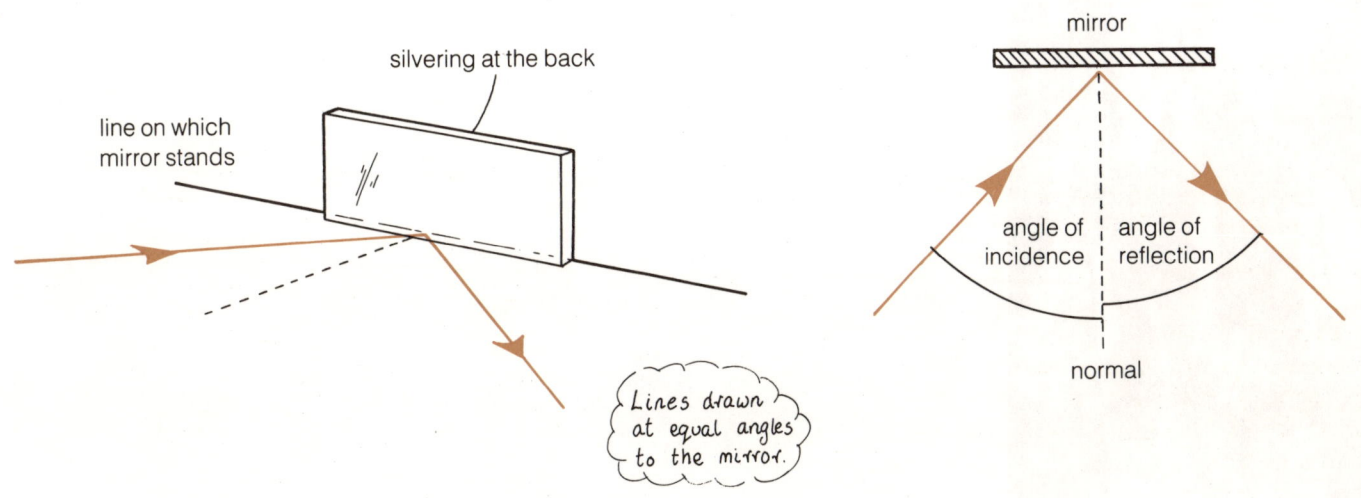

Reflections of a light ray by a mirror

Light levers

If you move the mirror slightly in the experiment on p.17, you will see the reflected ray move through a much larger distance. A long light ray reflected from a mirror like this greatly magnifies the movement of the mirror. Such an arrangement is called a light lever.

7 Explain how a cup of tea in a sunny room can produce a flickering patch of light on the ceiling.

8 A boy is using a mirror to flash a signal to his friend.
(a) How does he know when the Sun's reflected light rays will be seen by his friend?
(b) What will his friend then see?
(c) How can the boy send a series of quick flashes of light to his friend?

Seeing by scattered light

In question 8 the girl sees the bright image of the Sun because she is in the right position to receive the light reflected by the mirror. The old man would not be dazzled by this light. But both people see the boy equally well from different angles. This is because he scatters light from the Sun and sends it out in all directions. The scattered light makes him visible from different directions.

■ When light is reflected, the angle of incidence equals the angle of reflection.

Images formed by a mirror that is not flat

5 Curved mirrors

The inside surface of a shiny spoon can make two different sorts of image. One is small and upside down; the other is magnified and the right way up. Can you find these two images?

Concave mirrors – these curve inwards

A concave mirror, like the inside of a spoon, forms two sorts of image. Hold the mirror at arm's length and you will see a **small**, **upside-down** image of your face. (It is also reversed.) Hold the mirror close to your eye and you will see a **magnified** image that is the **right way up**.

Experiment. Concave mirror images

Line up a concave mirror, lamp and screen then search for an image by moving the screen. This image, when you find it, will be **upside down** and **reversed**. Move the lamp closer to the mirror, keeping the image focused on the screen. Notice how the image gets larger as it moves further away. When the lamp gets very close to the mirror, the image on the screen disappears. But if you look into the mirror you will see an image of the lamp that is **magnified** and **upright**.

Other properties

Concave mirrors can collect a wide beam of light from the Sun and concentrate it to a bright spot at its focus. They can also reflect light from a small lamp (placed at this focus) and send it out as a nearly parallel beam. Concave reflectors are widely used with other radiation. Radio, infra-red and microwaves can be focused or sent out as nearly parallel beams.

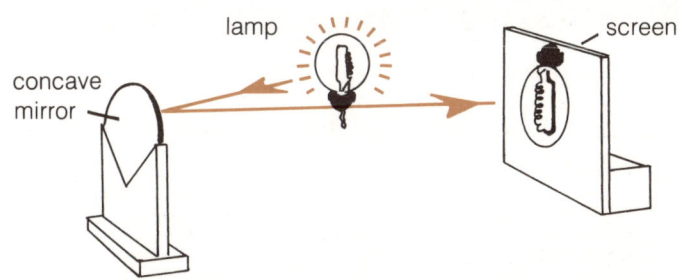

A concave mirror can form a real, upside-down image

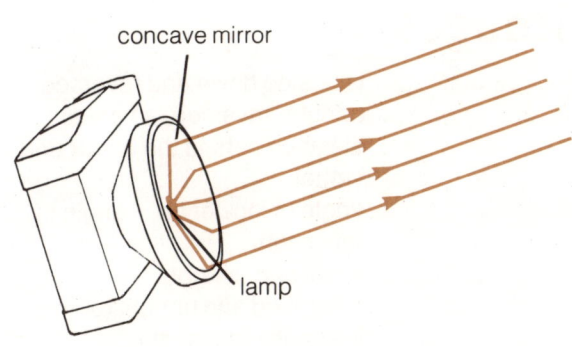

A concave reflector used to focus microwaves from a satellite

19

Convex mirrors – these curve outwards

The back of a shiny spoon forms an image that is different from those formed by its inside surface. See if you can spot the differences. A convex mirror, like the back of a spoon, can only form a small, upright image of things, whether they are near or far away. Because the images are small, the view in the mirror covers a wide area. This wide view makes convex mirrors useful in shops, as rear-view driving mirrors and at some 'blind' road junctions.

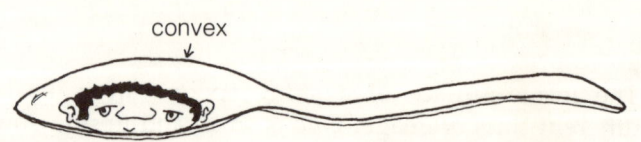

convex mirror

plane mirror

1 Copy this table and fill in details about the images formed.

Mirror	Position of the object	What the image is like	A use for this type of mirror
Concave	Object very near		
	Object far away		
Convex	Object near		
	Object far away		

- A convex mirror always forms a small, upright image.
- A concave mirror can form an upright, magnified image (object close) or an upside-down image (object far).

Summary of pinhole and mirror images

- A pinhole camera forms an image that...is upside down and reversed.
- The image in a plane mirror is...upright, reversed, an equal distance behind the mirror and virtual.
- The law of reflection is ....angle of incidence = angle of reflection.
- A convex mirror always forms an image that is..small and upright.
- A concave mirror forms two sorts of image ....magnified and upright (object inside the focus) or upside down (object outside the focus).

20

Further questions

2 This diagram shows the image in a plane mirror of a clock face. What is the correct time? (a) 2.35 (b) 8.35 (c) 9.25 (d) 2.25.

3 Draw diagrams to represent (a) a convex mirror (b) a concave mirror. Which would you use to form a magnified image, and which to form a small upright image?

4 Put the following items into two lists, one headed **concave mirrors**, the other **convex mirrors**. Shaving mirror, driving mirror, torch mirror, dentist's inspection mirror, car headlamp mirror, staircase mirror on a double decker bus, make-up mirror.

5 Draw rays on these two diagrams to show the shadow cast by each object. Mark the parts that are called **umbra** and **penumbra**. (E. Anglia. Part question)

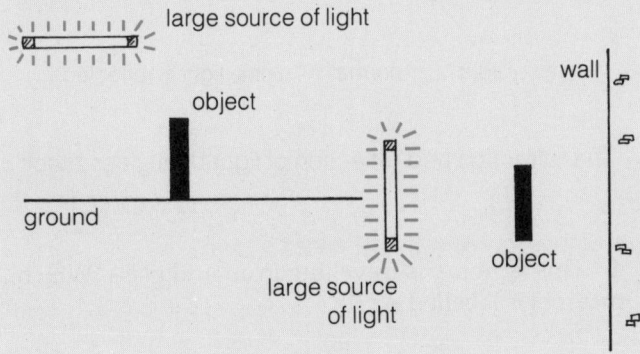

6 Which letter in the diagram below shows the position of the image of the girl's toes? Explain why she cannot see her hair-do in the mirror.

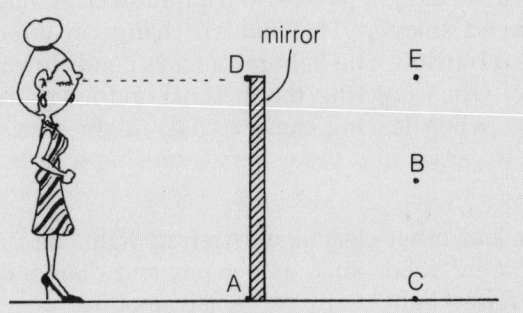

7 Copy this diagram and trace the path of the ray as it is reflected by the two mirrors. Name a device that uses two mirrors arranged like this.

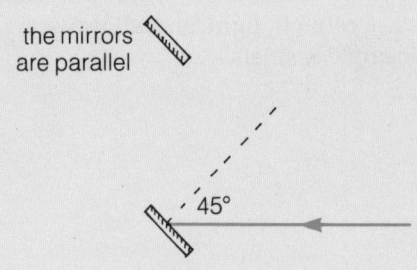

6 Refraction of light

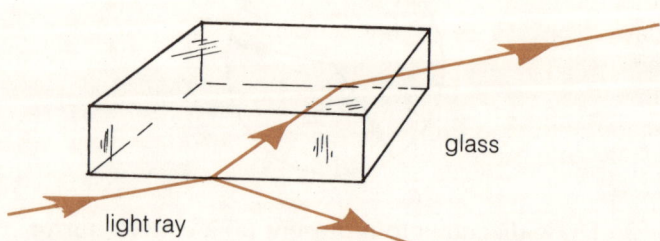

When a ray of light passes from air into a clear material, it may bend sharply. This sudden change in direction is called **refraction**. The light ray always bends towards the normal when entering the material and away from the normal when leaving the material. (Light slows down when it passes into the material, causing it to bend like this.)

Water and other clear liquids refract light. So do other transparent solids such as perspex and diamond. Even gases refract light but by very small amounts.

Experiment. Refraction and reflection of light by a glass block

Pass a ray of light into a block of glass and look for the reflected and refracted rays. Change the angle and notice how well glass reflects light when the angle is large, and how well it refracts light and allows it to pass through when the angle is small.

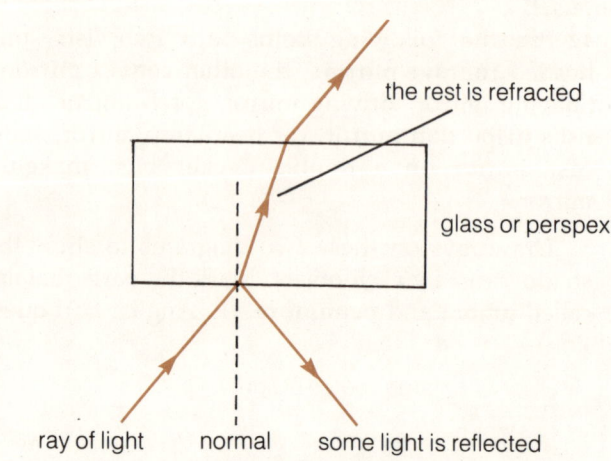

The refraction and reflection of light by a glass block

1 Explain the terms **refraction** and **reflection**.

2 Copy and complete. When light enters glass from air it is refracted _____ the normal. When light leaves glass it is refracted _____ from the normal.

3 Copy this diagram and continue the light ray into the air and the next block of glass.

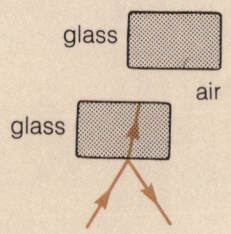

4 This light ray is travelling in air and glass. Which material is labelled A?

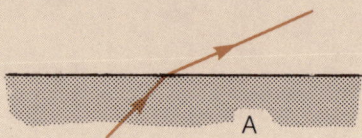

5 How can you make a light ray enter glass without changing direction?

■ The sudden change in direction of a ray of light when it passes into or out of a transparent material, is called refraction.
■ It is caused by a change in the speed of light.

Real and apparent depth

Experiment. Looking through water and glass

Place two coins on the bench and cover one with a block of glass. Look at both coins. Does looking at the coin through glass change its appearance? Try covering one coin with water. Does water have the same effect as glass? You will perhaps remember that looking at your feet through clear water makes them seem closer to you than they really are. Objects in clear materials appear nearer to us than they really are.

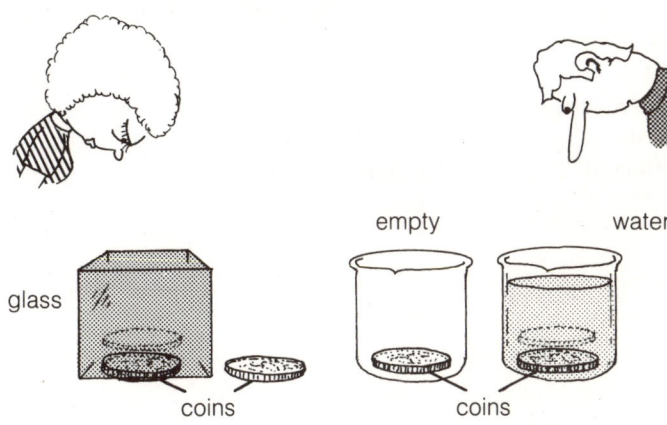

The light from objects at the bottom of water or glass is refracted as it leaves the surface. The rays form a virtual image that is above the object. Our eyes tell us that the bottom, and objects on the bottom, are closer to the surface than they really are. The material appears to be less deep than its true depth.

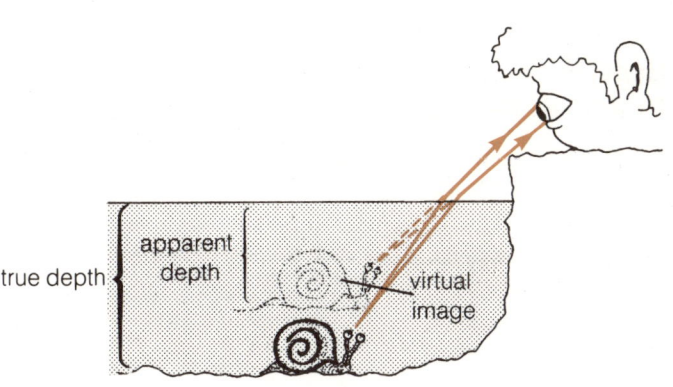

6 A pencil placed in water appears to be bent. Use the diagram to explain why this is so.

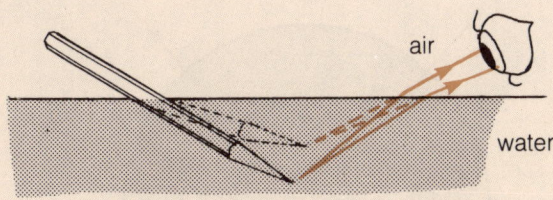

7 A coin that cannot be seen at the bottom of a cup, comes into view if water is poured into that cup. Use the diagrams to explain this illusion.

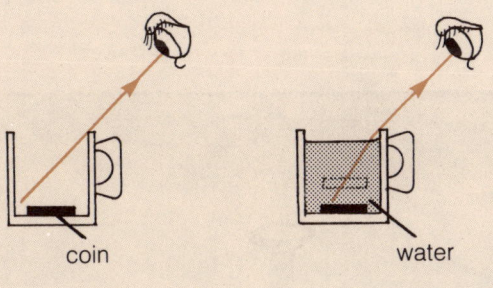

8 Explain why, in spear fishing, you do not aim your spear at the place where the fish appears to be.

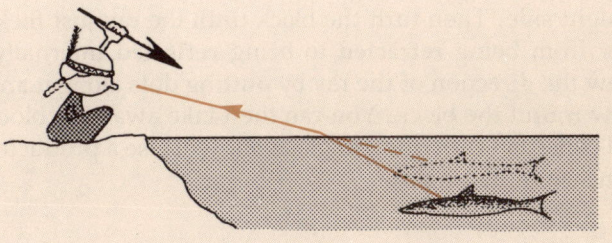

9 Explain why the boat-man appears to be rowing with broken oars

- Refraction makes clear materials look less deep than they really are.
- Refraction makes straight objects look as if they bend when they pass through the surface of a clear material.

Critical angle

It should be possible to make light emerge from glass so that it just skims along the surface. The angle the ray then makes with the normal inside the glass is called the **critical angle**. If the ray hits the surface at an angle greater than the critical angle, then all of the light is **reflected**. This is called **total internal reflection**. The glass surface acts as a perfect mirror.

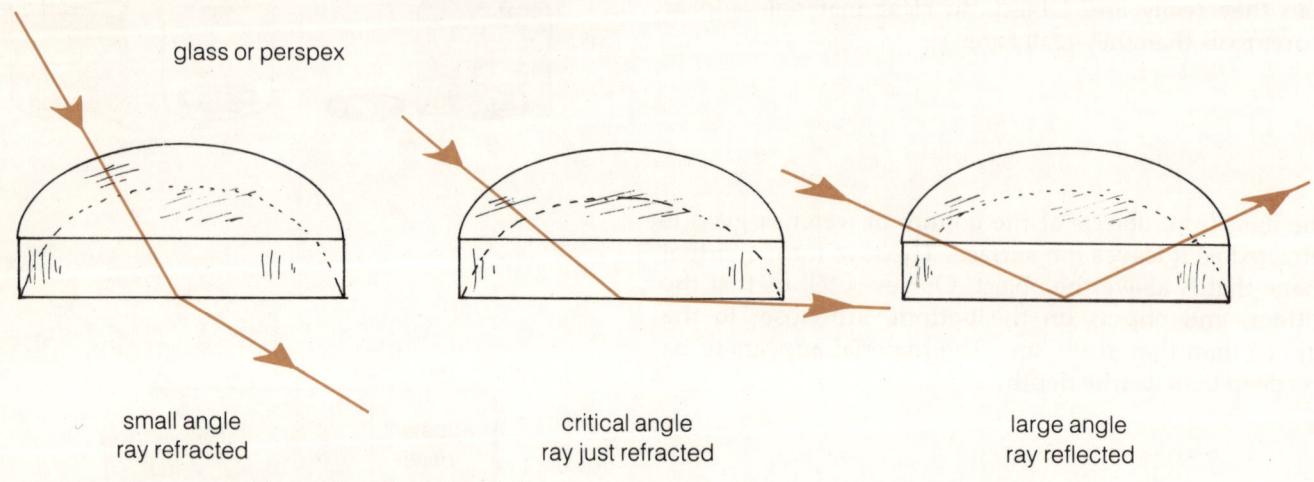

small angle
ray refracted

critical angle
ray just refracted

large angle
ray reflected

Experiment. Measuring the critical angle of perspex

Place a semicircular block of perspex on a sheet of paper. Aim a ray of light through the block at the centre of the straight side. Then turn the block until the ray just flicks over from being **refracted** to being **reflected** internally. Draw the direction of the ray by putting dots along it and draw round the block. You can then take away the block and construct the critical angle as shown. Use a protractor to measure this angle.

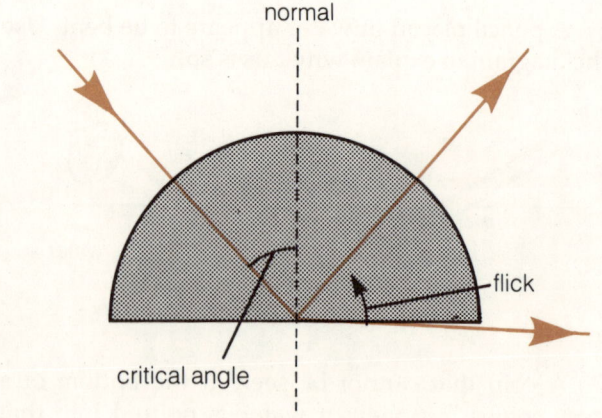

10 Copy and complete. Total internal reflection takes place if the angle of incidence of light inside a material is _____ than the _____ angle.

11 The diagram shows rays of light from an underwater torch hitting the surface. Explain why some of the rays cannot get out of the surface.

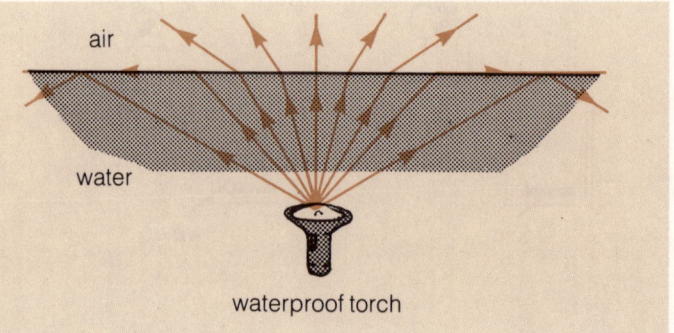

■ Total internal reflection happens inside materials if the angle of incidence of light is greater than the critical angle.

Total internal reflection by a prism

Experiment. Reflection by a prism

Pass a ray of light into a glass or perspex prism as shown in the diagram. You will notice that the light passes straight through the first surface but is totally reflected at the second surface. The light hits this surface at an angle greater than the critical angle and so is **reflected**. With the prism shown the light is turned through 90°. Prisms are sometimes used to reflect light instead of mirrors because they reflect more light, do not have silvering and do not give double images.

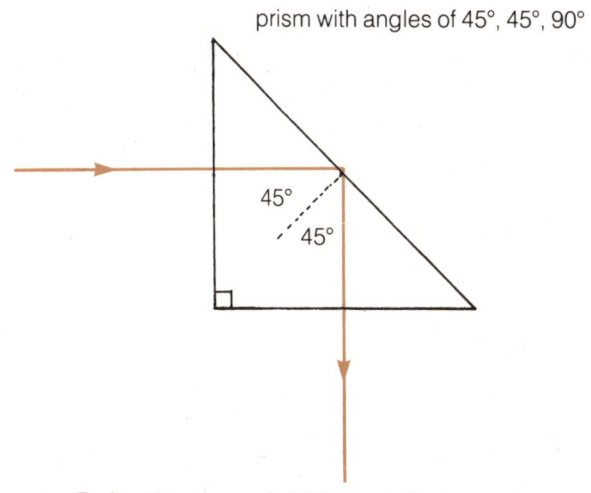

Reflection through 90° by a prism

Experiment

Use the same prism as in the experiment above to reflect light through 180°, back the way it came. Notice how the bottom ray comes out on top.

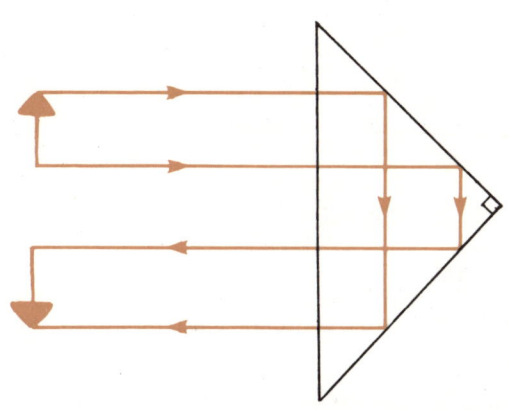

Reflection through 180° by a prism

12 Is the critical angle for the glass of the prism above more or less than 45°?

13 Draw diagrams to show a prism reflecting light rays in the directions shown.

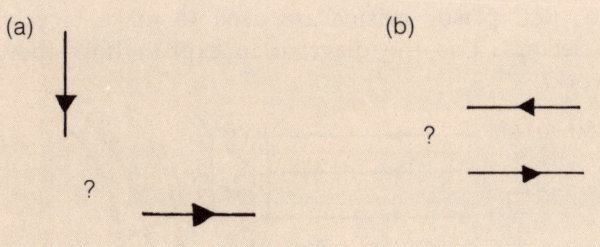

14 Use a prism to read a book from behind and from the side. In each case say whether the words are upside down or upright; reversed or the right way round.

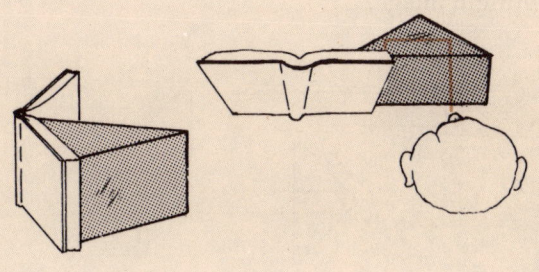

■ Glass prisms with angles of 45°, 45°, 90° can be better at reflecting light than mirrors.

Uses of totally reflecting prisms

Periscopes

– useful at crowded meetings, for looking round corners and for submariners.

Two prisms or mirrors reflecting rays of light in a periscope

15 Copy this diagram and draw the path of the ray from the top of the arrow through the periscope. Would you expect a periscope to give an upright image?

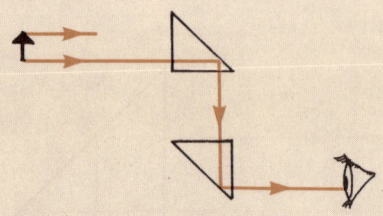

16 Draw the same two prisms in the positions of the ?'s so that the man can see light coming from behind.

17 Draw a diagram of a periscope being used upside down.

Binoculars

– useful for bird-watchers, plane-spotters, spies and military men.

Each side of the binocular is a telescope (p. 41). The prisms 'fold up' the rays of light so making the instrument short enough to hold in the hands. The prisms also turn the image the right way up – a telescope forms an inverted image.

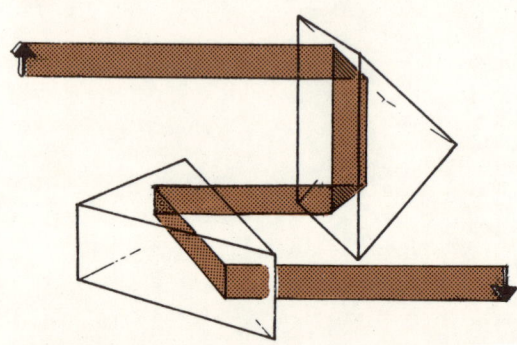

Two prisms reflecting light in binoculars

18 Copy this diagram of a ray of light passing through a binocular. Draw in the path of the ray from the bottom of the arrow through both prisms. Would you expect this prism arrangement to give an upright image?

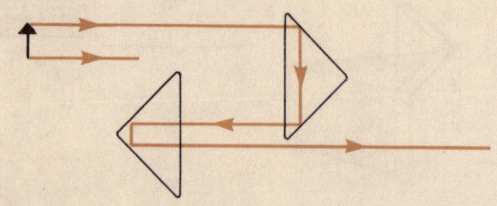

19 Two prisms placed flat on the table as in Q18 form an upright image. Yet two prisms in binoculars' turn the image upside down. What is the difference in the way the prisms have been arranged?

20 Red plastic prisms are used to make bicycle reflectors. Use the diagram to explain how they work.

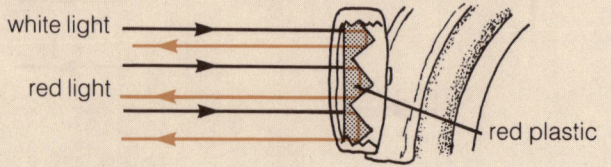

■ Reflecting prisms are used in periscopes, binoculars and bicycle reflectors.

7 The image formed by a lens

We have seen (p. 14) that the image formed by a pinhole camera can be sharp or bright, but not sharp and bright at the same time.

Experiment. Using a lens to form an image

Fit a pinhole camera box with a lens in a tube that can slide in and out of the box. Point the lens at a lamp and move the tube until a sharp image is formed on the tissue screen. You will notice that the image is much brighter than the pinhole's image and you can see more of the lamp. A lens forms an image that is bright and sharp but that has to be focused.

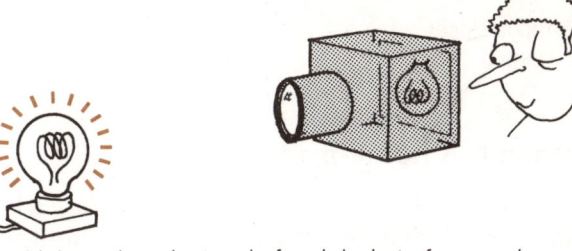

Using a lens instead of a pinhole to form an image

Experiment. Investigating the image

Point your simple camera at an interesting view and focus the image. Check the following observations:
(a) The image is upside down, reversed (left to right), coloured, not as bright as the object and (usually) smaller in size.
(b) The lens must be moved nearer to the screen to focus distant objects.

1 What are the advantages of using a lens, rather than a pinhole, to form an image?

2 Draw a diagram of the image that this camera would form of a brightly lit EXIT sign. Could this image be turned the right way up by turning the camera upside down?

Experiment. Using a lens to form an image on a screen

Arrange a lamp, lens and screen along a metre rule on the bench, so that a focused image of the lamp is formed on the screen. Move the lens and screen about and make the largest image you can. And then make the smallest possible image. Notice that the image is upside down and reversed as above.

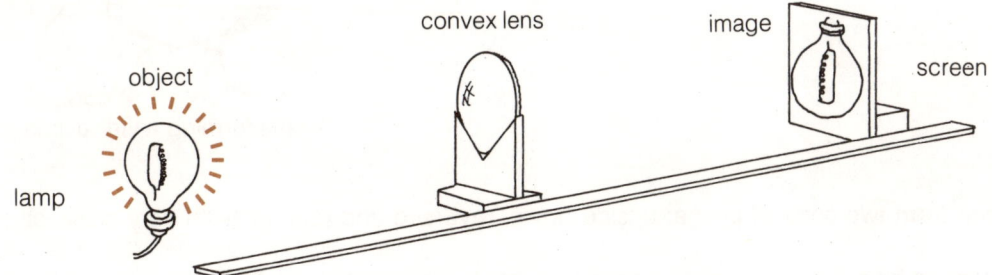

A lens forming a real image

3 (a) Which arrangement will make the largest image?
(b) What must you do to make the image larger (two things)?

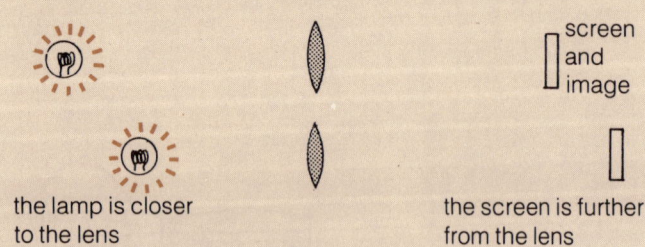

4 Are the following the same or different for the object and its image? Copy and put 'same' or 'different' in the table.

Colour	Brightness	Shape	Way up	Way round

Experiment. A home-made projector

Use a colour slide, lit by a lamp, as an object. Place a lens and screen as shown and move them about until you have a large image of the slide on the screen. You will notice that this image is upside down and reversed. Since it is formed on a screen, it is a **real** image.

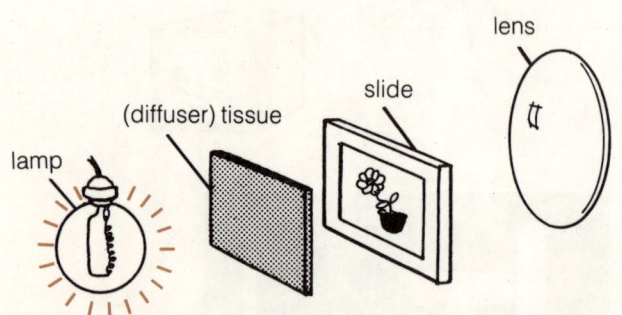

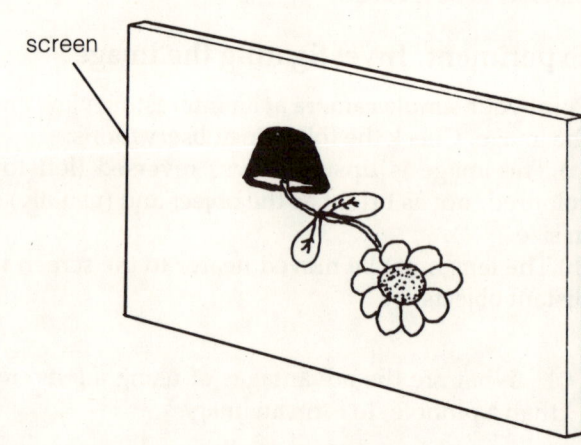

A home-made slide projector

5 Criticize your home-made projector.

Magnifying glass

If a convex lens is close to an object, an image is not formed on a screen. An image can be seen by looking into the lens. This image is upright, magnified and the right way round. It cannot be shone onto a screen and so is a **virtual** image.

A lens forming a virtual image

■ A convex lens can form two sorts of image: upside down, reversed and real, or (with very close objects) magnified, upright and virtual.
■ The real image formed by a convex lens can be made larger by moving the screen away and moving the lens towards the object to refocus.

8 Lenses and rays

Experiment. A lens can focus light

Pass parallel rays of light from a ray box through a convex lens. You will see that the rays are refracted through a single point called the **focus** of the lens. The distance from the focus to the lens is called the **focal length**. Draw round the lens, mark the focus and measure the focal length. Repeat with a stronger lens (one that is more curved). You will find that a strong lens has a short focal length and a weak lens has a long focal length.

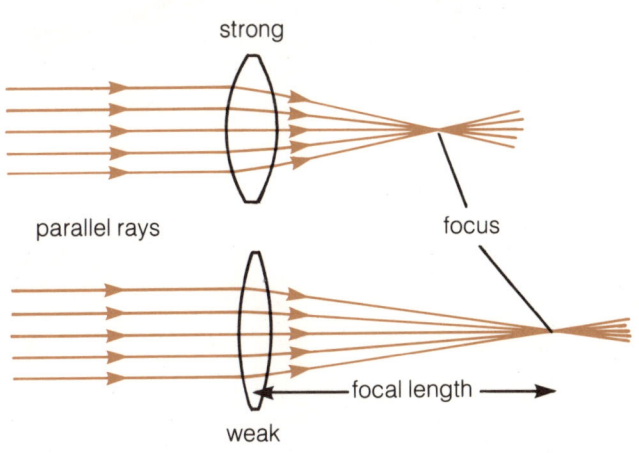

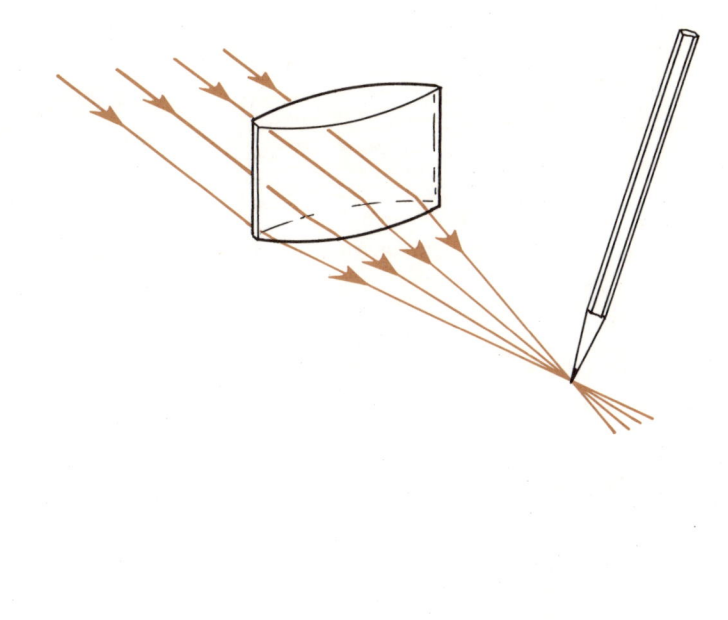

The principal focus of a convex lens

Experiment. Measuring the focal length of a concave lens

Concave lenses are thinner in the centre than they are at the edges and make parallel rays of light spread out (diverge). To find the focus of a concave lens you must mark the diverging rays with dots and then draw the rays back until they meet. This type of lens has a negative focal length. Measure the focal length of a concave lens. Then put a concave and convex lens together and measure the focal length of the combined lens.

1 Choose a focal length for each lens from the value given. Copy and complete the table.

Lens	◗	(	I	)(
Focal length				
Strong or weak				

Choose from 20 cm; 5 cm; -5 cm; -15 cm.

The principal focus of a concave lens

- A convex lens has a positive focal length.
- A concave lens has a negative focal length.
- A strong lens has a shorter focal length than a weak lens.

How are images formed?

Real images

If a multiple slit is placed in front of a ray box, several rays of light will spread out from the lamp. If these rays are reflected by a concave mirror or pass through a lens, they can form into a cone of rays that travel towards a point. A real image is formed when light rays travel and meet like this.

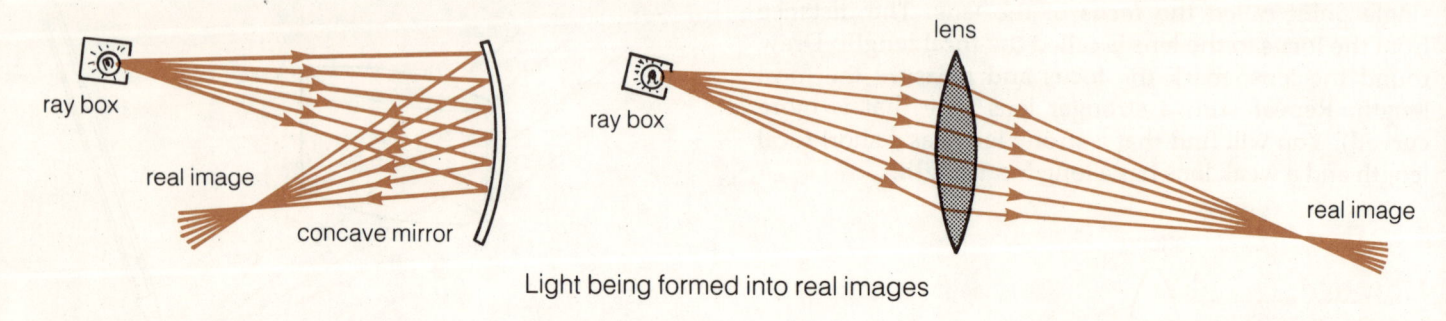

Light being formed into real images

How to draw light rays through a lens to find a real image

Of the many light rays that leave the top of an object, two can be traced easily through the lens.

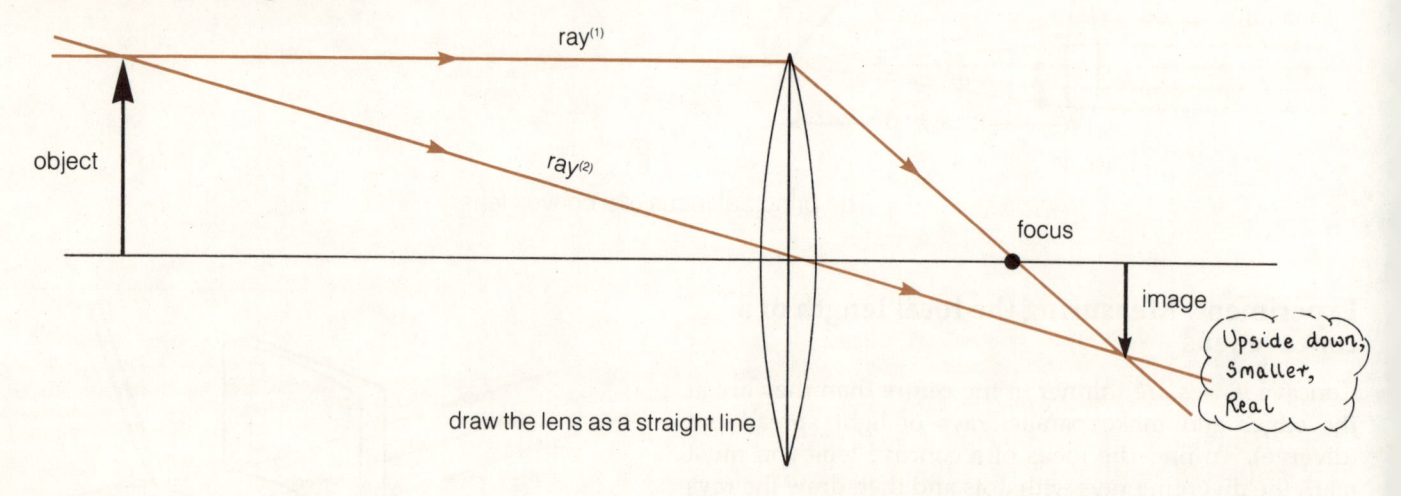

Ray 1.
Draw this ray from the top of the object parallel to the axis until it hits the lens, then bend it down through the focus.

Ray 2.
Draw this ray from the top of the object to the centre of the lens and then carry it straight on. (A thin lens has almost parallel sides at its centre.) The place where these two rays meet is where the top of the image will be formed. It is best to draw ray diagrams on centimetre graph paper.

2 For each question draw ray diagrams to find the position and size of the image. The focal length is 3 cm in each case and the object distances are given. Copy and complete the table.

Focal length	Object distance	Image distance	Object height	Image height
3 cm	7 cm		2 cm	
3 cm	6 cm		2 cm	
3 cm	5 cm		2 cm	

Virtual images

Sometimes light rays leave a mirror, lens or water surface as a cone, but are moving away from a point. Although the rays never meet, they can be received by the eye and appear to be coming from a point. The eye 'sees' an image at that point although nothing is actually there. This is a virtual image.

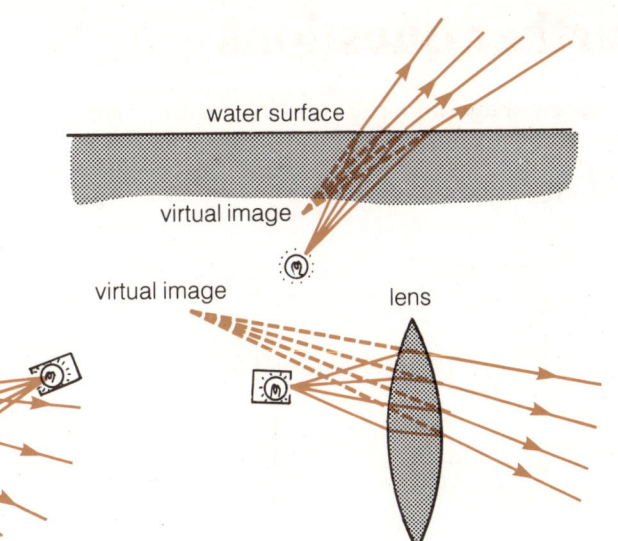

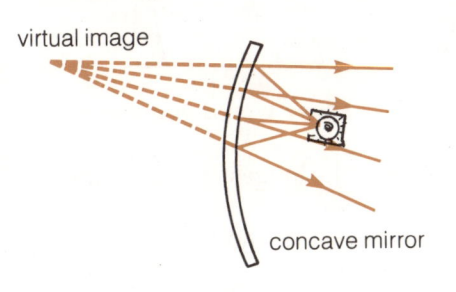

Light being formed into virtual images

How to draw light rays through a lens to find a virtual image

Draw rays 1 and 2 as before (p. 30). If the object is between the focus and the lens, the two rays do not meet after they leave the lens. However they do meet if you produce them backwards. The virtual image is formed at this meeting point. It is upright, magnified and virtual.

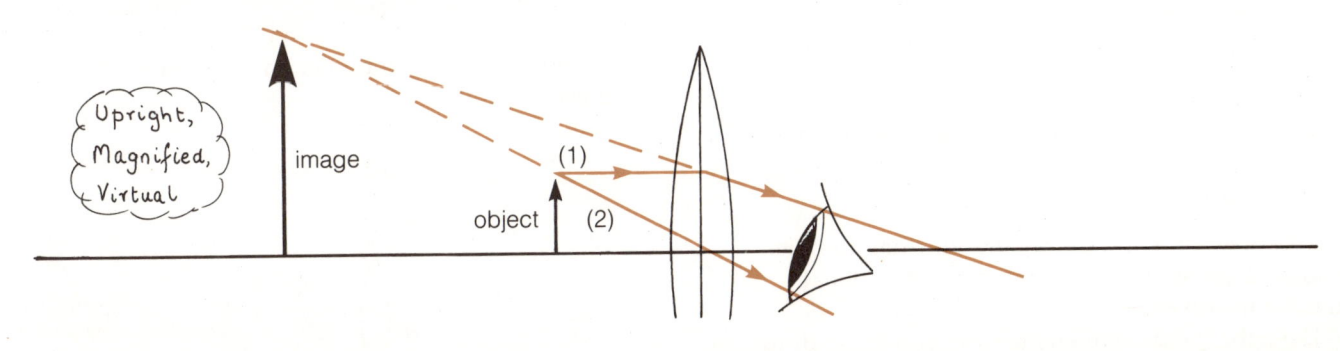

3 Find the image position and size for objects placed at the following distances from a convex lens. The focal length of the lens is 3 cm in each case. Copy and complete the table.

Focal length	Object distance	Image distance	Object height	Image height
3 cm	2 cm		1 cm	
3 cm	1 cm		1 cm	

Summary of refraction and lenses

- Light is refracted towards the normal when it .... enters a denser medium.
- Refraction makes clear materials look .... less deep than they really are.
- Total internal reflection occurs when the angle of incidence inside a material is .... greater than its critical angle.
- Totally reflecting prisms (45°, 45°, 90°) are used in .... periscopes, binoculars, cycle reflectors.
- A convex lens forms two types of image. When the object is outside the focus the image is .... real, upside-down, reversed.
- When the object is inside the focus the image is .... virtual, upright, magnified.
- The focus of a convex lens is the point through which .... parallel rays are refracted.

Further questions

4 Draw diagrams of: a concave mirror; a concave lens; a convex mirror; a convex lens.

5 Copy and complete these ray diagrams.

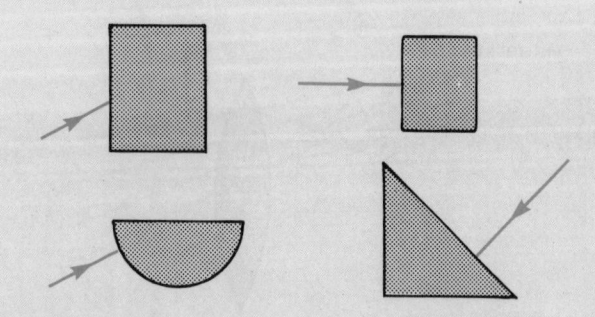

6 Explain why the underside of a water surface can act like a mirror.

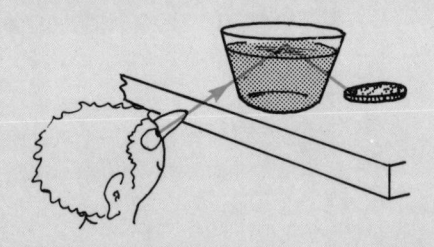

7 Draw a diagram to show how two prisms can be used to make a periscope. Give two reasons why prisms are preferred to mirrors when making a high quality instrument.

8 The diagram shows a ray drawn from an object A through an optical component (mirror or lens).
(a) Is it a mirror or lens?
(b) Describe the path of another ray you could draw to help find the position of the image.
(c) Describe the image that would be formed in this case.

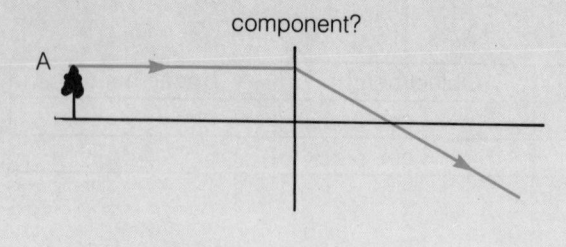

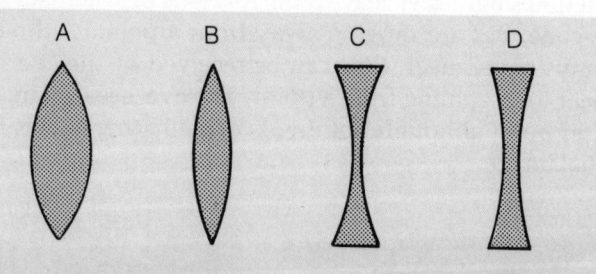

9 (a) Which of the lenses above would you choose as a magnifying glass?
(b) Which lens would have the longest positive focal length?
(c) Which lens would have the shortest negative focal length?

10 The eye cannot see the coin at the bottom of the tank. Draw a diagram and explain how filling the tank with water brings the coin into view.

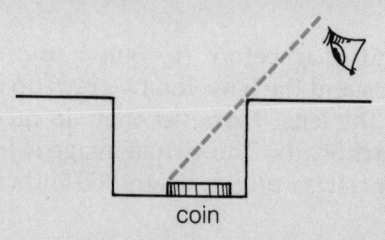

11 Copy and carry the rays on through the lenses in these diagrams.

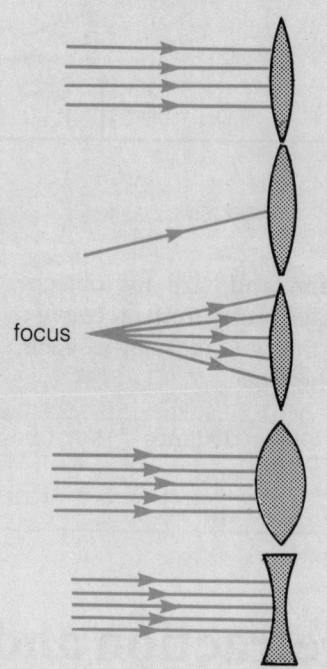

9 Optical instruments

Lenses are used to form images in a number of important instruments.

The lens camera

A camera is a light-proof box with a lens at one end and photographic film at the other.

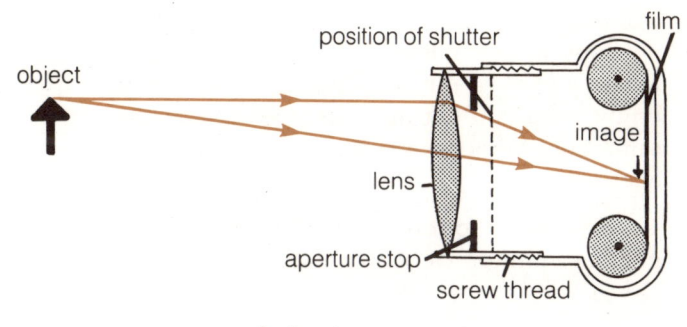

A simple camera

Focusing

The lens forms a small, real, upside-down image on the film (p. 27). This image must be focused by moving the lens 'out' for a close object and 'in' for an object in the distance. Marks on the lens help to set the lens for the correct distance.

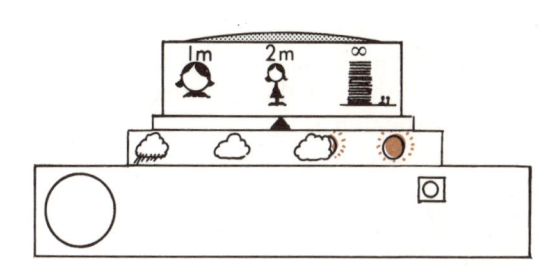

A camera has marks on the lens ring to help with focusing

Light control

It takes very little light to activate photographic film and capture an image. Too much light will spoil the film so it is important to control the amount of light that falls on the film. There are two ways of doing this.

(a) The shutter time control

The shutter stops light from reaching the film. The shutter can be opened for short times (e.g. 1/250 s) or longer times (e.g. 1/30 s). More light will fall on the film with long opening times than with short ones. Note that moving objects will appear blurred unless the opening times are very short.

Shutter opening times	1/30 s	1/60 s	1/125 s	1/250 s
	'long'			'short'

1 Which of these words correctly describes the image formed on the film of a camera: upright; reversed; upside down; coloured; small; black and white; the right way round; large?

2 Copy and complete table.

Shutter opening times	1/30 s	1/250 s
Is this a long or short time?		
How much light will fall on the film, a lot or a little?		
Will the image of a moving cyclist be sharp or blurred?		

33

(b) The aperture control

The amount of light that reaches the film can also be controlled by the size of a hole or **aperture** placed behind the lens. A large hole will allow a bright image to form on the film. The aperture control is marked in f-numbers or pictures. (An aperture with a value of f/8 means the diameter of the hole is ⅛ of the focal length of the lens.)

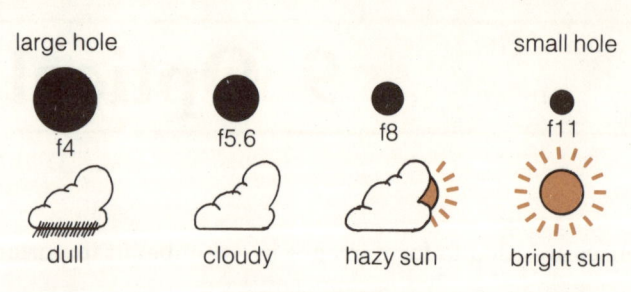

The apertures needed for different lighting conditions:
- f4 — dull
- f5.6 — cloudy
- f8 — hazy sun
- f11 — bright sun

(large hole → small hole)

3 Copy and complete. A _____ aperture is needed to take a photograph on a dull day in order to form a bright image on the film. To form an image of the same brightness on a sunny day requires a _____ aperture.

4 Write down four things that this lens camera has got that a pinhole camera (p. 14) has not got.

5 Which of the combinations of shutter times and apertures would you choose to give:
(a) the largest amount of light on the film,
(b) the smallest amount of light on the film?

	1/30 s	1/250 s
f/11	A	B
f/4	C	D

Taking a photograph

Decide on the picture you want to take and then:
(i) Choose a shutter time. (This will depend on the brightness of the light, whether the object is moving and the sensitivity of the film.)
(ii) Choose an aperture.
(iii) Focus.
..... then squeeze the trigger gently until it clicks.

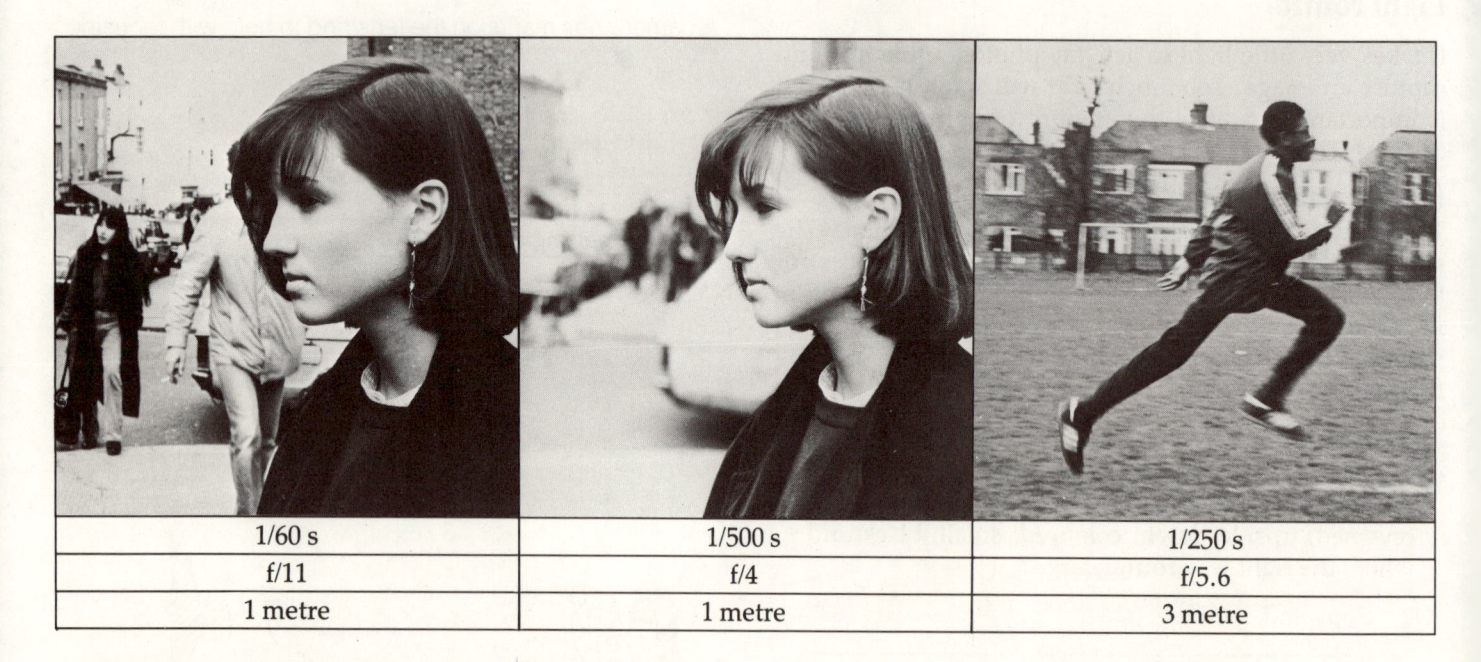

shutter time, aperture, focus, shoot

1/60 s	1/500 s	1/250 s
f/11	f/4	f/5.6
1 metre	1 metre	3 metre

6 Why was a shutter speed of 1/250 s chosen for the photograph of the sprinter?

7 Describe the difference between the portrait taken with an aperture of f/4 and the same picture taken with an aperture of f/11.

Depth of field

You will notice in the photographs above, that the scene is sharp for a long distance behind the person when a small aperture (f/11) is used. A small aperture is said to give a large **depth of field**. (The photo is sharp right into the distance). A large aperture gives a small depth of field and the photo is only sharp over a small distance, making it more important to focus the lens carefully.

■ A camera forms a small, real, upside-down image on sensitive film. The brightness of the image can be controlled by the shutter opening times and the aperture size.

The slide projector

Properly designed projectors give a much brighter and clearer image than the home-made projector on page 28.

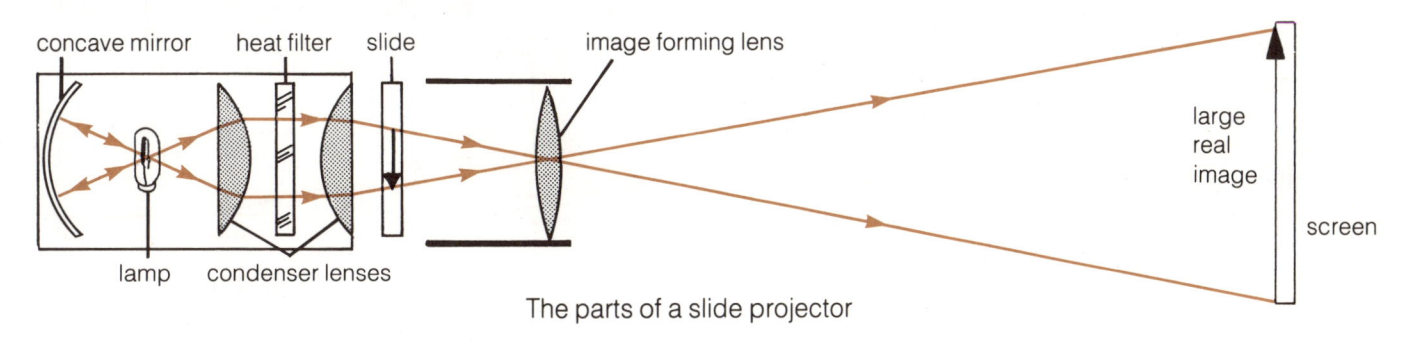

The parts of a slide projector

To get as much light as possible onto the slide, to produce a bright image, the designer has:
(a) used a very powerful (500 W) lamp,
(b) put a curved mirror behind the lamp to reflect the light forward,
(c) used two cheap lenses (called condenser lenses) to bend the light onto the slide.

To remove heat and prevent it reaching and buckling the slide, the designer has:
(d) built in a cooling fan and put slots in the lid,
(e) used a piece of special glass, called a heat filter, that lets light through but stops infra-red radiation (p. 93). (This radiation carries much of the heat away from the lamp.)

Finally a good quality lens is used to form an image of the brightly lit slide on a screen.

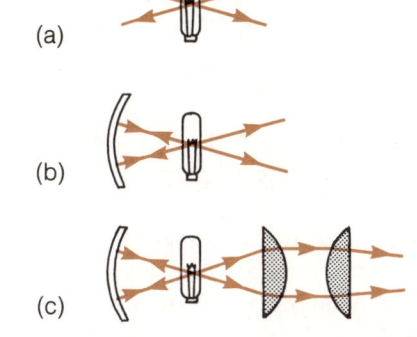

8 How must a slide be put into a projector to give an upright image, the correct way round?

9 What two things must be done to get a larger image?

10 What difference, other than size, is there between a large and small image?

11 What would happen if the heat filter were removed?

12 What would you do to the slide to correct these images of the letter R? Say whether to turn it upside down, to turn it round sidways, or both.

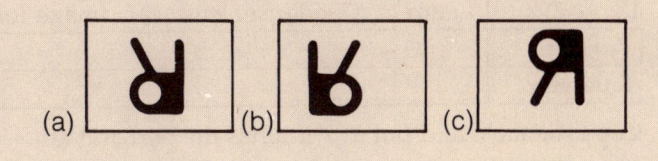

35

Back projection

The image can be much brighter if it shines onto a tissue screen and is viewed from the other side to the projector. Try it and see. Why do you think a brighter image can be seen this way?

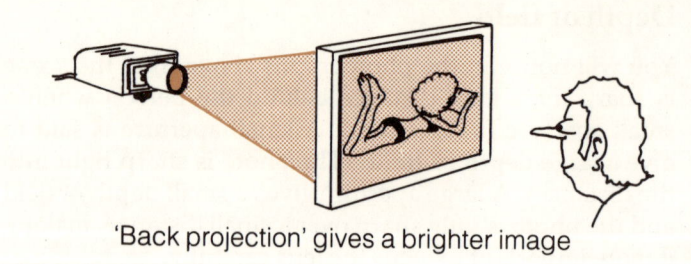

'Back projection' gives a brighter image

- A projector produces a real, magnified, upside-down image on a screen.
- The further away the screen is, the larger and less bright the image is.

The enlarger

The photographic enlarger uses a convex lens to form a magnified image of a small 'negative'. This image is used to make a large photograph from a small negative. The negative is evenly lit by passing light from a 'pearl' lamp through a condenser lens. A good quality convex lens then forms a real image of this bright negative on photographic paper. There are two controls for changing the size of the image; one that moves the head of the enlarger away from the base, one that focuses the image. The lamp is completely enclosed in its house so that light cannot escape into the darkroom except through the lenses. Black cooling fins (p. 96) on the outside of the lamp-house help to remove heat produced by the lamp.

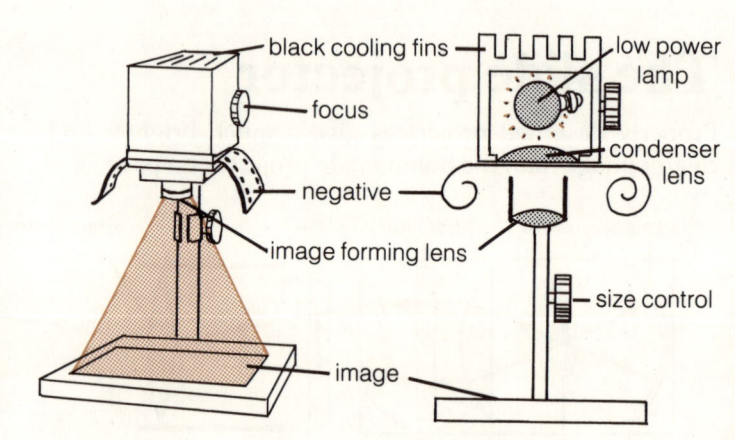

A photographic enlarger

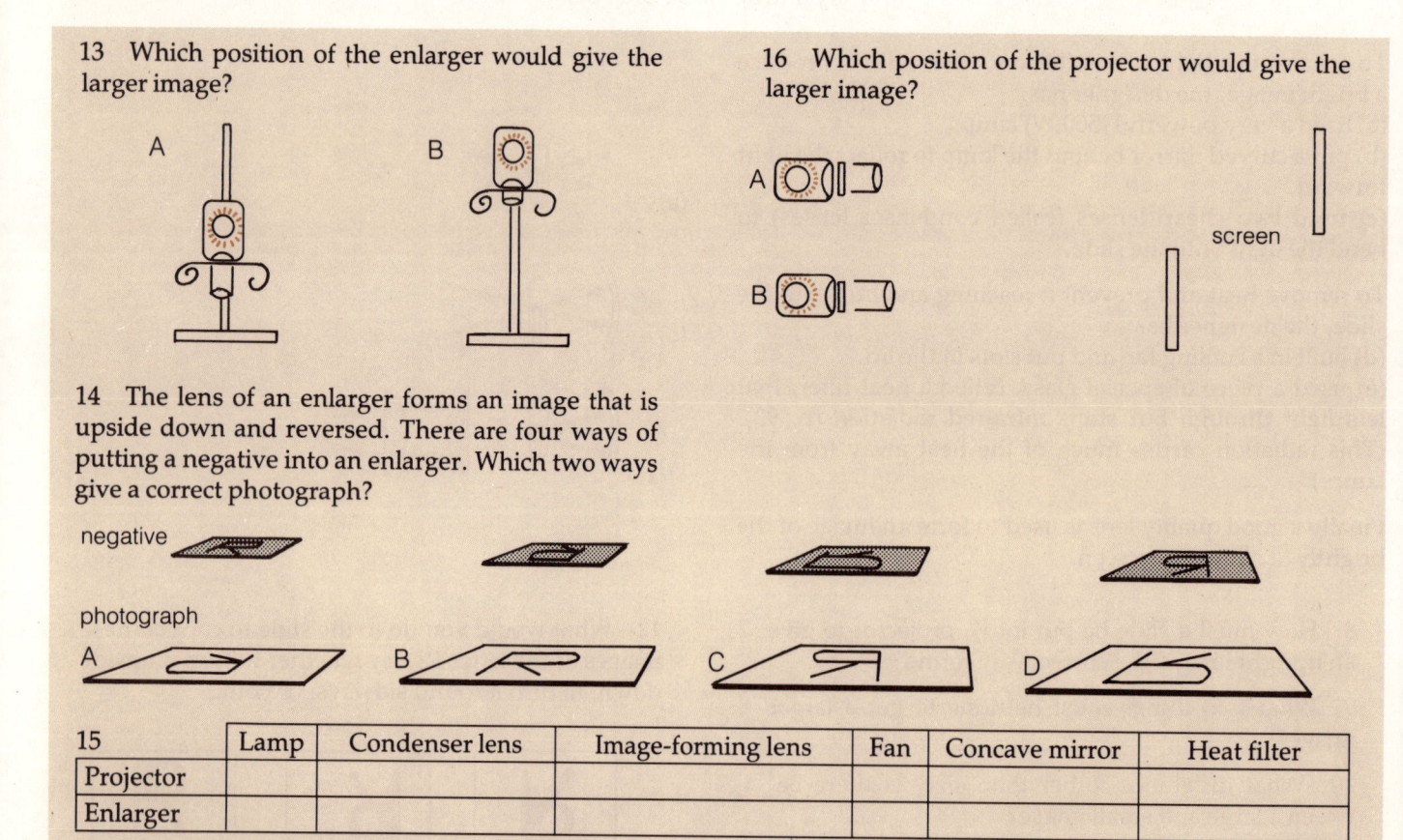

13 Which position of the enlarger would give the larger image?

16 Which position of the projector would give the larger image?

14 The lens of an enlarger forms an image that is upside down and reversed. There are four ways of putting a negative into an enlarger. Which two ways give a correct photograph?

15	Lamp	Condenser lens	Image-forming lens	Fan	Concave mirror	Heat filter
Projector						
Enlarger						

Copy the table and put a ✓ if it has the part and an × if it has not.

The eye

Our eyes use lenses to form images of the world for us to see. The clear front part of the eye-ball (1. the **cornea**) and the clear liquid behind it (2. the **aqueous humour**) form a liquid lens of fixed strength. The second **lens** (3) is flexible so that its focal length can be changed. These two lenses form a small, real, upside-down image on the **retina** (4). The retina is sensitive to light and sends messages to the brain about the image. The **vitreous humour** (5) – a clear jelly – prevents the eye-ball from collapsing.

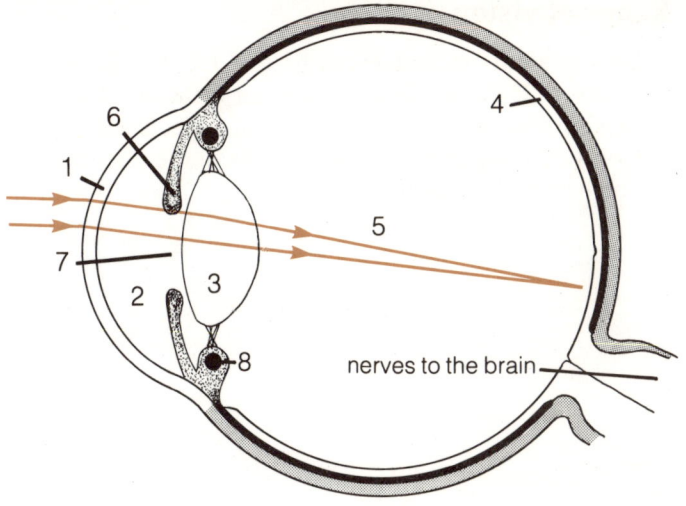

The image-forming parts of the human eye

The effect of bright light on the eye

The coloured **iris** (6) automatically controls the amount of light entering the eye by changing the size of the **pupil** (7). The brighter the light, the smaller the hole. The aperture of a camera is a copy of this natural device.

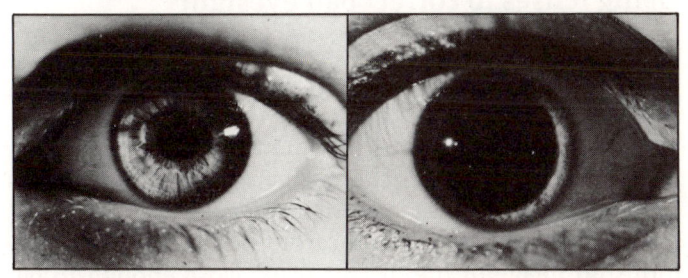

Pupil in bright light   Pupil in dim light

The effect of distance on the eye

The eye can form clear images on the retina of close or distant objects. It does this by changing the thickness of its lens. The **ciliary muscles** (8) bulge, relaxing the tension on the lens, which becomes more convex. The eye can then focus close objects.

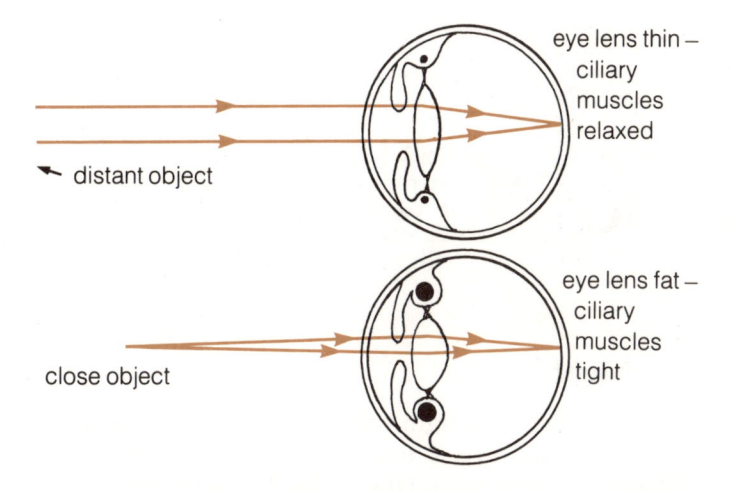

distant object — eye lens thin – ciliary muscles relaxed

close object — eye lens fat – ciliary muscles tight

How the eye lens changes shape as it focuses on near and distant objects

17 Copy this table and fill in details of what each part of the eye does.

Number of part	Name	What it does (see text)
1	cornea	
2	aqueous humour	
3	lens	
4	retina	
5	vitreous humour	
6	iris	
7	pupil	
8	ciliary muscle	

■ Lenses in the eye form small, upside-down images of the things we look at.

Range of vision

A person with normal eyesight can focus comfortably from about 25 cm to objects in the far distance. A person with **short sight** cannot see distant objects clearly. A person with **long sight** can see objects in the distance but not objects that are near.

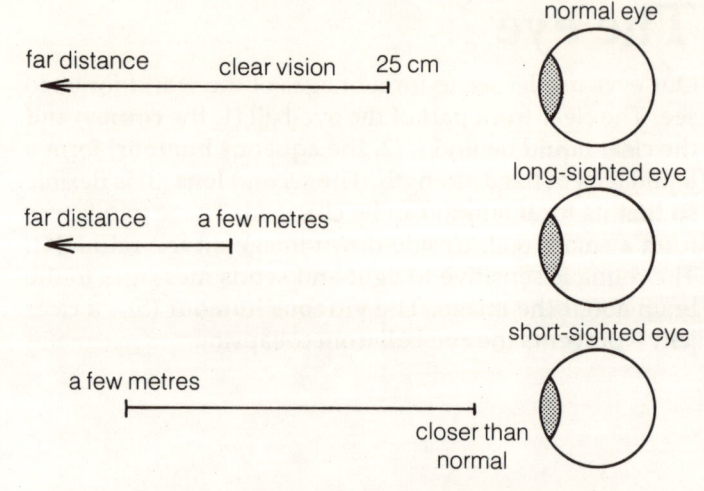

The focusing ranges of the three types of sight

Using lenses to correct bad eyesight

Short sight

A person with short sight cannot focus distant objects. The lens of the eye is too strong and forms an image in front of the retina. To enable such a person to see distant things, a **concave** lens (a lens that spreads out the light) of suitable strength, is placed in front of the eye. This lens forms an image of the distant scene close enough to be focused clearly. This image is upright, reduced in size and virtual.

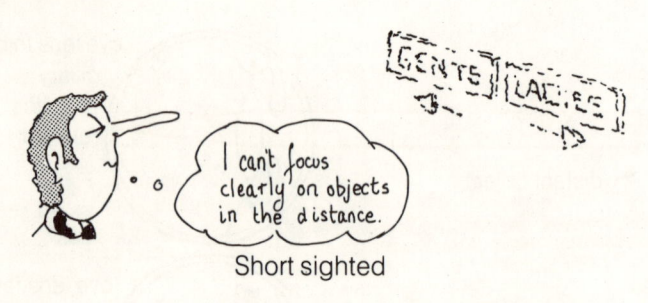

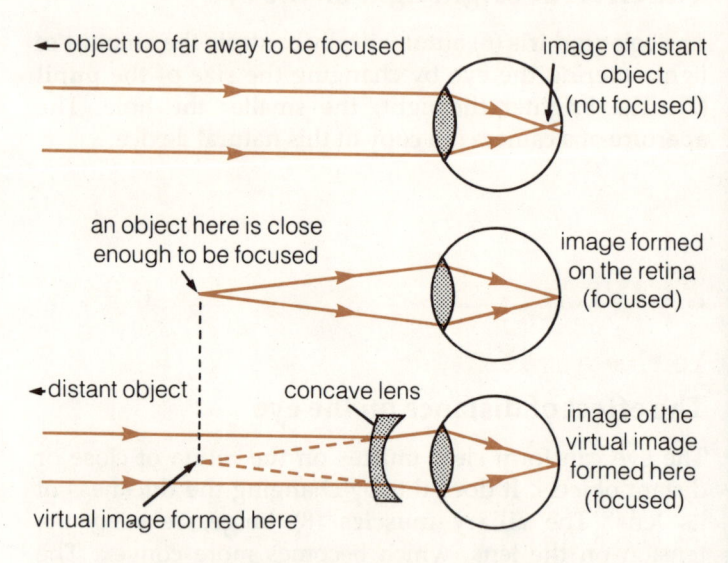

Short sighted

The use of a concave lens to correct for short sight

Long sight

A person with long sight cannot focus on close objects. The lens of the eye is too weak and focuses the rays towards an image behind the retina. To enable the person to see close things, a **convex** lens of suitable strength is used to form an image far enough away for it to be focused by the eye. This image is upright, slightly enlarged and virtual.

Long sighted

The use of a convex lens to correct for long sight

38

18   Copy and complete table.

Defect	Name of defect	Type of lens used to correct the defect
Eyes cannot focus on distant objects		
Eyes cannot focus on nearby objects		

19   The lens of a short-sighted eye is too _____ and forms an image of distant objects in _____ of the retina. To be seen clearly the object has to be moved _____ _____ the eye. The lens of a long-sighted eye is too _____ and focuses the rays from a close object to a point that lies _____ the retina. To be seen clearly the object has to be moved _____ from the eye.

■ Short-sighted eyes cannot focus on distant objects.
■ Concave lenses are used to correct short sight.
■ Long-sighted eyes cannot focus on nearby objects.
■ Convex lenses are used to correct for long sight.

Playing tricks on your eyes

You have a blind spot

Close your left eye, hold the book at arm's length and look at the spot. Move the book towards you, still looking at the spot and the rabbit will disappear. The eye has a blind spot and when the rabbit's image falls on that spot, the image disappears. There is a gap in the retina where the optic nerve leaves the eye.

Two eyes are better than one

Try to make two pencil points touch while using only one eye. It is rather difficult to tell when the two pencil points are the same distance away. Two eyes give us two pictures of an object from different angles (called binocular vision) and allow us to make a better guess of its distance away.

20   Why is binocular vision particularly important in driving a car or stepping off a kerb?

21   Why is it useful for hunting animals (including man) to have two eyes at the front of the head? Why do many of the animals they hunt have eyes at the sides of their heads?

Optical illusions

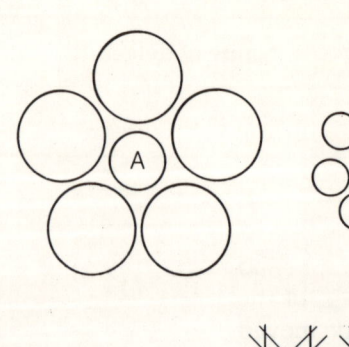

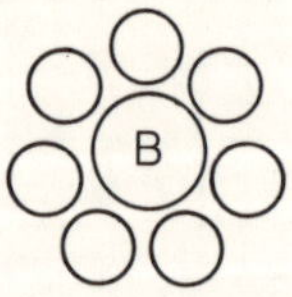

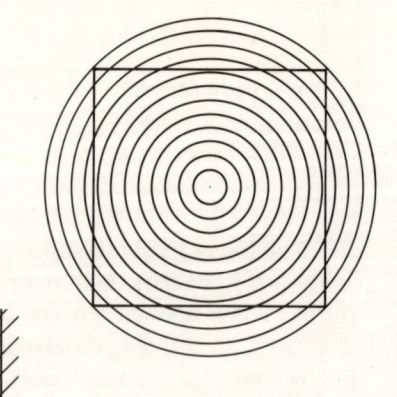

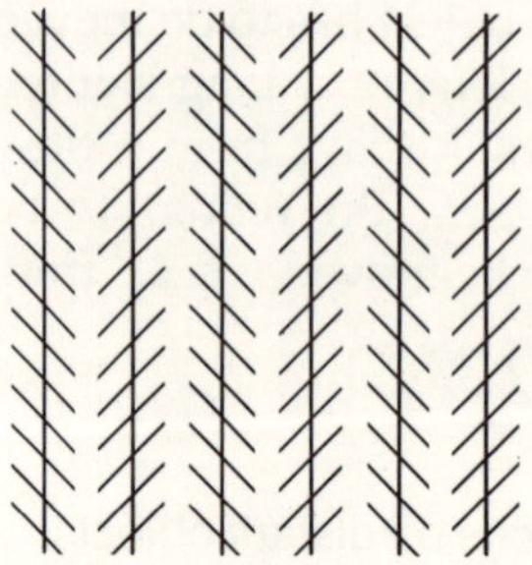

Do your eyes tell you that:
the circles go round when you rotate the book,
circle B is bigger than circle A,
the lines of the square are curved,
the lines are not parallel?
If they do, you have been tricked. Sometimes we cannot rely on our eyes to tell us the truth!

Brightness and vision

If you look at a written page and a coloured picture in bright light and then dim the light, it becomes more difficult to read the writing. The colours also disappear becoming shades of grey. The eye cannot see colours when the light is dim. Check this when you are in a dimly lit place.

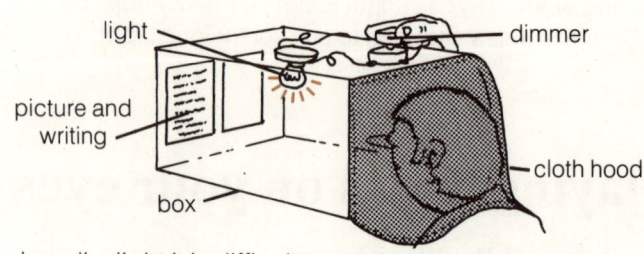

In a dim light it is difficult to read and colours cannot be seen

Persistence of vision

The image on the retina is held by the eye for a fraction of a second, even after the object has been removed and there is nothing to be seen. This is called **persistence of vision**. If a second picture (slightly altered) replaces the first, the two images merge, appearing to have moved slightly. If image follows image rapidly enough, it looks as if the pictures are moving. The illusion of moving pictures uses the persistence of vision of the eye. Home movies project 18 still pictures per second. To prevent flicker, professional movies and television pictures are projected rather faster than this.

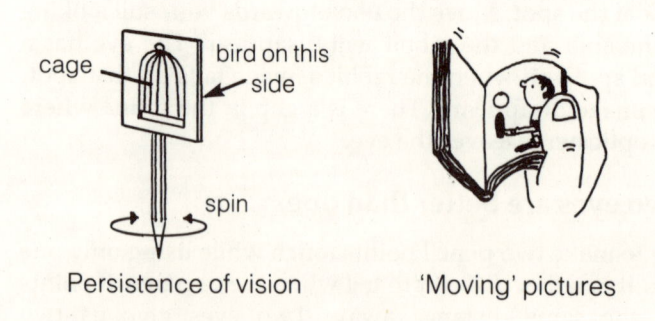

Persistence of vision

'Moving' pictures

22 Explain how to draw pictures on the pages of a notebook that can be made to look as if they are moving. How does the illusion work?

Animation

Plasticine models (or drawings) can be made to look as if they move, by filming them with a cine camera. To animate like this, take one picture of the model, move it slightly and then take another. Keep this up until you have finished the movement you have in mind. When you run the finished film through a projector, it will look as if the model is moving smoothly.

Making an animated film

23 A boy took 720 separate pictures, on movie film, of a plasticine dragon, which he moved slightly in between each shot. He then projected the film at 18 frames (pictures) per second. How long would his film last? What differences would you notice if he changed the projector speed to 9 frames per second?

The telescope

The telescope uses two lenses to make distant objects look closer.

Experiment. Making a telescope

Take a convex lens with a long focal length and fix it to a metre rule with plasticine. Point the rule at a distant lamp and find the image that the lens forms. Do this by moving a grease-proof paper screen along the rule until the image is focused. (Note that this image is real, small and upside down.) Use a second, short focus lens as a magnifying glass to view this image. Then remove the paper screen and look through both lenses at the lamp. The lamp looks closer than it really is and so seems bigger. This arrangement of lenses is a simple telescope. Use your telescope to look at other distant objects.

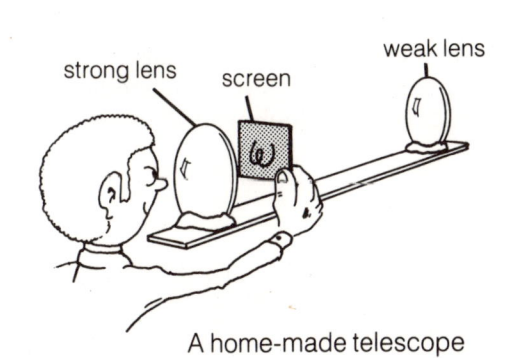

A home-made telescope

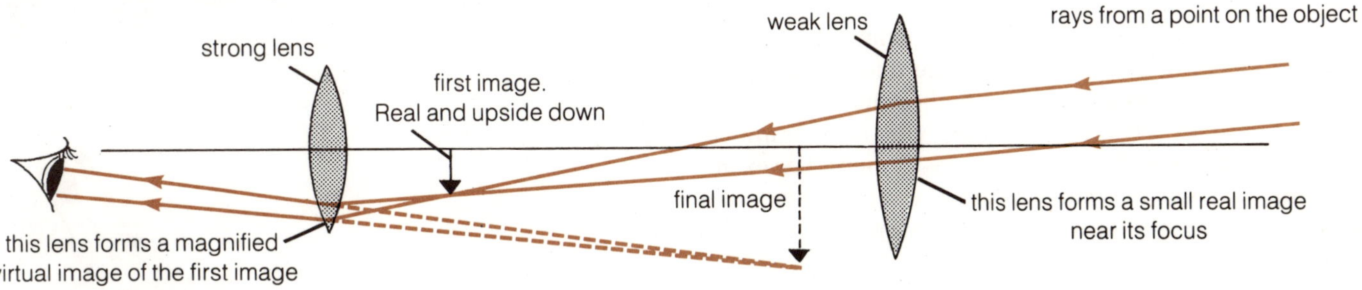

The image formed by a telescope

Magnifying power

It is useful to know the focal lengths of each lens of a telescope because the

$$\frac{\text{long focal length}}{\text{short focal length}} = \text{magnifying power.}$$

It is also useful to know the diameter of the front lens because the larger it is, the brighter the image will be.

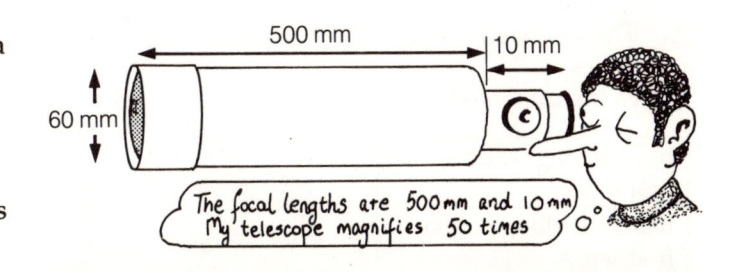

The focal lengths are 500mm and 10mm. My telescope magnifies 50 times.

24 Copy and answer these questions about the lenses of a telescope.

Lens	Is it a weak or strong lens?	Has it a short or long focal length?	Does it form a real or virtual image?
The front lens			
The lens near the eye			

■ A telescope has a weak lens that forms a small, real, upside-down image and a strong lens to magnify this image. The final image is upside down and virtual.

41

The microscope

We have seen that a convex lens can form a magnified image (p. 28). For greater magnification two convex lenses must be used.

Experiment. Making a microscope

Take two convex lenses with focal lengths of about 5 cm. Fix them to a metre rule with plasticine so that they are 15 cm apart. Look through one lens at your finger nail placed just outside the other lens. Then slowly move your finger away until you see a large upside-down image of your nail. With simple lenses the image is not perfect. Notice how distorted it is and how sometimes it has coloured edges. If you want greater magnification put the lenses 20 cm apart. You will have to look more carefully for the image, but it will be much larger. How many times do you think your microscope magnifies? If you can, use a real microscope to look at small interesting objects.

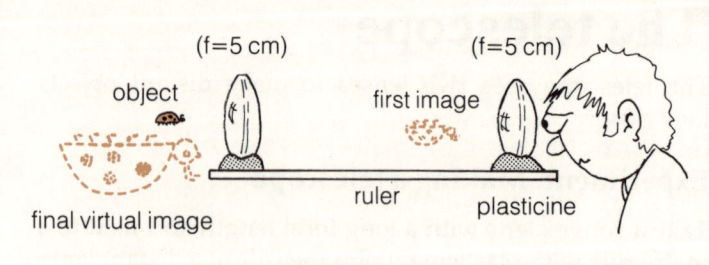

How it works

The first lens forms a real magnified image of the object. The second lens acts as a magnifying glass, forming a virtual, upside-down, final image.

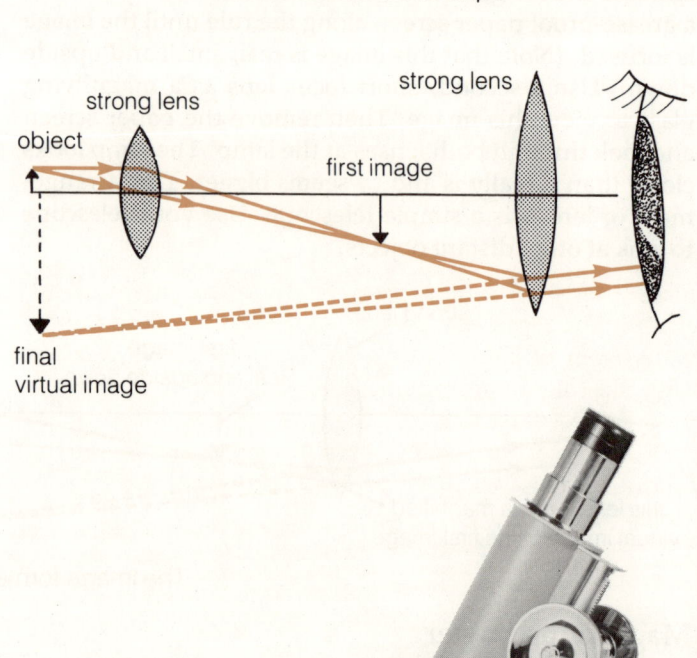

Real microsocopes

Microscope lenses are properly designed and should give a better image than your home-made microscope. Each lens is usually marked with a number that tells us the number of times it magnifies. Multiplying these numbers gives the total magnification of the instrument. For example if the first lens magnifies 10 times and the other lens 5 times, the two together will magnify 50 times.

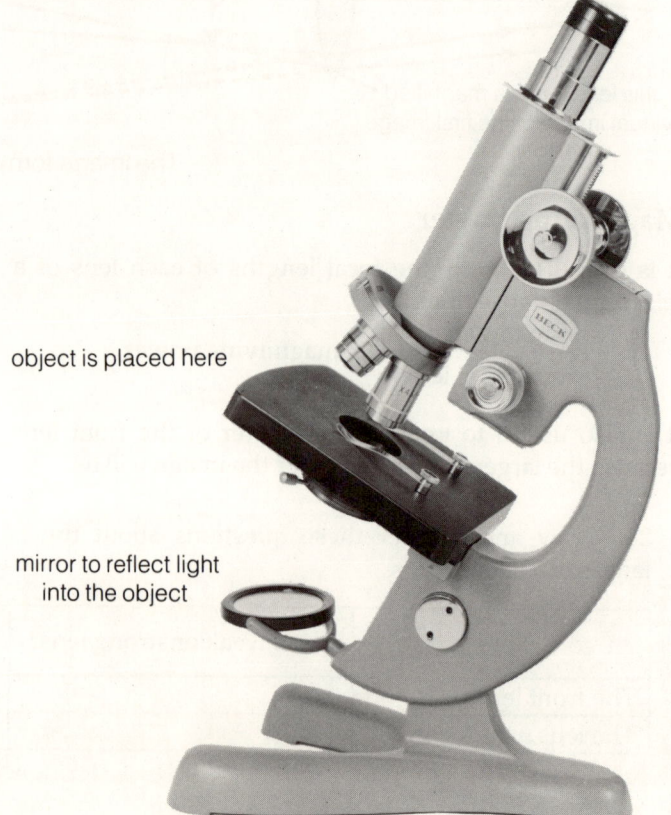

A home-made microscope

object is placed here

mirror to reflect light into the object

25 These questions are about microscopes and telescopes.
Which instrument(s):

has a strong (short focus) first lens?	
has weak (long focus) first lens?	
have a strong second (eye-piece) lens?	
has a nearby object?	
has a distant object?	
form an intermediate real image?	
form a virtual, upside-down, final image?	

Copy the table and put in microscope, telescope or both.

10 Colour

Have you noticed that when you look through the corner of a prism, you see a world with multicoloured edges? The following experiments examine those colours more closely.

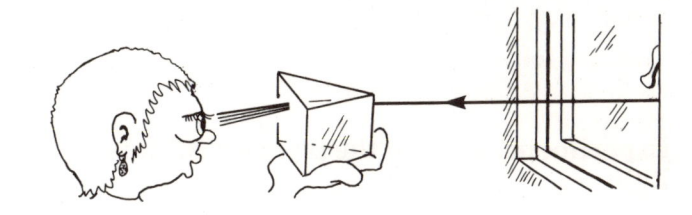

Experiment. Getting colours from white light

Use a ray box (or projector) with a slit to shine a ray of light through a prism as shown. Arrange a white screen to collect the light after it has passed through the prism. What do you notice about the light on the screen? How many colours can you see? White light seems to be made up of coloured lights and can be split up into these colours by a prism. The prism separates the colours into what is called a white light **spectrum**.

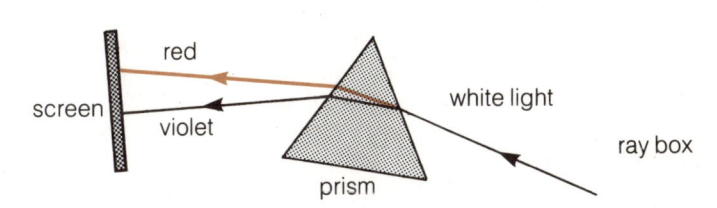

A prism can split white light into a spectrum

Experiment. Making a brighter and purer spectrum

Place a lens between the ray box and the prism of the experiment above. (It is best to remove the slit and use a wide beam of light.) Move the lens and turn the prism until the colours on the screen are as bright and sharp as possible. All the colours of the spectrum should be there with no white light in between. Check you can see the following colours: red, orange, yellow, green, blue, violet.

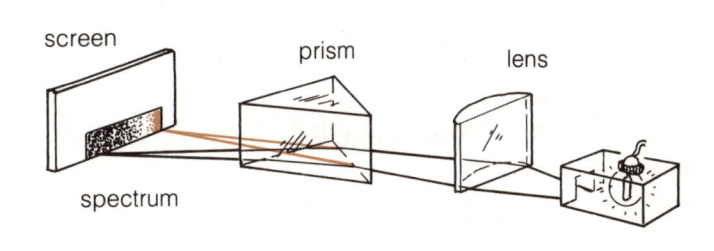

Making a brighter and purer spectrum

1 Which of the following diagrams is correct? They show a prism splitting white light into a spectrum.

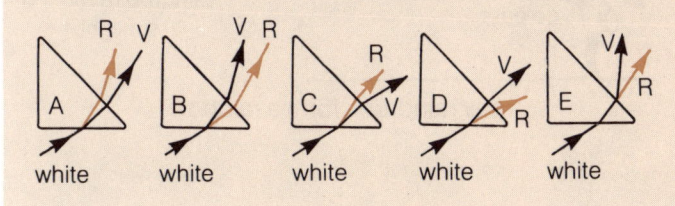

2 'Rely on your gruff bass voice' is a sentence where the first letters of the words stand for the colours of the spectrum. It may help you to remember those colours. Can you think of a better sentence than this?

The primary colours of light

Colour television and colour film use only three colours to produce all the colours of the spectrum. These colours are called primary red, primary green, and primary blue. They can be obtained by passing white light through coloured plastic filters. A filter is a piece of plastic that has been coloured by a dye but that is still clear enough to see through.

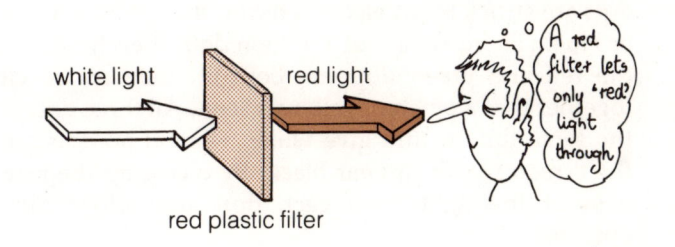

The strange case of the yellow filter

You would expect a yellow filter to allow only yellow light to pass. In fact most yellow filters allow red and green light to pass through as well. And yet the light from the filter looks as yellow as the pure yellow found in a spectrum. The eye sees a mixture of red and green light as the colour yellow, no different from pure yellow itself.

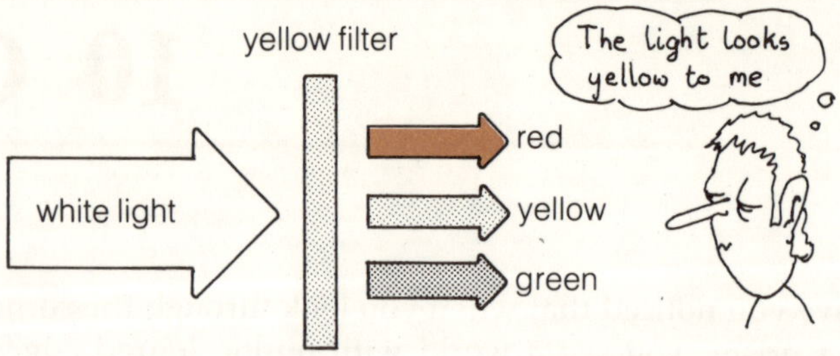

Experiment. Mixing the primary colours of light

Fit two ray-boxes with red and green filters and shine red and green beams onto a white screen. Make these beams overlap and notice that red and green really do look yellow. Add a blue beam by using a third ray box with a blue filter. By switching the ray-boxes on and off check that the following observations are true:

red light mixed with green light looks **yellow**
green light mixed with blue light looks **cyan** (turquoise)
blue light mixed with red light looks **magenta** (pink).
These new colours are called **secondary** colours.
You can also check that where blue, green and red lights overlap a **white** patch of light is seen. Red+Green+Blue=White. (Circles of coloured paint act quite differently and would not give these secondary colours, p. 45.)

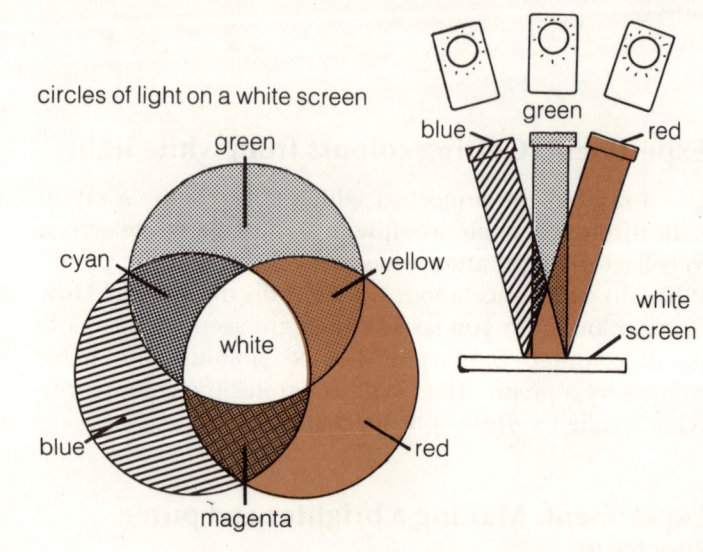

Other ways of breaking white light up into its separate colours

(a) Bright colours can sometimes be seen on soap bubbles, insect wings and patches of oil on water. These all consist of thin layers of clear material. The colours come from a rather complicated double reflection from these layers.

(b) The rainbow.
Raindrops refract sunlight and split it into the colours of the spectrum. As the drops also reflect the light, you have to stand with your back to the Sun to see a rainbow.

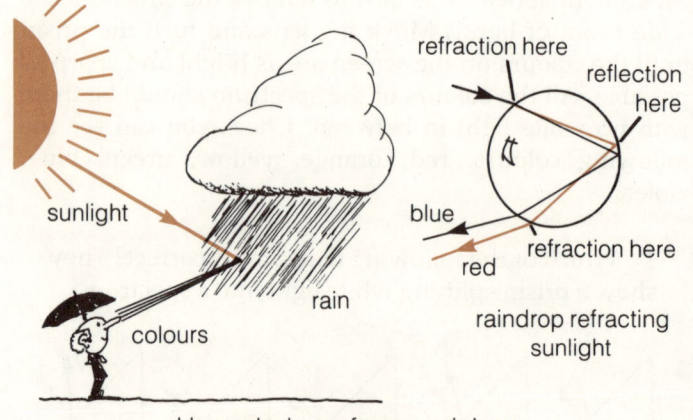

Colour television

The screen of a colour television set is made up of very small fluorescent dots, arranged in threes. When these dots are struck by an electron beam, they glow red, green or blue. (There are about 1 million dots of each colour.) If the red and green dots are both lit, they are so close together that a patch of yellow is seen. All three dots lit at the same time would give white, while if no dots are lit the screen would appear black. By changing the brightness of the light from each dot, any colour can be obtained.

3 Copy and complete these sentences.
The three primary colours of light are _____, _____, and _____. When mixed together with the right brightnesses they make _____ light. Blue light mixed with green light looks _____. Red light mixed with _____ light looks magenta. _____ light mixed with _____ light looks yellow.

4 If red and green lights mixed together make yellow light, how would you change them to make orange light?

5 A pencil stands where red and green strips of light cross. It casts two shadows. What colours would be seen in the places where the numbers are?

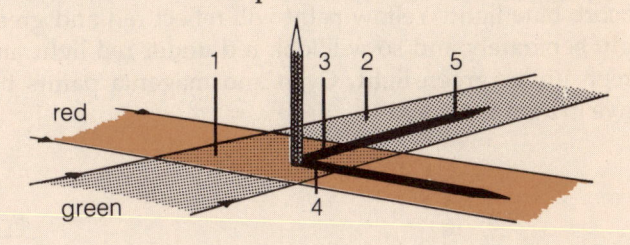

■ 'White' light is a mixture of the coloured lights of the spectrum. The three primary coloured lights can be used to make all the natural colours in a scene.

Why do things look coloured?

It is helpful for this work to think of white light as a mixture of red, green and blue lights.

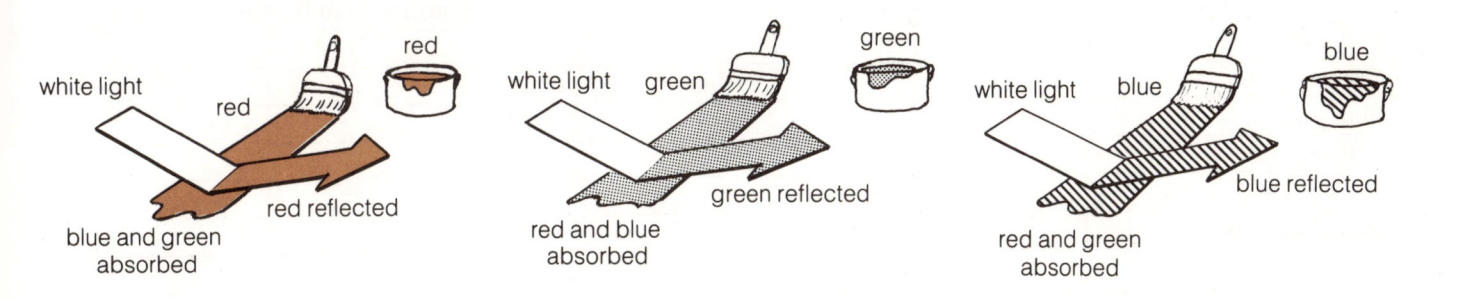

Red paint or dye

The chemicals of the paint are able to absorb (soak up) green and blue light, so that only red light is reflected. The paint therefore looks red when white light falls on it. Note that the red colour comes from the light that strikes the paint. If that light contains no red, the paint would reflect nothing and look black. Green and blue paints act in a similar way.

6 A dancer is lit by a spotlight that keeps changing colour. She has blue hair and is wearing a green blouse and a red skirt. Copy the table and write in the colour each of these items would look, as the colour of the spotlight changes. (Remember, red material only looks red if the spotlight contains red light, otherwise it will look black.)

Spotlight colour	Red skirt	Green blouse	Blue hair
White			
Red			
Green			
Blue			
Yellow (red + green)			

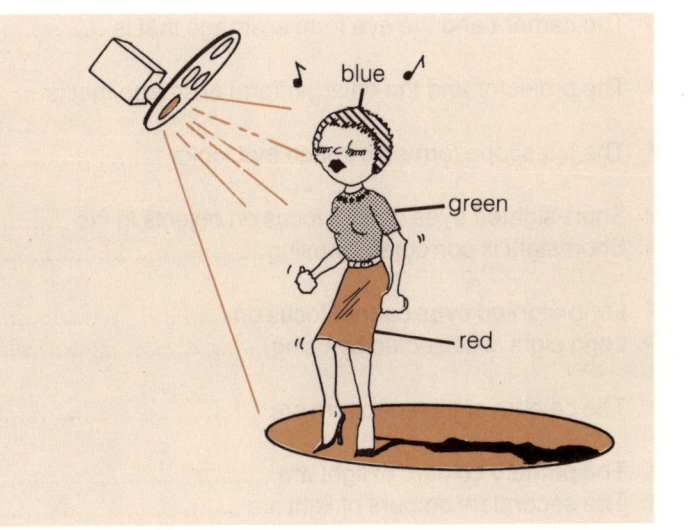

Yellow, cyan and magenta paints

Yellow paint reflects red and green light which combine to look yellow to our eyes. Yellow paint must therefore absorb blue light. Yellow paint will reflect red and green light separately and so will look red under red light and green under green light. Cyan and magenta paints behave in a similar way.

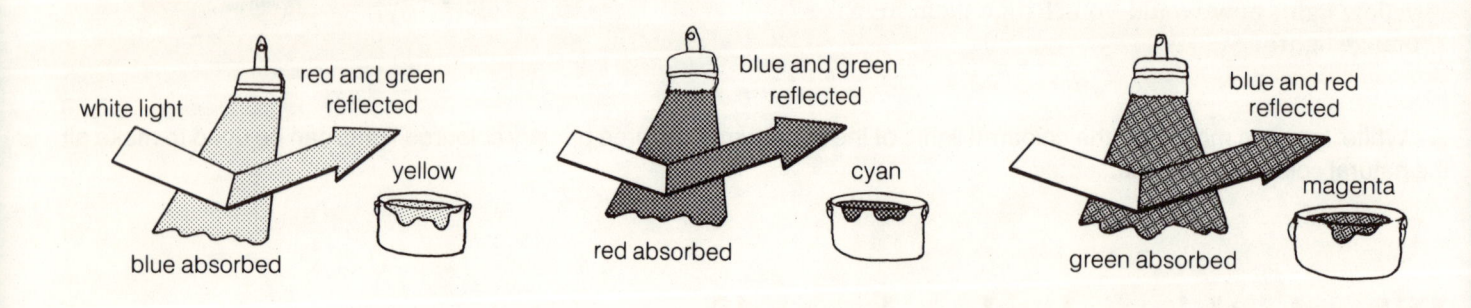

7 Copy and complete.

Colour of paint	The colours of light that are reflected	The colours of light that are absorbed
Red paint		
Green paint		
Blue paint		
Yellow paint		
Cyan paint		
Magenta paint		

8 This diagram is a way of showing how yellow paint absorbs blue light and reflects red and green. Draw similar diagrams for cyan, magenta, red, green and blue paints.

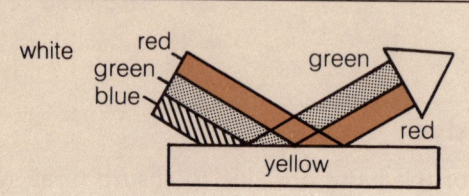

Summary of 'image makers' and colour

- The camera and the eye form an image that is .... small, upside down, reversed and real.
- The projector and the enlarger form an image that is .... large, upside down, reversed and real.
- The telescope forms an image that looks .... large, upside down, reversed and is virtual.
- Short-sighted eyes cannot focus on objects in the .... distance.
- Short sight is corrected by using .... concave lenses of suitable strength.
- Long-sighted eyes cannot focus on .... nearby objects.
- Long sight is corrected by using .... convex lenses of suitable strength.
- The colours of the spectrum are .... red, orange, yellow, green, blue, violet.
- The primary colours of light are .... red, green, blue.
- The secondary colours of light are .... yellow, cyan, magenta.

Further questions

9 What do the following controls on a camera do:
(a) the focusing control,
(b) the aperture control,
(c) the shutter speed control?

10

Part	Camera	Eye
Image-forming lens		
Light-sensitive surface		
Aperture control		
Flexible lens		
Shutter		

Copy and put ✓ if it has the part; × if not.

11 Explain how the following focus on an object:
(a) a camera,
(b) a human eye.

12 Which part(s) of a human eye:
(a) play a part in converging the light from a distant object?
(b) adjusts the amount of light that enters the eye?
(c) play a part in changing the strength of the eye lens?

13 Copy this table of the parts found in a slide projector and number them correctly.

Part	Number
Image-forming lens	
Slide	
Condenser lenses	
Heat filter	
Lamp	
Concave mirror	

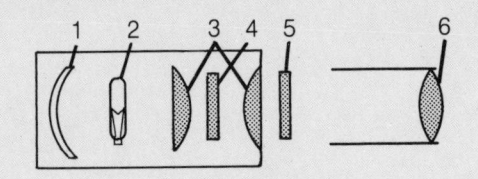

14 Explain the job of the following parts commonly found in a slide projector:
(a) the reflector,
(b) the condenser lenses,
(c) the heat filter,
(d) the projection lens.

15 If the picture from a projector has the image of a piece of dirt in the top right-hand corner, where would you look for the dirt on the slide?

16 Copy this diagram of light passing through a prism. Draw in the path of the red part of the white light.

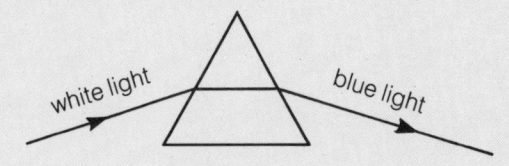

17 A pencil stands in front of a screen in overlapping beams of red and green light. Each beam casts a shadow of the pencil on the screen. What colour would each shadow be?

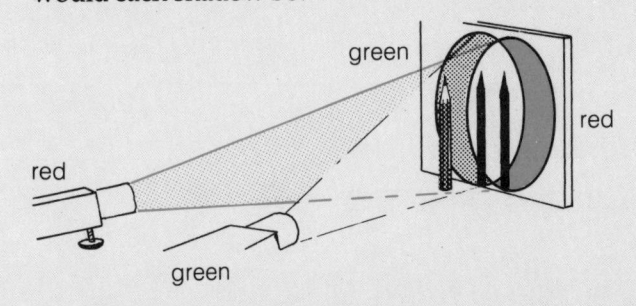

18 Draw a diagram to show how you would use lenses with focal lengths of 50 cm and 5 cm to make a telescope. Draw two rays through the telescope to show how it forms an image.

Wave and sound energy

11 Waves

What is a wave?

Experiment. Travelling vibrations

Fix one end of a rope and move the free end up and down. A hump is formed that travels along the rope, carrying energy from the hand with it. It is clear that the rope does not move along, but moves up and down as the hump passes. This moving disturbance of the rope is called a wave. When the wave reaches the wall it is reflected but some of its energy is taken by the wall.

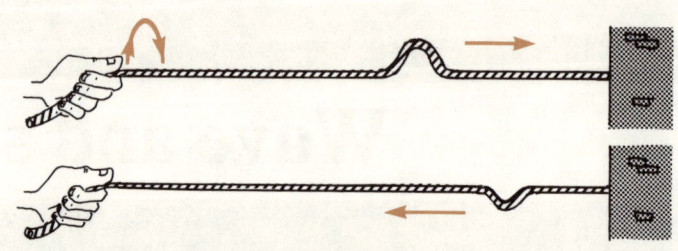

A moving disturbance (wave) on a rope

1 Give one reason why the hump is smaller after reflection.

2 Write down three changes that happen to the hump when it is reflected.

3 Which of the following will make the hump travel faster along the rope?
(a) moving the rope up and down faster.
(b) pulling the rope and making it tighter.
(c) making the rope slacker.

Waves carry energy

Drop a stick into still water and a circular ripple will spread out from the stick. A duck on the water will move up and down as the ripple passes. Continue to move the stick and ripple will follow ripple making a series of humps and dips in the water surface, that travel across the water. These are travelling water waves. The distance between humps (or crests) is called the **wavelength** of these waves.

Travelling waves carry energy

4 What proof is there that water waves carry energy?

5 Why does the duck get so little of the energy you gave to the stick?

6 From where do ocean waves get their energy?

7 Give an example of what the energy of ocean waves can do.

Waves carry vibrations

To make wave follow wave, the bar in the diagram has to be vibrated up and down. The waves carry these vibrations from place to place.

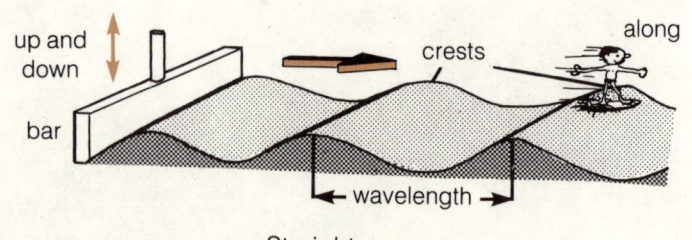

Straight waves

- These waves carry energy and vibrations from place to place without the rope or water moving along.
- The wavelength of a wave is the distance from one crest to the next.
- If a wave moves at right angles to the disturbance as in these examples, it is called a **transverse** wave.

A closer look at water waves

Water waves move rather quickly across the surface. If they are viewed by a light flashing at the right speed, they appear to stop and can be studied more carefully.

Some properties of water waves

Reflection

Waves are reflected when they hit a rigid barrier. The reflected waves make the same angle to the barrier as the incoming waves, and travel at the same speed. Light and sound also obey this law of reflection.

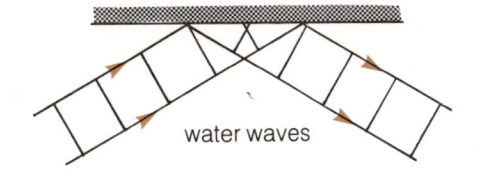

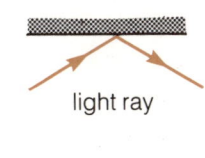

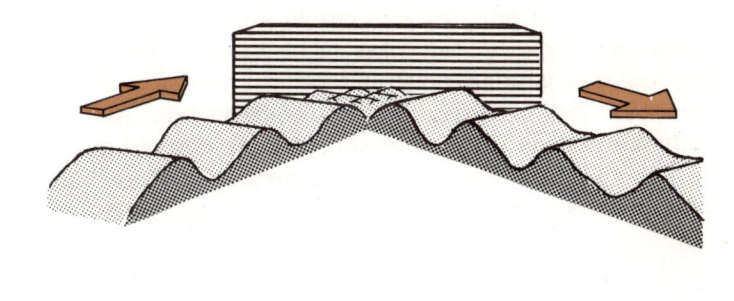

The reflection of waves

Refraction

If straight waves cross a line where they suddenly change speed, the waves change direction. Light changes direction like this when it enters or leaves glass. This is called refraction.

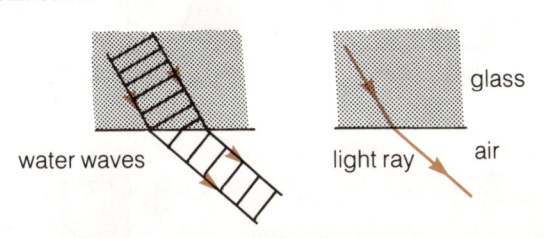

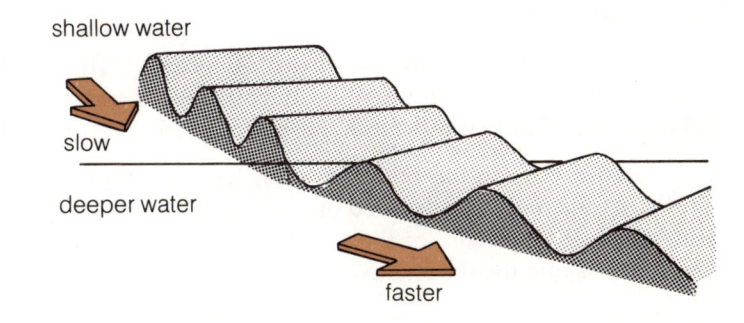

The refraction of waves

> 8 If light is a wave, does it travel faster in air or glass?

Diffraction

When straight waves hit a barrier with a gap in it, some of the waves' energy passes through the gap. The waves on the other side become curved and spread beyond the edges of the gap. This is called **diffraction**.

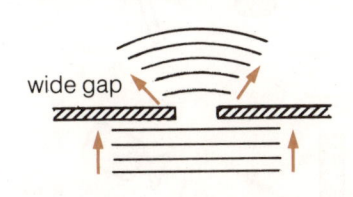

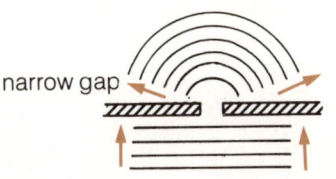

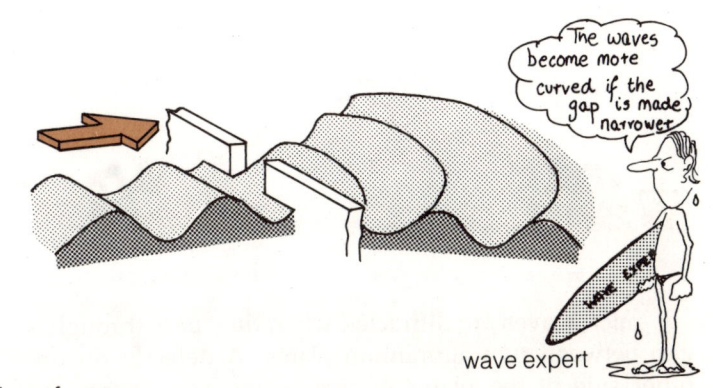

The diffraction of waves

The waves become more curved if the gap is made narrower

wave expert

> 9 Why are the waves not so high after they have passed through the gap?

> 10 Describe three differences between waves diffracted by narrow and wide gaps.

■ Waves can be reflected, refracted and diffracted.

Electromagnetic waves

Some waves are carried by material things such as rope, water and air. There is another sort of wave that can cross space where there is no material. It is called an **electromagnetic** wave. The space around us is full of electromagnetic waves of different wavelengths, coming at us from all directions. These waves carry energy that they deliver to suitable receivers. Waves of certain wavelengths enable us to see. Electromagnetic waves of these wavelengths are called **light**. Waves with other lengths are especially good at warming the skin (called **infra-red**) or turning the skin brown (called **ultra-violet**). Some wavelengths can pass right through the body (**X-rays** and **gamma rays**) and others need a radio or television set to receive them (**radio waves**). All this radiation travels at the same speed – the speed of light. It is the length of the wave that determines the effect it has on materials in its path.

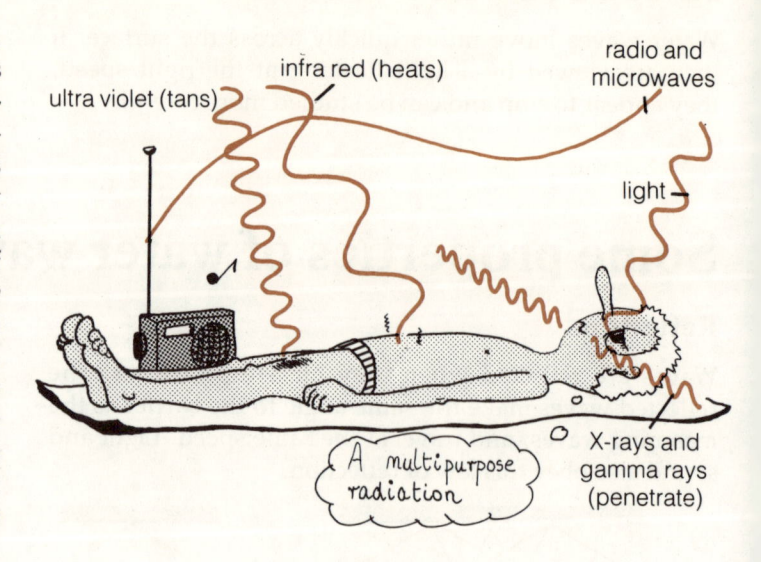

A multipurpose radiation

- ultra violet (tans)
- infra red (heats)
- radio and microwaves
- light
- X-rays and gamma rays (penetrate)

11 Use the sketch above to list the named radiations in order of wavelength.

Microwaves

Microwaves are electromagnetic waves with a wavelength of a few centimetres. If you have a microwave transmitter, you can check these properties . . .

. . . microwaves can pass through a thick book although a little of the energy is absorbed on the way through, and a little is reflected. Rain (or the spray of water from a tap) also absorbs microwave energy.

. . . metal sheets reflect microwaves allowing none to pass through. All materials will absorb some microwave energy, getting warmer as they do so.

. . . microwaves can be reflected by a sheet of aluminium and focused by concave aluminium dishes.

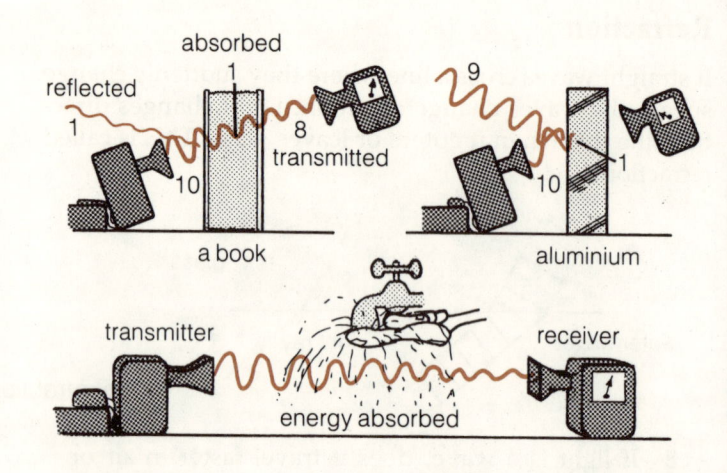

Reflection, absorption and transmission of microwaves (the numbers give an idea of what happens to the wave energy)

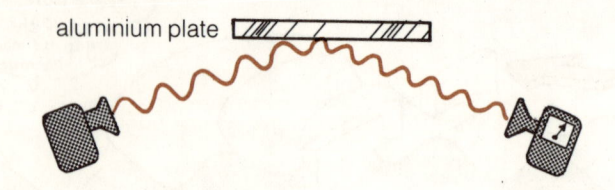

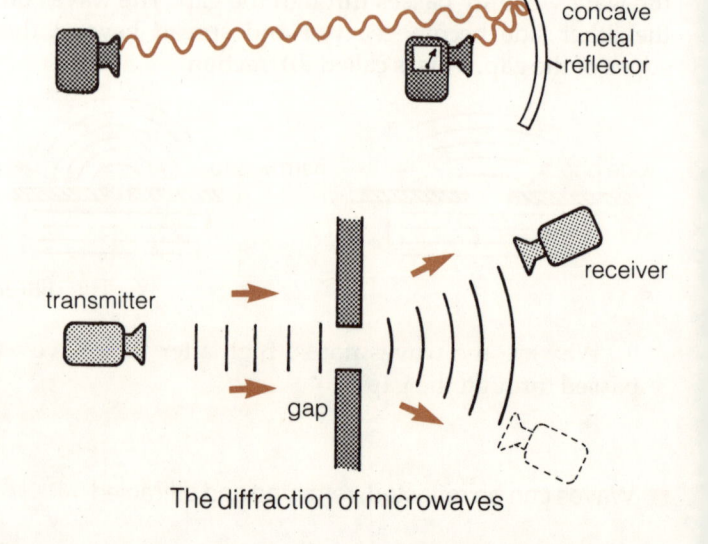

. . . microwaves are diffracted when they pass through a gap between two aluminium plates. A detector on the other side of the plates receives microwave energy far beyond the edges of the gap. This is evidence that microwave energy is carried by waves.

The diffraction of microwaves

12 This diagram shows what can happen to microwaves (and other electromagnetic waves) when they strike matter. They can pass through, be reflected, or absorbed. Copy the diagram and put these phrases into the correct boxes.

13 What happens to the microwave energy that is absorbed?

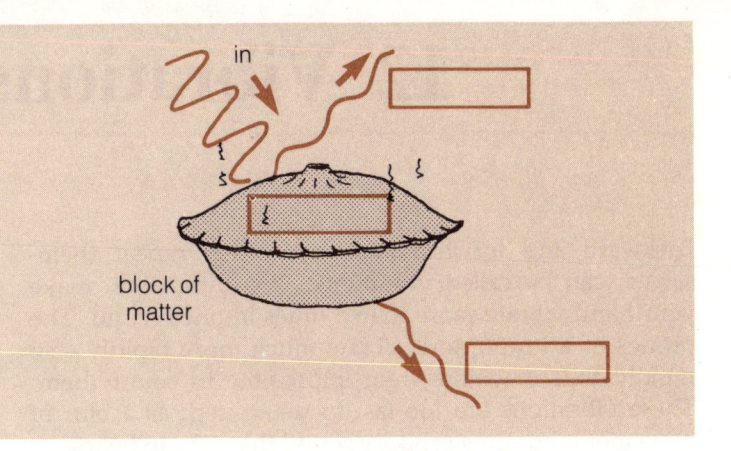

block of matter

Uses of microwaves

i) Intercity telephone links.
A microwave beam is used to carry telephone conversations between cities. The beam can carry many more conversations than a wire.

ii) Satellite links.
A microwave beam, carrying television pictures, can be aimed at a satellite positioned between two continents. The satellite receives and amplifies the beam before sending it back to receiving aerials on the ground. 'Live', world-wide TV coverage is achieved in this way.

iii) Cooking.
Microwaves are used in special ovens to cook food. They cook food right through very rapidly. They would also cook our brains and internal organs if we got in their way. Microwave energy should be treated with caution.

Microwave transmitters and receivers on the Post Office Tower

- Electromagnetic radiation fills the air around us and has many properties.
- Radio, microwaves, infra-red, light, ultra-violet, X-rays and gamma rays are all electromagnetic waves.

12 Vibrations we can hear

Backward and forward movements that repeat themselves, can be called **vibrations**. It is difficult to make your hand vibrate more than 5 times in one second. The prongs of a tuning fork vibrate much more rapidly – so rapidly that it would seem impossible to count them. These vibrations are too fast to see, except as a blur of movement, but they produce sound that we can hear.

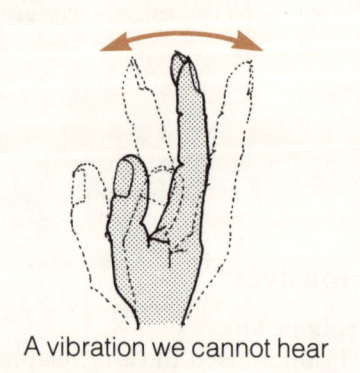

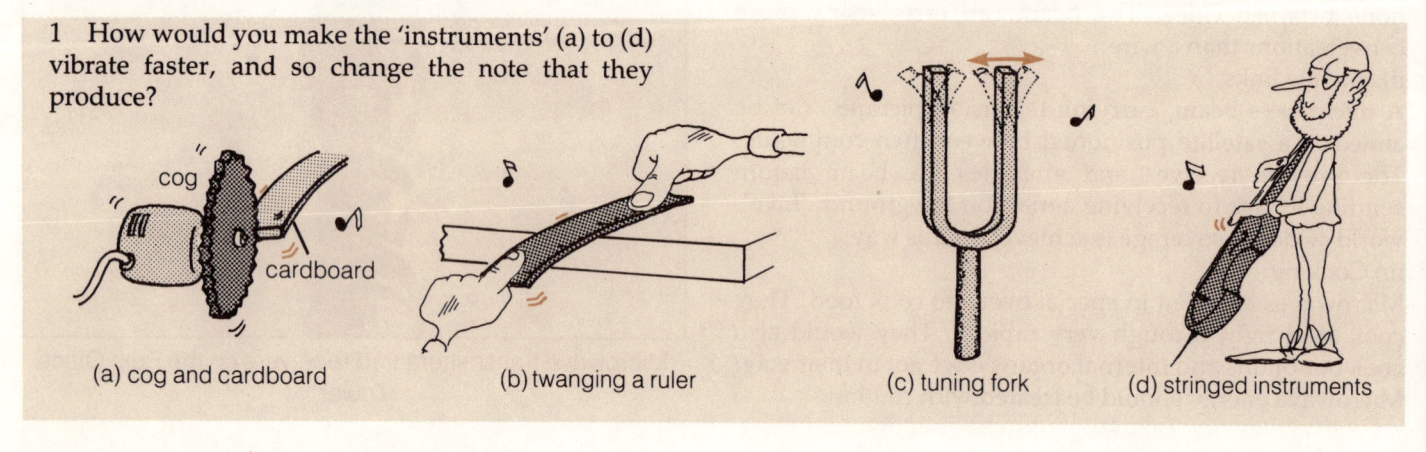

A vibration we cannot hear

1 How would you make the 'instruments' (a) to (d) vibrate faster, and so change the note that they produce?

(a) cog and cardboard   (b) twanging a ruler   (c) tuning fork   (d) stringed instruments

How many vibrations does a tuning fork make in one second?

Experiment

Here is a way of showing up the vibrations of a tuning fork so that we can count them. Fix a piece of wire to the prong of the fork and cover a metal disc with an even coat of soot. Put the disc on a record turntable, strike the fork and touch the wire on the revolving disc. As the prong vibrates, the wire will draw a circle of small waves in the soot. Count how many waves there are in a complete circle. Find out how long it takes to draw a circle of waves by finding the time it takes for the disc to go round once. (As this is less than one second, it is best to time 100 revolutions and divide this time by 100.)

Results (get your own if you can)
Time for 100 revolutions = 80 s
Time for 1 revolution = 80/100 = 8/10 s
Number of waves in 1 rev. = 200
Number of waves in one second = 200 ÷ 8/10 = 250

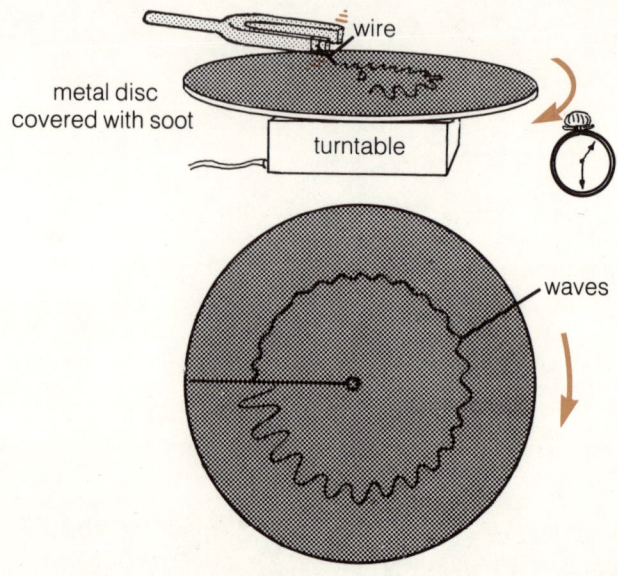

Drawing waves on a sooty disc with a tuning fork

2 Why are the waves at the end of the trace smaller than the ones at the beginning?

3 Explain why the waves are shorter if they are drawn nearer the centre of the disc.

4 The number of waves in a complete circle is the same whether you draw the circle in the centre or near the edge. Explain why this is.

5 Why is the number of vibrations measured in this way likely to be slightly less than the true value? (It is something to do with the wire prong.)

■ A tuning fork vibrates several hundred times per second. It makes a musical note when struck.

Frequency and hearing

We often need to know how frequent vibrations are. So we call the number of vibrations made in one second the **frequency** of the vibrations. If something makes one complete vibration a second, its frequency is '1 per second' or '1 Hertz' (1 Hz). For higher frequencies, kilohertz – kHz (or 1000 vibrations per second) – can be used.

A signal generator is an electronic machine that can make a loudspeaker vibrate at different frequencies. The frequency can be read from its control knob.

Using this equipment we find that:
frequencies of less than 20 Hz (20 vibrations per second) are too slow for most human ears to hear as sound;
frequencies of more than 20 kHz (20 000 vibrations per second) are too high for most human ears to hear;
speech is a mixture of vibrations with frequencies up to about 10 kHz. Musical frequencies reach about 16 kHz.

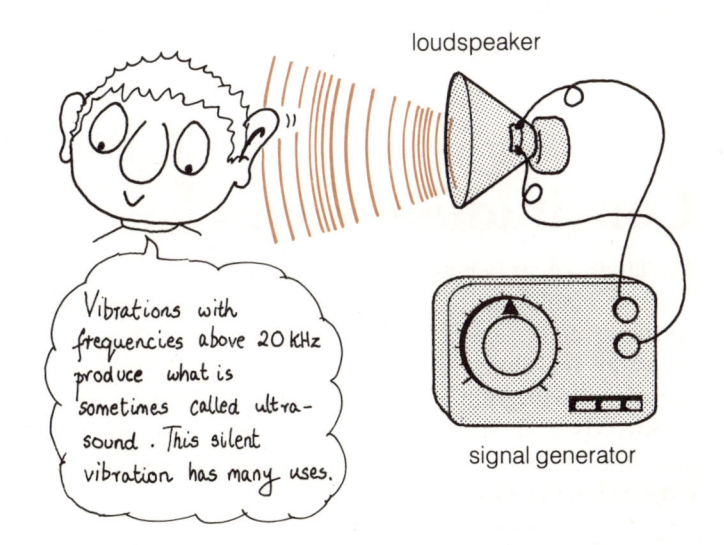

Vibrations with frequencies above 20 kHz produce what is sometimes called ultrasound. This silent vibration has many uses.

6 What is meant by frequency?

7 As the cone of a loudspeaker is made to vibrate at higher and higher frequencies, does the note it gives out get higher or lower?

8 Make a rough guess of the following frequencies. You could use the signal generator to match the sounds and get an idea of the frequency that way. Copy and complete the table.

9 If the cog in the diagram opposite has 25 teeth and the motor revolves 8 times a second, what is the frequency of vibration of the cardboard? Would we hear the vibration as sound?

The wings of a pigeon in flight	A fly's wings	The hum of a transformer	The highest note you can make	The lowest note you can make

■ Frequency is the number of vibrations made per second.
■ Frequency is measured in Hertz. One hertz is one complete vibration in one second.
■ Sound frequencies range from about 20 Hz to 20 000 Hz.

13 Sound waves

Sound waves carry vibrations from the sound source to our ears and make our ear-drums vibrate.

As the prongs of a tuning fork move out, layers of air are pushed closer together, forming a patch of compressed air. Once formed, this compression moves on through the air until it reaches our ear and pushes the ear-drum inwards. The vibrating prongs send out compression after compression, bombarding the ear-drum and making it vibrate in step with the tuning fork.

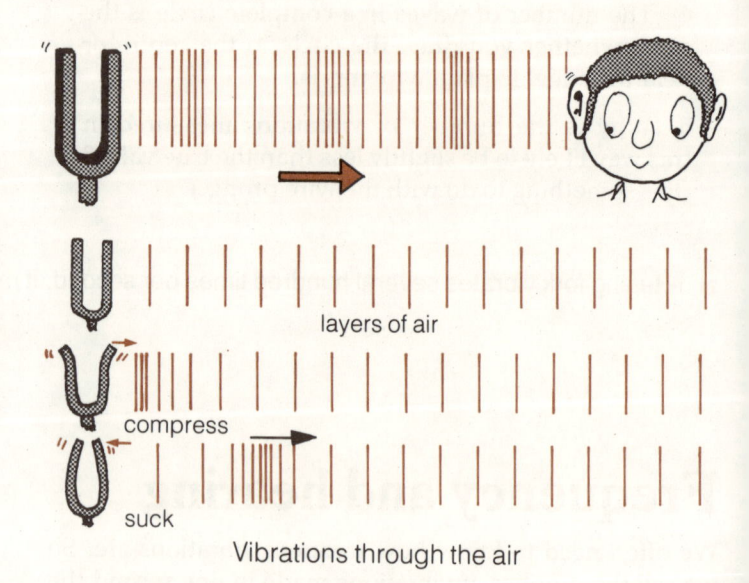

Vibrations through the air

Longitudinal waves

The layers of air behave rather like the links of a spring. If the hand holding the spring is moved to the right, the spring is compressed over a small distance. This 'compression' will then travel along the spring. Further compressions will follow if the hand continues to move backwards and forwards. Such travelling compressions are called a **longitudinal** wave. Sound waves are also longitudinal waves.

1 Which way does one particular coil of the spring move, as the wave passes by?

2 How would you move your hand to make humps travel along the spring? Which way would one particular coil move in this case?

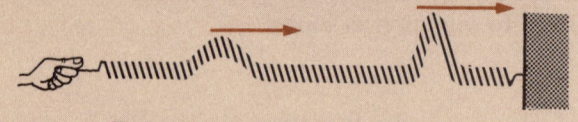

Transverse waves in a spring

3 How can you make the wave travel faster along the spring?

4 What is the difference between a longitudinal and transverse wave?

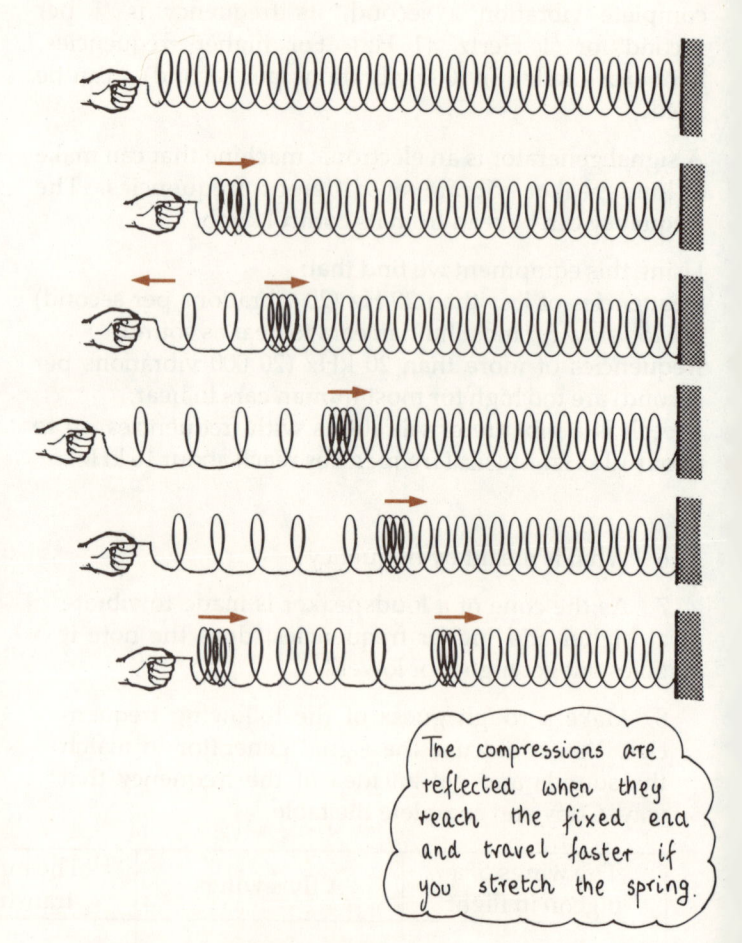

The compressions are reflected when they reach the fixed end and travel faster if you stretch the spring.

Longitudinal waves in a spring

- When a longitudinal wave travels along a spring, the links move in the same direction as the wave.
- Sound energy is carried through air and other materials by a longitudinal wave.

The speed of sound

Experiment

How fast does sound travel? Here is a way of measuring its speed.

Stand 50 metres from a wall that gives a good echo. Make a loud clap and listen for the echo. It takes less than a second for the sound to get back to your ears – too short a time to measure with a stop-watch. So make a second clap the moment the echo is heard. Keep this up, clapping with a rhythm that makes each clap cover the echo of the previous clap. Time 20 of these claps, counting the first clap as '0'.

Measuring the speed of sound

Results (get your own if you can)
Time for 20 such claps = 6 seconds
Time between clap and echo = 6/20 s
Distance travelled in this time = 100 metres

Speed of sound = $\frac{\text{distance}}{\text{time}}$ = 100 ÷ 6/20 = 333 m/s
(As the time measurement is only approximate, this result should be given as 330 m/s.)

5 Why is it difficult to measure the time between a clap and its echo using a stop-watch?

6 Give two reasons why the echo is quieter than the clap (see p. 50).

7 How far must you stand from a wall if you want the sound of your clap to reach your ears after a journey of 200 m?

8 If the BBC used sound waves instead of radio waves for broadcasting, how long would it take the programme to reach Perth from London (666 km)? (Take the speed of sound as 333 m/s.) What other problems would there be?

■ Sound takes time to travel from its source to a listener. The speed of sound in air is about 330 m/s (740 mph) at 0°C and gets less if the temperature drops.

Can sound travel through . . .

. . . wood and metal?

Try the experiments shown in the pictures. You will find that sound travels very much better through wood and metal than through air. It also travels much faster (3600 m/s for steel). Sound can travel easily around a building along pipes and wooden beams.

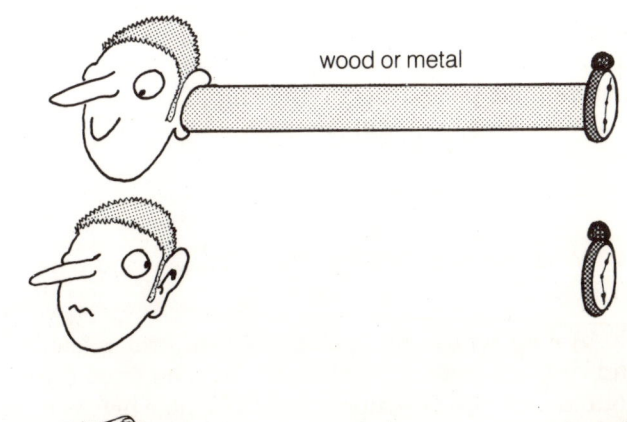

. . . wire, rubber and string?

String or wire can carry the vibrations of the voice. The pots help to transfer the vibrations of the air to the string. You will notice that a lot of energy is lost and the quality of the sound may change.

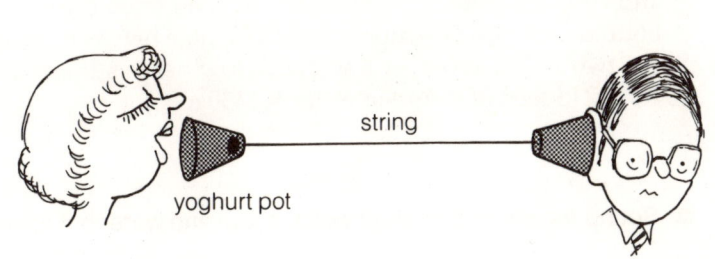

. . . a vacuum?

Sound cannot travel through a vacuum. There must be a solid, liquid or gas to carry the sound vibrations to our ears. A vacuum is a perfect insulator of sound.

9 Why did American Indians put their ears to the ground when listening for approaching horses?

10 Why are the gurgles and clunks of a central-heating system often heard throughout the house?

11 Give a reason why astronauts use radio waves to talk to each other on the moon.

12 Describe how you would show that sound cannot travel through a vacuum.

13 Give two reasons why you can hear sounds from the **inside** of an engine if you listen to it through a stick.

. . . water?

Sound waves travel well through water, but special loudspeakers and microphones are needed to generate and pick up the vibrations.

Passive sonar

Underwater sounds made by submarines or even whales can be picked up by underwater microphones (hydrophones). Sound is a powerful way of detecting objects that are hidden from us by water.

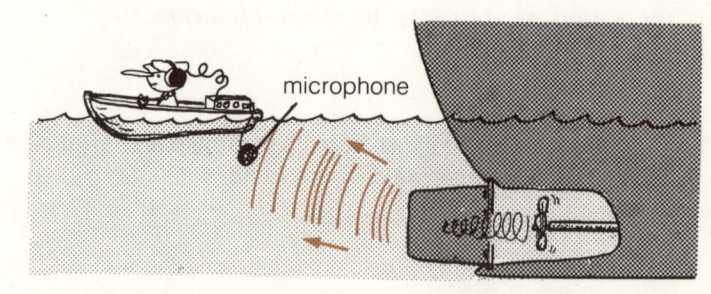

Active sonar

To detect silent objects such as a shoal of fish or a submarine lying on the bottom, sound pulses can be sent out by a ship or buoy. These pulses are reflected by the submarine and picked up by the ship. The echo gives away the position of the submarine.

14 What is the difference between active and passive sonar?

15 A ship sends out a pulse of sound underwater and displays both the pulse and its echo from the bottom on an oscilloscope screen. The time between the two is measured as 1 second. How deep is the water? (Speed of sound in water = 1430 m/s.)

16 List some of the uses of sound under water.

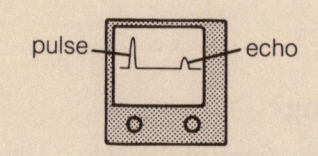

■ Sound travels well through wood, metal and water but cannot travel at all through a vacuum.

The shape of sound

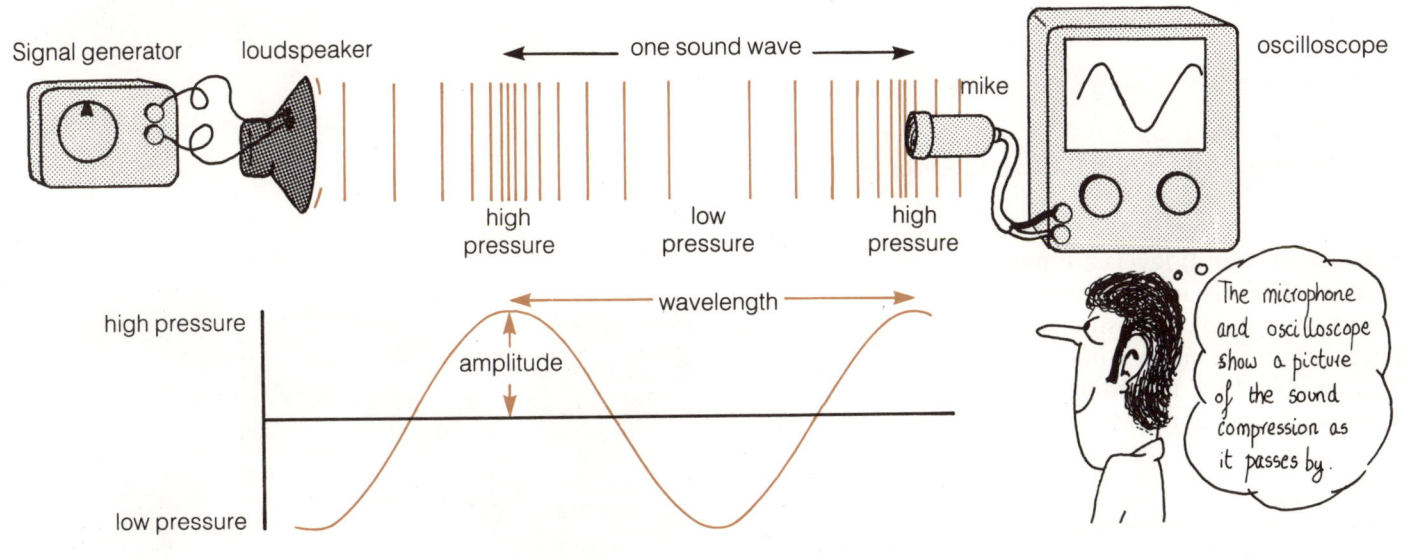

Looking at the shape of sound

Signal generator — loudspeaker — one sound wave — mike — oscilloscope

high pressure — low pressure — high pressure

wavelength, amplitude, high pressure, low pressure

The microphone and oscilloscope show a picture of the sound compression as it passes by.

The pressure changes through a simple (pure) sound wave look like this. Such a wave has a **wavelength** (distance from crest to crest) and an **amplitude** (height of the wave above the centre line). Using the equipment above we find that:
LOW notes have LONG wavelengths.
HIGH notes have SHORT wavelengths.
LOUD notes have a LARGE amplitude.
SOFT notes have a SMALL amplitude.
Notes from different instruments have different shapes (see diagram). It is the shape of a sound wave that enables us to identify the instrument it came from.

17 Say whether the sound waves shown have the same or different wavelengths and amplitudes. Copy and put same or different.

The two sound waves	Amplitude	Wavelength
(a) (b)		
(c) (d)		

18 Which of the four sounds shown above would be:
(a) the softest (b) the highest note?

19 A note played on a piano sounds different from the same note played on a violin. Explain why this is so.

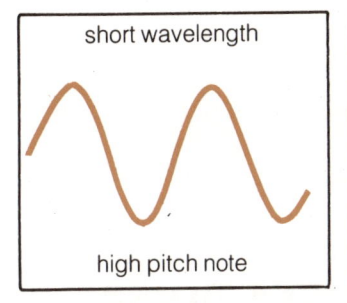

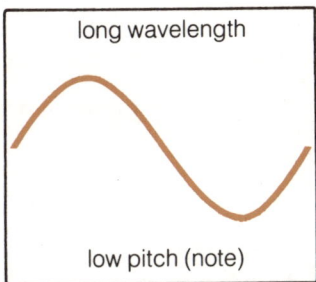

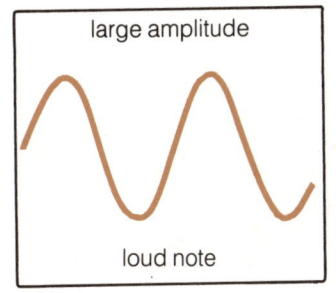

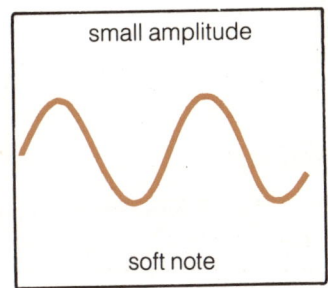

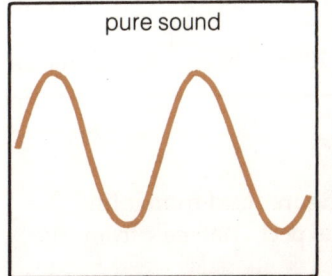

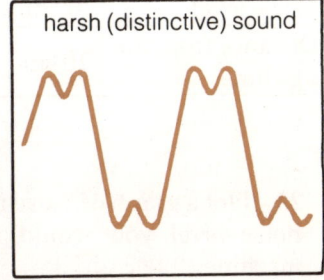

short wavelength — high pitch note

long wavelength — low pitch (note)

large amplitude — loud note

small amplitude — soft note

pure sound

harsh (distinctive) sound

these two notes differ in quality

How changes in a sound alter the shape of its wave

59

Noise annoys

What is noise? What one person calls unpleasant sound, may be 'music' in another's ears.

> 20 Write a list of noises that some people would call pleasant.
>
> 21 Write down some of the bad effects of noise.

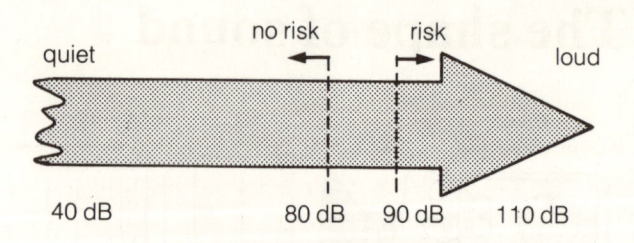

The decibel scale of noise levels

Noise (and sound) levels are measured in **decibels** (dB) and usually range in level from about 40 dB (very quiet) to 110 dB (very loud). Exposure to a noise level of 90 dB for 8 hours (e.g. working in a noisy factory) can damage your hearing. Levels of 110 dB for more than 2 minutes (as at some concerts) can result in permanent hearing loss.

> 22
>
> | Vacuum cleaner* | Radio playing very loud* | Normal speech* | Noise level in class with everyone talking |
> |---|---|---|---|
> | 80 dB | 95 dB | 55 dB | 90 dB |
>
> *taken from 1 metre away.
>
> Plot these examples of noise levels on a block graph.

Using ear muffs to reduce noise level

Distance reduces noise

These figures show how the noise level can drop if you move further way from the source of the noise.

Noise level	100 dB	94 dB	88 dB	82 dB	76 dB
Distance from the machine	10 cm	20 cm	40 cm	80 cm	160 cm

> 23 Plot a graph of these figures and from it find the noise level you would expect 100 cm from the machine.

- Noise makes life unpleasant and can damage our ears if it is too loud.
- Noise levels are measured in decibels.

More noise

Experiment. Insulation reduces noise

Take a noisy motor and design screening to reduce the noise it makes. Take a noise level reading for each step you take to make it quieter. The results below show an example of how you might insulate the motor.

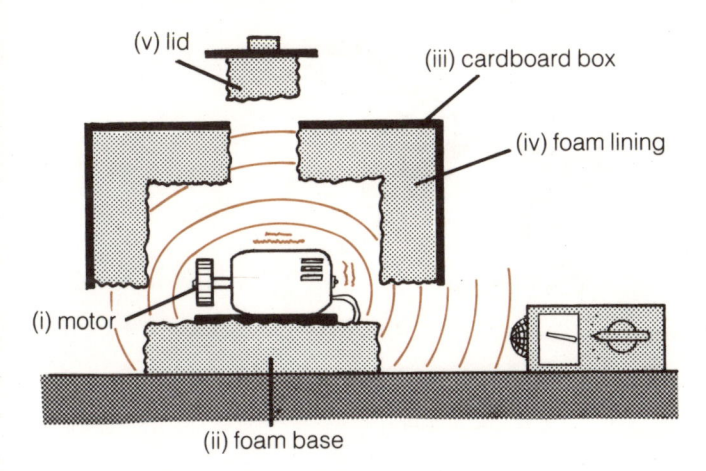

Ways of reducing noise from a motor

Results (get your own if you can)
i) the motor on its own 99 dB
ii) the motor on a foam base 96 dB
iii) ... with a cardboard box on top 87 dB
iv) ... with a foam lining in the box 81 dB
v) ... with a lid 78 dB

This experiment shows how simple steps can greatly reduce the noise heard from a motor. Other noises that affect our lives can often be reduced in a similar manner.

Note that, because of the scale used to measure sound levels, a drop of 3 dB means that the sound energy reaching the meter has been almost halved.

24 Can you suggest why so much noise reaches the noise meter when the motor and the meter both lie on the bench?

25 A thick carpet in a car reduces the noise level inside from 86 dB to 80 dB. Has the carpet reduced the sound energy inside the car by ½, ¼ or ⅙ th of what it was before?

26 Can you show that the insulation in the experiment above has reduced the sound energy to 1/128 th of what it was without it?

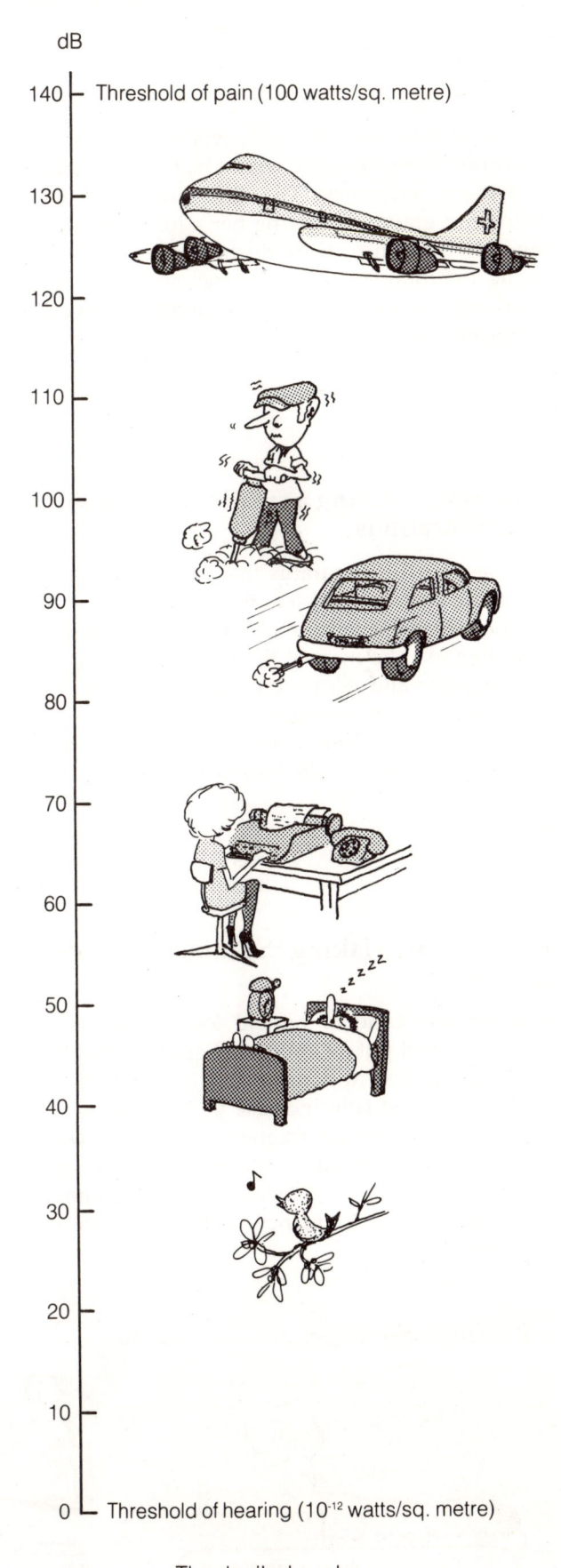

The decibel scale

Threshold of pain (100 watts/sq. metre) — 140 dB

Threshold of hearing (10^{-12} watts/sq. metre) — 0

14 Resonance

A swing, if pushed and left, will move backwards and forwards. The frequency with which it does this is called its **natural frequency**. The little girl in the picture can swing her granny by giving her a lot of small pushes at the right frequency. If the pushes have the rhythm of the swing's natural frequency, a large amplitude movement builds up. 'Working up' a swing like this is an example of using **resonance**.

Experiment. Using a small force to build up large vibrations

Put together the apparatus that is shown in the picture. When the switch is pressed, the coil magnetizes and pulls the magnet with a very small force. See if you can use this force to make the magnet bounce on its spring. You will have to press and release the switch at the right frequency, matching the natural frequency of the bouncing magnet. The build up of large vibrations by small rhythmic forces like this is called resonance.

Experiment. Making the cone of a loudspeaker resonate

Connect the cone of an old loudspeaker to a signal generator, and put a handful of light plastic balls into the cone. Switch on and make the cone vibrate at a low frequency. Gradually increase the frequency and watch the balls. At a certain frequency, the cone will start to vibrate wildly and throw the balls into the air. This is resonance. The signal generator forces the cone to vibrate at its own natural frequency, and large amplitude vibrations build up.

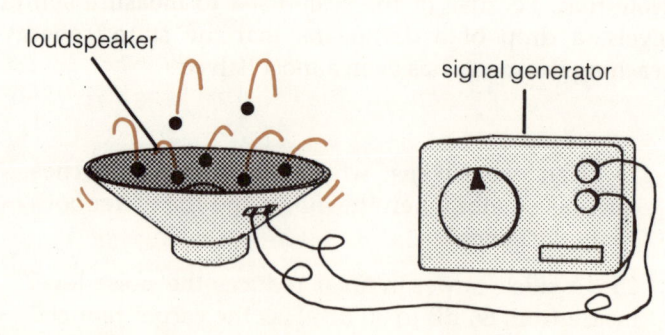

1 Which speech goes in which balloon?

A: If I jump up and down on this diving board at its natural frequency......

B: ....large amplitude vibrations will build up — an example of resonance

C: If bent and released, I vibrate at my own natural frequency.

Other examples of resonance

Bouncing a car

Several people, lifting at the natural frequency of the spings of a car, can work up a large amplitude bounce. When it is bouncing the car can be moved sideways fairly easily. This is one way out of a tight spot.

Cracking a glass by singing

If you 'ping' a glass with your finger, it will ring at its natural frequency. A singer, singing this same frequency, is supposed to be able to make the glass vibrate so much that it cracks.

Talking to a piano

If you sing a note to a piano, the string that makes the same note will begin to vibrate. Press the loud pedal and the string will carry on vibrating even after you have stopped singing.

Rattling windows

Loose window panes have a natural frequency. If the vibrations from a passing car or lorry contain this frequency, the windows will be made to rattle. Even the walls and floors of buildings can vibrate. Passing vehicles or trains produce vibrations that can make whole buildings resonate.

Bridges and blocks of flats are often springy and rapid gusts of wind of the right frequency can produce dangerously large vibrations. Resonance can be dangerous because small forces can produce large movements and cause structures to collapse.

> 2 A plank across a stream has a natural frequency of 1 Hz. A boy with heavy boots marches across the plank at one step per second. What is likely to happen?

Summary of waves and sound energy

- A moving wave carries .... energy.
- Waves are refracted (change direction) when .... they suddenly change speed.
- When waves squeeze through a narrow gap .... they are diffracted, spreading beyond the edges of the gap.
- If a wave moves at right angles to its disturbance it is a .... transverse wave.
- If a wave moves in the same direction as its disturbance it is a .... longitudinal wave.
- A vibration is a movement that .... repeats itself regularly.
- The frequency of a vibration is .... the number of vibrations per second.
- The unit used to measure frequency is .... Hertz (Hz).
- We can hear sound frequencies that range from about .... 20 Hz to 20 000 Hz.
- The speed of sound is about .... 740 mph (330 m/s) at 0°C.
- Supersonic means .... faster than the speed of sound.
- The amplitude of a wave is .... its height above the centre line.
- The loudness of a sound is fixed by .... the amplitude of its wave.
- The wavelength of a wave is the .... distance from one crest to the next.
- The pitch of a note (high or low) is fixed by its .... frequency.
- Noise levels are measured in .... decibels.
- Damage can occur to ears at noise levels .... above 90 dB.
- Noise levels can be reduced by .... moving away from the source or by insulation.

Further questions

3 Why can you not hear a plane flying at supersonic speeds towards you?

4 Why is it easier to break the sound barrier at high altitude where the air temperature is about −50°C?

5 A valley is 660 m wide. How long would it be between making a sound and hearing the echo from the other side? (Take the speed of sound in air to be 330 m/s.)

6 Give two facts that show that sound waves are not electromagnetic waves.

7 If thunder is heard 10 seconds after a lightning flash, how far away is the storm (speed of sound = 340 m/s)? What do you assume about the light from the flash?

8 (a) What effect does plucking a guitar string harder have on (i) the pitch of the note, (ii) the amplitude of the sound wave produced?
(b) State two ways of raising the pitch of the note from the string.

9 The blade of an electric saw has 80 teeth and rotates 16 times each second when sawing a piece of wood. What is the frequency of the note produced?

10 Compare the sound A, shown by its oscilloscope picture, with the other four sounds. Say what is the same about the sounds and what is different.

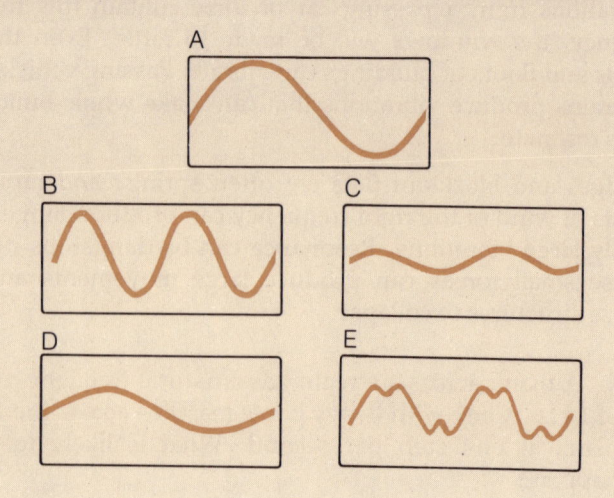

Heat energy

15 Heat at work

Some of the things that heat can do

In the following experiments, heat passes from a hot flame into a colder substance. The substance warms up and a number of things are seen to happen. Set the experiments up if you can, watch them carefully and answer the questions.

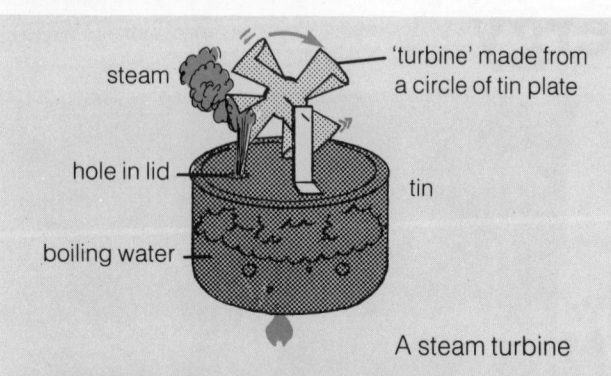

A steam turbine

1 Put these sentences about the steam turbine into the correct order:
Water warms up and boils.
The steam jet turns the turbine.
Heat passes from the flame into the water.
Steam is produced and escapes through the small hole.

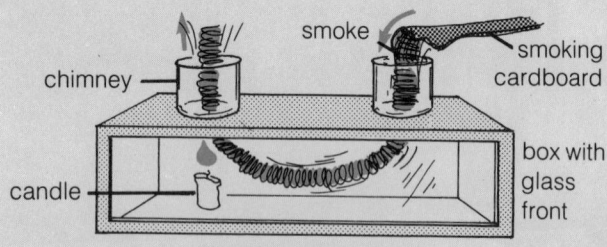

Hot air and cold air

2 Copy and complete these sentences:
Heat from the candle flame _____ the air. This _____ air moves _____ one chimney and cold air moves _____ into the other chimney.

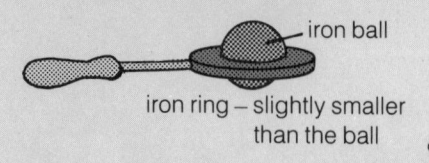

Using heat to make things bigger

3 Copy and complete.
The iron ball can be made to fall through the ring by heating the _____. As it gets warm the _____ expands and the _____ falls through.

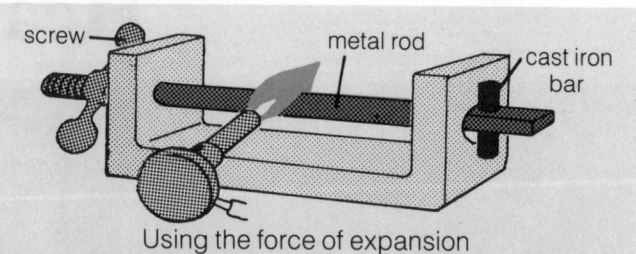

Using the force of expansion

4 To use heat to snap the cast iron bar you must:
Let the bar cool. Tighten the screw. Heat the metal rod.
Put these instructions in the correct order.

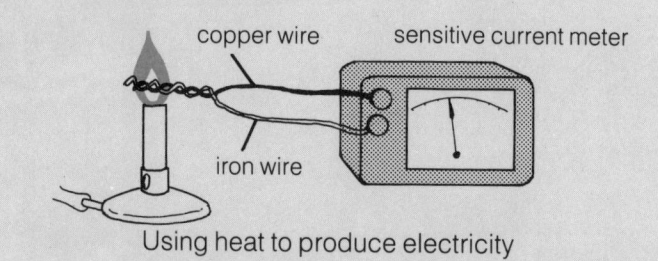

Using heat to produce electricity

5 Describe how heat can produce electricity.

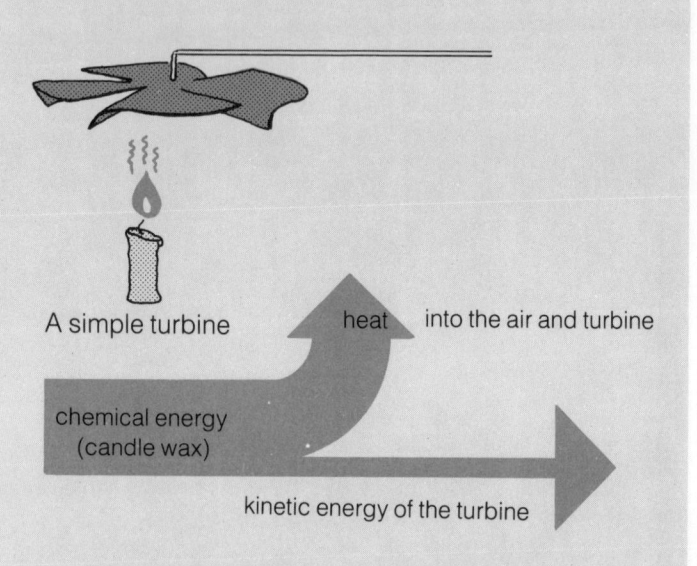

A simple turbine

chemical energy (candle wax) → heat into the air and turbine → kinetic energy of the turbine

6 Describe the energy changes that take place as this turbine starts to move.

■ In these experiments, heat energy from the hot flame generates electricity, causes movement of the turbines and air, and makes metal expand.
■ Heat is a form of energy that passes from hot to colder objects.

Hot gas engines

We would not get far without 'heat engines'. They have helped to put men on the Moon (rocket engines), power cars and boats (petrol and diesel engines), fly aeroplanes across continents (jet engines) and drive generators that make the electricity we use (steam turbines).

Steam turbines

At the heart of this heat engine is a turbine wheel. This has a set of blades fixed to a revolving shaft. Water is boiled under great pressure, producing very hot, high pressure steam. This steam (the hot gas that the engine uses) is made to hit the blades of the turbine wheel. As the steam shoots off the curved blades, it pushes the wheel round. A carefully designed steam turbine can change about 1/3 of the energy of the steam into the circular movement of the wheel.

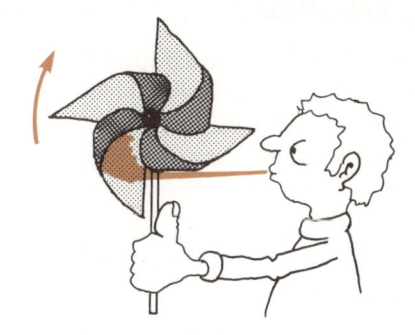

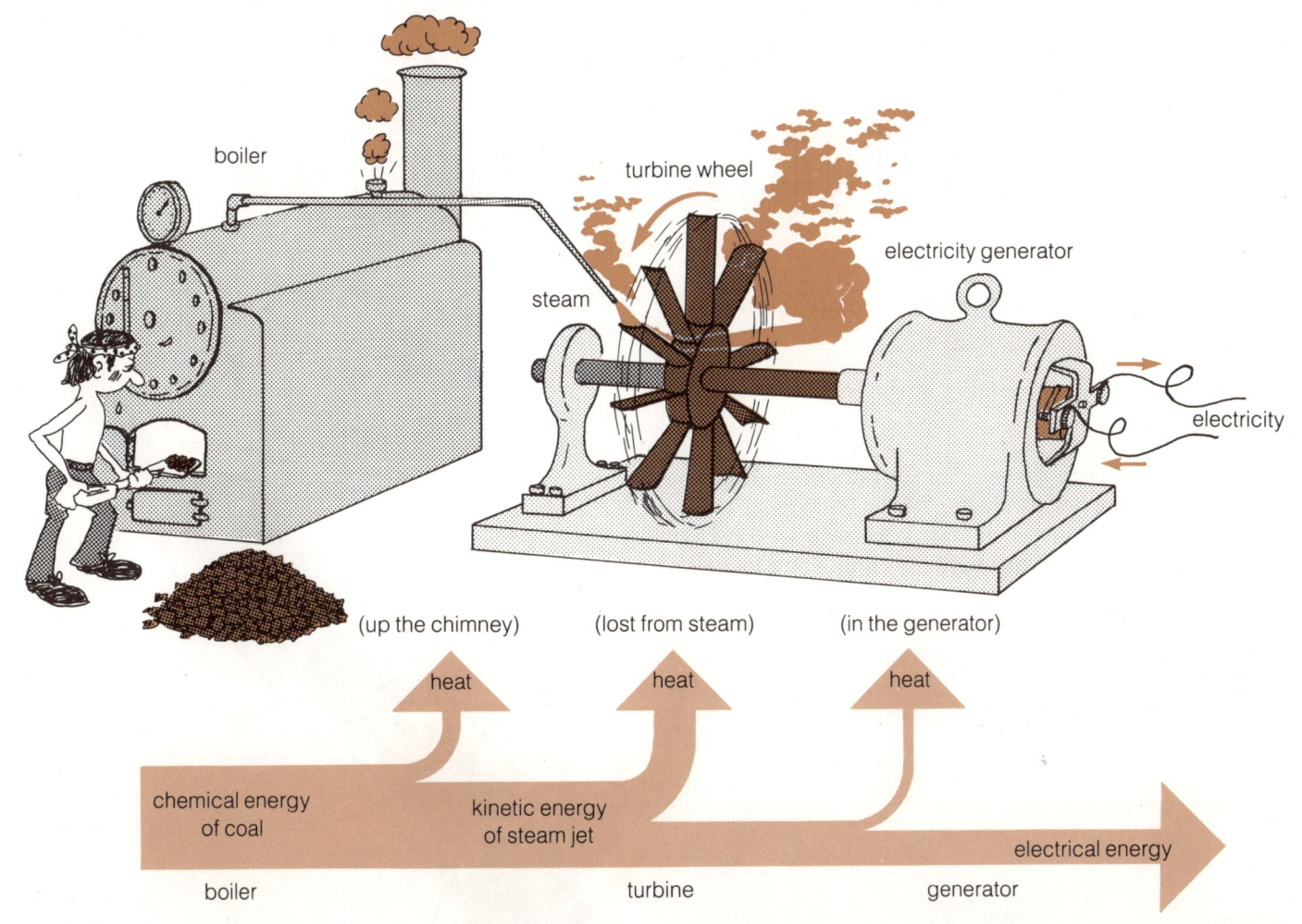

7 Look at the energy change diagram and describe what happens to the energy as it is changed by the machinery in the picture.

8 Does most energy escape in the boiler, the turbine or the generator? Give a reason why this might be.

Jet and rocket engines

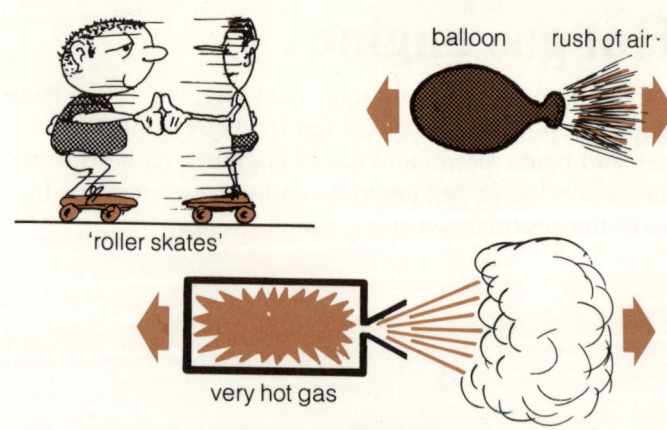

What will happen if the small boy in the picture tries to get moving by pushing against the big boy? The same force that moves the small boy acts on the big boy and he moves too – although not quite as fast.

Blow up a balloon and let go of the neck. The air rushes out, pushing against the balloon and making it fly about the room.

Jet and rocket engines produce very hot gas in a container and let it out through a hole at the rear. As the hot gases rush out backwards, the container is pushed forwards.

'roller skates'

balloon   rush of air

very hot gas

High pressure gases producing movement

Jet engines (gas turbines)

These engines can develop tremendous power and are especially suitable for aircraft. They take air, compress it and squirt in paraffin. The paraffin and air burn, producing very hot gas. This gas rushes out of the jet nozzle and the engine is forced forwards.

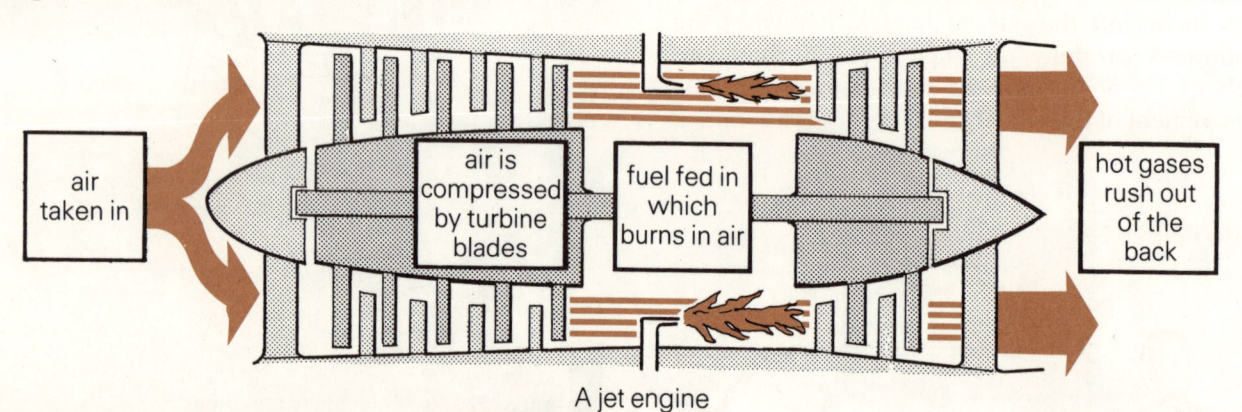

air taken in | air is compressed by turbine blades | fuel fed in which burns in air | hot gases rush out of the back

A jet engine

9   Why are jet engines not used in space or on the Moon?

Rocket engines

Rocket engines carry fuel and air (or rather oxygen). The fuel and oxygen burn producing hot gas that escapes and gives the forward movement. A rocket will work where there is no air. It gets much lighter as it flies and its fuel is used up.

10   As a rocket flies, it becomes easier to make it fly faster. Why is this?

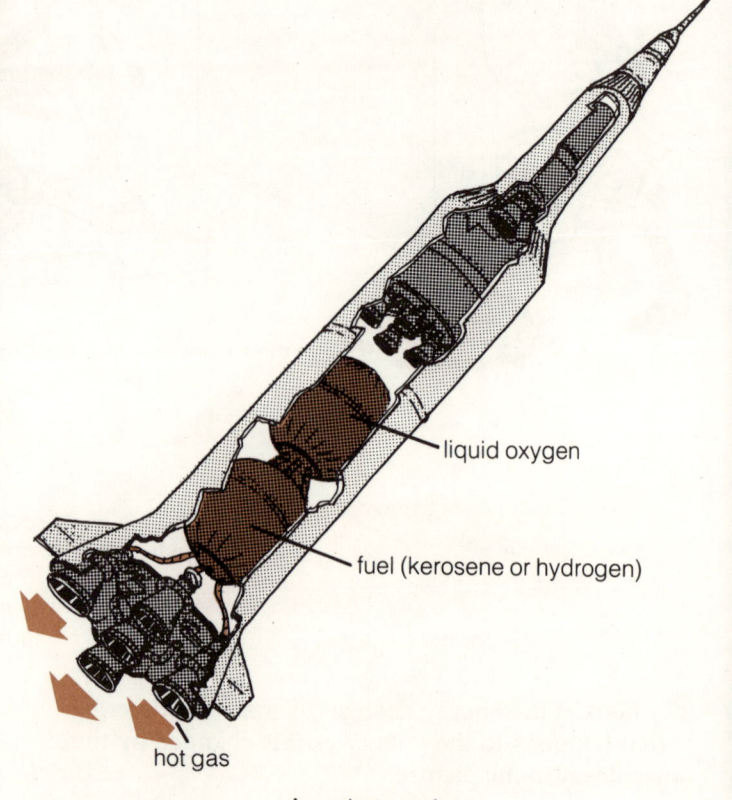

liquid oxygen

fuel (kerosene or hydrogen)

hot gas

A rocket engine

Petrol engines

Petrol engines produce hot gas from an explosion. The gas does not rush out but is made to move a piston instead. Small air-cooled petrol engines come in many shapes and sizes but they all have the following main parts:

Petrol tank and tap
Air intake and filter
Carburettor
Throttle cable
Cylinder block and crankcase
Spark plug
High voltage lead
Cooling fins
Exhaust and silencer

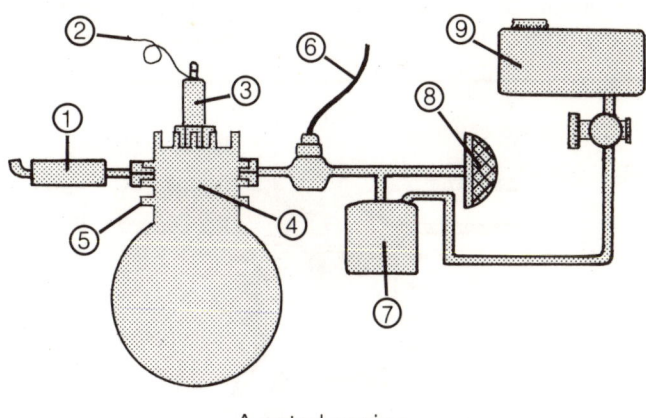

A petrol engine

11 Draw this diagram of a single cylinder petrol engine. Write down the list of parts and try to number them correctly*.

The fuel used in this sort of engine is a mixture of petrol droplets and air. This mixture is exploded in the cylinder by a spark, producing a very hot gas. The gas expands, pushing the piston down.

This table shows what some of the parts do.

Part	The job it does
Air filter	Removes dirt from the air sucked into the engine
Carburettor	Mixes small drops of petrol with the air
Throttle	Controls how much air and petrol enter the engine and so the speed of the engine
Spark plug	Sparks at the right moment and explodes the petrol/air mixture

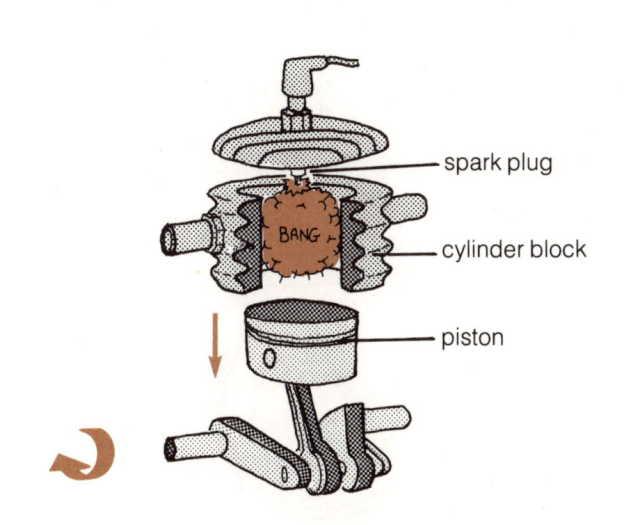

Rotation from up and down motion

12 Would a petrol engine work on the Moon? Explain.

13 Copy this energy flow diagram for a petrol engine starting up. Write in these forms of energy instead of the question marks: kinetic energy; chemical energy; heat energy.

14 What happens to a petrol engine if you place your hand over the air intake when it is running? Explain why.

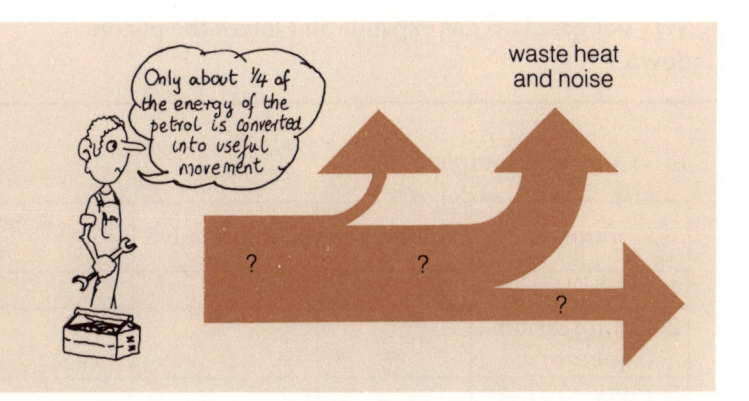

*the parts are numbered 9, 8, 7, 6, 4, 3, 2, 5, 1, starting from the top.

69

What happens inside a common type of petrol engine?

The piston of a 'four stroke' engine goes down, up, down, up, each stroke having a different effect on the gases in the cylinder. The four stokes are then repeated, always in the same order.

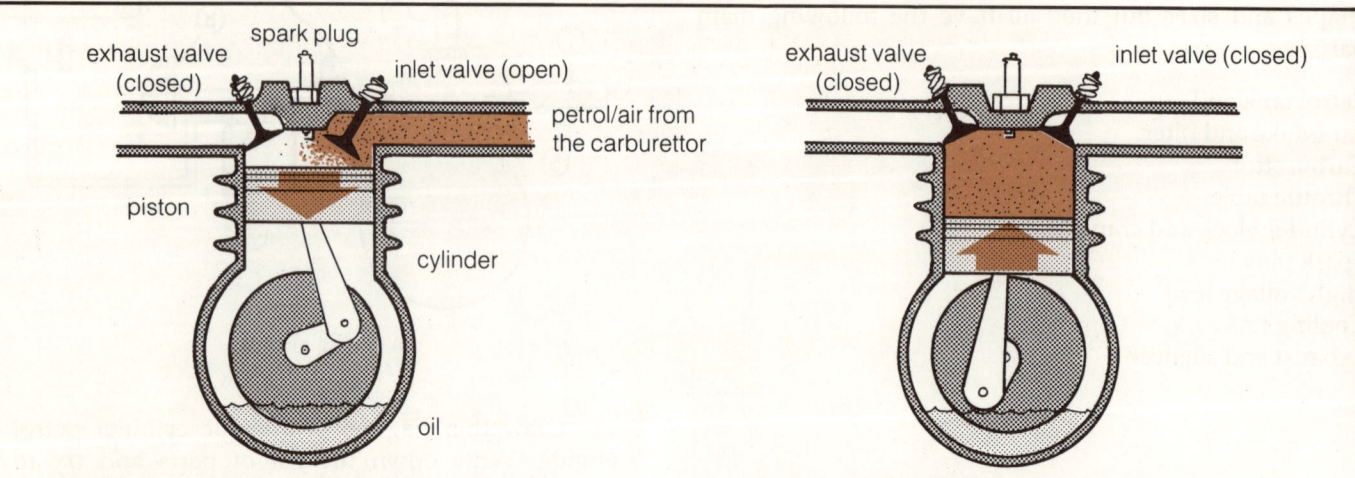

1. Intake stroke
A 'four stroke' engine has two valves. As the piston moves down, the inlet valve opens and petrol/air mixture is sucked into the cylinder.

2. Compression stroke
Both valves close and the petrol/air mixture is compressed to about 1/10 th of its starting volume.

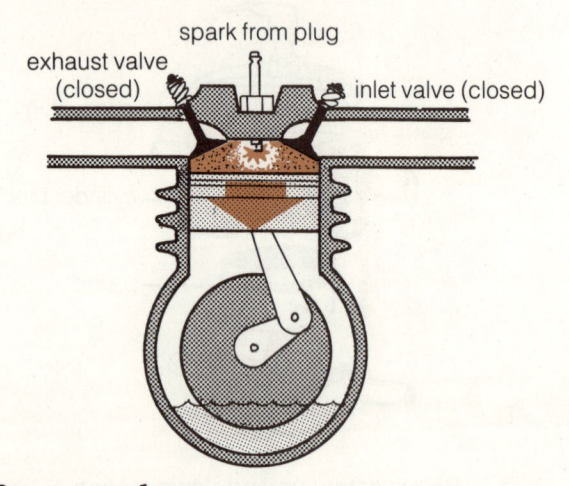

3. Power stroke
The spark plug sparks just as the piston is starting to move down. The petrol and air explode, producing a very hot gas. This gas expands and forces the piston down.

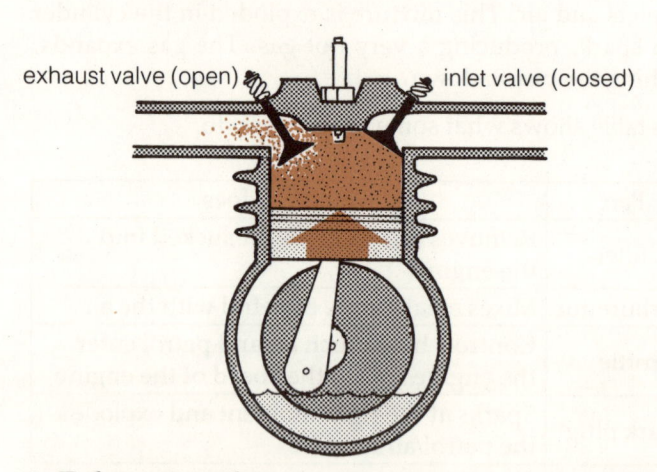

4. Exhaust stroke
The movement continues pushing the piston up. The hot gas is driven out through the open exhaust valve.

---

15 Copy and complete.

Stroke	Inlet valve	Exhaust valve	What is happening to the fuel	Which way the piston is moving
1. Intake (suck)				
2. Compression (squeeze)				
3. Power (bang)				
4. Exhaust (blow)				

Open or closed? Up or down?

16 Which stroke provides the useful energy?

16 Heat and the change of state

What can heat do to materials?

Set up these heating experiments and watch what happens.

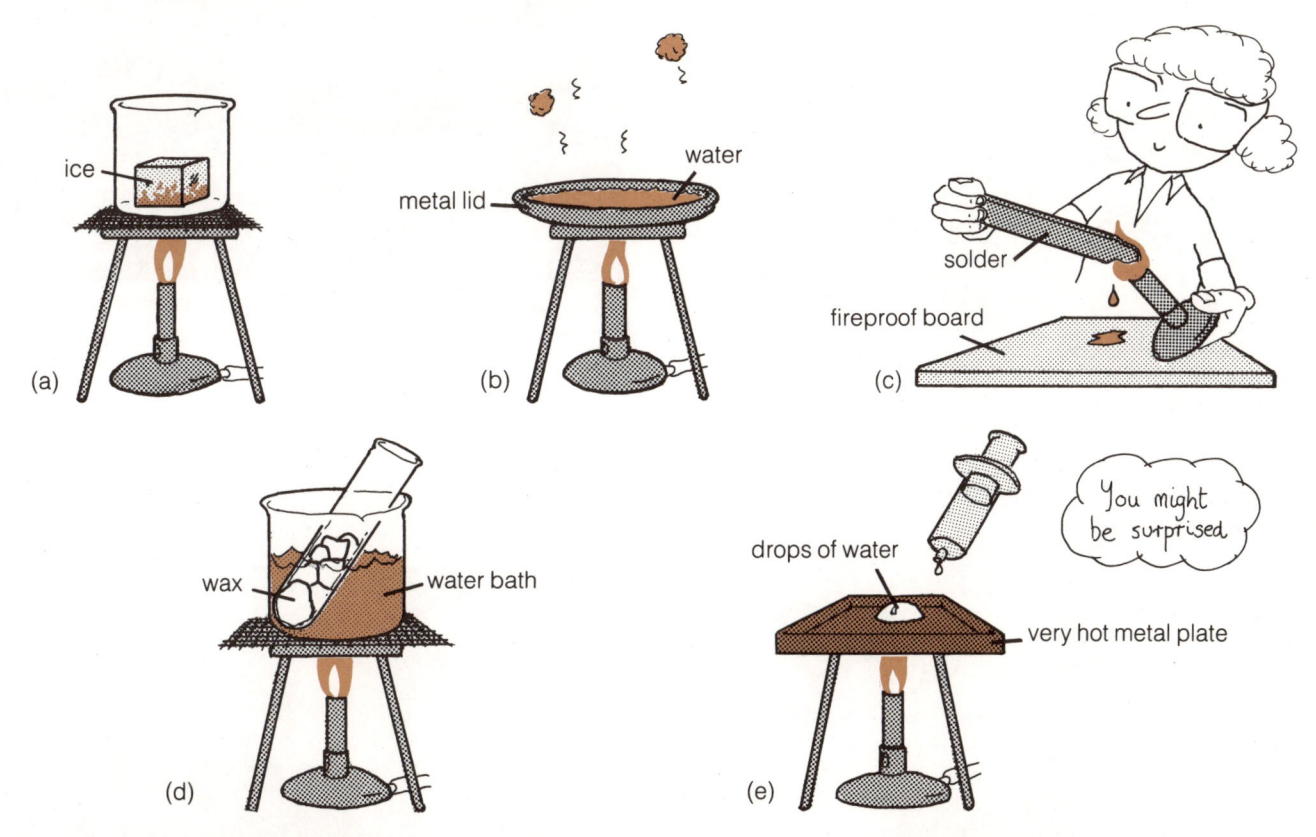

(a) ice
(b) metal lid, water
(c) solder, fireproof board
(d) wax, water bath
(e) drops of water, very hot metal plate — You might be surprised

1 What will happen in these experiments? Copy the table and fill in the spaces.

Material that is heated	Is it solid, liquid or gas at first?	Does it boil?	Does it melt?	What else happens?
Ice				
Water				
Solder				
Wax				
Drops of water				

Materials are either solids, liquids or gases. These are the three states of matter. Heat can change matter from solid to liquid and from liquid to gas.

2 What must be done to change a gas into a liquid or a liquid into a solid?

solid →(energy) liquid →(energy) gas
      melting   boiling

■ Heat can make materials change state.

71

The particles of matter

What are materials made of and what happens to them when they change state? To find out we must examine them in different ways. An electron microscope can magnify 80 000 times, and materials looked at in such detail seem to be made up of small particles. A beach looks smooth from a distance but is seen to be made of particles when looked at close up.

If we are curious about what things are made of, we examine them carefully to try and find out

Electron micrograph showing protein molecules

Crystals

If we pack balls or oranges in neat rows, a regular shape builds up. Some substances form crystals that have the same regular shape. This suggests that they too are built from rows of particles.

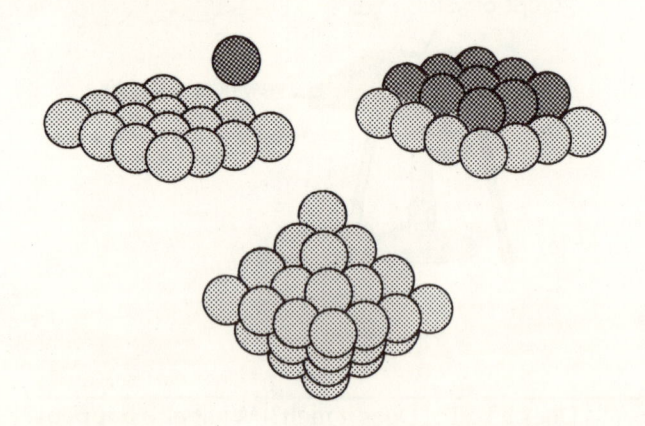

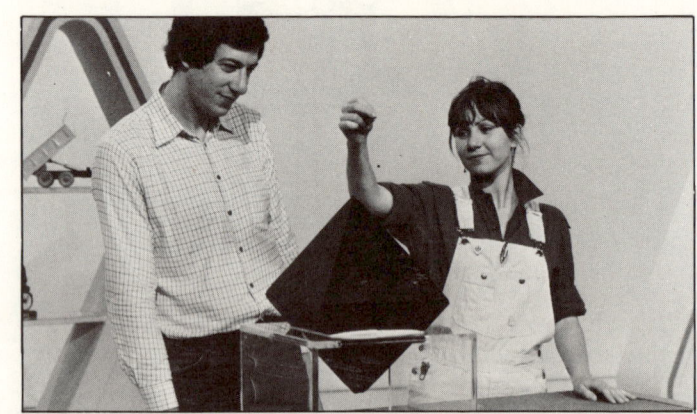

A giant crystal of chrome alum (Ray Gluckman with *Blue Peter* presenter, Sarah Greene)

Chemists use the idea of particles

John Dalton revived the age-old idea that matter consists of particles. After many years examining how substances react chemically he became convinced that the simplest substances are made up of tiny particles of matter called **atoms**. Modern chemists use the idea of atoms and **molecules** (groups of atoms) to explain what happens when substances react.

Atoms have never been seen – they are too small – and it is hard to believe in something you cannot see. As you experiment, watch carefully and ask yourself: does the idea of atoms fit in with these happenings?

Most atoms combine with others to form groups of two or more. These groups of atoms are called molecules

- All materials, whether they are solids, liquids or gases, are thought to be made of atoms.
- Molecules are groups of atoms.

Gases

Some well known facts about gases are:
(a) A gas can be compressed.
(b) A gas is 'thin'. It has a low density.
(c) When a substance turns into a gas, there is a great increase in its volume.

These observations can be explained if we imagine a gas is made of molecules that are spaced out far from each other with nothing between.

A gas can be compressed

solid carbon dioxide

after the carbon dioxide has turned into a gas it fills a larger space

The particles of gas are spaced out

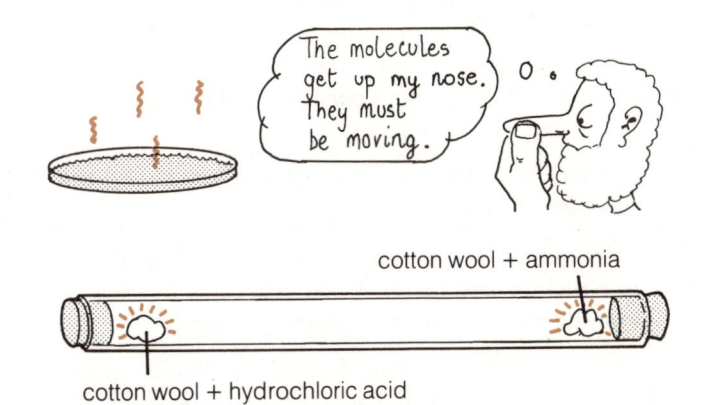

Experiment. To show that the particles of a gas are moving

(a) Place a dish of after-shave, scent or ammonia solution on the bench. The molecules will soon reach your nose.

(b) When hydrogen chloride gas meets ammonia gas, a white smoke is formed. Place a drop of concentrated hydrochloric acid at one end of the tube and a drop of ammonia solution at the other. After a while white smoke appears some distance from the ends of the tube.

> 3 What do these experiments suggest about the molecules of a gas?
>
> 4 Solids and liquids cannot be compressed like a gas and have a much greater density. What does this suggest about the particles of solids and liquids?

cotton wool + ammonia

cotton wool + hydrochloric acid

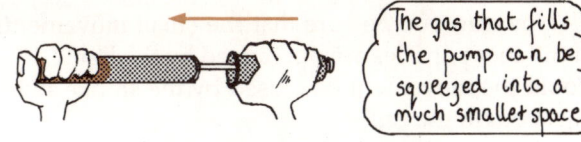

■ The molecules of a gas are spaced out and move about.

Brownian motion

Experiment. Looking at smoke

Look at smoke through a microscope. The smoke will have to be held in a small plastic cell and lit from the side by a small lamp. Smoke is made of tiny pieces of soot floating about in warm air. Even under the microscope these pieces of soot only look like specks of light. Watch the soot particles carefully. Can you see them moving? How would you describe the movement of one of the particles?

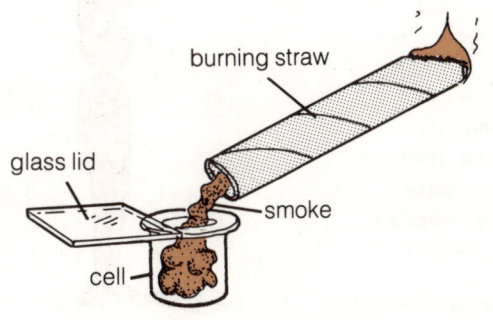

Filling a smoke cell

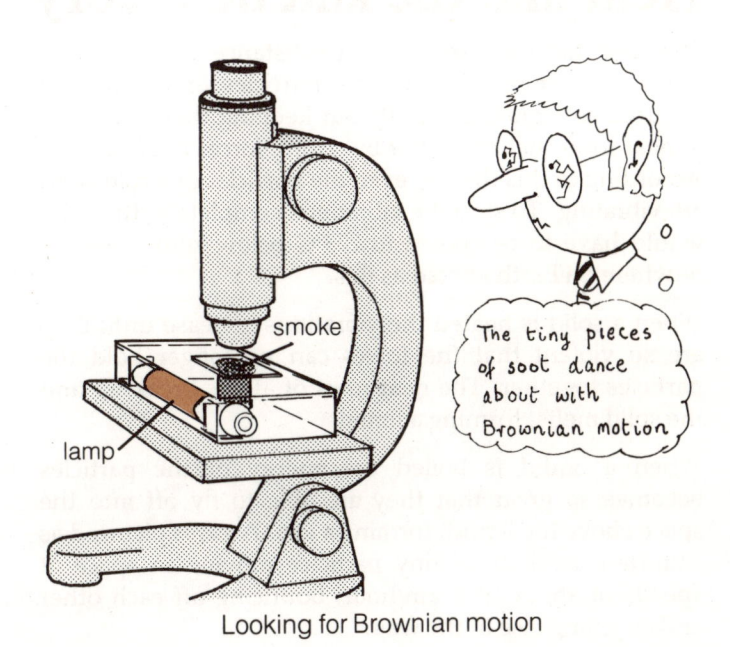

Looking for Brownian motion

5 How can you be sure that the small movements of the soot particles are not caused by the light? Could the movement be caused by the smoke swirling about in the cell?

6 The moving specks of light are:
A. Molecules moving in a regular way.
B. Molecules moving in a haphazard way.
C. Smoke particles colliding.
D. Smoke particles moving in a regular way.
E. Smoke particles moving in a haphazard way.
Which is the most likely?

What causes the motion?

The smoke particles are surrounded by air. If air is made up of moving molecules then these molecules would hit the smoke particles. If a smoke particle gets hit harder on one side than the other, it would move. The molecules are extremely small, explaining why we cannot see what is causing the movement. Can you think of a better explanation of why the soot particles move as they do?

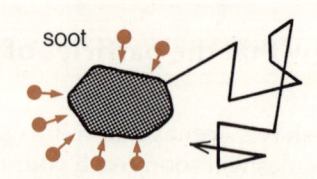

7 What does this experiment tell us about the molecules of a gas?

8 At higher temperatures, the smoke particles move further and faster. What else does this tell us about the movement of the gas molecules?

9 Small bits of carbon, floating in liquid, show Brownian motion. What does this tell us about the molecules of a liquid?

■ Brownian motion, first reported by Robert Brown in 1827, is evidence that the molecules of a liquid and gas are moving.

Heat and the kinetic theory

The idea that the particles of a substance are moving is called the **kinetic theory**. The particles of a solid are pictured as vibrating rapidly but keeping their positions in neat rows, held together by strong forces of attraction. According to this theory, even the particles of a cold solid are vibrating. To stop the vibrations completely, the solid would have to be cooled to 273°C below zero. There is nowhere on Earth as cold as this.

When a solid is heated the vibrations increase until they are so violent that the forces can no longer hold the particles together. The neat rows of atoms break up and the solid melts, forming a liquid.

When a liquid is boiled the energy of the particles becomes so great that they are able to fly off into the space above the liquid, forming a gas. A gas is pictured as countless millions of tiny particles moving in space at speeds of about 1000 km/hour, bouncing off each other and anything else in the way.

A model of the particles of a solid

10 Copy and put solid, liquid or gas in spaces.

What the molecules are doing	The state
The molecules are free from each other and moving at high speeds	
The molecules are vibrating and are loosely held together but not in a neat pattern	
The molecules are vibrating and held in neat rows.	

11 As steam changes to water and then to ice, does the energy of its molecules increase or decrease?

Experiment. Solid to liquid to gas – a model of what happens to a substance when it changes state

Set up this apparatus and run the motor at different speeds. Watch what happens to the balls as their energy of vibration increases.

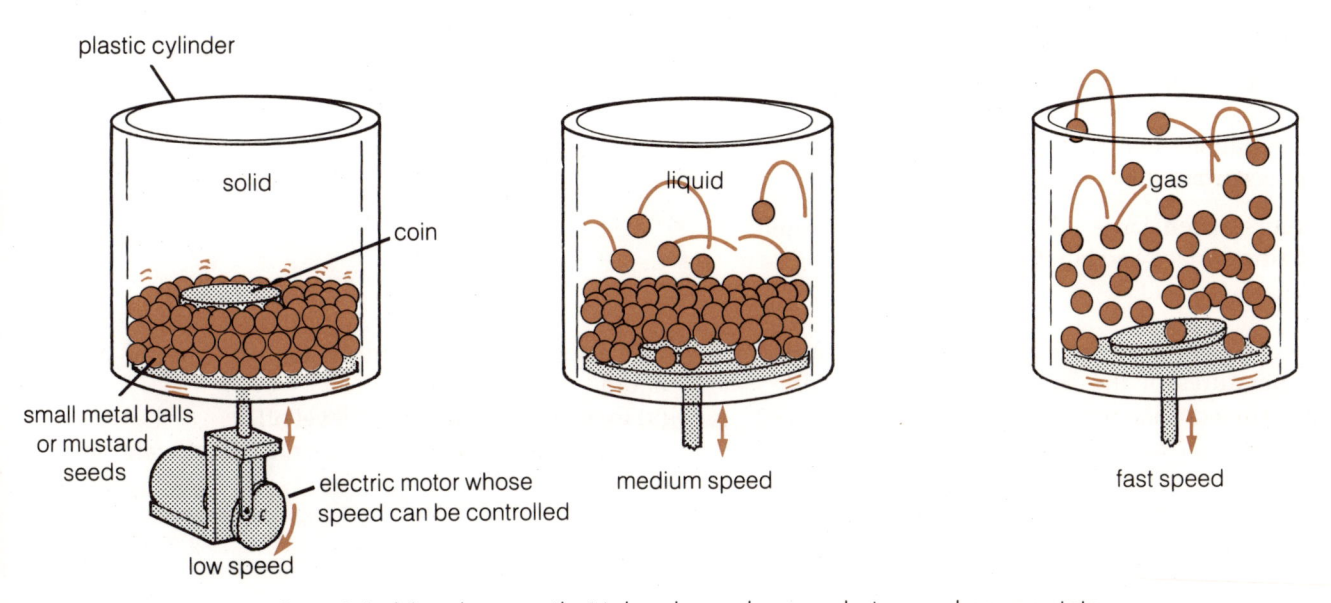

A model of the changes that take place when a substance changes state

12 Describe the changes that take place as the balls are given more and more energy.

13 What would you feel if you put your hand into the cylinder?

14 Why do high speed gas molecules not break windows and glass bottles?

15 Can we feel the collisions of the molecules of gas in an air bed? What would happen if they suddenly stopped moving?

This bag of air is mostly empty space

air bed

■ Heat energy can change the state of a material because it increases the energy of its molecules.

17 Boiling and freezing

Boiling

We often boil water. Heat warms the water to its boiling point and then changes it from liquid to gas.

Experiment. Watching water boil

Heat a beaker of fresh tap water and watch it carefully until it boils. Put a thermometer in the water and write down the temperatures when you see the following things happen:

(a) Mist appears on the outside of the beaker.
(b) Small bubbles rise from the bottom of the beaker to the top.
(c) Wisps appear above the surface.
(d) Large bubbles appear and disappear on the bottom of the beaker.
(e) The large bubbles get to the surface where they burst, whipping the surface into a turmoil.

Boiling occurs when large bubbles form in the liquid, then rise to the surface and burst.

It's surprising how much happens

1 Water and alcohol were heated separately and the temperatures of the liquids were taken every minute.

Time	0	1	2	3	5	8	11	14	minutes
Water temp.	20	27	35	42	61	83	100	100	°C
Alcohol temp.	20	40	57	70	78	78	78	78	°C

Plot a graph of temperature against time for each liquid.
(a) Explain why the graphs level off.
(b) What are the boiling temperatures of water and alcohol?

Hidden heat

If you continue to heat water when it is boiling, its temperature does not rise. So what is the heat energy doing? Heat energy changes the boiling water from a liquid to a gas. This enegy is held by the steam and is released when the steam turns back into water. Steam at 100°C has more energy than the same amount of water at 100°C. The extra energy needed to change water into steam is called **latent** (hidden) heat.

2 Describe two differences, according to the kinetic theory, between molecules in boiling water at 100°C and molecules in steam at 100°C.

Boiling water needs latent heat before it can change into steam.

■ Energy is needed to change a liquid into a gas.

Changing the boiling point of water

If you boil water in a pressure cooker and measure the temperature of the steam inside, you will find that it is more than 100°C. The steam is made to lift a weight before it escapes. This greatly increases the pressure inside the cooker. The extra pressure raises the boiling temperature (boiling point) of the water. If more weights are added, the pressure of the steam rises still further. Water can be made to boil at temperatures up to 120°C in this way.

3   Why do you think pressure cookers cook food faster?

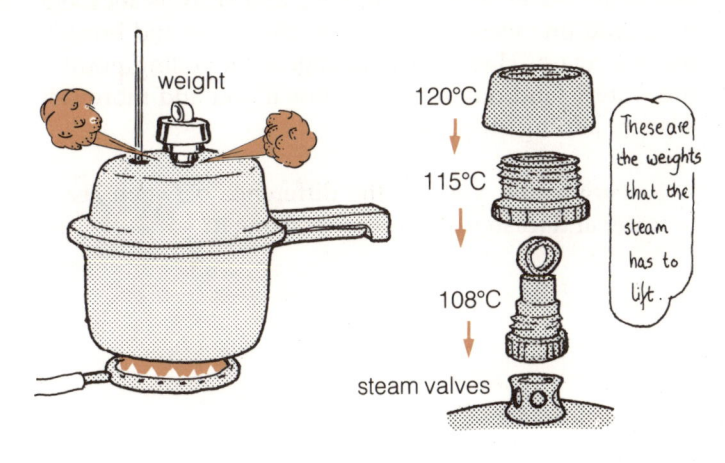

Water boiling under high pressure

Why extra pressure raises the boiling point

The steam bubbles find it difficult to form under the crushing effect of the extra pressure. So the bubbles cannot form until the temperature is higher and the steam inside the bubbles has a high enough pressure. The boiling point is raised.

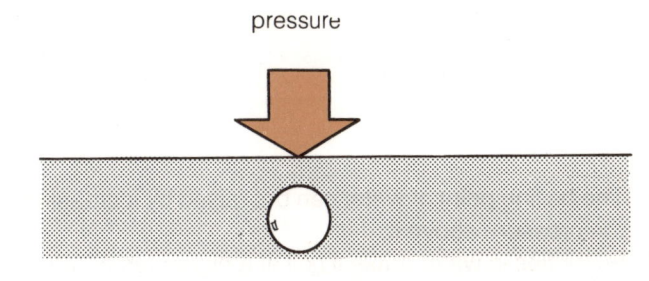

Experiment. Boiling water under low pressure

Connect a flask of water to a vacuum pump. Pump the air from the flask and heat the water until it boils. Measure its boiling temperature. You will find that water can be made to boil at temperatures as low as 20°C or 30°C.

Water boiling under low pressure

4   Copy and complete these sentences:
'When the pressure above water is low, the steam bubbles find it _____ to form. The boiling point of the water is _____. Increasing the pressure, _____ the boiling point of water a little; decreasing the pressure, _____ the boiling point of water a lot.

5   Why does the mountaineer find that his tea does not brew properly?

Experiment. Impurities raise the boiling point

Boil some water in a boiling tube and read its temperature. Add one teaspoon of salt to the water and bring to the boil again. Has the salt changed the boiling point of the water? Find out what happens if you add more salt. Also try adding other substances.

> 6 How could you tell the difference between sea water and fresh water without tasting it?

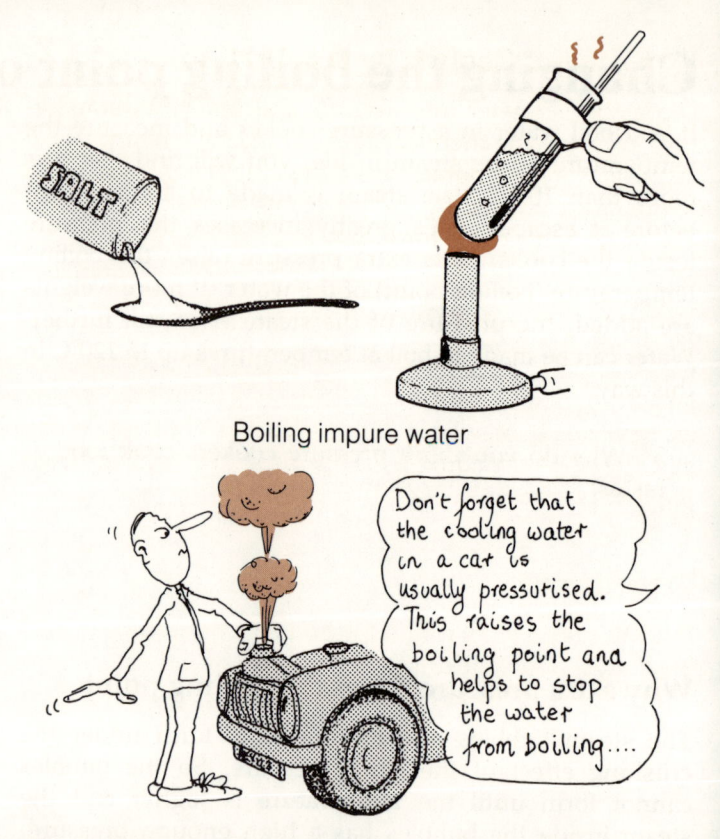

Boiling impure water

Don't forget that the cooling water in a car is usually pressurised. This raises the boiling point and helps to stop the water from boiling....

- The boiling point of water can be: raised by increasing the pressure above it or adding impurities; lowered by decreasing the pressure above it.
- Impurities in water make it boil at a higher temperature.

Evaporation

Wet clothes dry in the wind and puddles of water disappear. What happens to the water? The liquid water must turn into an invisible vapour that is carried away by the wind.

The more energetic water molecules manage to escape from the liquid and move around among the air molecules. This happens even if the water is not boiling.

When a liquid turns into a gas without boiling, it is said to be evaporating. It is hard to detect water vapour but when scent or aftershave evaporate we can smell the vapour.

> 7 Does water have to be at its boiling point before it can evaporate? Give an example that proves your answer.

Experiment. Evaporation

Dip a finger into acetone. Lift it out and watch the acetone evaporate. The liquid disappears but do any of the molecules reach your nose? Notice that your finger feels a little cooler as the liquid evaporates.

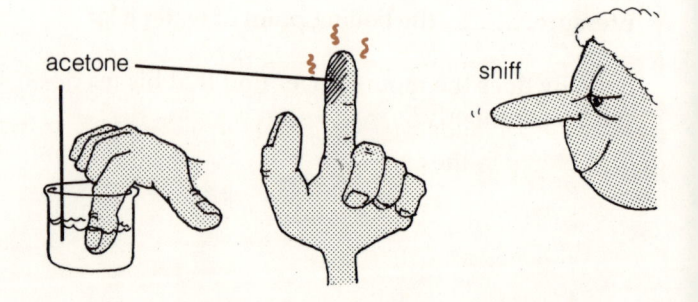

Experiment. Cooling by evaporation

Dip a thermometer into acetone and read the temperature. Remove the thermometer and read the temperature as the acetone evaporates from the bulb. Find the drop in temperature caused by the evaporation of other liquids. Try water and alcohol for example.

Why does evaporation cause cooling?

Gas molecules have more energy than the molecules in a liquid. A liquid cannot turn into a gas unless it gets energy from somewhere. If the energy is not supplied by a heater, then the liquid will take the energy it needs from the things around, cooling them down.

Experiment

Put wet cotton wool round the bulb of a thermometer and place it in a stream of cold air alongside a thermometer with a dry bulb. Read both thermometers.

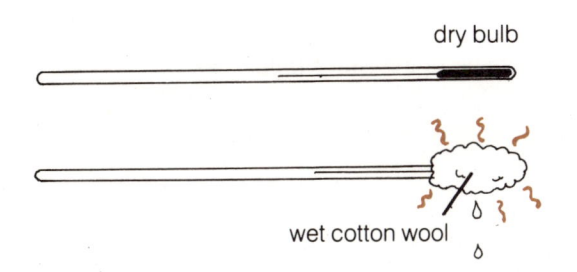

8 Do both thermometers give the same reading? If not explain why not.

9 Explain why you feel cold when you get out of a pool or bath, especially if it is draughty. Note – the water itself is not cold. Why do you feel cold for longer if you are wearing wet clothes?

Experiment. Making ice

Put a little acetone into a tin and stand the tin in a puddle of cold water. Blow air through the acetone to evaporate it quickly. The puddle of water should freeze after a time.

10 Explain why the water freezes and fixes the can to the wooden block.

11 Why does the outside of the can mist up?

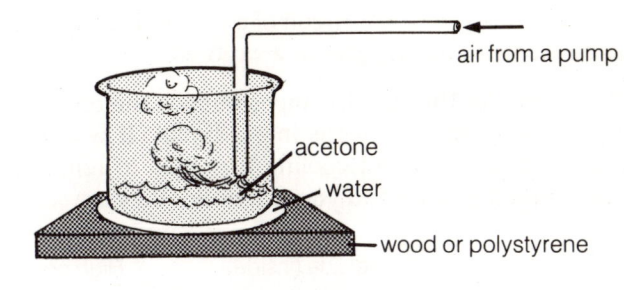

Examples of condensation – the reverse of evaporation

Clouds

If water vapour enters cool air then the vapour turns back into liquid, not as a puddle but as many tiny drops of pure water. Clouds are made up of millions of water drops held up in the air.

Dew

During the day the warm air collects water vapour. In the night the air cools down. Vapour condenses and forms drops of water on the ground. Dew drops like to form on sharp points or edges.

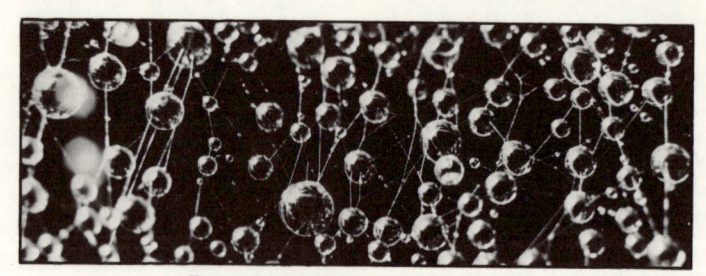

Dew drops on a spider's web

12 Explain why a person's glasses mist up when he walks into a steamy bathroom from a cold passage. Or when he sips hot soup.

13 Copy and complete.

	Evaporating	Condensing
What change of state takes place?		
Does energy have to be supplied or removed?		
Are the particles moving further apart or closer together (on average)?		

- When a liquid changes into a gas without boiling, it is called evaporation.
- Evaporation can take place at any temperature.
- Evaporation causes cooling if warmth is not supplied by a heater, warm air or the Sun's rays.

Refrigerators

Cooling by evaporation is used in a refrigerator to keep food cold. A substance called **freon** is used in refrigerators.

1) It is pumped round a circuit of pipes and spends part of its time as a liquid and part as a vapour.

2) As it passes through the pipes outside the refrigerator, it is compressed and turns into a liquid. It warms up a little as it does so and cooling fins help to remove this heat. (Feel the pipes and you will notice they are warm.)

3) The liquid freon then squirts through a valve into pipes that surround the freezing compartment. This is inside the refrigerator.

4) The liquid evaporates, taking the heat it needs from the metal and air inside the cabinet. The vapour is then drawn into the pump and pumped round the circuit again.

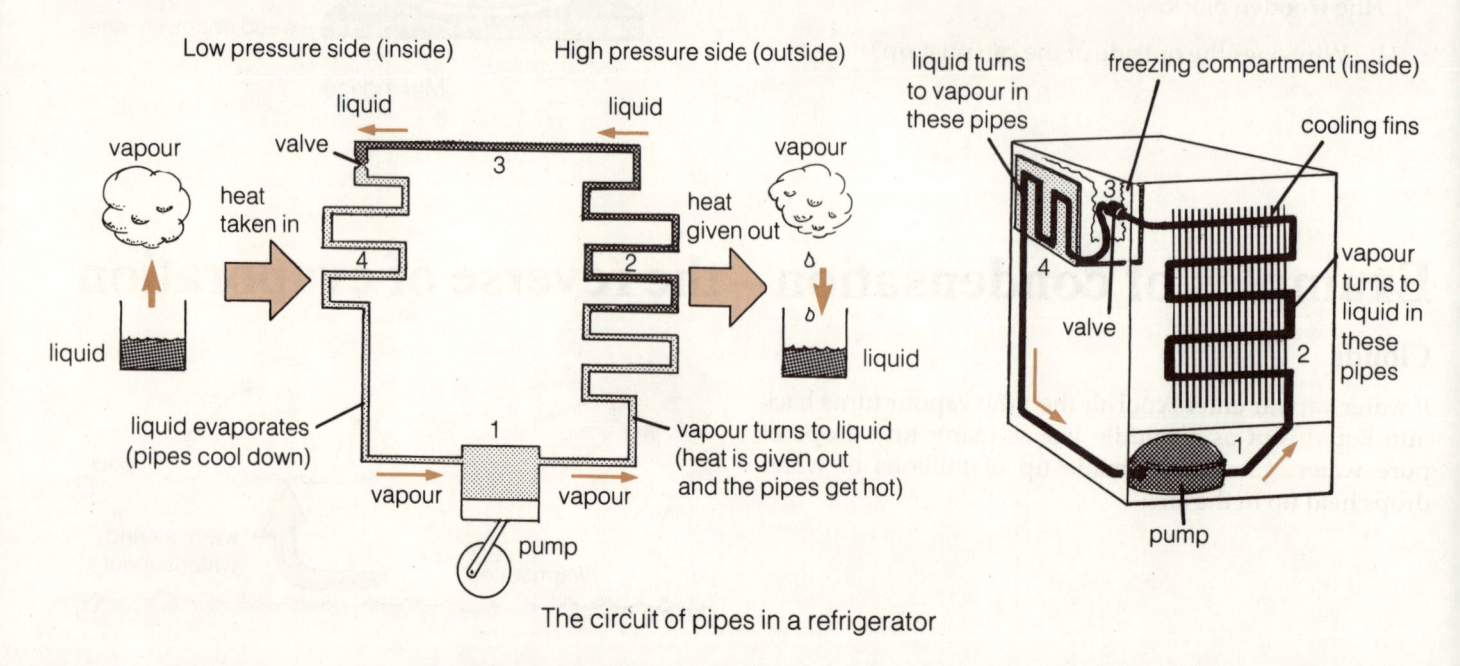

The circuit of pipes in a refrigerator

14 Refrigerators and electric irons are controlled by thermostats. Copy the table below and write in the boxes whether the thermostat is on or off.

	Electric iron thermostat	Refrigerator thermostat
Temperature too high		
Temperature too low		

15 Why is it important to insulate the cabinet of a refrigerator?

16 What happens to the energy that is taken from the inside of a refrigerator?

Melting

Experiment. Melting ice

Melt some crushed ice in a beaker. Use a bunsen with a small flame and take the temperature of the ice every half minute. Stir gently before you take each reading. Plot a temperature/time graph of your readings.

Ice needs latent heat before it will melt.

17 The temperature of the ice and water stays around 0°C for quite a long time. What is the heat energy from the flame doing during this time?

18 Describe two differences between the movement of the molecules in ice and the molecules in water.

Experiment. Making very low temperatures

Crush some ice and measure its temperature. Add one teaspoon of salt. Stir the mixture and measure the temperature again. What happens to the ice?
How low can you make the temperature? How does salt affect the freezing point of water?

Explanation. Salt water freezes below 0°C. Salt sprinkled on ice makes the ice melt. Melting needs heat and so heat is taken from the rest of the salty ice mixture. A salt/ice mixture is a handy way to produce very low temperatures.

19 Why is salt sometimes spread on roads in the winter?

20 Ice sometimes forms on the outside of a beaker of salt and ice. Where does this ice come from?

Experiment. Melting and freezing wax

Melting. Boil some water in a beaker. Put a tube containing wax into the water and start the clock. Read the temperture of the wax every half minute until it has melted.

Freezing. Take the tube of liquid wax out of the boiling water and take the temperature of the wax every minute as it cools in the air. Plot a temperature/time graph of your readings. Put arrows on the graph to show where the wax is melting and freezing.

21 Copy and complete.	Melting	Freezing
What changes of state take place?		
Does energy have to be supplied or removed?		

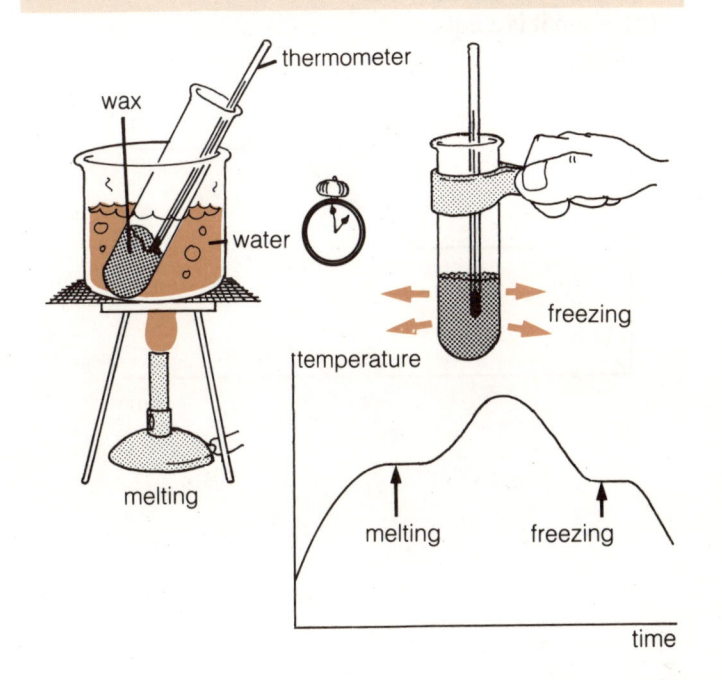

81

Summary of change of state

- The three states of matter are .... solid, liquid and gas.
- The kinetic theory supposes that the molecules of materials are .... moving.
- As a material changes from solid to liquid to gas, the energy of its molecules .... increases.
- The temperature at which a liquid boils can be raised by .... increasing the pressure and adding impurities.
  and lowered by .... decreasing the pressure.
- When a liquid changes to a gas without boiling it is .... evaporating.
- The energy that is needed to make a liquid boil or evaporate is called .... latent heat.
- The energy that a solid needs to melt is also called .... latent heat.

Further questions

22 Use the kinetic theory to explain:
(a) why a puddle dries up on a windy day;
(b) why a large volume of steam condenses to a small volume of water;
(c) why energy is needed before water can change into steam.

23 Explain why perfume can be smelt some distance from the person wearing it.

24 What is meant by the 'Brownian movement' of smoke particles in air? What does it tell us about the molecules of air?

25 Describe the motion of molecules in:
(a) a solid;
(b) a liquid;
(c) a gas.

26 The graph below shows how the temperature of a pure crystalline substance changes as it is heated. Copy the graph and label it to show:
(a) when the substance is melting;
(b) when the substance is boiling;
(c) when it is a solid;
(d) when it is a liquid.

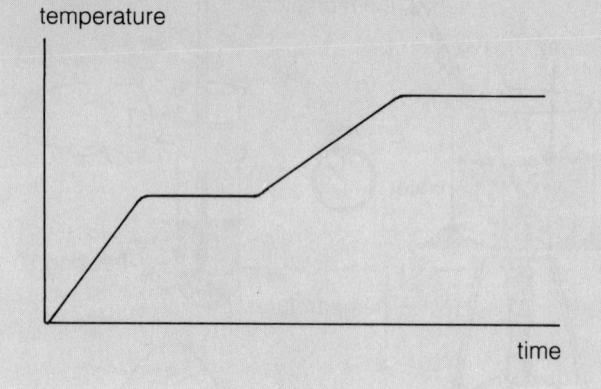

27 Write down two differences between boiling and evaporation.

28 Describe two ways of making a puddle of water evaporate more quickly.

29 Explain the following:
(a) salt is sprinkled on icy roads;
(b) motorists put 'anti-freeze' in the cooling water of some cars;
(c) wet clothes feel cold;
(d) tea is cooled more rapidly by blowing on it;
(e) perspiration helps to cool the body.

18 The expansion of solids

Experiment. Heat causes expansion

Build this piece of apparatus and watch the pointer as the bar is heated. Notice how the roller and pointer show up the tiny expansion (growth) of the bar. Which way does the pointer move?

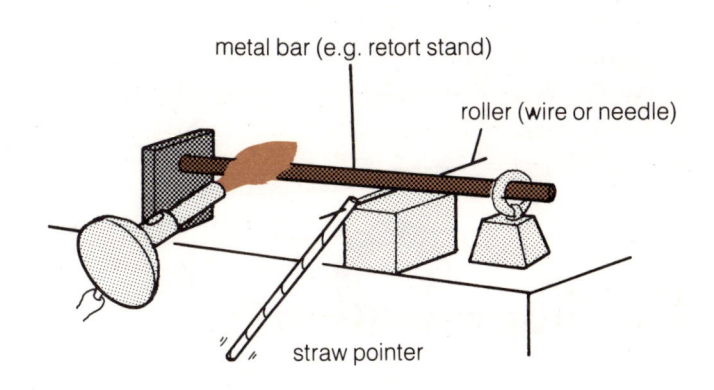

Experiment. Measuring the expansion of metals

In this apparatus, steam is used to heat the metal. The levers magnify the expansion about 50 times, making it easy to see and measure. Measure the expansion of different metals using this or similar apparatus.

Results. Tubes or bars of metal 1000 mm long and heated from 0°C to 100°C would expand by the following amounts:
Copper 1.7 mm
Steel 1.2 mm
Aluminium 2.3 mm
Other materials expand too:
Glass 0.9 mm
'Pyrex' glass 0.05 mm
Concrete 1.2 mm

The expansion is small. It can cause problems and it can be useful.

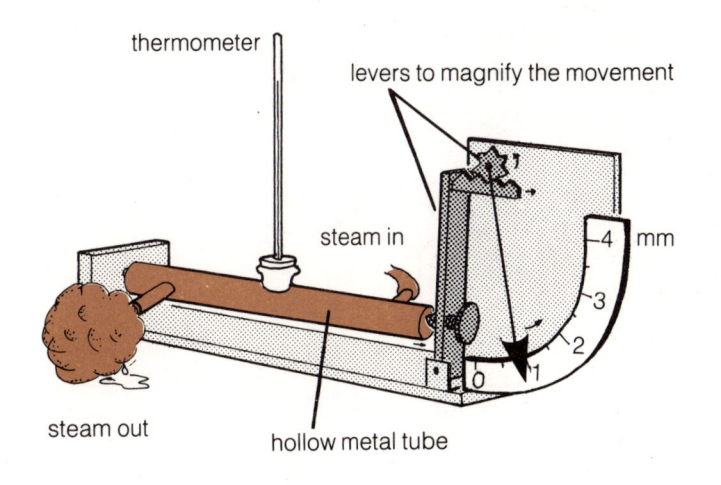

1 When a steel ruler is heated we have seen that it increases in length. Would you expect it to increase in width and thickness too?
Would a hole in the ruler get bigger or smaller?
If you measured a length using a hot steel ruler, would the value you get be too long or too short? Explain your answer.

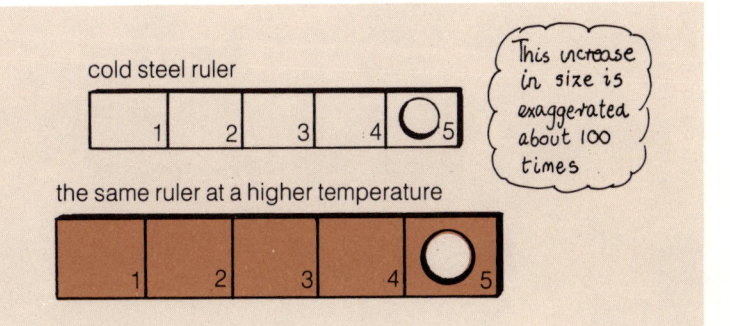

This increase in size is exaggerated about 100 times

■ Heating makes materials expand in every direction.

Problems caused by expansion

2 We have seen that the force of expansion is strong enough to break an iron bar (p. 66). What do you think will happen to each of these metal tubes when they are heated? Their ends are firmly fixed. (Steam and oil pipelines in hot countries sometimes have loops in them to allow for expansion.)

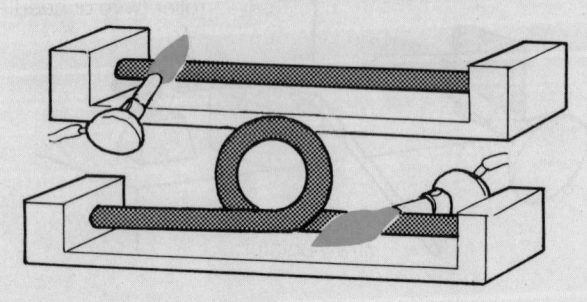

3 If you pour boiling water into a thick glass jar, it will probably crack. The inside expands, the outside does not and the stress cracks the glass. There are two ways of preventing glass containers from cracking:
(a) by using thin glass   (b) by using Pyrex glass.
Explain why these methods work.

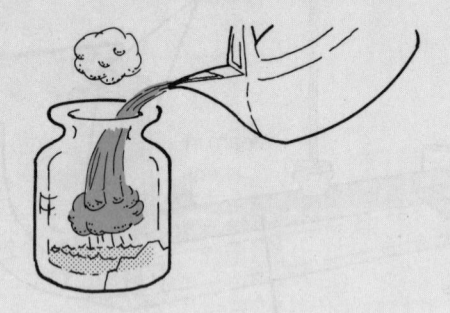

4 Why are gaps left between the slabs of a concrete road? Why is tar such a good material to use to fill these gaps? What would happen if no gaps were left? Should gaps be left at the edge of the road?

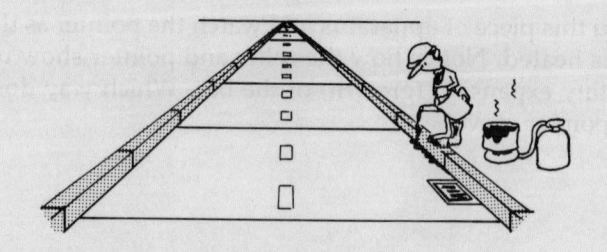

5 A steel cap, screwed tight on a glass bottle, can sometimes be loosened by pouring hot water over it. Look at the expansion figures for glass and steel and explain why this should work.

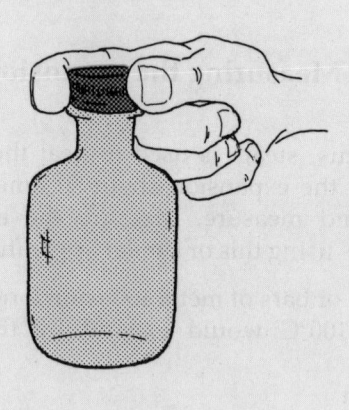

Why does heat make solids expand?

When a solid is heated its molecules vibrate with more energy and move further away from each other. The solid gets a little larger in every direction.

The 'expansion' of a line of people

■ Expansion is caused by molecules gaining energy and moving further away from each other.

The bimetal strip

A bimetal strip is made of two metals firmly welded together. Steel and copper are examples of two metals that could be used.

6 If you heat a bimetal strip, it bends. Look up the expansion figures for steel and copper (p. 83) and explain why this happens.

7 If the strip is straight at room temperature and you plunge it into ice, what will happen?

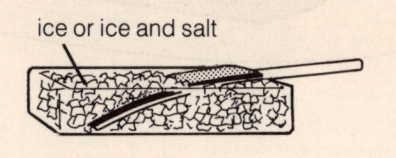

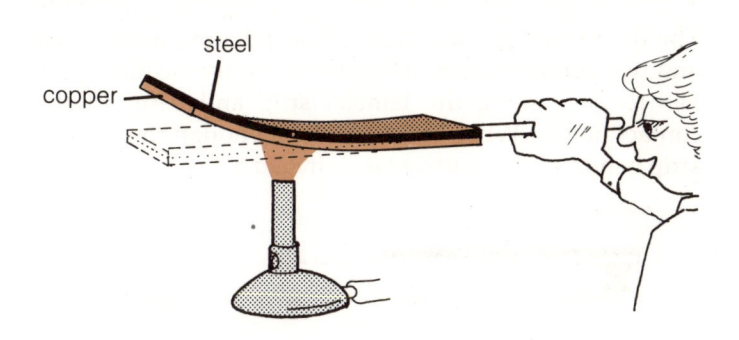

Bimetal strips bend when heated or cooled

Experiment. Thermostats – automatic temperature controllers

Obtain an electric iron with a light that shows when the iron is on. Switch on (the light will come on) and start the clock. After a while, when the iron is hot enough, the light will go off. Note the time when this happens. The iron will then continue to go on and off by itself. Write down the times when it goes on and when it goes off. The iron has a thermostat inside; a switch that goes on when the temperature is too low and off when the temperature is too high.

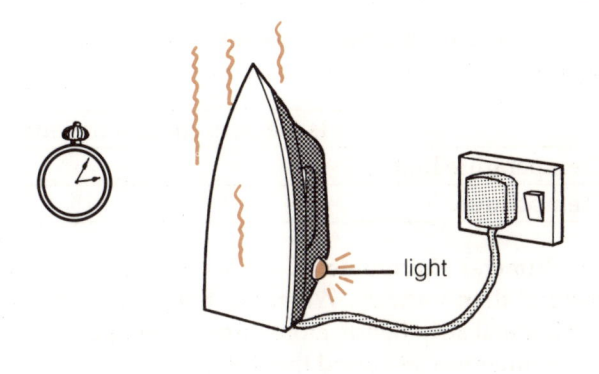

Investigating the action of a thermostat

8 An electric iron was found to go on and off at the following times:

On	Off	On	Off	On	Off	On	Off
0	3min 15s	3.30	4.00	4.10	4.20	5.00	5.05

Plot an on/off time diagram on graph paper. Calculate the time that the iron is on. Work this out as a percentage of the total time.

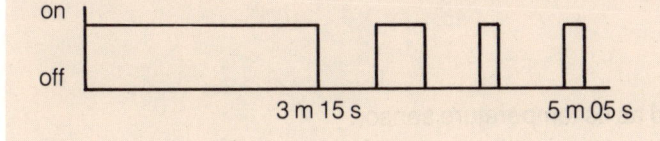

9 Write down two advantages of having a thermostat in an iron.

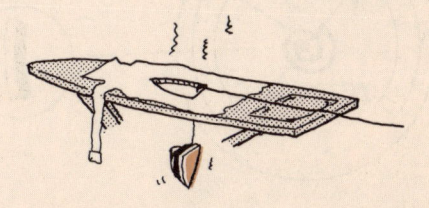

10 Why is the iron on so long at first compared with later.

■ A bimetal strip bends because one metal expands more than the other.

How does the thermostat work?

The thermostat is made from a bimetal strip, a metal bar and two contact points. The current for the heating plate has to pass along the bimetal strip and between the contact points. When the plate is hot enough the bimetal strip bends and the current is switched off.

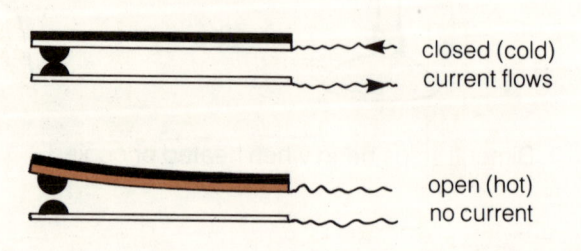

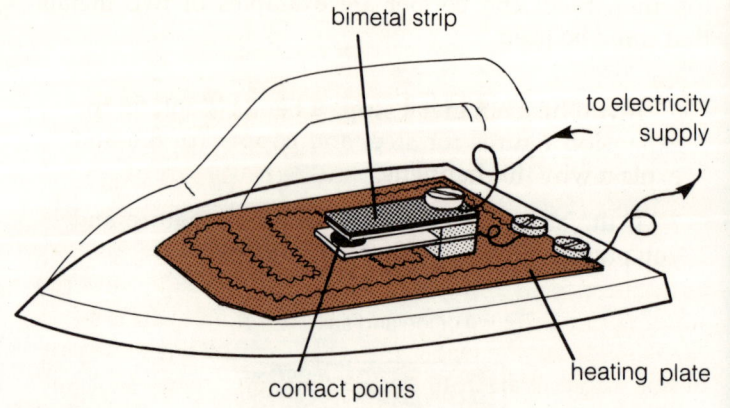

closed (cold) current flows

open (hot) no current

A bimetal thermostat

11 Continue this account by explaining what happens as the heating plate cools.

12 Copy and complete this table. It is about the action of a thermostat in an electric iron.

	Is the strip straight or bent?	Is the current on or off?	Are the points in contact?
Temperature high			
Temperature low			

13 **Bimetal thermometer.** This diagram shows a bimetal thermometer. When the temperature rises, the bimetal strip bends more (into a tighter coil) and the pointer moves round the scale.
(a) Should the metal that expands the most be on the inside or the outside of the coil?
(b) Write down two advantages that this thermometer has over a mercury in glass thermometer.*

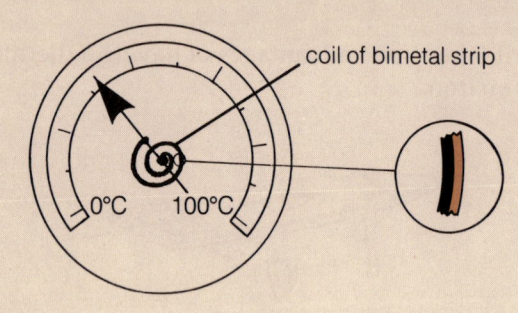

*It is easy to read; less easy to break.

■ A thermostat controls temperature. A bimetal strip can be used as its temperature sensor.

19 Expansion and convection

The expansion of liquids

Experiment. Comparing the expansion of liquids

Completely fill a flask with coloured water and push in a bung fitted with a tube and thermometer. Make sure the water goes a little way up the tube and that no air is left in the flask. Mark the water level then put the flask in a bath of hot water. Wait until the thermometer reads 40°C and measure how far the water moves up the tube. (Note that the mercury moves up the tube of the thermometer because mercury expands when it is heated.)

Put methylated spirits in the flask instead of water and measure its expansion for the same temperature rise. You will see that liquids expand by differing amounts. However, they all expand much more than solids.

Even warmth from the hand makes the liquid expand

1 The experiment above shows that methylated spirits expands more than water. Why is it important to heat the same volume of liquid through the same rise in temperature?

2 Which thermometer, A or B, will be the most sensitive? (Show the most expansion for the same rise in temperature.) Explain your answer.

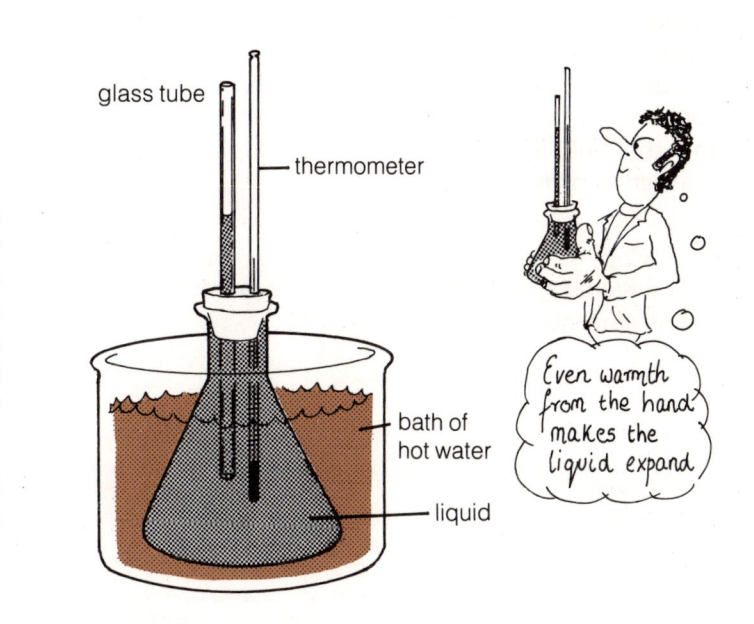

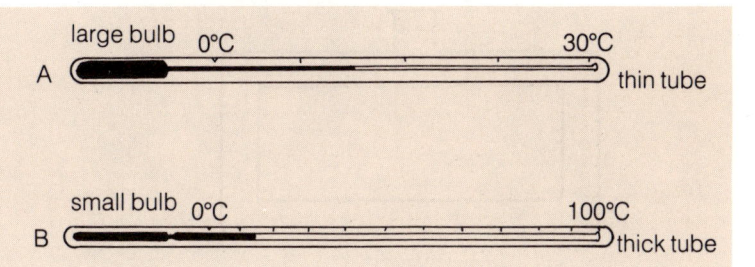

A — large bulb, 0°C to 30°C, thin tube
B — small bulb, 0°C to 100°C, thick tube

Experiment. Convection currents

Put water in a flask, add a pinch of fine aluminium dust (care!) and two drops of washing-up liquid. The aluminium dust forms a 'snow storm' that shows up any movement of the water. Heat or cool the water by the different ways shown below. Watch the moving currents of warm and cold water (convection currents). Draw simple diagrams of these convection currents. Which way do hot water currents move? Which way does the cold water move?

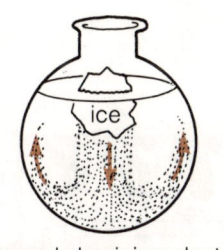

water and aluminium dust and washing-up liquid

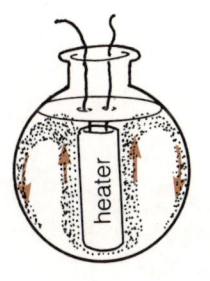

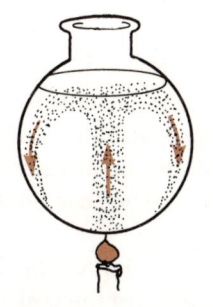

Watch carefully

Looking at convection currents

- Liquids expand more than solids.
- Cold liquid falls downwards, forcing warm liquid to rise.

87

Expansion and the convection of heat

'Convection' is the movement of heat energy by currents of hot liquid (or gas).

When a drop of liquid is heated it expands – its volume increases. The amount of material (its mass) does not change. Since its mass is more spread out, hot liquid is less dense than cold liquid around it. So in a mixture of hot and cold liquid, the cold liquid will sink to the bottom and the hot liquid will rise to the top. This is why convection currents flow.

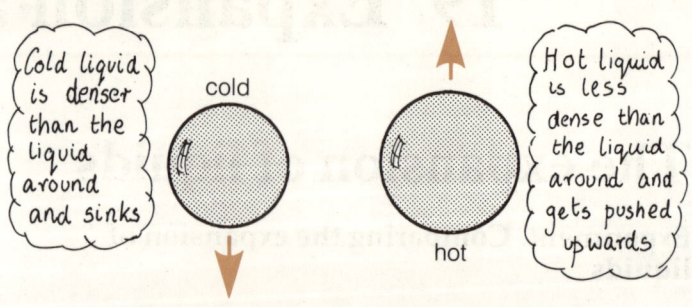

Cold liquid is denser than the liquid around and sinks

Hot liquid is less dense than the liquid around and gets pushed upwards

3 Copy these diagrams and put an arrow where you would have to heat the water to get the convection currents shown.

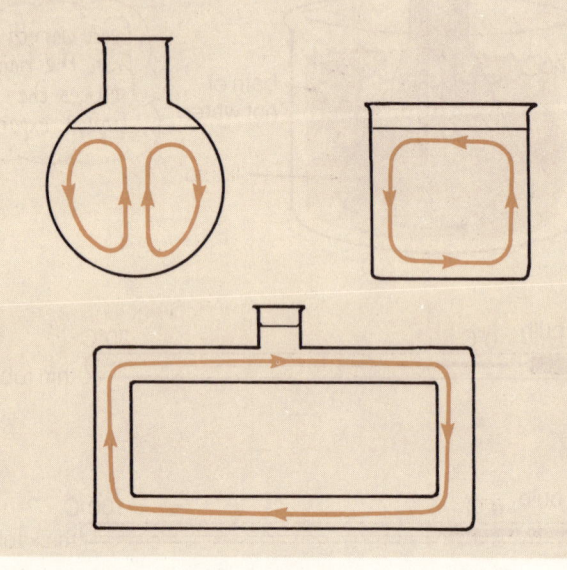

4 (a) Explain how the water at the top of this kettle gets heated by a heater that is at the bottom.

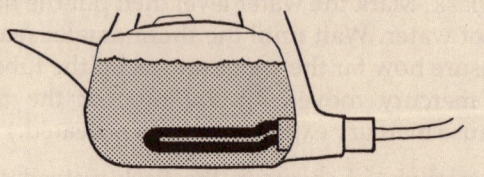

(b) Explain why the water in this tank that is below the immersion heater cannot be heated by convection currents of hot water. (See p.91 also.)

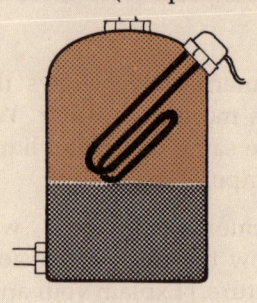

■ Convection is caused by expansion.

A hot and cold water system

Nearly all homes have 'running' hot and cold water. Convection plays a useful part in a household hot and cold water system. The one shown here has an electric heater in the hot water storage tank to heat the water. There are some special points to remember in designing such a system.

Special design feature	Reason
The cold water from the storage tank must enter the bottom of the hot tank.	The cold water falls to the bottom so with this design the hot and cold water do not mix. The hot water stays on top.
The hot water must be piped from the top of the hot tank.	The 'lighter' hot water will be at the top of the tank.
There must be a 'vent' pipe.	This allows steam or air bubbles to escape from the hot tank.

88

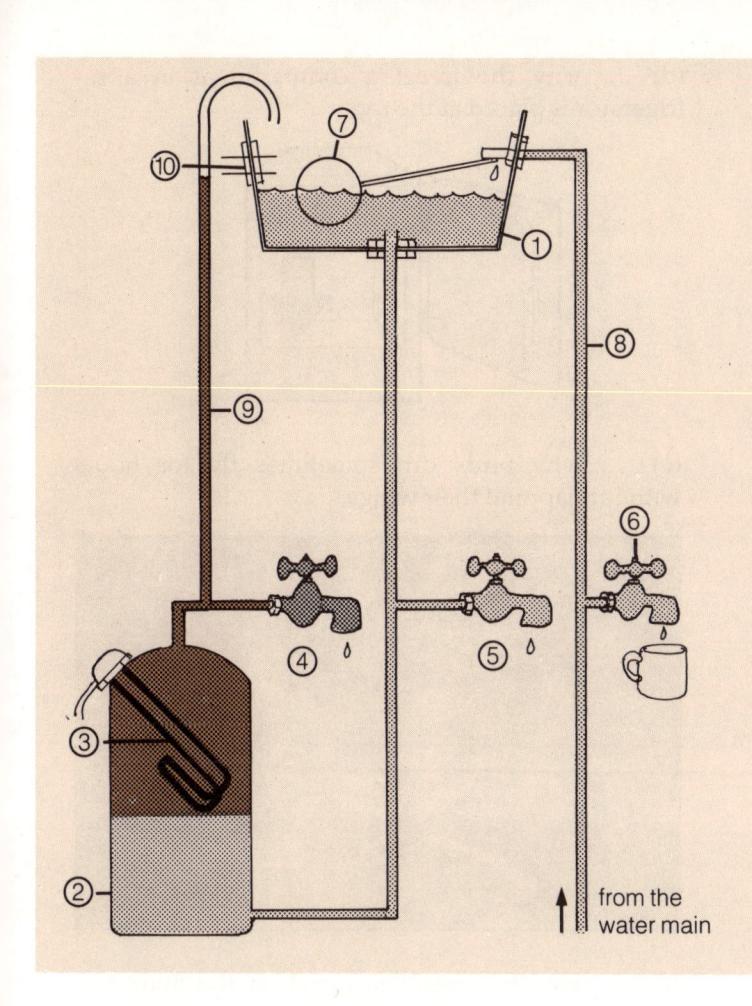

5   Copy this diagram and list of parts. Put the right number against each part*.
Cold water storage tank
Hot water tank
Heater and thermostat
Hot tap
Cold tap
Drinking water tap
Ballcock
Rising main
Vent pipe
Overflow pipe

6   Why is the drinking water tap, usually the one in the kitchen, connected to the rising main?

7   Draw in one stop tap that can shut off all the water. Draw in a second stop tap that can shut off just the hot water.

8   Why is the (hot) water level in the vent pipe slightly higher than the water level in the cold storage tank?

9   What is the job of the thermostat and what would happen if it stopped working?

*The parts are numbered: 1, 2, 3, 4, 5, 6, 7, 8, 9, 10, starting from the top.

Convection of air
Experiment

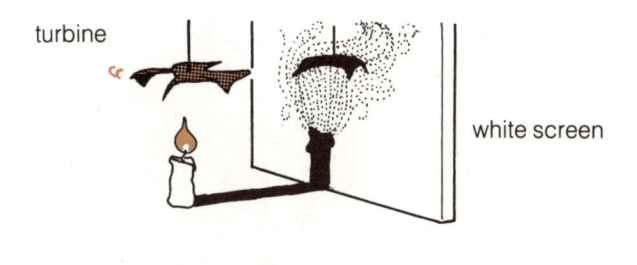

Showing up convection currents in air

Arrange a projector so that it casts the shadow of a candle on a white screen. The shadow of the hot gases from the flame and the liquid wax should also be visible. Which way do the gases move? Experiment with this current of hot gas and air:
(a) Place a turbine blade over the flame.
(b) Place a heat-resistant board over the flame to act like the ceiling of a room.
(c) Place a chimney over the flame.
In each case notice what happens to the rising warm air. Air expands when heated and becomes less dense. Cold dense air then falls and makes the warm air rise.

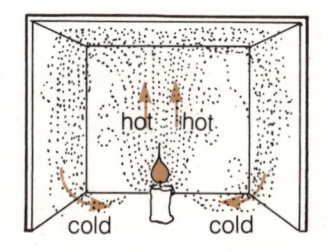

■ Cold air falls making warm air rise.

10 It is clear that warm air rises and so must be lighter than cold air. Can you explain . . .
(a) . . . how a flame can lift a man into the sky.

(b) . . . why a kilt keeps a Scotsman's knees warm.

(c) . . . why a fire or heater keeps air moving around a room.

(d) . . . why the freezing compartment in a refrigerator is placed at the top.

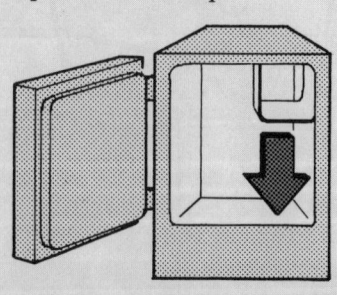

(e) . . . why birds can sometimes fly for hours without flapping their wings.

(f) . . . why it is better to crawl on the floor of a smoke-filled room.

20 Conduction of heat

Experiment

Hold a piece of wire in the flame of a burning match. Which do you have to drop first, the copper or the match? Heat travels quickly through the copper wire. It cannot be seen as it travels but it can be felt when it reaches your fingers. The movement of heat energy like this, without any obvious movement of the material, is called **conduction**

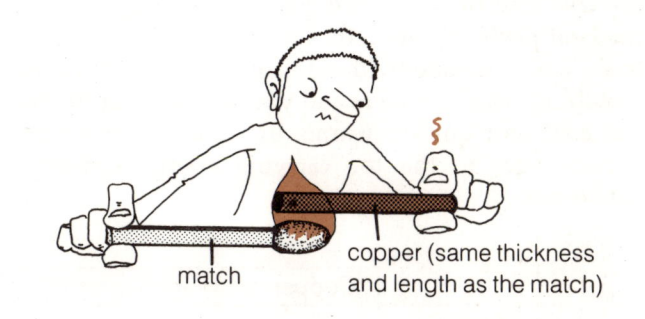

Experiment. How well do materials conduct heat?

Put rods of copper, iron and glass on a tripod and heat the ends with a small bunsen flame. (The rods should be the same length and thickness.) Run your finger carefully along the rods from the cold end to get an idea of how far the heat has travelled in each material. You will find that copper conducts heat much better than iron and that very little heat travels along the glass.

1 Which of our senses can tell us whether heat is being conducted through a material?

2 How would you use a match to show that wood does not conduct heat as well as a brass screw?

3 Should these things be good or bad conductors of heat?
Copy and complete.

	Hot water bottle	Saucepan	Blanket	Radiator	House bricks	Gloves
Good or Bad?						

4 Explain why the heated end of the iron rod in the experiment above glows red hot while the end of the copper rod does not.

Water

You will find that you can boil water at the top of a tube and hold the tube comfortably at the bottom. Very little heat is conducted down through the water to the hand. Water is a bad conductor of heat.

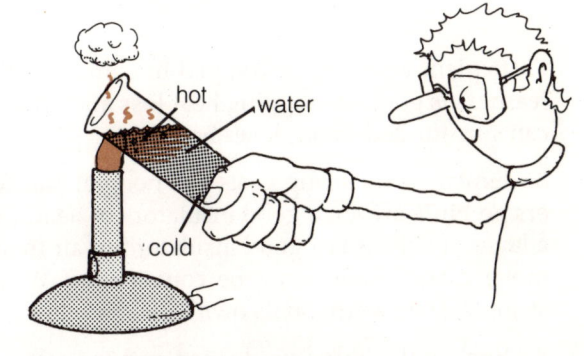

Water is a bad conductor

■ Conduction is the movement of heat through a material without any obvious movement of the material.

Experiment. The conduction of heat by air

Place a heater at one end of a cardboard tube fitted with two thermometers. When the air is hot at one end, cover the ends with cardboard lids. Leave the apparatus for a while and watch the thermometers. The thermometer at the cold end does not rise quickly showing that little of the heat passes through the air. Air is a bad conductor of heat. Turn the tube (without its lids) so that it is vertical. Watch the thermometers and you will see that the one at the cold end quickly warms up. The warm air at the bottom rises to the top carrying energy upwards by convection.

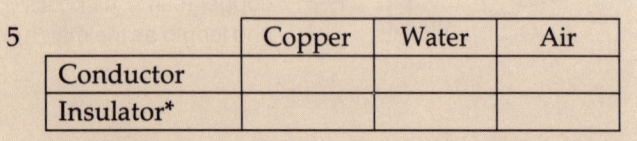

Air is a bad conductor

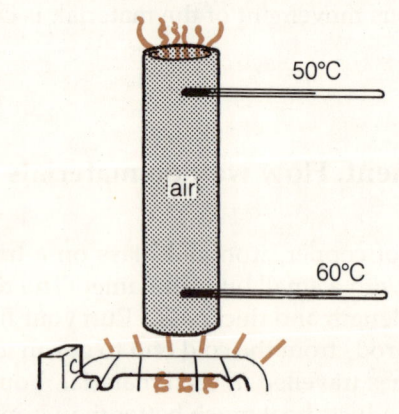

Air carries heat well by convection

5

	Copper	Water	Air
Conductor			
Insulator*			

*An insulator is a material through which heat passes very slowly.

Copy the table and put 'good' or 'bad' in the boxes to show whether copper, water and air are good or bad conductors and insulators.

6 Why can no heat pass by convection or conduction through a vacuum?

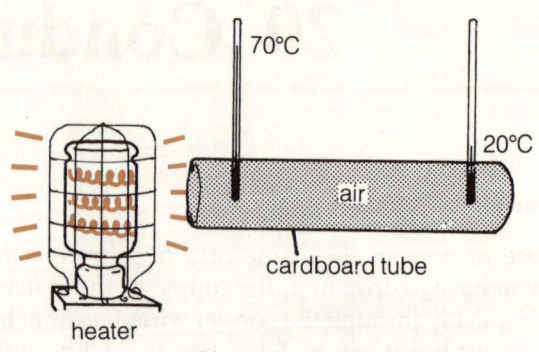

Experiment. Testing insulators

Find out how well cotton wool and feathers stop heat escaping by using them to insulate cans full of boiling water. Have one can without any insulation as a control and find out how long each can takes to cool from 90°C to 70°C. Which material is the best insulator?

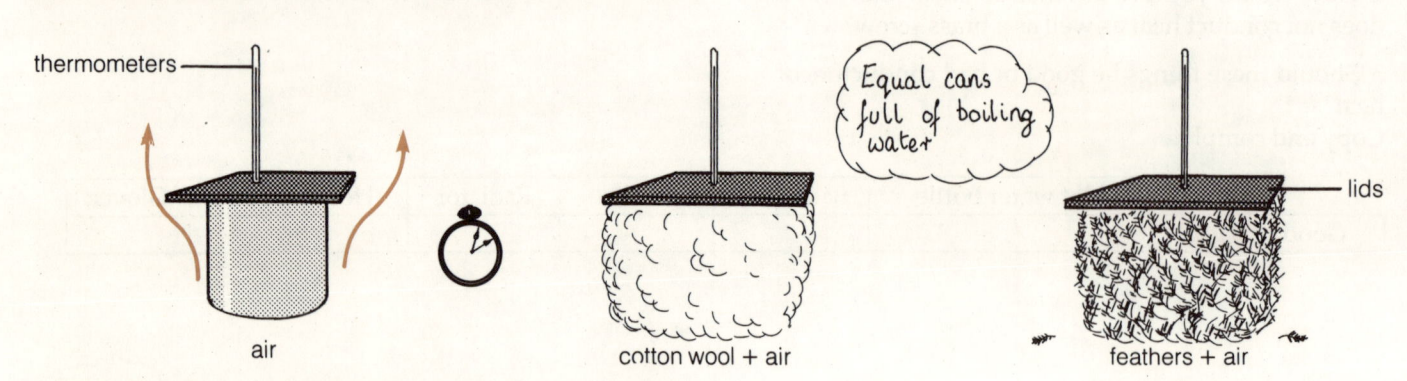

7 Explain why the air trapped in cotton wool and feathers is good at stopping heat loss and why a hot can surrounded by air, loses heat so quickly.

8 Explain why string vests (on people) and feathers on birds are such good insulators of heat. (Note: a layer of still air is a good insulator but air than can move carries heat away be convection.) Would a string vest be warm on its own?

9 Explain the terms conduction and convection.

■ Air and water are bad conductors of heat but transfer it well by convection.

21 Radiation

Experiment

Place the back of your hand by the side of an electric heater. Very little heat reaches the hand by conduction or convection and yet the skin gets very warm. There is a third way that heat energy can travel and that is by electromagnetic waves. We have seen that these waves carry energy (p. 52). Hot objects such as this heater and the Sun give out electromagnetic waves. This radiation then passes through air and space, spreading energy around at the speed of light. When the radiation falls on things, some of it soaks in and warms them up. The hot Sun warms the Earth by radiation in this way.

1   Why can we be sure that:
(a) very little heat reaches the skin by conduction and convection?
(b) heat does not reach the Earth from the Sun by conduction and convection?

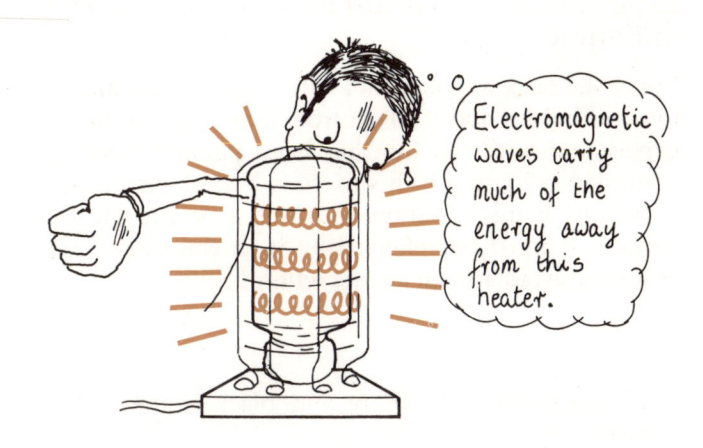

Experiment. Can radiation be reflected and focused?

Place the heater at the focus of a large concave mirror. Look straight into the mirror and you will feel and see the reflected radiation. The mirror reflects the waves from the heater into a nearly parallel beam that can be felt all over the face (cf. p. 19).

Use a second mirror to collect the beam and focus it into a hot spot. Find this spot by hand and then hold a live match there. The temperature should be sufficient to light a match. Radiation can be reflected and focused by mirrors.

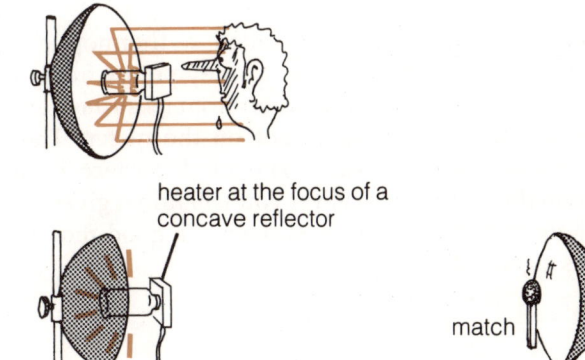

Reflecting and focusing radiation

2   Which of the heaters shown:
(a) focuses radiation;
(b) reflects radiation into a broad beam?

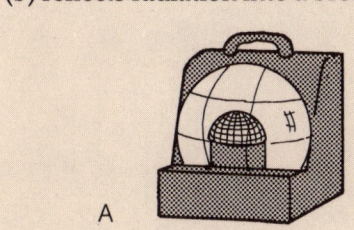

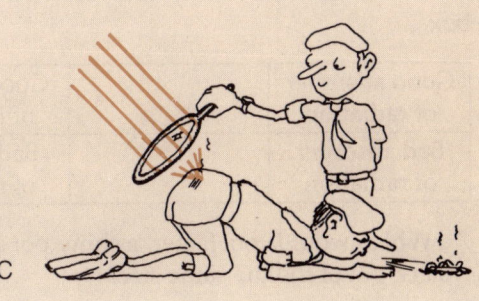

■ Heat energy can be transferred by conduction, convection and radiation.

Black is best

When radiation falls on a surface, some of its energy is absorbed and warms up that surface.

Experiment. Which surface is best at absorbing radiation?

Cover the back of your hand with a square of aluminium foil and hold it about 10 cm from a heater. Do the same experiment with foil that has been painted black. Can your skin tell you which surface is best at absorbing the radiation? If the radiation does not soak into the shiny surface, it must be reflected by it. If the black surface absorbs the radiation it cannot reflect it.

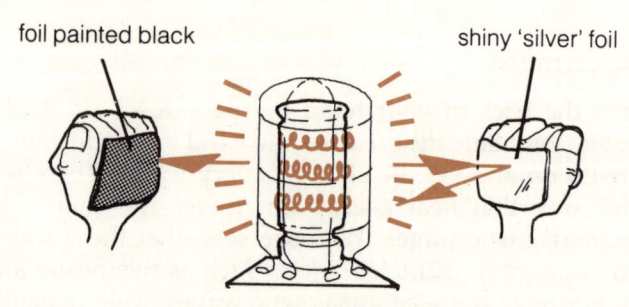

Black absorbs more than silver

3 Copy and write 'shiny' and 'black' in the correct box.

Good absorber		Bad reflector
Bad absorber		Good reflector

4 Which surface colour (black or shiny) would be best for:
(a) a Rolls Royce in a hot country (no expense spared);
(b) a space suit for the Moon (very hot in the Sun);
(c) a solar water heater (used to collect the Sun's heat).

Experiment. Which surface sends out the most radiation?

A sensitive radiation detector called a thermopile is needed for this experiment. Heat a shiny pot by filling it with hot water. Pick up the radiation from its surface and note the position of the light spot on the meter. Then paint the shiny surface black. The black surface is no hotter than the shiny surface, yet you will find it gives out much more radiation. A black surface is a good radiator as well as a good absorber.

Black radiates more than silver

5 Copy and complete. A shiny surface is a _____ emitter of radiation as well as a _____ absorber.

6 Copy and write 'shiny' and 'black' in the correct box.

Good absorber of radiation		Good radiator of radiation
Bad absorber of radiation		Bad radiator of radiation

7 Which would cool faster, a shiny pot of hot tea or a black pot of the the same size?

8 Why are the cooling wires at the back of a refrigerator painted black?

The vacuum flask

Experiment. How good is a vacuum flask at keeping things hot?

Put some hot water in a cup and an equal amount in a vacuum flask. Leave to cool and measure the temperatures after 30 minutes. Does the vacuum flask stop heat escaping from the water? Does it make any difference if you put a stopper in? Do an experiment to find out.

How does a vacuum flask work?

The flask has a double glass wall with a vacuum between the walls. The inside surfaces of the glass are silvered. The flask is designed to reduce the three ways that heat can escape.

Conduction

The vacuum stops all conduction through the walls. A little heat is conducted up the walls and out that way.

Convection

The cork stops the air, heated by the water, from escaping with its energy. The cork will get warm and conduct a little heat out.

Radiation

This can cross the vacuum. The hot inside silver surface is a bad radiator so only a little radiation sets off across the vacuum. When it reaches the other side it is reflected back by the silvering on the outer wall. Very little radiation escapes.

Put an ice/salt mixture into a vacuum flask and you will find that it is just as good at stopping heat from getting in.

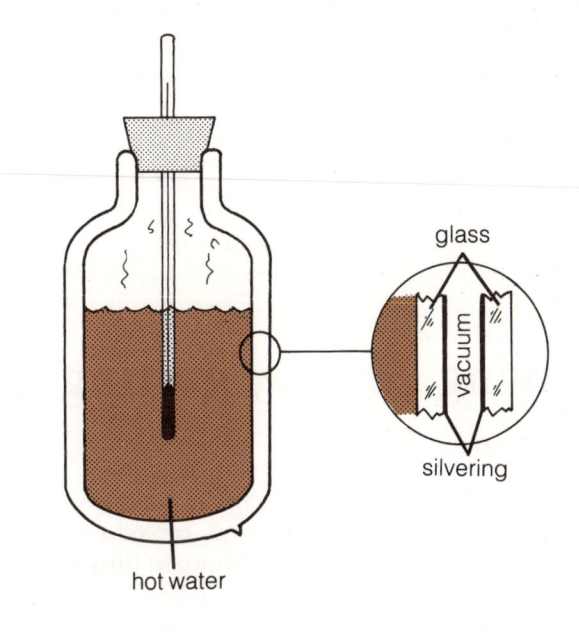

9 Why does the liquid in a vacuum flask not wash the silvering off the walls.

10 Liquids in vacuum flasks do not stay hot for ever. Explain three ways that heat can escape.

11 Explain why the two silver surfaces are good at stopping radiation from getting into the flask when it is holding cold liquid.

Keeping warm

Insulation in your home can save a lot of money. Insulation in the loft reduces the large amount of heat that otherwise escapes through the roof. Cavity walls, sometimes filled with plastic foam, and double-glazed windows reduce loss of heat through the sides of the house. Carefully sealed doors and windows stop cold draughts and the escape of warm air. Reducing the amount of heat that escapes in this way means that you have to provide less heat inside the house to keep warm.

12 List four ways of reducing the heat loss from your house.

13 List four other good insulators found in the picture.

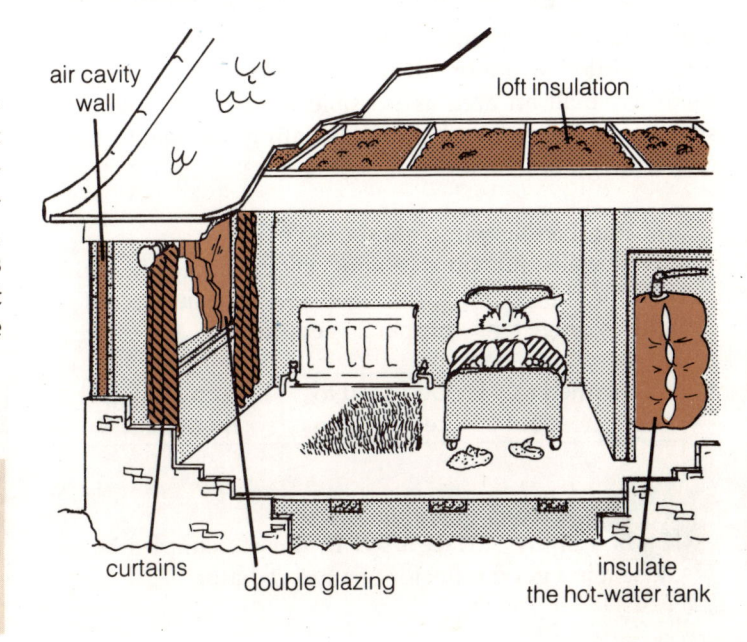

House radiators

Convection makes sure that hot water reaches the top of the radiator. The 'radiator' does radiate a little heat but most of its heat is taken away by **convection** of the air that it heats.

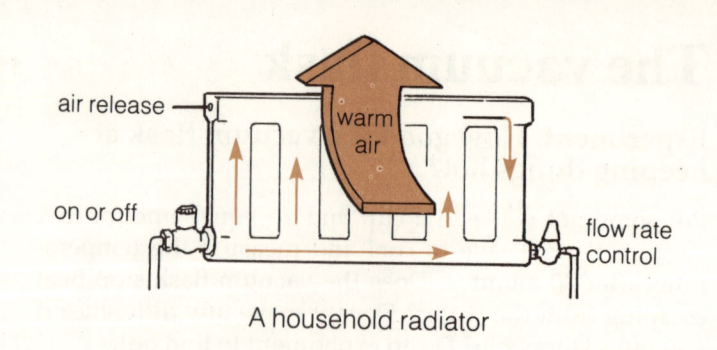

A household radiator

Staying cool by getting rid of heat

Car radiators

Car engines overheat if they are not cooled. Water is usually used and the water itself is cooled by passing it through a radiator. The water is pumped through narrow pipes that are joined to black cooling fins. These are then cooled by the air flow from a fan and by radiating a little heat. The cool water then returns to the engine block.

Cooling fins

These are found on air-cooled engines, at the back of refrigerators and in car radiators. Their job is to get rid of heat. The fins make a large area of hot metal for the cooling air to flow over. The fins also radiate heat.

14 Why are cooling fins usually painted black?

15 Explain how conduction, convection and radiation take part when cooling fins cool a hot engine.

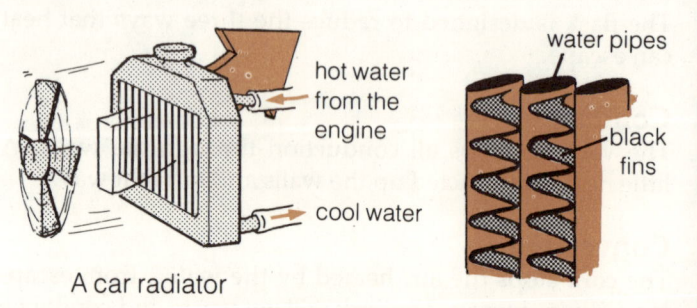

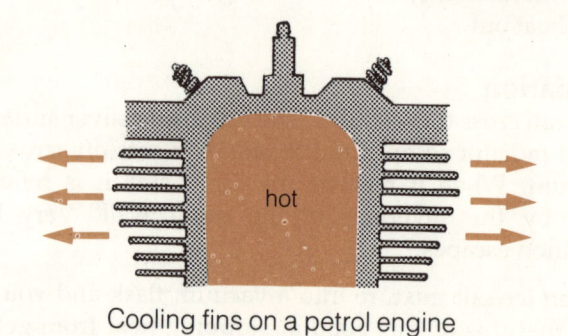

A car radiator

Cooling fins on a petrol engine

Staying cool by keeping heat out

Tanks that store chemicals that must not get too hot, are often painted white or silver. Some are spherical to give them as small an area as possible. Fire-proof suits and space suits are made of shiny insulating material to stop heat from getting inside.

16 Put the following into the table below:
Cavity walls, fins on an engine, silver space suit, car radiator, house radiator, silver tea-pot, silver cold liquid storage tank, slippers, vacuum flask.

Designed to keep heat out	Designed to keep heat in	Designed to get rid of heat

17 Is a shiny surface used in these examples because it is a good reflector or a bad radiator?

Summary of expansion and heat transfer

- Expansion is caused by the molecules of a material gaining energy and .... moving further apart.
- A bimetal strip bends because .... one metal expands more than the other.
- Convection is the transfer of heat energy .... by the movement of hot liquid or gas.
- Convection is caused by .... expansion.
- Conduction is the transfer of heat through a material without .... any obvious movement of that material.
- Radiation transfers heat energy at the speed of .... light.
- The best type of surface for absorbing and emitting radiation is .... black.
- The best type of surface for reflecting radiation is a .... shiny one.

Further questions

18 (a) Explain how the bimetal strip would look at −30°C.

(b) Which of the metals A and B expands the most when heated?

(c) The metals are fixed end to end. Draw how they would look at 500°C. (E.Midlands)

19 A metal sheet with a hole cut in it is heated. The distance AB increases. What difference, if any, is there in: (a) AC (b) D?

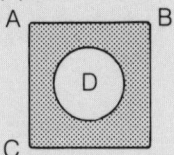

20 Draw a labelled diagram of a thermostat and explain how it works. Say whether it would be suitable for use in an electric iron or a refrigerator.

21 The diagram shows a cross-section through a metal radiator filled with hot water.
(a) How does the heat travel from the hot water to the air of the room?
(b) How does the radiator eventually heat all of the air in the room? (E.Midlands)
(c) How does a person sitting in front of the radiator get warmed up?

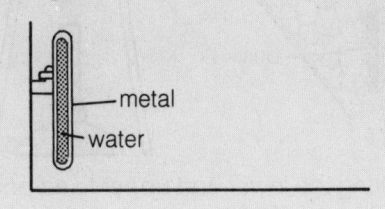

22 If water in a test tube is heated at the top, the water at the bottom stays cool. If the water is heated at the bottom, the water at the top soon gets hot. Explain these observations.

23 A thick sheet of copper, blackened on one side and polished on the other, is heated by a bunsen burner. The bunsen is then removed and a person puts his hands on either side of the sheet, equal distances away. Which hand will feel hotter? Explain your answer.

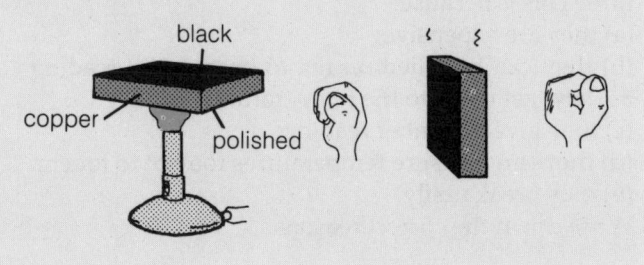

24 Explain the following observations in terms of conduction, convection and radiation:
(a) a vacuum flask keeps tea hot;
(b) a cold liquid stays cool in a vacuum flask even without a cork;
(c) the blackboard in a classroom does not warm up even though it absorbs more radiation than the rest of the room;
(d) the metal head of a hammer feels colder than the wooden handle on a cold day;
(e) the metal head of a hammer feels hotter than the wooden handle if it has been standing in the sun for some time;
(f) it is warmer to wear a woollen jumper under a shirt rather than over it;
(g) on a sunlit beach, black pebbles feel warmer than white ones.

22 Temperature

We often say 'it is hot today' or 'this tea is cold'. The scientific word for the level of hotness of things is **temperature**. It is important to know the temperature (hotness) of things like water, the air outside, our bodies or an oven. We have a sense that tells us when things are too hot or too cold, but can we trust our senses?

It is important to know temperature

Experiment

Put one finger into hot water and another finger into cold water. After 1 minute put both fingers into some warm water. Both fingers are now at the same temperature but do they feel the same temperature? The skin can be 'conditioned' and cannot be trusted to measure temperature properly. A swimming pool feels cold when you first dip your toe in, but feels warm after you have been in the water for a while.

Can we trust our sense of hot and cold?

1 **Thermometers** are used to measure temperature. This is because:
(a) they are expensive;
(b) they can be relied on not to change the reading as they 'get used' to the temperature;
(c) they give a number reading;
(d) they can measure temperatures too hot to touch;
(e) they break easily.
Write down the correct reasons.

Thermometers are marked to read temperatures in degrees Celsius (°C). Pure melting ice is always at the same temperature. This temperature is called 0°C (the lower fixed point). The steam above boiling water under normal pressure is always at a fixed temperature too. This temperature is called 100°C (the upper fixed point). These two temperatures are marked on a thermometer and the distance between the marks is divided into 100 degrees.

Experiment

Take a thermometer and check its fixed points (0°C and 100°C). Then use it to measure other interesting temperatures.

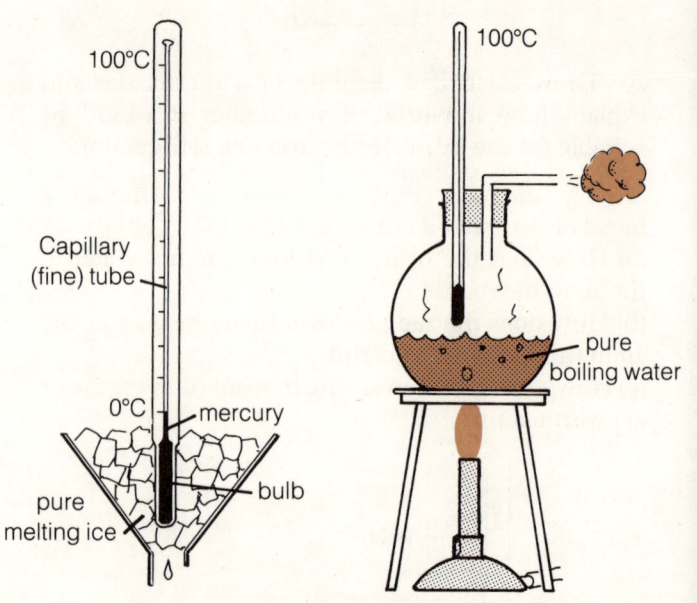

Checking the lower and upper fixed points of a thermometer

■ Thermometers measure temperature.

2   Alcohol (usually coloured red) is sometimes used as the liquid in thermometers. Alcohol boils at 78°C and freezes at −115°C. It expands much more than mercury and is cheaper. Which liquid would be the best to use in these thermometers?
Copy the table and insert 'mercury' or 'alcohol' into the correct box.

(a) A laboratory thermometer that is often used to measure the temperature of steam	
(b) A cheap household thermometer that is used to measure the temperature of the air in a house	
(c) A thermometer used to measure very low temperatures	
(d) A very sensitive thermometer that measures small changes in temperature	

3   Which of these properties of mercury make it a good liquid to use in thermometers? Copy the list and put 'good' or 'bad' against each property.

(a) Mercury is a good conductor of heat	
(b) Mercury expands evenly as the temperature rises	
(c) Mercury boils at 357°C and freezes at −39°C	
(d) Mercury is poisonous	
(e) Mercury is expensive	

Clinical thermometers – used to measure body temperatures

Experiment. Using a clinical thermometer

1. Clean the thermometer bulb in an antiseptic solution.
2. Flick the mercury down into the bulb. Look carefully at the capillary tube and you will see it becomes very narrow indeed just above the bulb. The mercury can force its way up through this narrow section but cannot get back when it cools. The mercury is returned to the bulb by a flick of the wrist.
3. Place the thermometer under your tongue for one minute.
4. Take the thermometer out of your mouth and read the temperature. You will notice that, because of the constriction, the mercury stays up the tube and the thermometer can be read away from the patient. The mercury thread is very fine to make the thermometer sensitive. Often the glass stem of the thermometer is triangular and magnifies the mercury thread when held at the correct angle – it does not roll so easily either.

4   Why does a clinical thermometer only measure temperatures from about 35°C to 42°C?

5   What are the advantages of a very fine capillary tube?

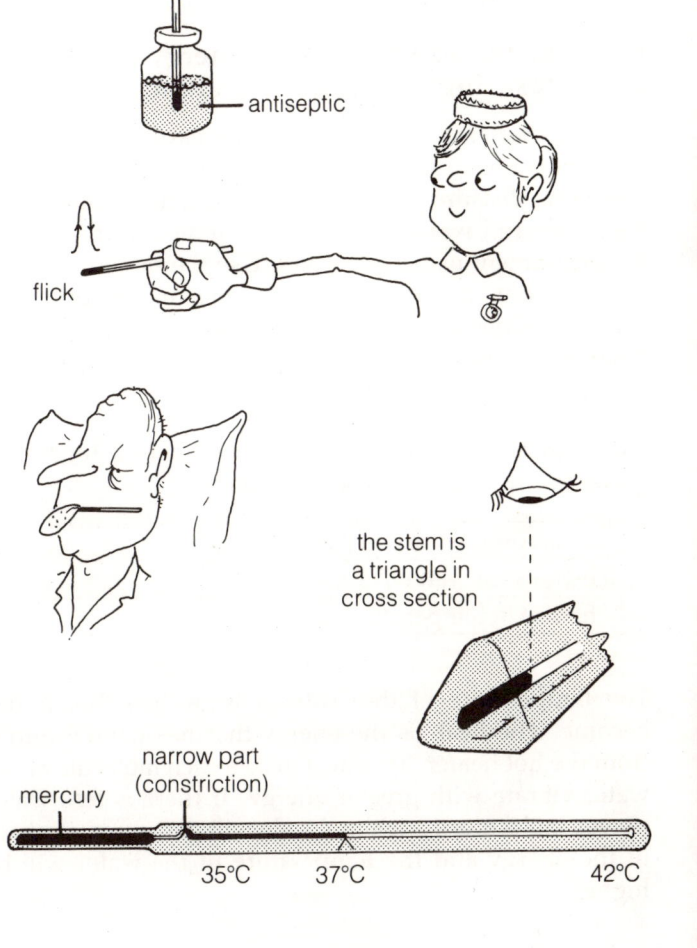

A clinical thermometer

23 Heat and temperature

Heat and temperature are not the same thing. Heat is the energy that you can give to an object to raise its temperature. A lot of heat energy does not always produce a high temperature. Which do you think has the highest temperature; a cup of boiling water or the white hot spark from a sparkler? Which do you think contains the most energy and would cause the nastier burn?

1 Think about the amounts of heat needed to make a needle red-hot and to warm up a bath of water. Copy and complete the tables.

	Amount of heat energy needed (lot or little)
To make a needle red-hot	
To warm a bath of water	

	Final temperature (moderate or hot)
Red-hot needle	
Bath of warm water	

For many experiments we have used a bunsen burner to supply heat energy. The chemical energy of the gas is changed into heat energy as it burns. In the next experiment an electric heater is used to supply the heat. This is because it supplies the heat steadily all the time it is on.

Experiment. Supplying heat energy to water and measuring its rise in temperature

Put some water in a plastic cup and measure its temperature. Submerge a heater in the water and switch on for 5 minutes. Measure the highest temperature reached by the water and work out the rise in temperature. Repeat the experiment using less water. Use the same heater for the same time to ensure that the same amount of heat is supplied. Does the water have the same rise in temperature?

Supplying the same heat to different masses of water

2 What is the same and what is different for the two lots of water in these experiments?

The amount of heat supplied	
The mass of water	
The rise in temperature	

The temperature of the water tells us how hot it has become. The **heat** is the energy that has passed into it from the hot heater. This heat makes each molecule of the water vibrate with greater energy. If there is less water (fewer molecules), each molecule will get a greater share of the energy and the temperature of the water will be higher.

■ When heat energy is supplied to water, its temperature rise depends on how much water there is.

Measuring heat energy

A **joulemeter** connected to an electric heater will measure the amount of energy that flows through to the heater. It is rather like a petrol pump that measures the amount of petrol flowing through. The amount of energy is measured in **joules** (p. 170).

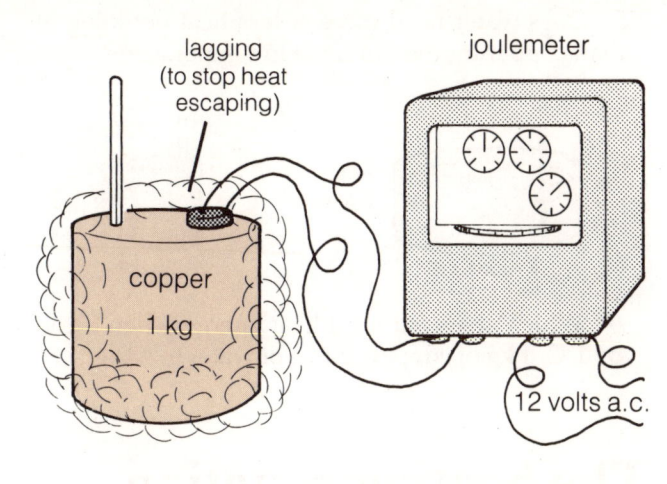

Experiment. Finding the amount of heat energy needed to warm up a 1 kg block of copper by 10°C

Put an electric heater into the block of copper. Read the joulemeter and the temperature of the block. Switch the heater on and off until the block has warmed up 10°C. From the new joulemeter reading find the amount of energy you have used.

Measuring energy with a joulemeter

> 3 In an experiment just like this, a student found he had used 3800 joules of energy to produce a 10°C rise in temperature of the copper block. How much heat energy would be needed to warm the block by only 1°C?

Specific heat capacity

The **specific heat capacity** of a substance is the amount of energy needed to make 1 kg of that substance 1°C hotter. The student in the question found that 1 kg of copper needed 380 joules of energy to raise its temperature by 1°C, so 380 J/kg°C is his value for the specific heat capacity of copper (note the unit used). It is a useful number to know because it tells us how much energy we have to spend to warm up that substance.

Experiment. Measuring the specific heat capacity of water

Use the method above to find out the amount of heat energy needed to warm 1 kg of water by 10°C. You can then easily work out the amount of heat energy needed for a 1°C temperature rise. It is important to keep the heater under the water and to stir well before reading the thermometer. Does it take more heat energy to warm the water than the copper?

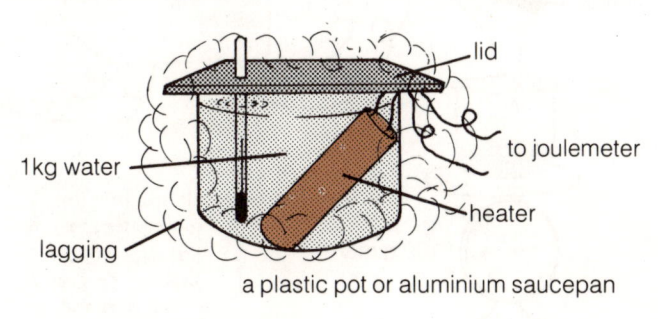

Heat needed to warm 1 kg of materials by 1°C

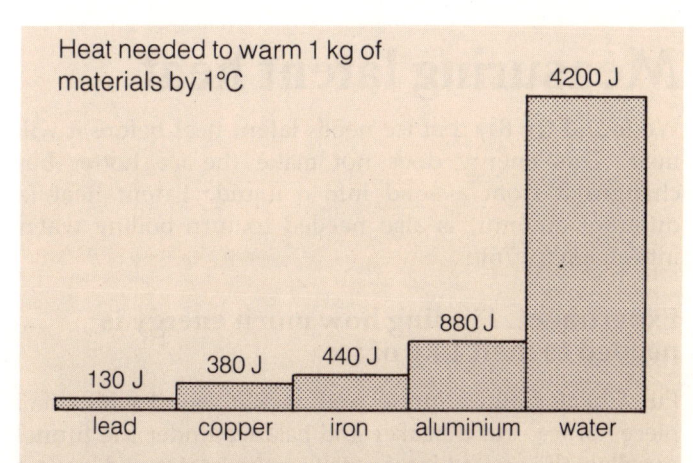

- lead: 130 J
- copper: 380 J
- iron: 440 J
- aluminium: 880 J
- water: 4200 J

> 4 Write down the specific heat capacities of these five materials in order, using the proper units.

■ The specific heat capacity of a substance is the amount of energy needed to make 1 kg of that substance 1°C hotter.

5 Does water need more or less heat per kilogram than copper for the same rise in temperature?

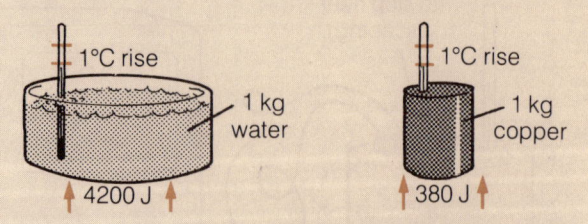

6 Which gives out most heat energy when it cools by 1°C, 1 kg of copper or 1 kg of water?

7 Would it take more or less time to boil a kettle of water if the specific heat capacity of water were the same as copper?

8 What properties should a metal have that is going to be used to make saucepans. Copy the table and write in high, low, good or bad.

Density	Specific heat capacity	Type of conductor	Cost

The heating equation

If 1 kg of copper needs 380 J for a 1°C temperature rise, then 2 kg would need twice as much heat for the same temperature rise (2 × 380 J), and if the temperature rise is to be 4°C this would need four times as much heat energy again (2 × 380 × 4 J). The heat needed can be worked out like this:

Heat needed = mass × specific heat capacity × temperature change.

Example
How much heat energy must you use to warm 200 kg of water for a bath from 20°C to 50°C?
Mass = 200 kg; specific heat capacity = 4200 J/kg°C; change in temperature = 30°C.
So heat energy needed = 200 × 4200 × 30 = 25 200 000 J.

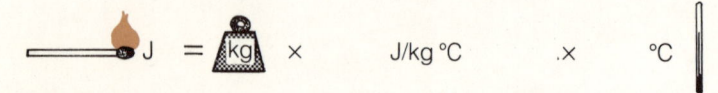

9 Copy this table and try and work out the missing numbers.

Material	Mass	Specific heat capacity	Temperature change	Heat energy needed
Copper	1 kg	380 J/kg°C	9°C	(a)
Iron	½ kg	440 J/kg°C	20°C	(b)
Water	2 kg	4200 J/kg°C	(c)	42 000 J
Lead	1 kg	(d)	10°C	1250 J

(a) 3420 J
(b) 4400 J
(c) 5°C
(d) 125 J/kg°C

Measuring latent heat

We found (p. 81) that ice needs latent heat before it will melt. This energy does not make the ice hotter but changes it from a solid into a liquid. Latent heat (a different amount) is also needed to turn boiling water into steam (p. 76).

Experiment. Finding how much energy is needed to melt 1 kg of ice

Put a heater into a funnel and pack it round with small pieces of ice. Put a beaker and balance under the funnel to collect the melted ice. Switch on the heater and leave it until the balance shows that 100 g of ice has melted. Use the joulemeter to measure the amount of energy you have used to melt this much ice. (You will have to read the joulemeter before and after the experiment.) Calculate the energy that is needed to melt **1 kg** of ice.

If you have no joulemeter, a 50 watt heater supplies 50 joules of heat a second

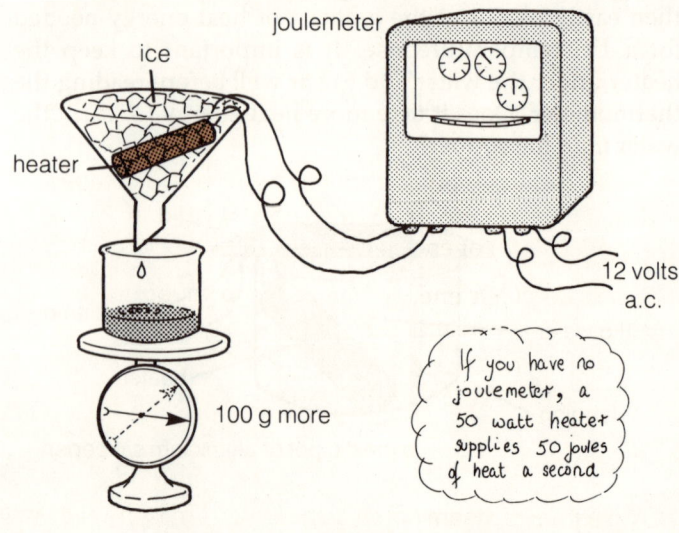

Measuring the latent heat of ice

10 A heater used 34 000 J of energy to melt 100 g of ice. How much is needed to melt 1 kg of ice?

Answer: 34 000 J of energy melt 100 g (=1/10 kg) of ice. Therefore 34 000 × 10 J would be needed to melt 1 kg. So the energy needed = 340 000 J for 1 kg. This quantity is called the **specific latent heat of fusion of water**.

11 How much energy is needed to melt 5 kg of ice at 0°C?

12 How much energy must be taken away to freeze 50 g of ice-cold water?
(Specific latent heat of fusion of water = 340 000 J/kg)

Experiment. Finding how much energy is needed to change 1 kg of boiling water into steam

Use a 3000 W electric kettle to boil some water. Put the kettle on a balance. When the kettle is boiling freely note the balance reading and start the clock. Let the water boil until the balance shows that 100 g of steam have been produced. Stop the clock at this point and note the time taken for this to happen. The energy supplied by the kettle = 3000 × time in seconds (p. 170). This energy changes 100 g of boiling water into steam. From your readings calculate the amount of energy needed to change 1 kg of boiling water into steam.

A 3000 watt heater supplies 3000 joules of heat per second.

Measuring the latent heat of steam

13 A thoughtful student was doing the experiment on p. 102 but used two funnels as shown. He ran the experiment until beaker B had collected 100 g of water more than beaker A. What was the purpose of the second funnel of ice?

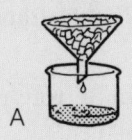

14 A heater used 240 000 J of energy when it changed 100 g of boiling water into steam. How much energy is needed to change 1 kg of boiling water into steam?

Answer: It took 240 000 J of energy to boil away 100 g (1/10 kg). Therefore 240 000 × 10 J would be needed to boil away 1 kg.
So the energy needed = 2 400 000 J for 1 kg.
(This quantity is called the **specific latent heat of vaporization of water**.)

15 How long would it take ½ kg of boiling water, in a saucepan, to boil dry if the heater it is on supplies 1200 J of energy to the water each second?

16 How much energy has to be removed to condense 100 g of steam into boiling water?
(Take the specific latent heat of vaporization of water to be 2 400 000 J/kg.)

17 (a) If you were boiling potatoes on a cooker and the specific latent heat of vaporization of water suddenly dropped to a much smaller value, what two differences would you notice?

(b) Explain one difference such a drop would make to ponds and puddles of water. Do you think it would affect the weather?

18 Explain why you would have to eat your lollipop faster if the specific latent heat of fusion of water was much smaller than it really is.

■ A kilogram of steam contains nearly 2½ million joules more of energy than a kilogram of boiling water.
■ Steam is a useful material for carrying energy from place to place.

Summary of temperature and heat

- Temperature is a measure of how .... hot or cold a body is.
- Temperature can be measured by a .... thermometer.
- The energy supplied by a heater to a material can be measured. The unit used is .... joule.
- The heat energy that is needed to make 1 kg of a substance 1°C hotter is called its .... specific heat capacity.
- The heating equation is .... heat energy = mass × specific heat capacity × temperature change.
- The heat energy needed to melt 1 kg of a solid at its melting point is called .... its specific latent heat of fusion.
- The heat energy needed to change 1 kg of a liquid to vapour at its boiling point is called .... its specific latent heat of vaporization.

Further questions

19 Choose the most likely temperature from this list for the following: 37°C; 120°C; 0°C; 20°C; 100°C.
(a) the temperature of a comfortably warm room;
(b) the melting point of pure ice under normal pressure;
(c) the temperature of steam in a pressure cooker;
(d) the normal body temperature of a healthy person.

20 Why does a clinical thermometer
(a) have a constriction just above the bulb?
(b) have a very fine tube?
(c) cover only a narrow range?

21 Explain why (a) a clinical thermometer should not be sterilized in boiling water; (b) its bulb may not be full at room temperature.

22 When a certain quantity of heat was supplied to 1 kg of water at 0°C, its temperature rose 5°C.
(a) What is the final temperature when the same amount of heat is supplied to 1 kg of water at 50°C?
(b) What is the final temperature when the same quantity of heat is supplied to 2 kg of water at 0°C?
(c) If the quantity of heat referred to in (a) is 21 000 J, calculate the specific heat capacity of water.

23 An immersion heater that supplies 1000 J of heat energy per second is placed into water and switched on. At the moment the water starts to boil, the mass present is 700 g. After 250 s of continuous boiling the mass of water is 600 g.
(a) Calculate the energy supplied by the heater in the 250 s.
(b) Calculate the specific latent heat of vaporization of water.

24 Give two reasons why energy must be given to a liquid before it will boil.

25 Give two reasons why engineers often use superheated steam (steam above 100°C) to transfer heat.

26 Give a reason why the jam in a roly-poly pudding stays hot longer than the pastry.

27 Write down three properties of (a) mercury, (b) alcohol, that make it a useful liquid to use in thermometers.

Force, matter and motion

24 Measuring matter

Mass

The mass of an object measures the amount of matter in it. Mass is measured in kilograms (kg) or sometimes grams (g). 1000 g = 1 kg. When we buy 1 kg of fruit we expect to get a certain amount. The shopkeeper measures this amount by balancing it on a scale against a 1 kg mass of metal. Modern balances give a direct reading but have to be checked with 'standard' 1 kg masses. These standard masses are the same all over the world.

Experiment. Measuring mass

Learn to use the balances you have in the laboratory. Find the masses of some of the things you have in your pockets.

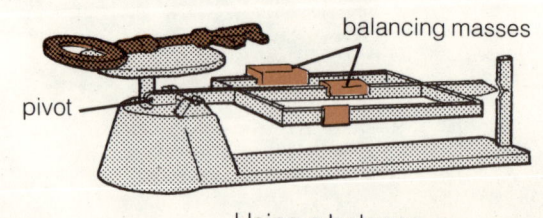

Using a balance

1 What are the masses of these objects? Choose from these values: 20 g; 110 g; 1 kg; 4 kg; 25 kg.

A sack of cement	A baby	A jar of coffee	A loaf of bread	An airmail letter

Volume

A cube with 1 centimetre sides has a volume of 1 cubic centimetre (1 cm^3). The volume of an object is the number of these centimetre cubes it contains. The block shown fills the same space as 24 of these cubes, so its volume is 24 cubic centimetres. Length × breadth × height (4 × 3 × 2 cm^3) also gives the volume.

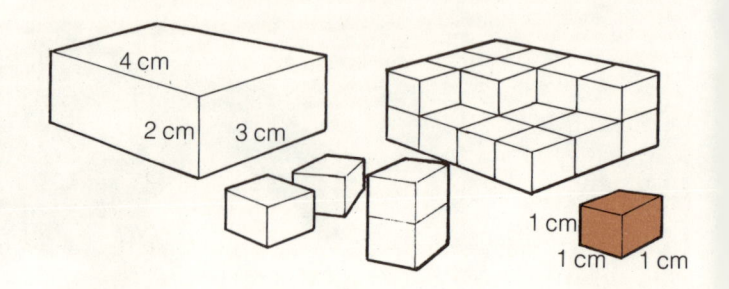

Experiment. Using a measuring cylinder to measure volume

Measuring cylinders are marked in cubic centimetres and so can be used to measure the volume of objects. Use a regular block and find its volume from change in water levels. Calculate its volume by measuring its sides and multiplying length, breadth and height. Are the two values the same?

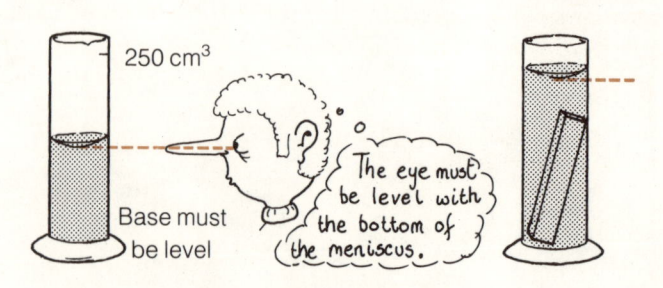

Using a measuring cylinder

■ Mass is measured in kilograms or grams; volume is measured in cubic metres (m^3) or cubic centimetres (cm^3).

2 How would you use a measuring cylinder to measure the volume of an object (a) that sinks, (b) that floats.

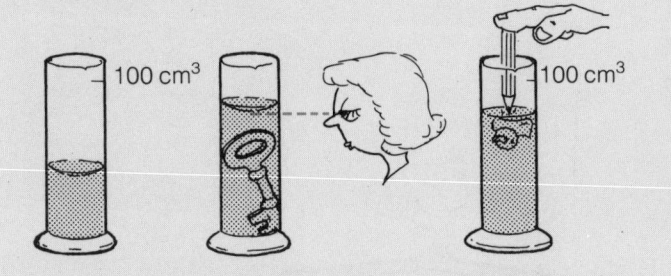

3 What happens to the water in the displacement can when the key is dropped in? How could you measure the volume of an object that will not go into the measuring cylinder?

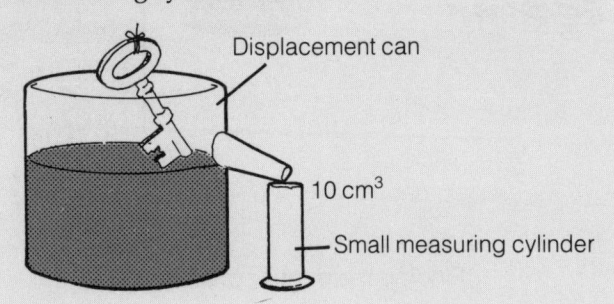

4 Volume can be measured in cubic metres (m^3). How many cubic centimetre blocks are there in a cube with 1 metre sides?

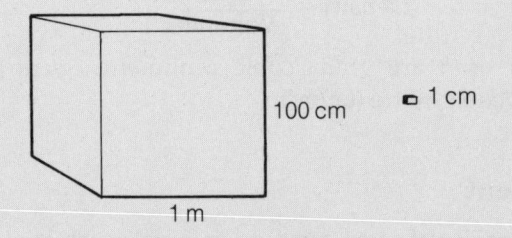

5 How would you find the volume of liquid held by a teaspoon.

Density

We must be careful before we say that steel is heavier than wood because it depends on the volume we are talking about. To compare the heaviness of materials we must take the same volume of each. A cube of steel has much more mass than a cube of wood with the same volume.

Experiment

Measure the masses of blocks of different materials. Use blocks that all have the same volume. Some materials have more mass per cubic centimetre than others. They are more **dense**. The **density** of a material is its mass per cubic centimetre. List your materials in order of their densities.

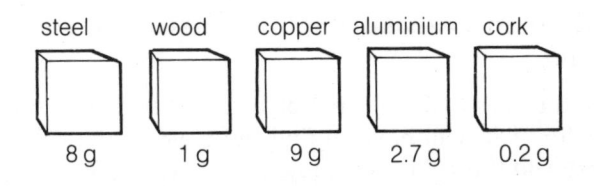

steel 8 g   wood 1 g   copper 9 g   aluminium 2.7 g   cork 0.2 g

6 Put the materials shown above in order of their densities, the most dense first.

7 A block of material measures 5 cm × 3 cm × 2 cm and has a mass of 270 g. (a) How many 1 cm^3 blocks would fill the same volume?
(b) What would be the mass of one of these blocks?
(c) What do you think the block is made of? (Look at the density figures in question 6.)

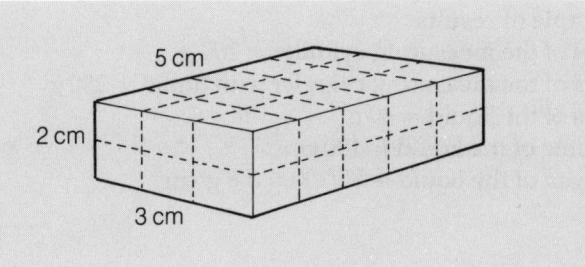

107

The density of any substance of any shape can be found by dividing its mass by its volume. This will give the mass of 1 cm³.

$$\text{Density} = \frac{\text{Mass}}{\text{Volume}}.$$

The units used are grams/cubic centimetre (g/cm³) or kilograms/cubic metre (kg/m³).

Experiment

Find the density of some common materials such as steel, glass, wood and aluminium. Find their volumes by measuring (length × breadth × height) or by using a measuring cylinder. Calculate density by **dividing mass by volume**.

Example. A king found his crown had a mass of 3 kg and a volume of 250 cm³. Could it be made of gold? (The density of gold is 19 g/cm³.)

Mass = 3000 g; volume = 250 cm³; density = $\frac{3000}{250}$ = 12 g/cm³.

It could not be gold.

Finding the density of an object

8 Copy this table and work out the numbers for the empty spaces.

Material	Mass	Volume	Density
Steel	160 g	20 cm³	
Wood	150 g	150 cm³	
Lead	110 g		11 g/cm³
Glass		50 cm³	2 g/cm³

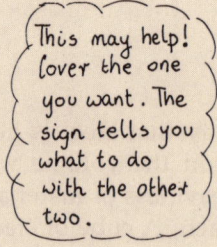

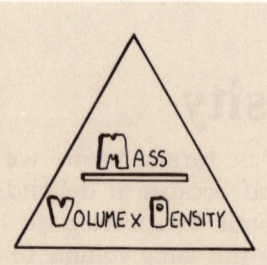

This may help! Cover the one you want. The sign tells you what to do with the other two.

$$\frac{\text{Mass}}{\text{Volume} \times \text{Density}}$$

Experiment. Measuring the densities of some liquids

Find the mass of 100 cm³ of a liquid in a measuring cylinder. You will have to find the mass of the cylinder empty and then with the liquid in it. Find the densities of water, oil, paraffin, methylated spirits if you can.

Example of results
Mass of the measuring cylinder = 200 g
Mass of the measuring cylinder with liquid = 280 g
Mass of the liquid = 80 g
Volume of the liquid = 100 cm³
Density of the liquid = 80/100 = 0.8 g/cm³

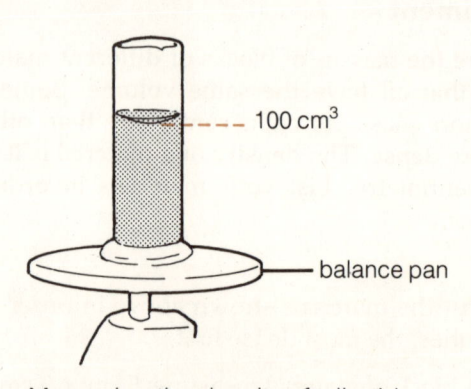

Measuring the density of a liquid

■ Density is mass/volume.

The density of air

Has air got mass? A sensitive balance shows that a bottle has a little more mass when full of air than when the air has been taken out.

Experiment. Measuring the mass of a 1 litre (1000 cm³) of air

Connect a 1 litre flask to a vacuum pump by a rubber tube that can be closed by a screw clip. Use the vacuum pump to remove the air from the flask. Then close the clip. Find the mass of the flask and its fittings by placing them on a sensitive balance. Open the clip and air will rush in and fill the flask. The balance reading should rise a little showing that air has mass. Work out the mass of this litre of air from the balance readings.

Results – using a 1 litre flask.
Mass of the flask and its fittings when empty of air = 340 g
Mass of the flask and its fittings when full of air = 341.2 g
Mass of air = 1.2 g

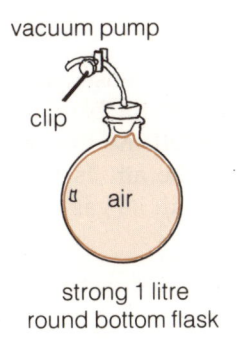

Measuring the density of air

9   The flask from the experiment above is emptied of most of its air and its tube is placed under water. Explain:
(a) what will happen when the clip is opened,
(b) how the water can show whether the flask was completely empty of air.

10   If a litre of air has a mass of 1.2 g, what will be the mass of 1 cubic metre of air? (1000 litres = 1 cubic metre)

11   A room measures 3 m × 4 m × 5 m. Calculate: (a) the volume of the room in cubic metres, (b) the mass of air in the room if the density of air = 1.2 kg/m³.

■ Air has got mass and density.

Floating and sinking

An object will float on water if its density is less than water. If its density is more it will sink, and if it is equal it will hang suspended in the water.

12   Three balls with their densities shown on them, are placed in a liquid with a density 1.0 g/cm³. The density of the liquid is changed to 1.1 g/cm³. Draw a diagram showing how the balls will settle.

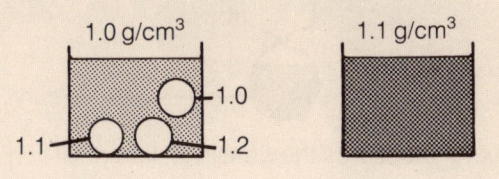

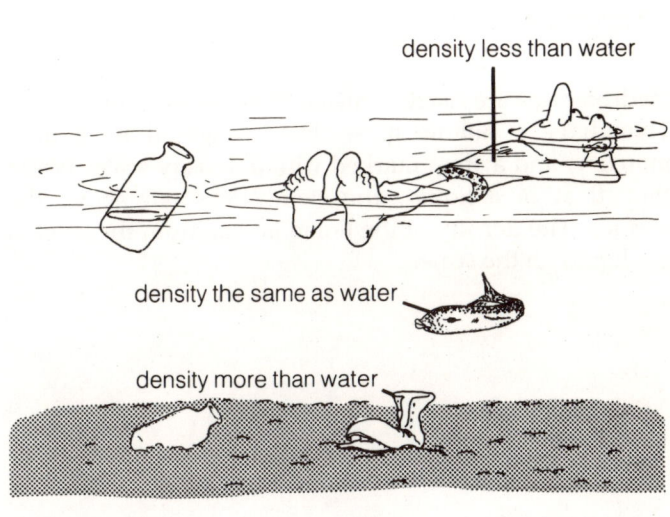

Floating or sinking depends on densities

Experiment. Floating in water

Make a 'diver' from a small test tube partly filled with water. The density of the diver can be changed by pressing on the rubber forcing more water into the tube. When its density is more than the density of water it sinks. When its density is less it floats on the surface. Can you make it float in the middle of the water? What is the density of the diver then?

Experiment. Floating in air

Use a pipette filler to pump natural gas (less dense than air) into a rubber balloon. Tie a long thread to the balloon to weigh it down. Then try to cut pieces off the thread until the balloon just hovers (floats) in the air. Is this easy? What is the density of the balloon with its gas and thread when it is hovering in the air?

Hydrometers

Experiment. Using a straw to compare densities

Seal the end of a straw by dipping it in molten wax. When the wax has set, drop lead balls into the straw until it floats upright in water. Mark the level of the water on the straw. Next put the straw in liquids of different density and mark the level for each liquid. The straw is a simple hydrometer. How can you tell which liquid has the lowest density?

13   Write down the liquids shown in the diagram of the straws in order of their densities, the most dense first.

14   Which sentence is true:
(a) The straw sinks deepest in the most dense liquid.
(b) The straw floats at the same level in all the liquids.
(c) The straw sinks deepest in the stickiest liquid.
(d) The straw sinks deepest in the liquid that has the lowest density.

Hydrometers are used to measure the density of liquids. They have a hollow glass float, weighted by a little mercury, and a stem marked with a density scale. When they float in a liquid, the stem sticks out above the surface. The density of the liquid is read from the level of the liquid on the scale.

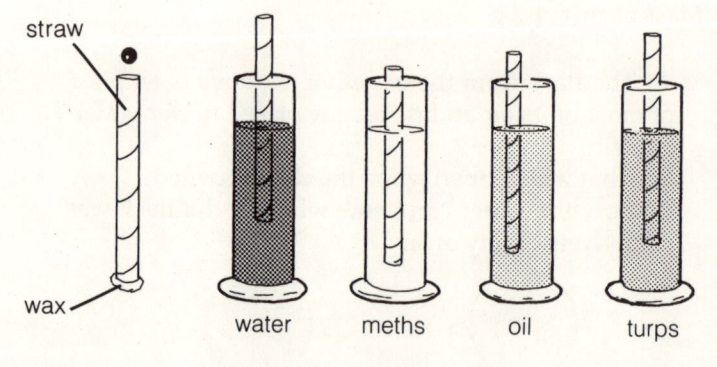

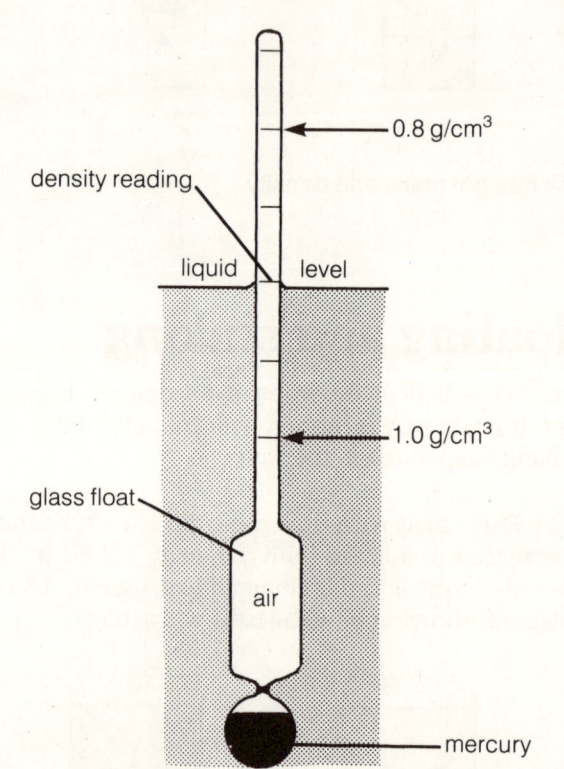

A hydrometer measures the density of liquids. It is quick and accurate

15 Why does the scale have small numbers at the top and large numbers at the bottom?

16 What is the density of the liquid shown by the hydrometer in the diagram?

17 What are the highest and lowest densities that this hydrometer can measure?

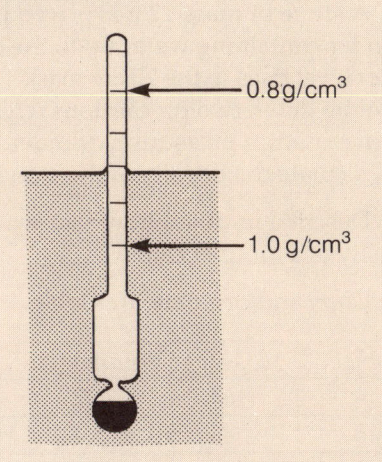

18 Which ball has the same density as the liquid? Which balls would weigh nothing when attached to a balance while still in the liquid?

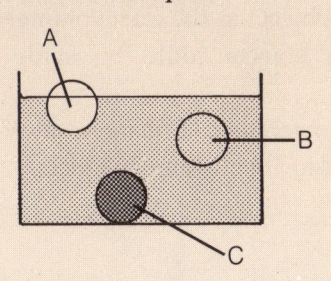

19 The following liquids and solids were put into a measuring cylinder and allowed to settle.

Oil	(0.8 g/cm³)	
Water	(1.0 g/cm³)	
Cork	(0.2 g/cm³)	
Polythene	(0.9 g/cm³)	
Mercury	(13 g/cm³)	
Steel	(8 g/cm³)	

Copy and put in the letter that shows the substance on the diagram.

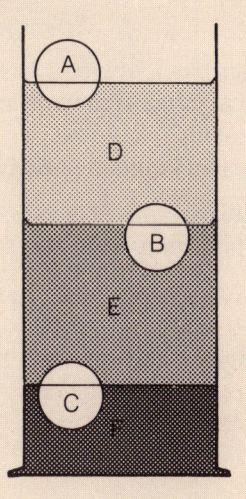

- Hydrometers measure the density of liquids.
- They sink deeper in liquids with a low density.

Summary of measuring matter

- The mass of an object is a measure of .... the amount of matter.
- Mass is measured in .... kilograms or grams.
- Volume is measured in .... cubic metres or cubic centimetres.
- Density is .... mass ÷ volume.
- An object will float in water if its density is .... less or equal to the density of water.
- Hydrometers can be used to measure .... the density of liquids.

Further questions

20 Two objects are balanced on a simple beam balance. Say whether the following quantities are the same or different for the objects: mass; volume; density.

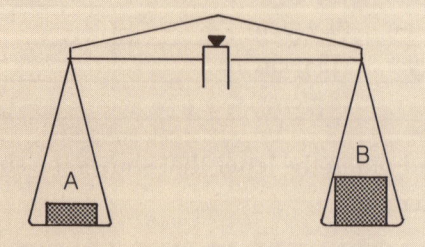

21 A rectangular block of wood has a mass of 32 g and measures 5 cm long, 4 cm wide and 2 cm thick.
(a) What is its density?
(b) Would it float in a liquid of density 0.9 g/cm^3?

22 Calculate the volume of a cube of side 2 cm. Find its mass if its density is 7 g/cm^3.

23 This hydrometer can be used to measure densities in the range 0.8 to 1.2 g/cm^3.
(a) Copy the diagram and mark on the positions of the scale readings 0.8, 1.0, 1.2 g/cm^3.
(b) Label the contents of x and y.

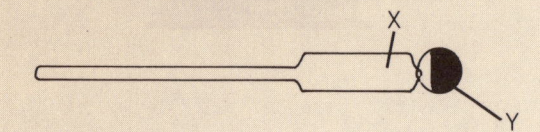

24 You have a number of sealed oil drums. Some are completely full of water and some completely full of petrol. Suggest a way of finding out which drums contain petrol without breaking the seals.

25 A stone of mass 22 g is placed into a measuring cylinder containing water up to the 61 cm mark. The water level rises to the 72 cm mark.
(a) Write down two precautions which are necessary when reading a measuring cylinder.
(b) Calculate the density of the stone.

26 Describe in detail how you would measure the density of a lump of coal.

27 Copy and complete this table.

Object	Mass (g)	Volume (cm^3)	Density (g/cm^3)
A	16	2	
B	8	4	
C	4		8
D	8	16	

(a) Which object has the greatest mass?
(b) Which object has the least volume?
(c) Which objects could be made of the same material?
(d) Which object would float on water?
(Take the density of water as 1 g/cm^3).

25 Measuring motion

Timers

We are always measuring time intervals. Here are some examples of timers.

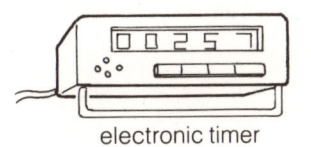

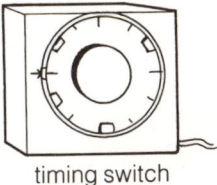

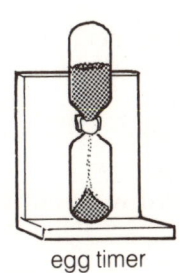

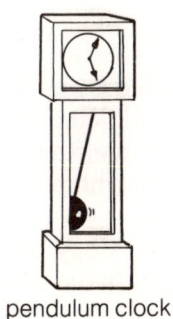

electronic timer   watch   timing switch   egg timer   pendulum clock

1 Copy this table and put in a tick in the box if the timer CAN measure that time (interval) and an X if it cannot.

Timer	Hours	Minutes	Seconds	$\frac{1}{10}$th of seconds	$\frac{1}{100}$th of seconds
Electronic timer					
Egg timer					
Stop watch					
Timing switch					
Pendulum clock					

2 Give an example of a use for each timer.

The ticker-timer

This very useful timer prints dots on paper tape that passes under its vibrating arm. It always prints 50 dots each second so by counting the dots we can work out time.

25 dots would take $\frac{25}{50}$ second (0.5 s) and 10 dots $\frac{10}{50}$ seconds (0.2 s) for example.

A ticker-timer

3 For each tape work out how long it took to print the dots.

4 Which tape was pulled through the timer fastest? Explain your answer.

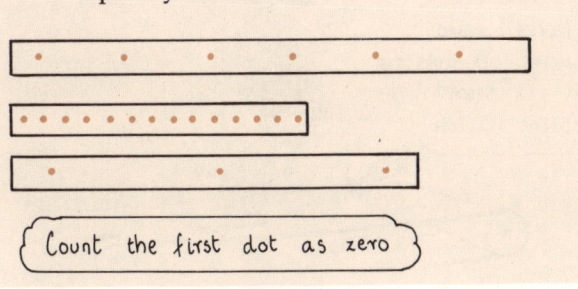

Count the first dot as zero

Note that the first dot is printed when the time is 0 s and so should be counted as dot 0.

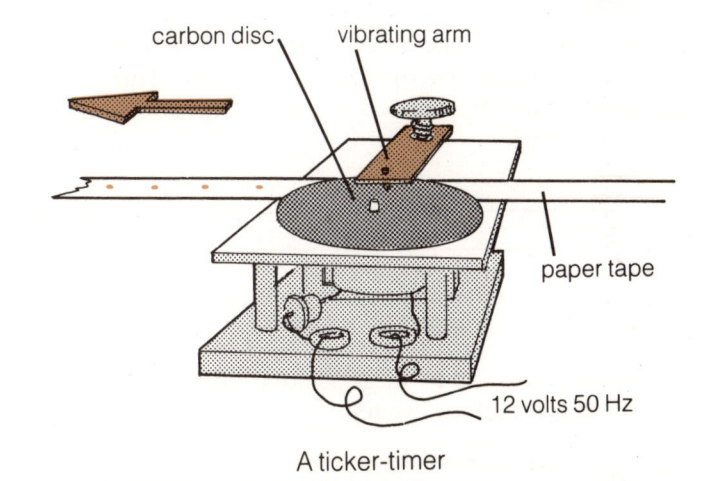

Speed

The speed of a body is the distance it moves in one second (or one hour). Speed can be worked out from this equation.

$$\text{Speed} = \frac{\text{Distance}}{\text{Time}}$$

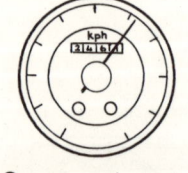

Speed is measured in miles per hour (mph)
or kilometres per hour (km/h)
or metres per second (m/s)
or centimetres per second (cm/s)

Car speedometer

A high-speed train

5 Copy this table and work out the numbers that go in the spaces.

Speed	Distance	Time
	100 m	5 s
5 m/s		10 s
8 m/s	96 m	

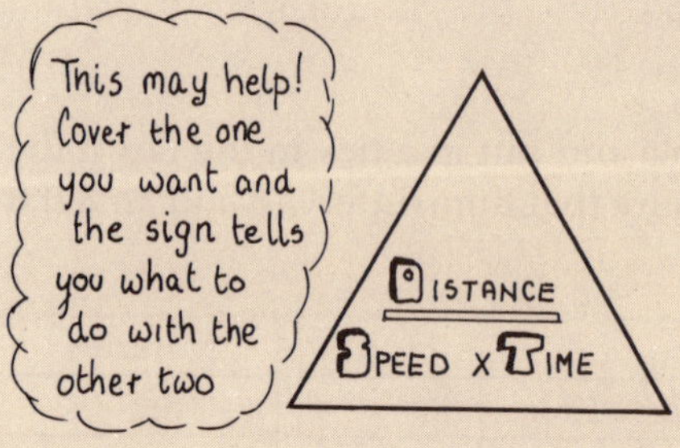

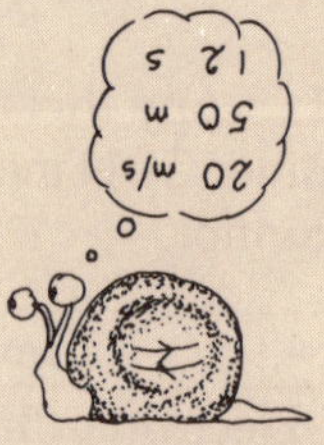

6 Copy this table and put these speeds into the correct spaces.

8 km/h; 25 km/h; 120 km/h; 1000 km/h; 2000 km/h; 24 000 km/h.

Car (top speed)	Bike	Passenger jet	Walking	'Concorde'	Satellite

This may help! Cover the one you want and the sign tells you what to do with the other two

$$\frac{\text{Distance}}{\text{Speed} \times \text{Time}}$$

Experiment. Using a ticker-timer to measure speed

Pull a paper tape through a ticker-timer at a steady speed. It takes 1 second for the timer to print 50 dots, so count 50 dots and measure the distance they cover. This is the distance the tape has moved in one second and so is the speed of the tape.

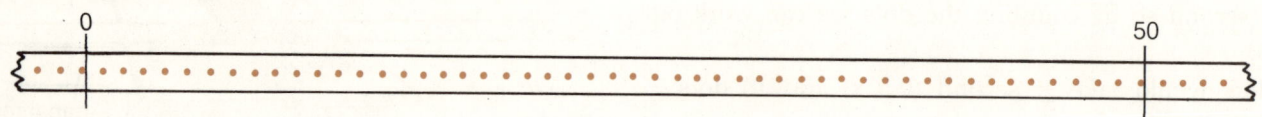

Example

The distance covered by these 50 dots is 15 cm. The speed of the tape is therefore 15 cm/s.

7 Work out the speeds of these tapes, shown full size

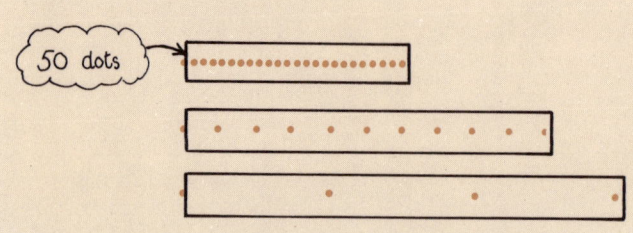

50 dots

It takes 1 second to print 50 dots and 1/5th second to print 10 dots

- Speed = distance/time.

Acceleration

If the tape is moved through the ticker-timer at a steady speed, the dots on it will be evenly spaced. If you cut the tape every 5 dots and stick the pieces side by side, they will all be about the same length.

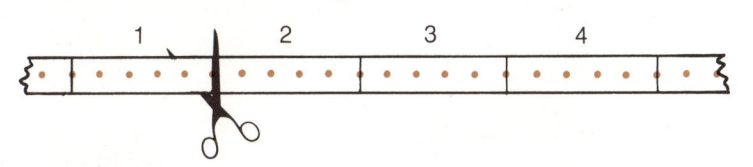

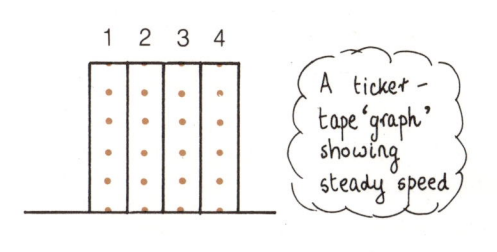

A ticker-tape 'graph' showing steady speed

Experiment

Pull a paper tape through a ticker-timer at an increasing speed. You could do this by sticking the tape to a trolley that can run down a sloping track. You will notice that the dots on the tape get further and further apart as the speed increases. Cut the tape every 5 dots as before and stick the pieces side by side. This time the lengths of the pieces increase, showing that the speed of the tape is increasing all the time. A body whose speed increases as time goes by is **accelerating**. A body is decelerating if it goes slower and slower – its speed dropping as time goes by.

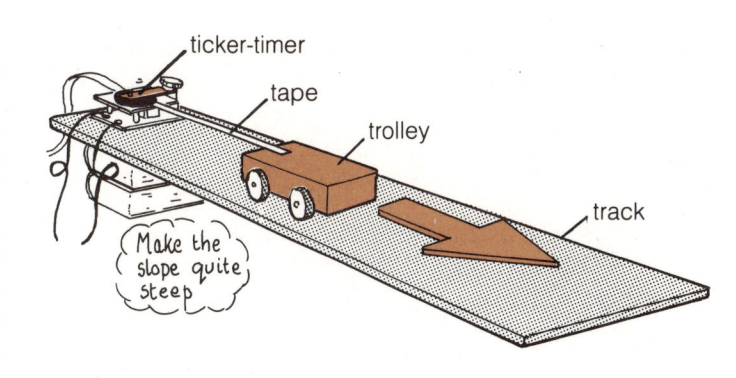

Make the slope quite steep

A trolley accelerating down a slope

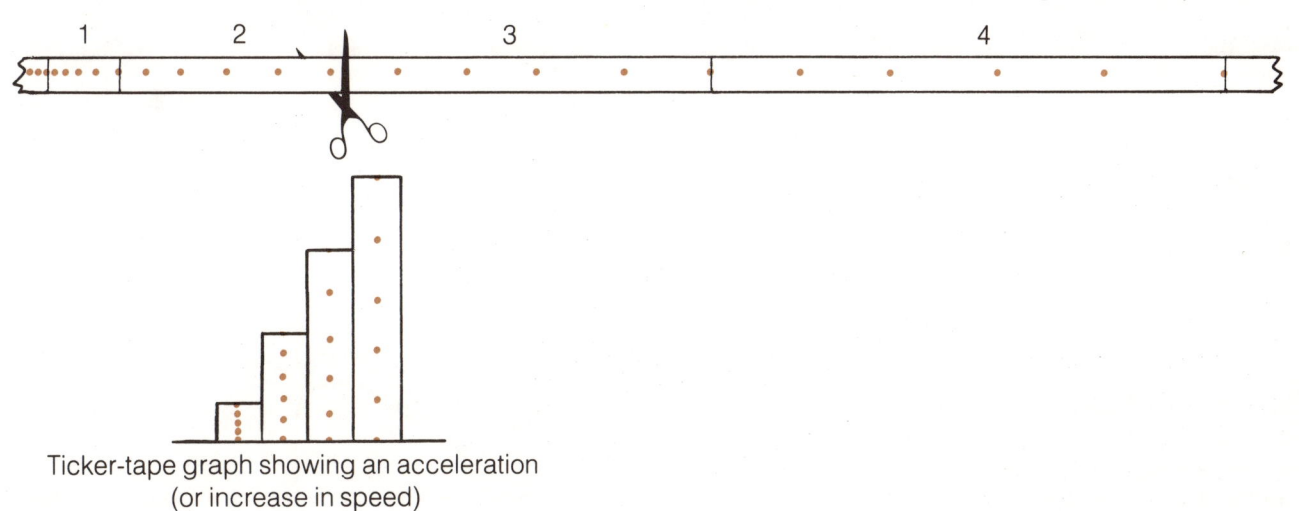

Ticker-tape graph showing an acceleration (or increase in speed)

■ An object whose speed is increasing, is accelerating.

---

8   These diagrams show ticker-tape graphs of moving trolleys Which diagram fits each of the following descriptions of movement?
(a) The trolley accelerates then decelerates.
(b) The trolley accelerates, travels steadily, then decelerates.
(c) The trolley accelerates, travels steadily, then accelerates again.

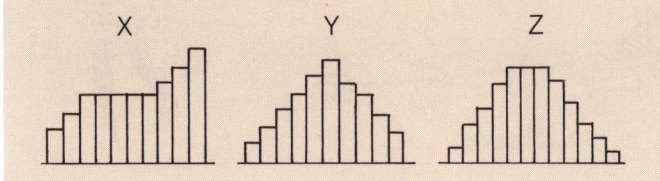

X   Y   Z

9   Draw a ticker-tape graph for a trolley that accelerates, travels at a steady speed, accelerates again and then decelerates.

10   A boy on a bicycle travels 300 m during one minutes and 420 m during the following minute. Calculate his average speed
(a) during the first minute,
(b) during the second minute,
(c) for the two-minute period.
(d) Did the boy accelerate or decelerate during the two-minute period?

26 Forces

We are always pushing, pulling and lifting. A push or a pull is called a **force**.

A force can get an object moving, or stop it from moving, or change the direction of its movement, or squeeze it and change its shape. Force is measured in **newtons** (N). A force of one newton is quite a small force. The drawings show people exerting forces and give a rough idea of the size of those forces.

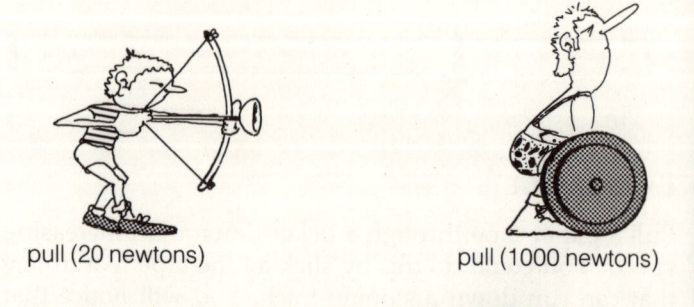

pull (20 newtons)

pull (1000 newtons)

push (1 newton)

squeeze (20 newtons)

pull (10 newtons)

push (1000 newtons)

■ Pushes and pulls are examples of forces.

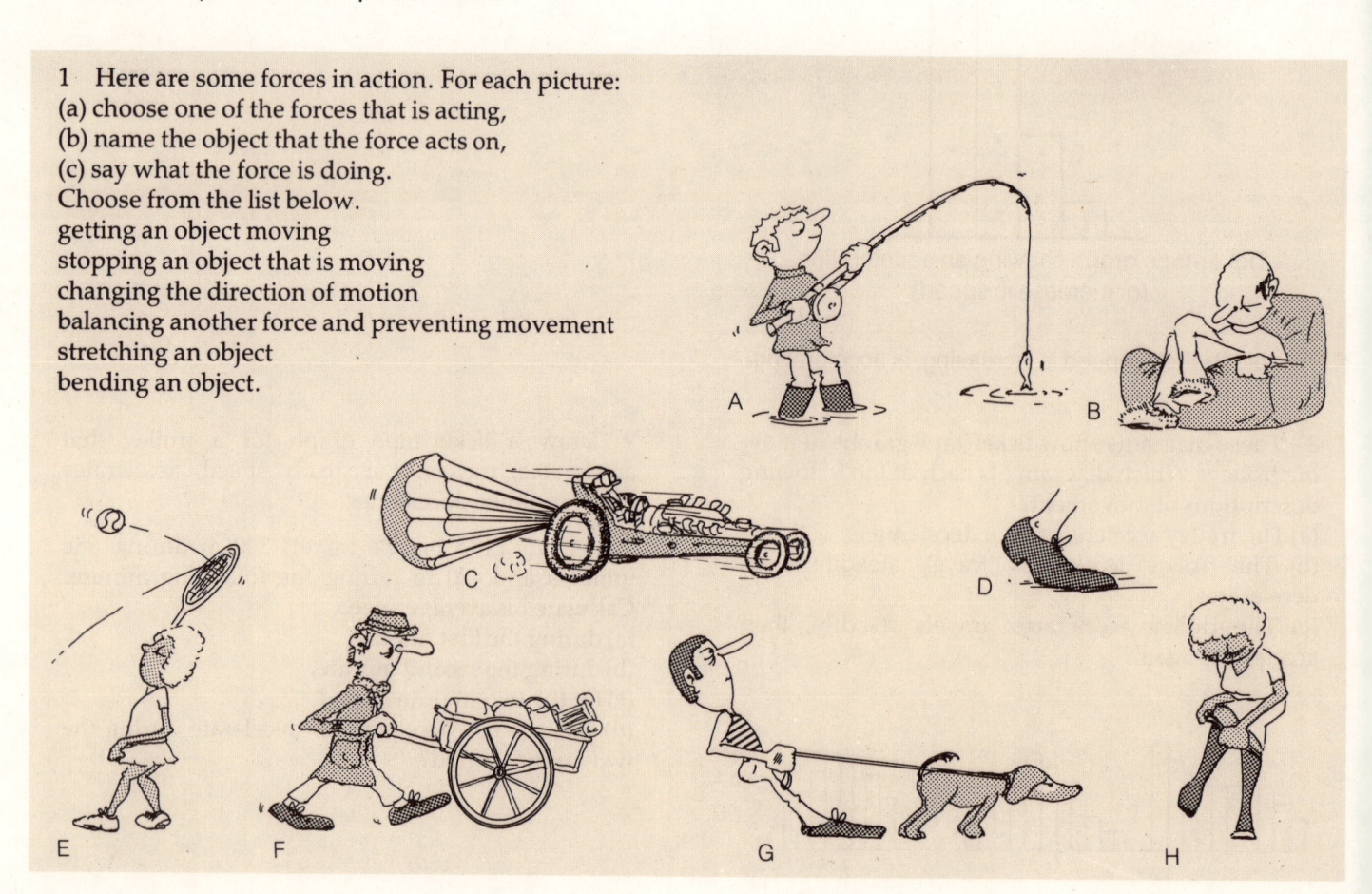

1   Here are some forces in action. For each picture:
(a) choose one of the forces that is acting,
(b) name the object that the force acts on,
(c) say what the force is doing.
Choose from the list below.
getting an object moving
stopping an object that is moving
changing the direction of motion
balancing another force and preventing movement
stretching an object
bending an object.

A   B

C   D

E   F   G   H

116

The pull of gravity – a most important force

There is a small force between any two bodies that pulls them together. Usually this force is very small, but when one of the bodies is the Earth, the force (close to) is far from small. The 'pull of gravity' is the pull of the enormous mass of the Earth on our bodies and any other object near the Earth's surface. The force gets less the further we travel from the Earth. It is the pull of gravity that:

(a) keeps things on the Earth;
(b) brings things down to earth when they are thrown upwards;
(c) holds the moon in its orbit round the Earth;
(d) captures returning space capsules and pulls them into orbit.

> 2   Write down three examples of things that the 'pull of gravity' can do.
>
> 3   The Moon has less mass than the Earth. Will the pull of gravity on objects on the Moon be more or less than those on the Earth?

Weight

The Earth pulls an object with a force that is called the **weight** of that object. As weight is a force it is measured in newtons. If there were no Earth to pull the object (say in deep space) it would have no weight, but it would still have mass.

The Earth pulls a hanger of mass 100 g with a force of very nearly 1 newton. So the weight of the hanger is 1 newton on Earth. On the Moon, the hanger would have less weight (about ⅙ newton) because the Moon is smaller than the Earth and pulls with less force. (The hanger's mass would still be 100 g.) In deep space the hanger would have zero weight although its mass would still be 100 g.

> 4   What is the weight (on Earth) of a 1 kg hanger?

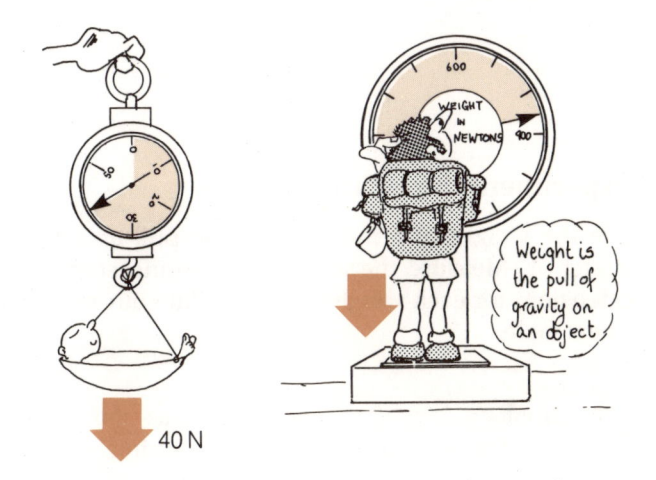

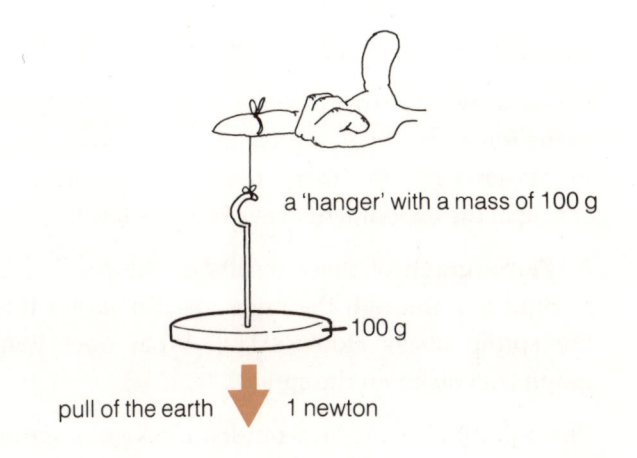

a 'hanger' with a mass of 100 g

100 g

pull of the earth   1 newton

Feeling a pull of 1 newton

5 A baby has a mass of 4 kg. What would the weight of the baby be on the Earth, on the Moon and deep in space? Choose from these values: 6 N; 0 N; 40 N; 400 N. Copy and complete the table.

	On the Earth	On the Moon	Deep in space
Mass of the baby			
Weight of the baby			

A spring balance can be used to measure weight. The weight of the object stretches a spring that moves a pointer over a scale.

Experiment

Find the weight of your body in newtons.

■ Weight is the pull of gravity on an object.

Spring force

A spring balance uses the extension of a spring to measure weight or pulling force. It should be marked in newtons. Sometimes spring balances have gears to change the stretch of the spring into the movement of a pointer.

Measuring forces with a spring balance

Experiment. Stretching springs

Use the weight of a metal hanger to pull a spring and stretch it. Measure the amount the spring stretches (its extension) for each weight you add. Put your results into a neat table.

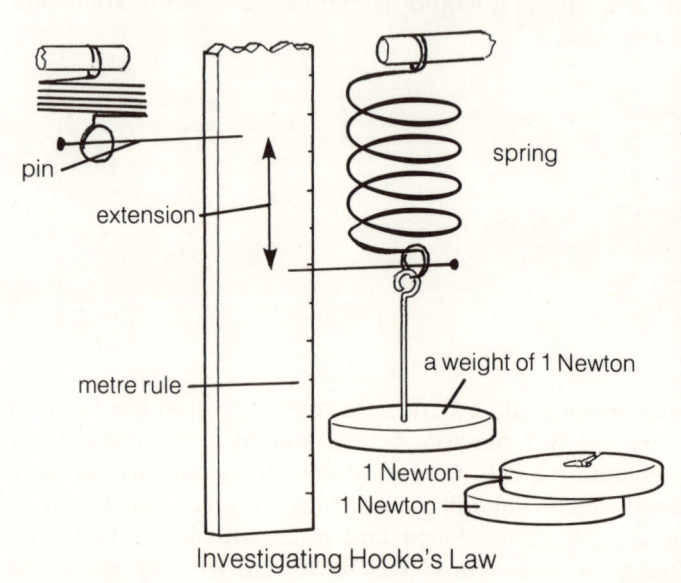

6 **Hooke's law**. The results in this table were obtained from an experiment with a spring.

Force on the spring	0	1	2	3	4	5	6 N
Extension		0	1.5	3.0	4.5	6.0	7.5	9.0 cm

Hooke's law says that the extension is proportional to the force (i.e. if you double the force, you double the extension). Do these results show that the spring in the experiment obeys Hooke's law?

7 Plot a graph of these results. If the graph is a straight line through the origin, it also shows that the spring obeys Hooke's law. What does your graph tell you about the spring?

Plot a graph of your own results. Does your spring obey Hooke's law?

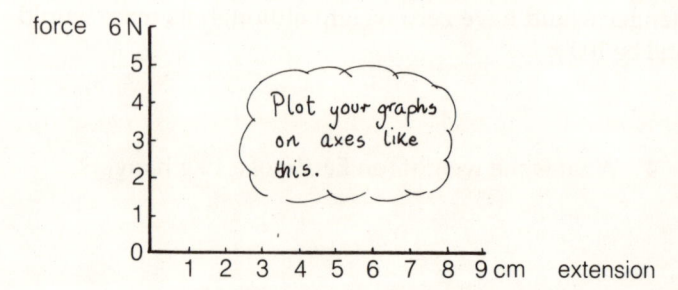

Investigating Hooke's Law

Plot your graphs on axes like this.

Experiment

Find out if pieces of elastic and strips of plastic obey Hooke's law.

Note that if a spring is stretched past a certain limit, it will not go back to its original length when the force is removed. Hooke's law is only obeyed up to this limit.

■ Hooke's law says that the extension of a spring is proportional to the force on it.

8   Here are some examples of springy objects in common use: car springs; catapult elastic; elastic bands; elastic in clothes; mattress springs; chest expanders.
For each one write a sentence explaining what the force that the spring exerts is used to do.

9   A force of 20 N stretches a 'chest expander' by 0.5 m. How much force must a man use to stretch it by 1.5 m if the spring obeys Hooke's law? Is this force exerted by each arm, or do they share the force between them?

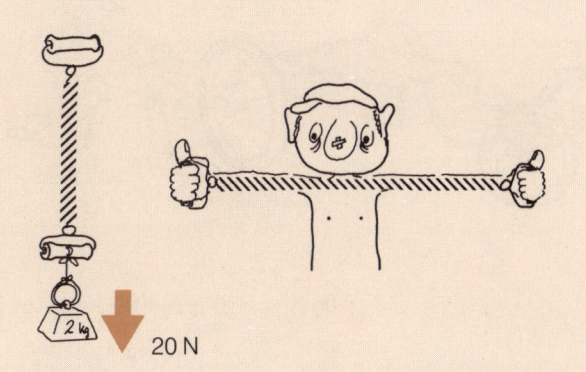

10   One of these arrangements of chest expanders is four times harder to stretch (through the same distance) than one of the others. Which one is hardest to stretch and which one easiest? Can you explain why one needs four times more force than the easiest one?

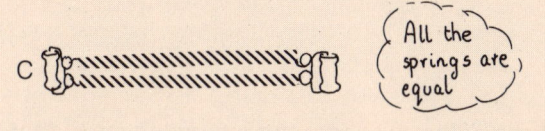

Friction

Friction is a very common force. When we slide a brick along a plank, the force of friction acts on the brick in the opposite direction to its movement.
Friction can be a drag . . .
The force we use to cycle along a level road is used to overcome friction. There is friction due to the air, as we force our way through it, and there is friction between the parts of the machine that move against each other. If the force we exert balances these forces of friction, then we move at a steady speed.
. . . . but friction is also a very necessary force.
It stops the feet slipping off the pedals. It stops the tyres slipping on the road, so that the bike moves forwards. It acts between the brake blocks and the wheel to stop the bike.

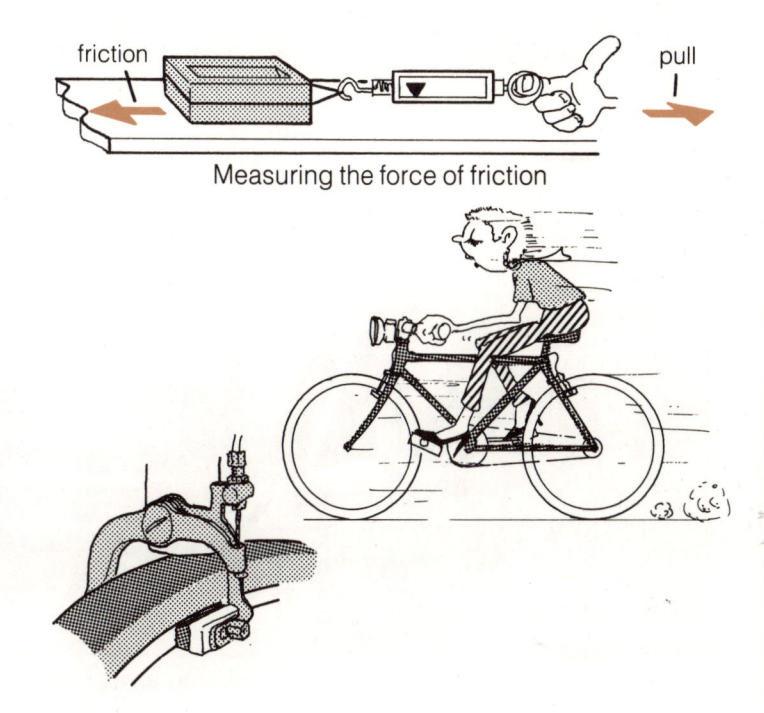

Measuring the force of friction

11 The examples (a) to (e) show the forces of friction in action. For each example:
(a) name two surfaces between which friction acts,
(b) say what the force of friction is doing,
(c) say what would happen if the friction force suddenly disappeared.

(a) pencil and rubber
(b)
(c) nail in wood
(d) a rubber belt turning a pulley
(e) shoes of all types gripping the ground

Reducing friction

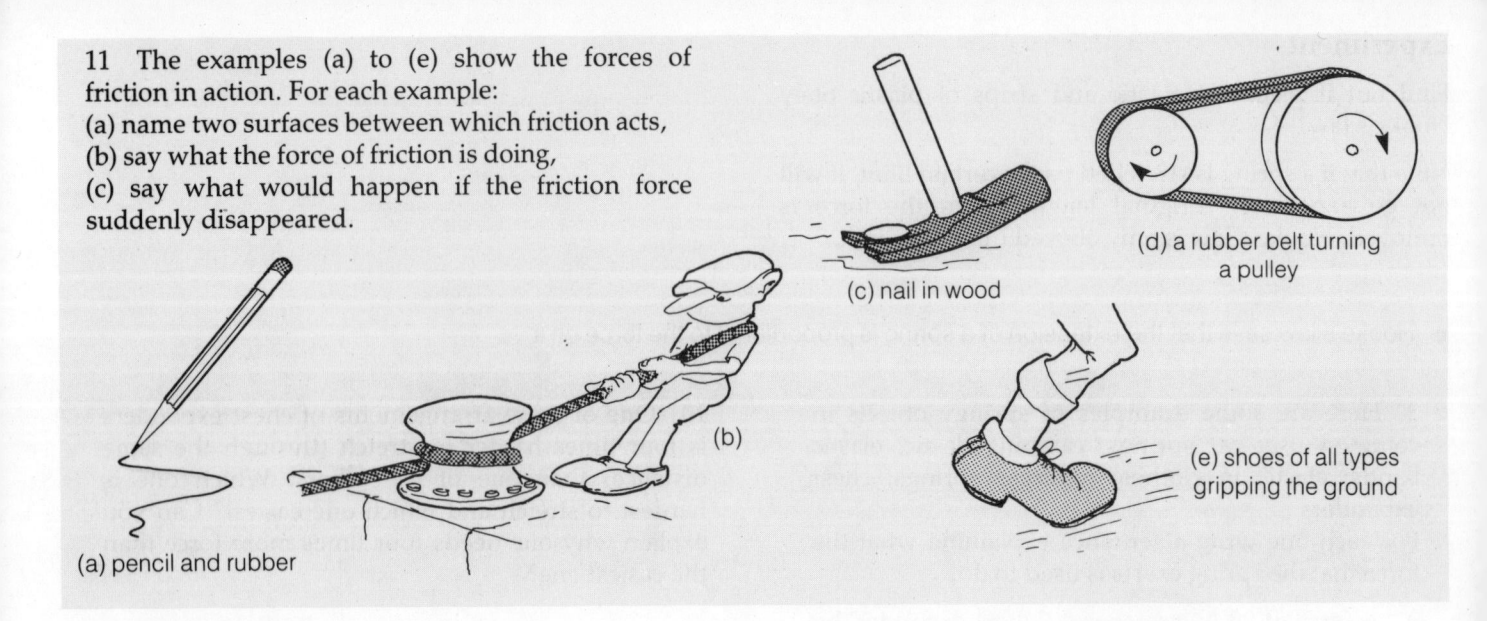

Reducing friction between the moving parts of a machine means that: (a) less energy will be needed to work the machine, (b) there will be less wear and tear, (c) the moving parts will be cooler.

More speed Less wear Less heat

12 These diagrams show the energy changes that take place in two machines. One machine is rusty and the other is well-oiled.
(a) Which is the energy diagram for the well-oiled machine?
(b) Explain why more energy has to be put into the rusty machine to get the same energy out as the well-oiled machine.
(c) Explain why the rusty machine gets hotter than the well-oiled one.

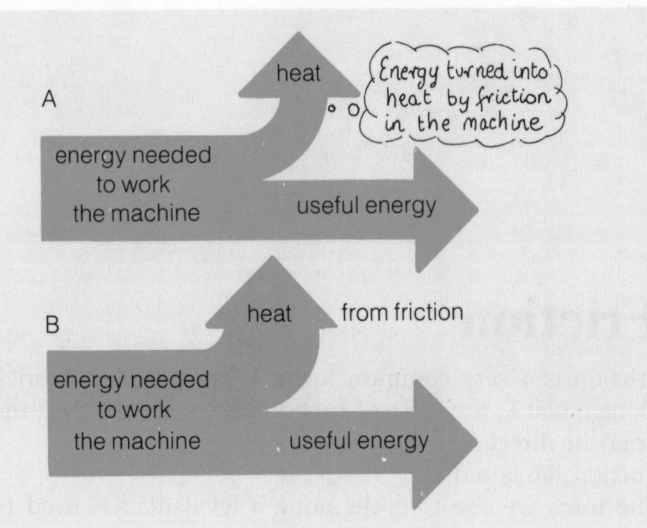

A: energy needed to work the machine → heat (*Energy turned into heat by friction in the machine*) / useful energy

B: energy needed to work the machine → heat from friction / useful energy

Using an air cushion to reduce friction

There are several ways of reducing friction.

Ball-bearings

Steel balls make the surfaces roll over each other instead of sliding. This greatly reduces friction.

Oiling

Oil gets between the moving parts and keeps them apart. This reduces friction.

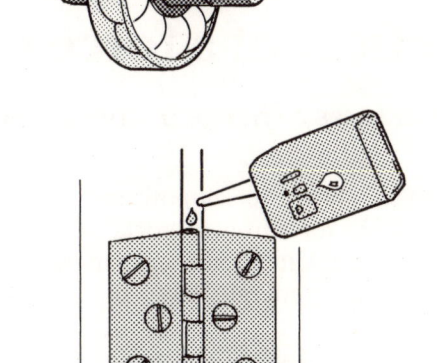

Air cushions

If the moving parts are kept apart by compressed air, friction is reduced to almost nothing. Hovercraft and 'air-bearings' use air cushions like this.

Streamlining

Streamlining cuts down wind resistance, making movement at speed much easier.

---

13   Give an example of the use of ball-bearings.

14   Give an example of where you would use oil to reduce friction.

15   Give an example of a 'streamlined' machine.

■ Friction can be a useful force; it can also be a nuisance.

27 Force and motion

The effect of a force on the motion of things

A force produces a change in speed (speeding things up)

Think about this brave rocket-powered skater shown in the drawings. The force from his rocket will speed him up – he will accelerate. Chemical energy in the rocket fuel is changing into kinetic energy.

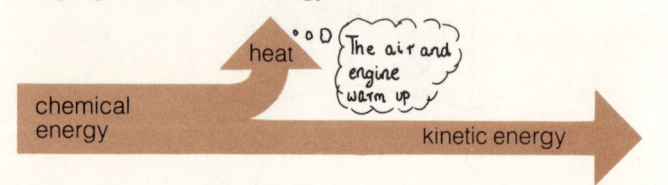

A force is not needed to keep an object moving at a steady speed

If the skater turns off the rocket, he will continue to move at a steady speed assuming there is no friction. (We do not often experience this because friction is nearly always present.) No energy changes take place and no work is done.

A force produces a change in speed (slowing things down)

The spring pushes against the skater and brings him to a stop. Kinetic energy is changed to strain energy in the spring. A force also acts on the spring, moving it and squeezing it into a different shape.

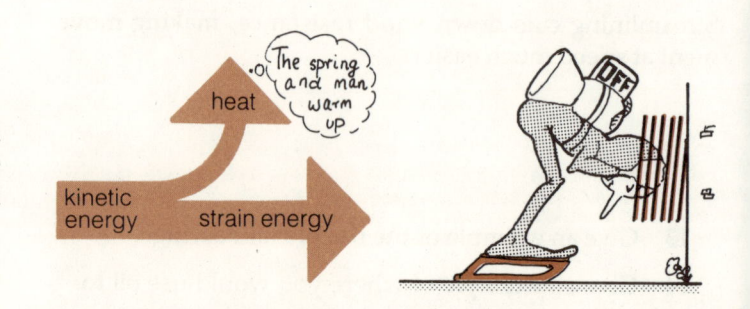

A force can be balanced by another force, in which case there will be no change in speed

A car travelling at a steady speed along a level road is rather like the skater dragging an anchor through ice. The engine exerts a forward force on the car in the same way as the rocket does on the skater. Wind resistance exerts a backwards force on the car, as does the drag of the anchor on the skater. These two forces are equal and balance, leaving no net force on the car. The car continues to move at a steady speed.

122

1 Copy and complete this table about the motion of a car.

Force and resistance	What happens to the car
Engine force greater than wind resistance	
Engine force less than wind resistance	
Engine force equal to wind resistance	

2 Sketch a speed/time graph for this brave skater.

■ A net force on an object will make it accelerate. If there is no net force on an object, it will stay put or continue to move at a steady speed.

Force and acceleration

The pull of gravity on the metal mass in the picture is felt by the finger.

Experiment

Use this force to accelerate a trolley as shown in the picture. Fix a paper tape to the trolley and use a ticker-timer to print dots on the tape as it accelerates by. Cut the tape every 5 dots and stick the pieces side by side. This will give a ticker-tape graph that shows that the trolley is speeding up (accelerating). Do the experiment again but this time use the weight of two of the masses to move the trolley. Again cut and stick the tape to give a ticker-tape graph.

You will see from your results that the acceleration gets larger as the force gets larger. In fact, careful experiments have shown that doubling the force doubles the acceleration. Force and acceleration are proportional. This is known as Newton's second law of motion.

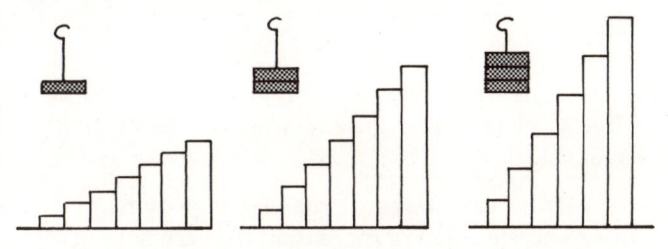

Ticker-tape graphs showing that acceleration increases with pulling force

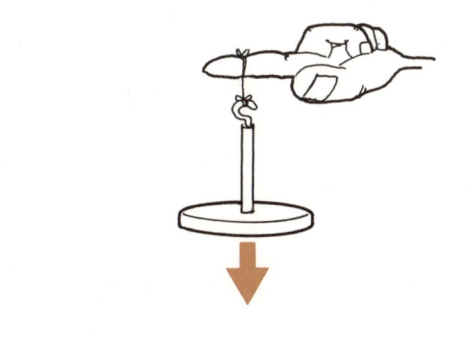

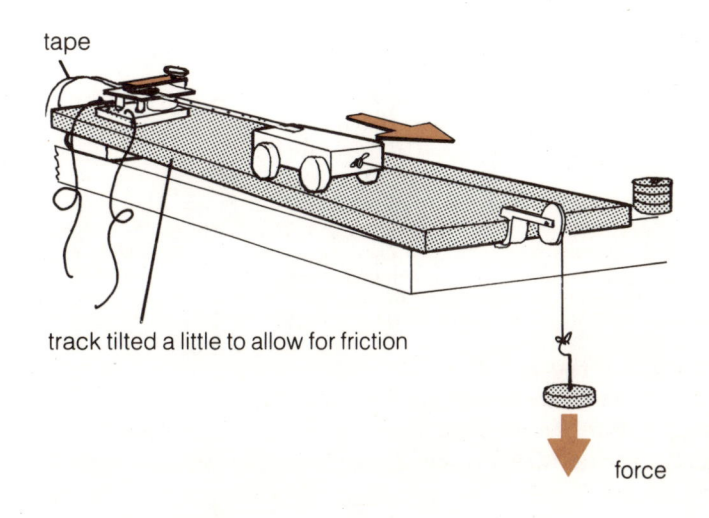

Using a force to accelerate a trolley

3 The following objects can accelerate: sprinter; car; bullet; skydiver. For each one say what it is that provides the force for acceleration.

4 When a weight accelerates a trolley which of them:
(a) loses potential energy?
(b) does work on the other?
(c) gains kinetic energy?
(d) has work done on it?

■ Force and acceleration are proportional.

The acceleration due to gravity

When you let go of an object above the ground, the pull of gravity makes it fall faster and faster. The pull of the Earth accelerates the object.

Experiment. Free-falling objects

If you drop a ball and a piece of paper, which will hit the ground first? Try it and you will find that they both hit the ground together (provided the paper is first crumpled into a ball). The pull of gravity gives heavy and light objects the same acceleration as long as air resistance can be neglected. This is called the acceleration of gravity.

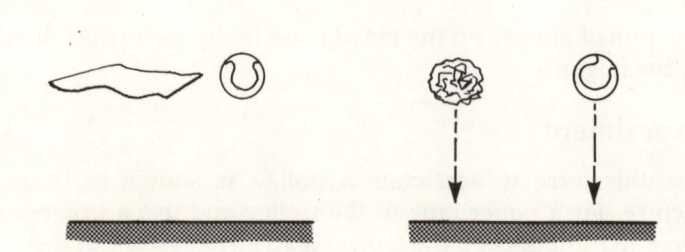

5 Describe three differences that we would notice if the acceleration of gravity was one tenth of its actual value.

6 Describe two ways of making a person move with an acceleration of more than the acceleration of gravity.

Getting things moving

. . . or stopping them once they are moving

Getting things to move

Getting things to stop

7   Copy this table and fit in the mass of each object, choosing from these values: 1000 kg; 1 kg; 10 kg.

Football	Baby in a pram	Car

Imagine you are trying to set the three objects above into motion. The one with the most mass would be the most difficult to get started. This is not because of friction. Even floating in space, the car would need nearly as much effort to start it moving. All bodies resist being set into motion, especially one with large mass. Once moving, these massive bodies are also difficult to stop. This property of mass is called **inertia**.

As an example, imagine a fat man and a thin man using identical rocket engines to get moving. The fat man gets less acceleration and takes longer to gain speed than the thin man. It is more difficult to get him moving because of his great mass. The fat man has more inertia than the thin man.

Collisions and blows

When we stop a moving ball we feel a blow. If the ball is large and moving fast, the blow is bigger. The ball has **momentum**. (The quantity of momentum is mass × speed.) The more momentum an object has, the bigger the blow it delivers when it is stopped. When we kick a ball, the blow gets the ball moving and gives it momentum. The bigger the blow, the greater is the momentum gained by the ball.

8   Write down these moving objects in order, with the one with greatest momentum first and so on: a lorry travelling at 80 km/h; a boy cycling at 30 km/h; an oil-tanker sailing at 15 km/h; a golf ball in flight at 100 km/h.

125

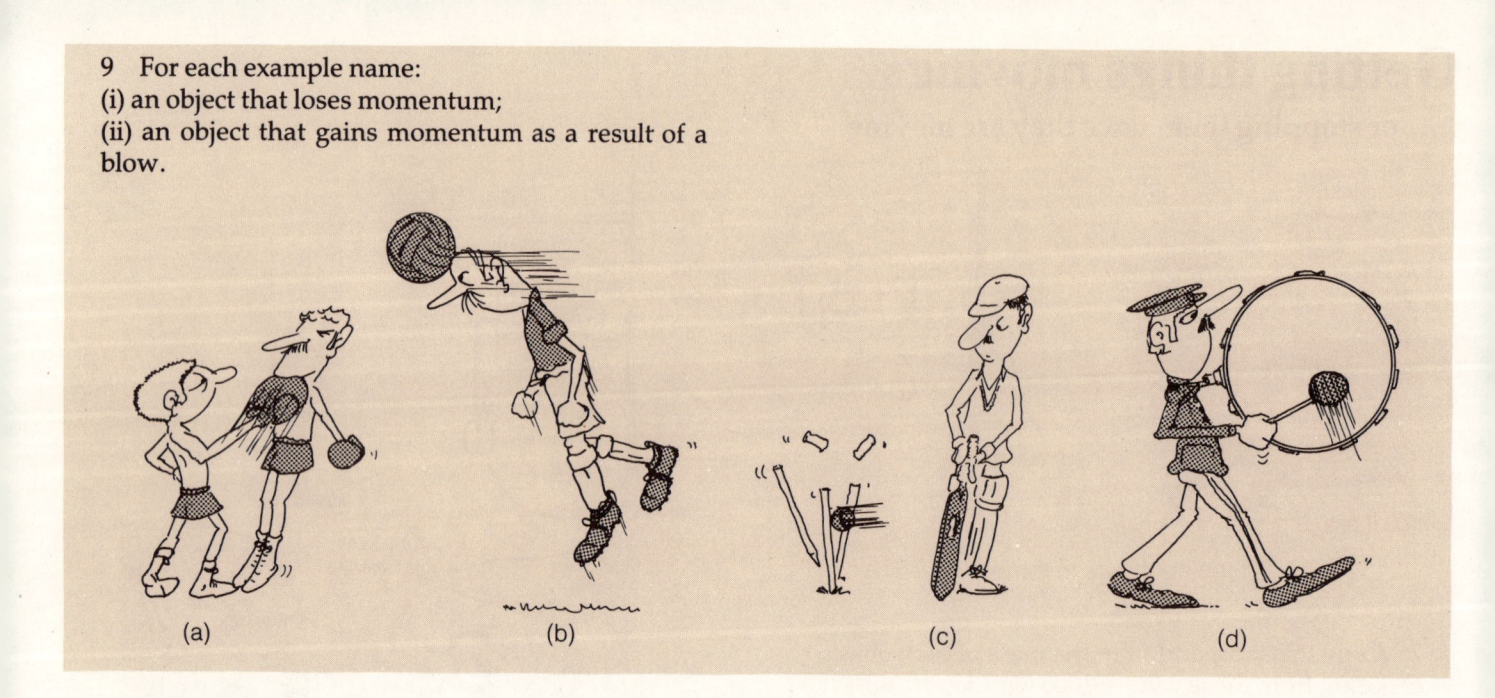

9   For each example name:
(i) an object that loses momentum;
(ii) an object that gains momentum as a result of a blow.

(a)   (b)   (c)   (d)

Summary of force and motion

- Pushes, pulls, weight and friction are examples of forces.
- A stationary body will not move unless a force acts on it.
- If no force acts on a moving body, it will continue to move at a steady speed in a straight line. (This can happen if there is no friction, or more usually, if the forces on a body balance.)
- If a force does act on a body it will accelerate. The greater the force the greater the acceleration will be. Force and acceleration are proportional.
- The same force produces less acceleration on a massive body than on a light body. A massive body is more difficult to get moving, or to stop once it is moving. It has a greater inertia.

No force, No acceleration No speed.

Force acts... Acceleration.. speed increases.

No force, No acceleration Speed constant

More mass... Same force... Less acceleration

28 Work

Often when we push or pull an object, it moves. When a force moves an object like this, we say that **work** has been done.

Examples of work being done

(a) A rocket-powered skater dragging an anchor!
(b) Striking a match.
(c) Lifting a load.

In these examples, a **force** is exerted by an 'engine' that has a supply of energy (the rocket engine, the hand and the man). This force equals the opposing forces of friction or gravity. The anchor, match and bricks move through a distance at a steady speed. The engines do work and as a result lose some of their energy.

The amount of work done is got by multiplying the force by the distance moved in the direction of that force.

Work = force × distance.

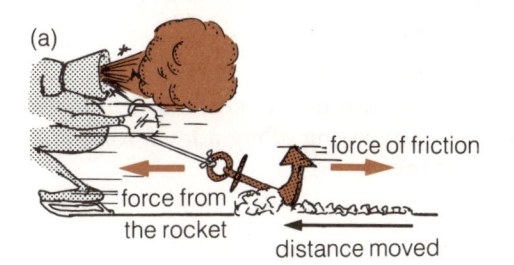

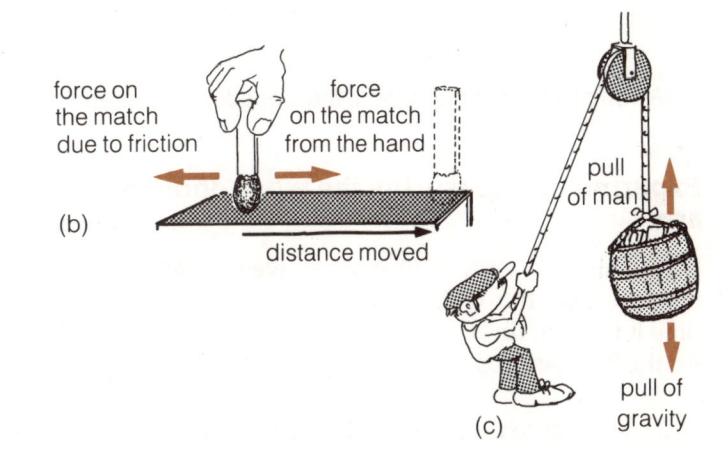

Experiment. Measuring the work done by a steam engine when it is made to lift a load of 1 N

Fix a thread over a pulley to the load that is to be lifted. Run the engine up to top speed and attach the thread so that the load is lifted. Let the engine lift the load by 1 metre and then cut the thread. For later use find the time that the engine takes to do this work. (If you have not got a steam engine, use an electric motor.)

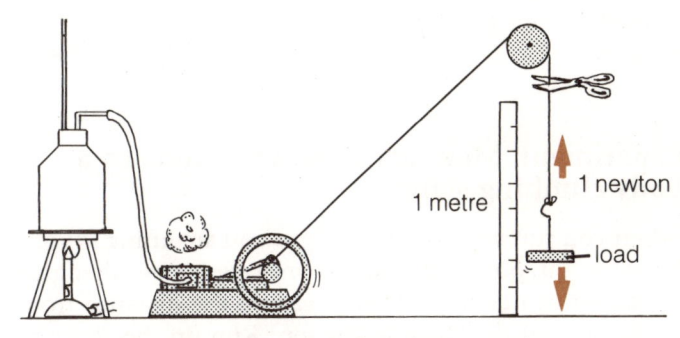

Measuring the work done by an engine

How much work is done

When the engine pulls with a force of 1 newton through a distance of 1 metre, the work it has done is
1 newton × 1 metre = 1 newton metre = 1 joule (joule is the same as 'newton metre')
Work is measured in **joules**.

1 Calculate the useful work done in the examples above. The forces and distances are given in the table below.

Example	Force	Distance moved	Work done
(a)	500 N	2 m	
(b)	1 N	1 cm	
(c)	200 N	3 m	

■ Work = force × distance moved in the direction of the force.

127

Energy and work

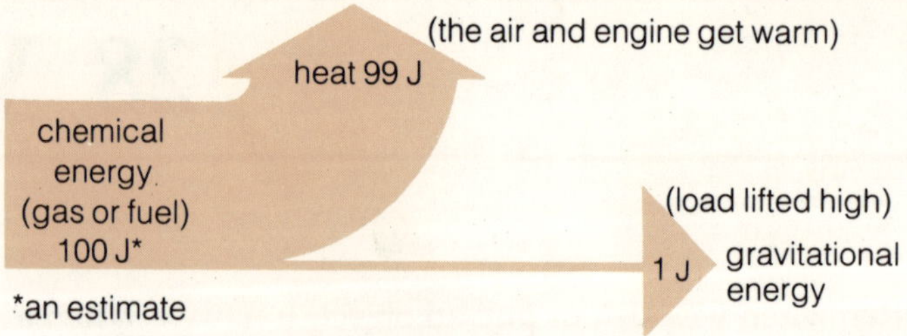

The steam engine in the last experiment changes chemical energy from its fuel into waste heat and gravitational energy of the load. The useful work done by the engine (force exerted × distance lifted) is 1 joule. This work tells us that 1 joule of chemical energy has changed into gravitational energy. The amount of chemical energy supplied by the fuel is much greater than this – it could be 100 J or more – because the engine changes a lot of chemical energy into 'waste' heat.

Note that when an engine works only against friction or wind resistance, all of the chemical energy used finishes up as waste heat. A car travelling along a level road at a steady speed is an example of this.

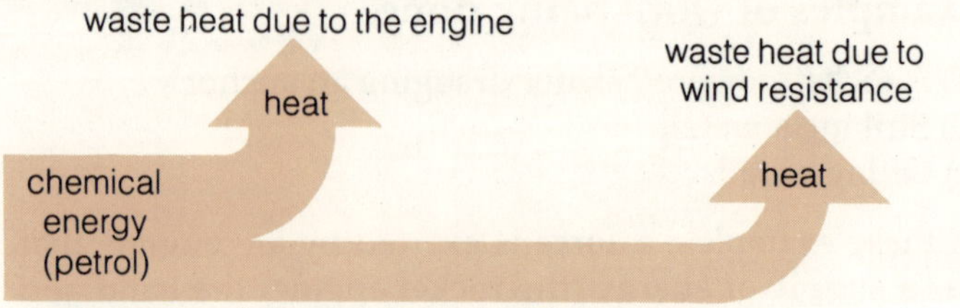

The energy changes that take place as a steam engine lifts a load

The energy changes that take place when a car travels at a steady speed on a level road

■ When energy changes form, the work done measures how much energy has changed.

Experiment. Measuring the work done by an arm

Do 'push-ups' with a 50 newton weight. Measure the distance that the weight moves, and for later use, the time it takes to do 20 'push-ups'. Calculate the work done for the 20 push-ups.

> 2 How much work is done for 1 push-up when a 50 N weight is pushed up 0.8 metre? How much work is done for 20 push-ups?

Measuring the work done by an arm

Experiment. Measuring the work done by a body climbing stairs

When you run up stairs the weight you are lifting is your body weight. So weigh yourself on scales – ones that give a reading in newtons. Then measure the distance from the bottom of the stairs to the top. Run up the stairs as fast as you can. (Note the time it takes to do this for later use.) Calculate the work you have done . . . body weight × distance from bottom to top.

> 3 How much work is done when a boy who weighs 500 N runs up 100 stairs, if each step is 0.5 m in height?

Measuring the work done by a body

Energy changes

The boy in Q3 does 25 000 J (25 kJ) of useful work. This shows that 25 kJ of chemical energy have changed into gravitational energy. The amount of chemical energy drawn from his muscles is greater than this since some chemical energy is changed into 'waste' body heat.

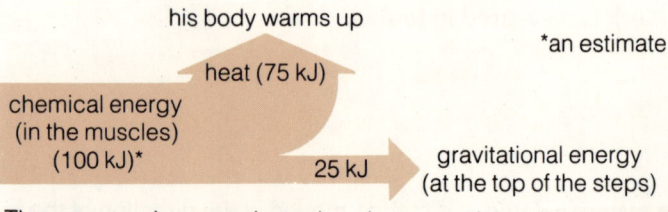

The energy changes that take place as a boy climbs stairs

29 Power

In the last two experiments, your friends may have done the same work as you in less time. If so, they did work faster than you and are more **powerful**.

A powerful engine or person is able to do work quickly. Power is defined as the work done per second. Power can be calculated from this equation:

$$\text{Power} = \frac{\text{work done}}{\text{time taken}}$$

Example
If 800 joules of work are done in 10 seconds by a person doing 'push-ups' with a weight, the power of that person's arm is $\frac{800}{10}$ = 80 joules/second = 80 watts (watts is short for joules/second).

Go back over the last three experiments and calculate the power of the steam engine, your arm and your body. Divide the work done in those experiments by the time it took to do that work.

Experiment. Finding the power needed (in watts) to keep a bicycle moving along a level road

Use a rope to pull a bicycle and rider at 'cycling pace' and a spring balance to measure the force needed to keep them moving. Find the time it takes to travel 10 metres from a flying start. The work done is the pulling force (newtons) × the distance (10 m). The power is this work divided by the time. Calculate the power that has to be put into the bicycle to keep it going at 'cycling pace'.

1 Copy this table and calculate the work done and power of the 'engines' from the figures given.

Engines	Force used (N)	Distance moved (m)	Work done (J)	Time taken (s)	Power (Watts) (W)
Steam engine	2	1		4	
Arm	40	15		10	
Body	600	10		6	

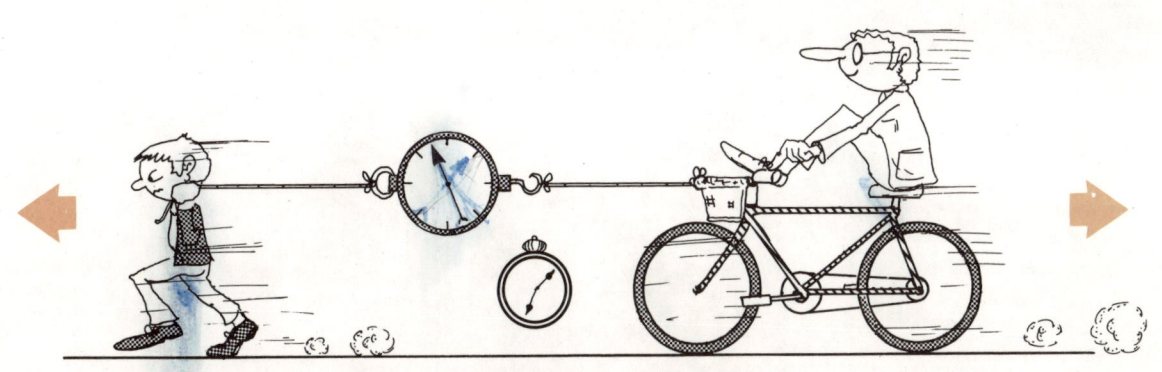

Measuring the power used in cycling

2 In an experiment like this a force of 40 N was used and it took 2 seconds to cover 10 metres. Calculate the power needed to keep the bicycle moving.

■ Power = work done per second.

Experiment. Measuring the power of a bunsen burner

This experiment gives a rough value of the (heating) power of a bunsen burner. How much do you think it will be? Use water to collect and measure the energy from the bunsen. Measure the temperature of 1 kg of cold water in a large tin. Put a roaring bunsen under it for 3 minutes. Remove the bunsen, stir and measure the temperature of the water. Work out how much the temperature has risen. We have found that it takes 4200 joules of heat energy to warm 1 kg of water by 1°C. Use this figure to calculate the heat supplied by the bunsen. (This energy has been changed into heat by the bunsen and is the 'work done'.) Calculate the heat supplied by the bunsen in 1 second – its power.

Example

In an experiment like this the temperature of the water rose by 30°C. So the heat supplied by the bunsen was 4200 × 30 = 126 000 J in 3 minutes (180 s) and the power of the bunsen = $\frac{126\,000}{180}$ = 700 watts.

Note that no force acts in this example so the work done cannot be calculated. In cases like this, power is calculated from energy changed/time taken (p. 170).

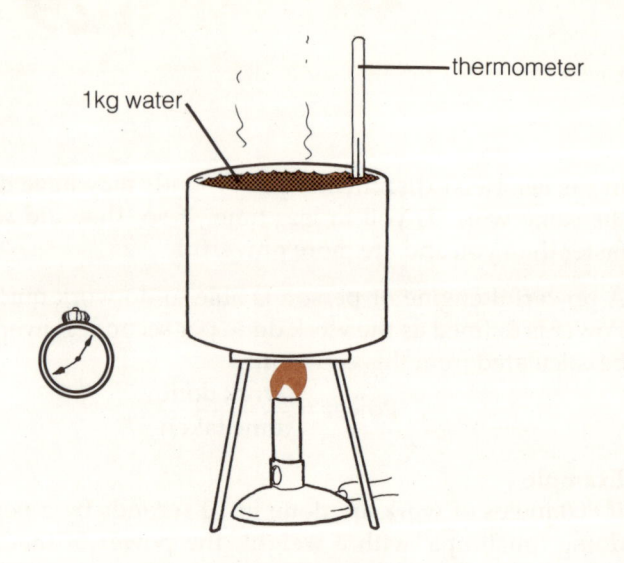

Measuring the power of a bunsen burner

Highly powered dragsters doing a large amount of work in a short time

30 Turning effects of forces

We often use forces to turn things.

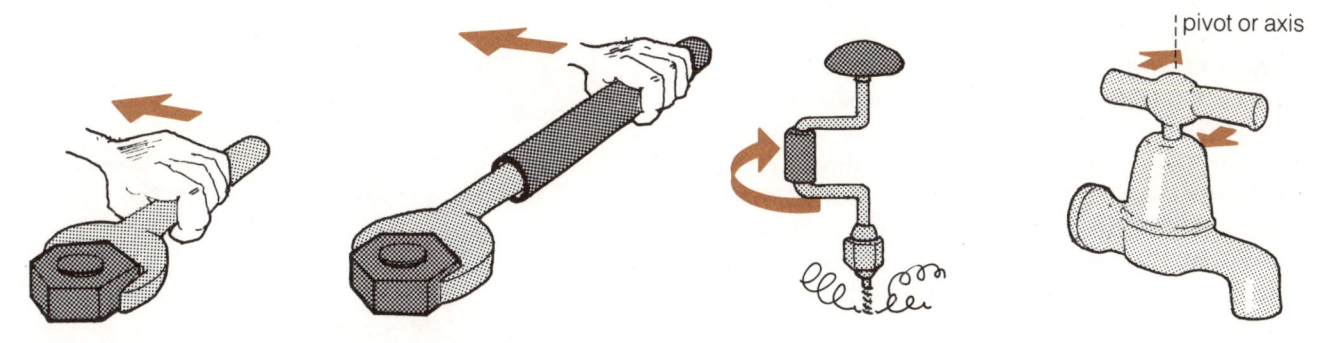

1 Look at the spanner being used to turn a stubborn nut. Explain two ways of increasing the turning effects of the force on the nut.

Experiment

Hang a weight on a rod and move it further and further from the hand (see diagrams). Try this with a larger weight. It is clear that the 'turning effect' depends on the **weight** and the **distance** from the weight to the hand.

The turning effect of a force is called its **moment** and is calculated by multiplying the force by the distance from where the force acts to the turning point.

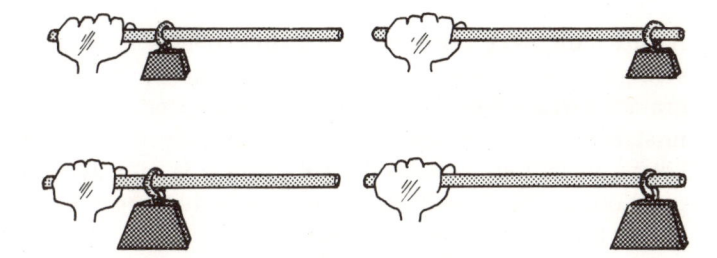

Increasing the turning effect of forces

2 Which of the forces below has the greatest moment about the pivot? Which moments will turn the ruler clockwise and which will turn it anticlockwise?

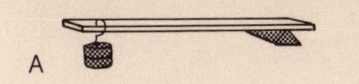

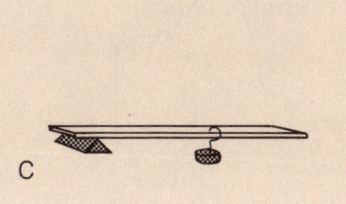

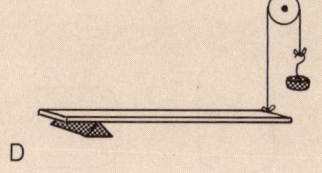

Balanced moments

Balance the beam on its centre line and then place weights on each side, moving them about until the beam balances. Each time you get it to balance, work out the moments of the weights on each side (the weight × its distance to the centre). Allowing for experimental difficulties, you should find that, when balanced:
the moment trying to turn the beam clockwise = the moment trying to turn it anticlockwise.

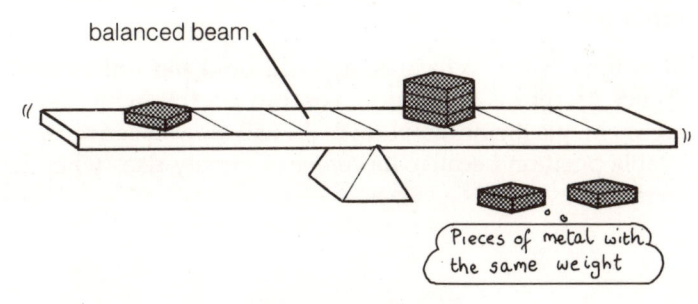

Balancing a beam

■ The turning effect of a force is called its moment and is calculated by multiplying force × distance to the pivot.

131

Stability and balance

We learn to balance things, including ourselves, at a very early age. We 'know' that a bottle of milk can be knocked over more easily than a loaf of bread, but what makes some objects more stable than others?

Experiment. Find the balancing point of a sheet of card

Take a sheet of card and hang it on a pin clamped in a stand. Make sure the card can swing freely. Make a 'plumb line' from a heavy nut and length of thread and hang it from the pin. Mark the line of the thread on the card. Do this twice more hanging the card from different holes. You should find that the three lines cross at one point, and that the card will balance on a pin at that point. The whole weight of the card acts at that balancing point. It is called the **centre of gravity** of the card.

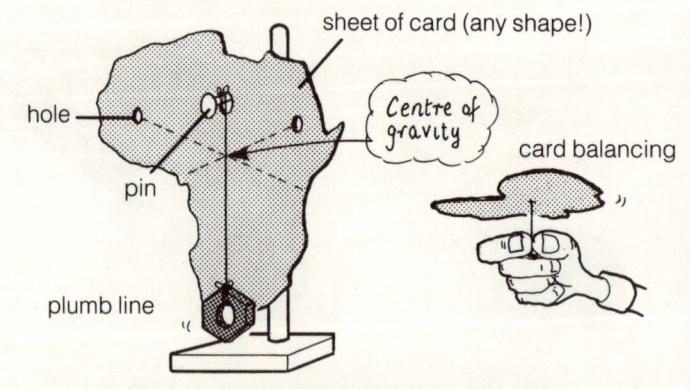

Finding the centre of gravity of a card

Stability and centre of gravity

A nut hanging on a thread is **stable**. If it is moved, it swings back to where it was. Note that its centre of gravity **rises** when it is moved. A balanced pencil is **unstable**. If it is moved its centre of gravity falls and it keeps on falling. A ball on level ground is in a **neutral** position. If it is moved, its centre of gravity does not rise or fall. It will stay where it is put.

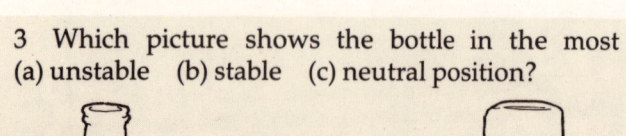

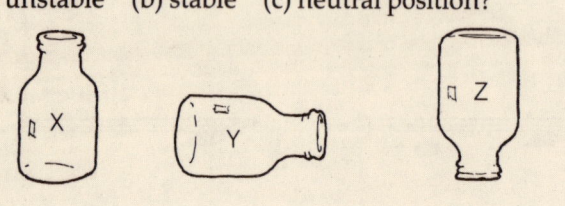

3 Which picture shows the bottle in the most (a) unstable (b) stable (c) neutral position?

An amazing balancing feat – balancing a pencil on a pin

It is impossible to balance a pencil on a pin unless you lower its centre of gravity. You can do this with 'sausages' of plasticine as shown. It will now balance in a stable position because its centre of gravity rises when it is moved.

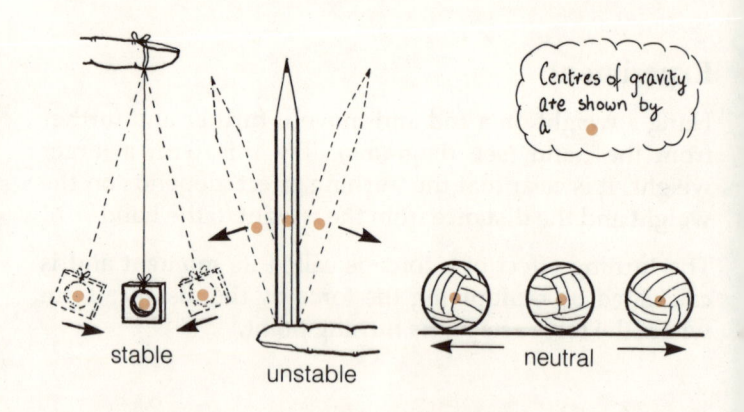

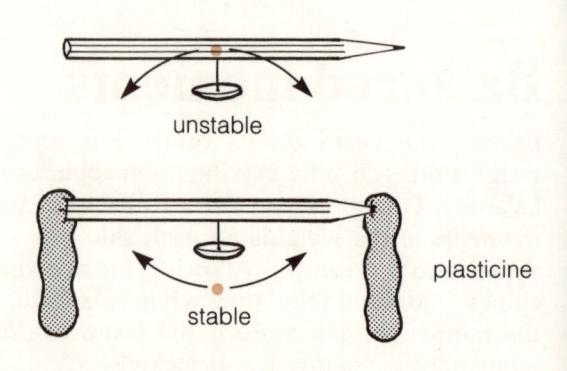

■ The centre of gravity of an object is the place where the whole weight of the object seems to act.

Toppling over

Experiment

Pin a plumb line to the centre of a heavy block of wood and tilt the block until it topples over. You will see that the block tips over when the plumb line (the line from the centre of gravity) passes the corner of the block. This happens most easily when the centre of gravity is high and the base is small.

Does not topple / Topples over

4 What has the designer done to make these objects difficult to tip over?

(a) A glass. Why is it less stable when it is full of liquid?

(b) A sailing boat. Why is a boat less stable when people stand up?

(c) A netball post on a stand. Why is it more likely to tip over if you climb up it?

(d) A table lamp. Suggest a good material for the base.

5 On which face would you lay a match box to make it as stable as possible? Explain why this position is best.

6 Give two reasons why racing cars are difficult to tip over.

7 What advantage is it to a boxer, to crouch low and stand with his feet apart?

8 Why is a stool easier to tip over than a deck-chair?

9 Why are steps rather easy to tip over sideways?

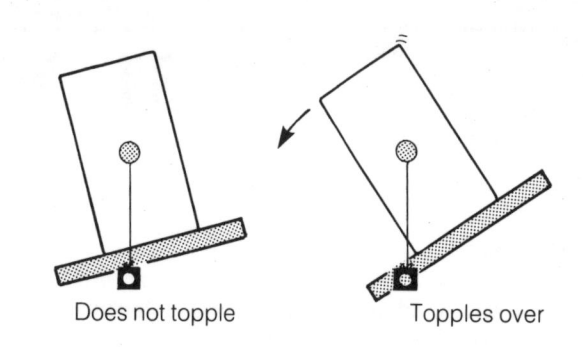

■ A wide base and a low centre of gravity give greater stability.

31 Machines

Levers

The man is trying to lift a **load** using a lever. He has arranged the bar and brick to make the force he has to use (his **effort**) as small as possible. The lever is a simple **machine**.

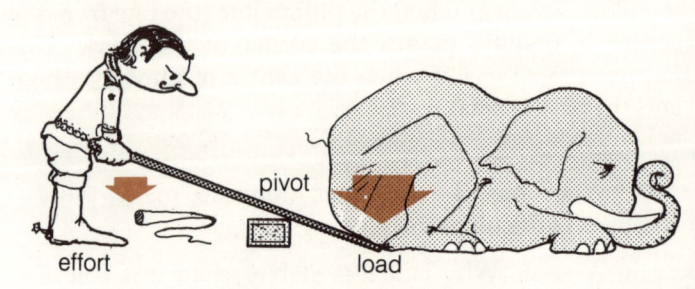

Using a lever to lift a load

Examples of levers

Build these levers and use the same load for each. Use the spring balance to measure the effort needed to just hold up that load. You will find that with two types of lever (1) and (2), the effort is less than the load. With the third type, the effort is greater than the load and a small movement of the effort causes a large movement of the load.

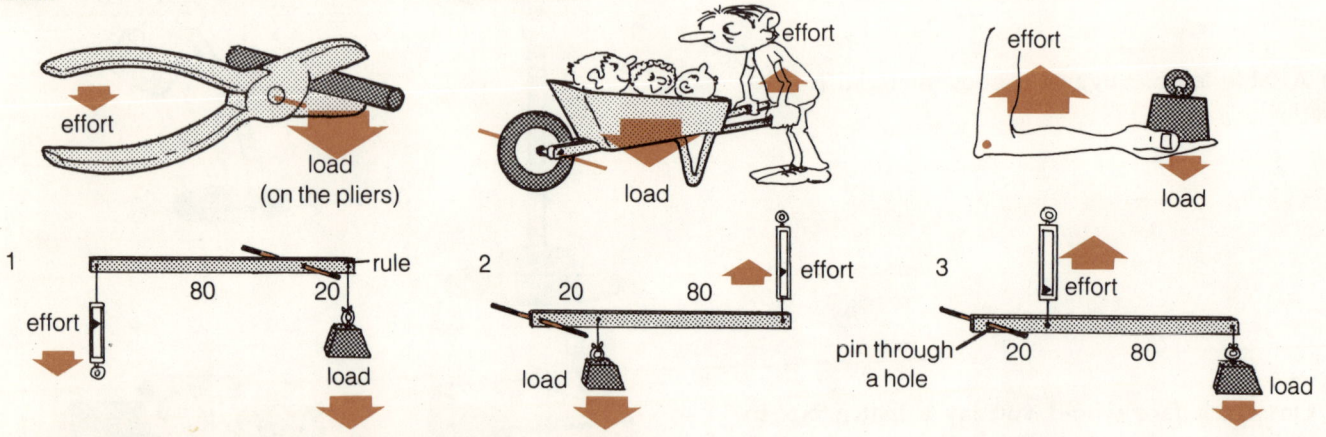

1. Explain why the pliers, the wheelbarrow and the arm are similar to the levers drawn below them.

It is usually an advantage to use a machine. Calculate load/effort for each of the levers in your experiment. This number tells you how many times the effort has been increased by the machine. $\frac{Load}{Effort}$ is called the **mechanical advantage** of the machine.

2. (a) Copy and calculate the mechanical advantage for each lever.

	Lever 1	Lever 2	Lever 3
Load	20 N	20 N	20 N
Effort	5 N	4 N	100 N
Mechanical advantage			

(b) What does it mean if a machine has a mechanical advantage of 1/5?

■ Mechanical advantage = load/effort.

Wheel and axle machines

With this type of machine the effort makes the machine go round. The load that is being lifted or turned is attached to a part of the machine that has a small radius. In this way a small effort can lift a larger load. However you will notice that the effort moves through a greater distance than the load.

The number that tells us how much further the effort moves than the load is called the **velocity ratio**. The velocity ratio of a machine is:

$$\frac{\text{the distance moved by the effort}}{\text{the distance moved by the load}}$$

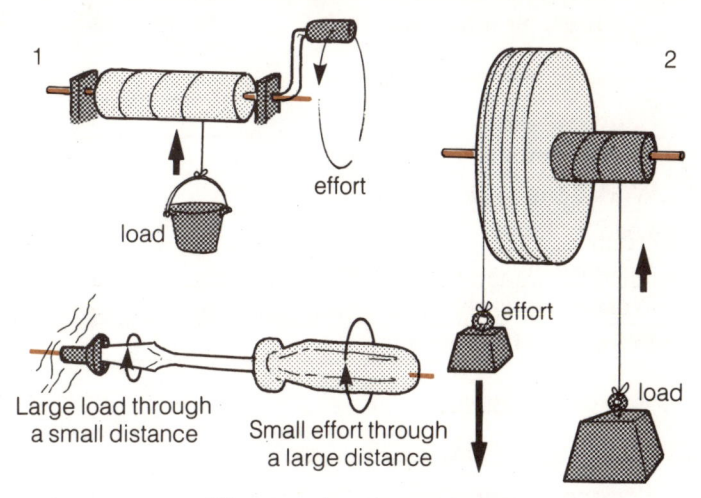

Wheel and axle machines

3   Calculate the velocity ratio and mechanical advantage for each machine.

	Machine 1	Machine 2	Screwdriver
Distance moved by the effort	100 cm	30 cm	10 cm
Distance moved by the load	20 cm	10 cm	0.5 cm
Velocity ratio			
Load	45 N	10 N	90 N
Effort	10 N	4 N	5 N
Mechanical advantage			

The efficiency of machines

Think about the energy changes that take place when the wheel and axle machine lifts the load shown. The effort loses 100 J of gravitational energy as it falls. We know this because it does 100 J of work (work = force × distance; 50 × 2 = 100 J). The load gains 90 J of gravitational energy as it rises. We know this because 90 J of work are done on it (90 × 1 = 90 J). 10 J of energy are wasted and are used to turn the machine against friction.

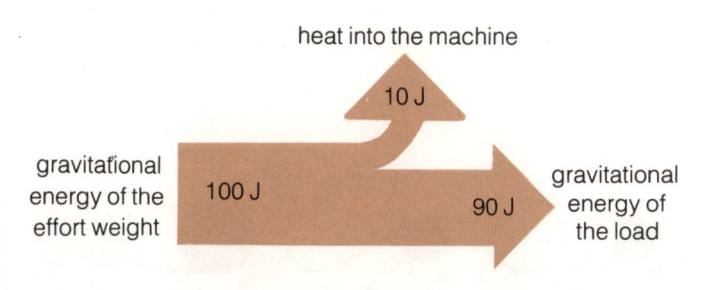

The ratio: energy gained by the load/energy lost by the effort is called the **efficiency** of the machine.

Also   efficiency = $\frac{\text{work done on the load}}{\text{work done by the effort}}$

In this example the efficiency = $\frac{90}{100}$ = 0.9

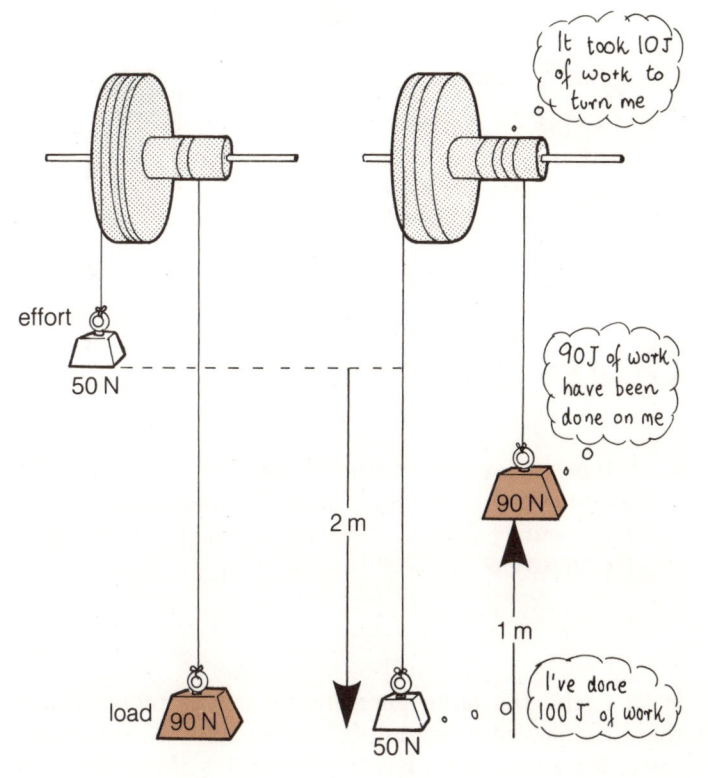

Work being done with a wheel and axle machine

4 This question refers to the same machines as Q1. Copy the table and complete.

	Machine 1	Machine 2	Screwdriver
Effort	10 N	4 N	5 N
Distance moved by the effort	100 cm	30 cm	10 cm
Work done by the effort			
Load	45 N	10 N	90 N
Distance moved by the load	20 cm	10 cm	0.5 cm
Work done on the load			
Efficiency of the machine			

- Velocity ratio = distance moved by the effort/distance moved by the load.
- Efficiency = work done on the load/work done by the effort.

5 These diagrams show different wheel and axle machines connected to the same load. Which of the machines will lift the load as the effort moves down? Which machine uses the smallest effort to lift the load (i.e. has the largest mechanical advantage)?

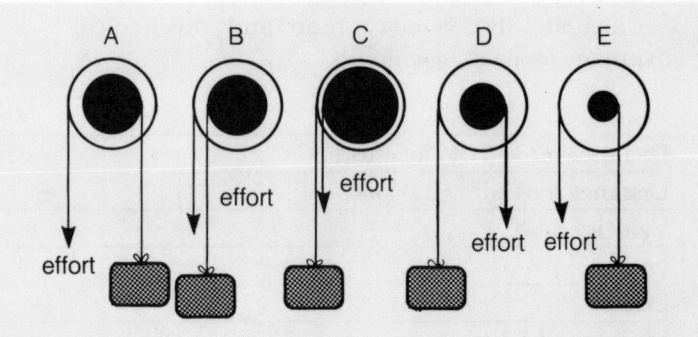

6 Which of these machines are wheel and axle machines?

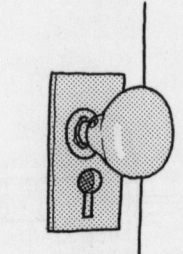

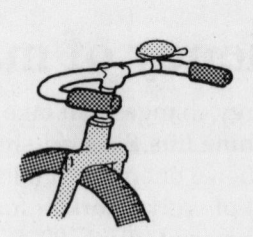

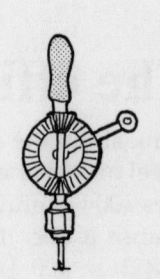

Gears and pulleys

7 In each case say whether the pulley that is being driven (white) goes round faster or slower than the driving pulley (black). Also say whether the white pulley goes clockwise or anticlockwise.

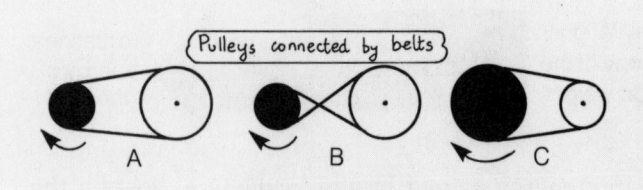

With gears, the large gear always moves more slowly than a small gear driving it, but is able to exert more force. If the small gear has 10 teeth and the large gear has 20 teeth, the large gear will go round half as fast as the small gear but will be able to exert almost twice the force.

8 In each case say whether gear X moves clockwise or anticlockwise.

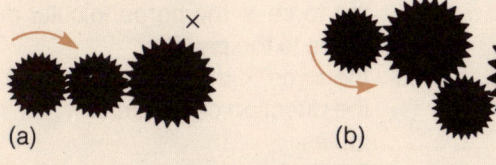

(a)

(b)

Now try this one.

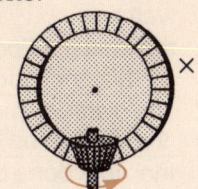

9 This diagram shows a 'two speed' gear box. In which case will the shaft X move slowest, (a) or (b)? This is bottom gear.

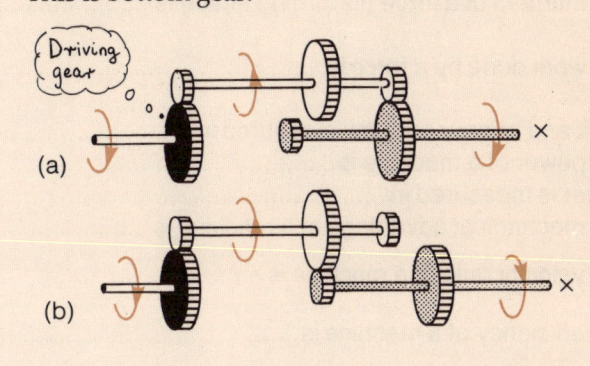

(a)

(b)

Pulleys for lifting

A pulley is useful for lifting things. It is easier to pull down than to pull up and you can use your weight to help you. Less effort is needed to lift a load if you use two pulleys like this. As rope is pulled from the top pulley wheel, the load and the bottom pulley wheel are lifted. If two metres of rope are pulled out the load will only go up 1 metre. (There are two ropes holding the bottom wheel and they both have to shorten.) This pulley has a velocity ratio of 2.

Experiment

Build these pulley machines and put the same load on each. Use a spring balance to measure the effort needed by each machine to lift this load. Which machine needs the least effort to lift the load? Work out the mechanical advantage of each machine from your results.

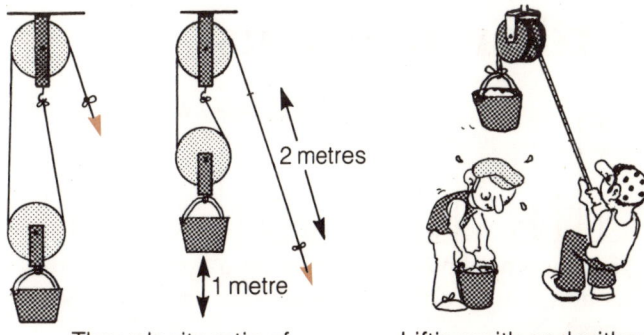

The velocity ratio of a pulley system

Lifting with and without a pulley

(a) (b) (c)

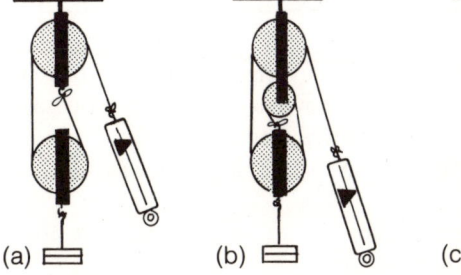

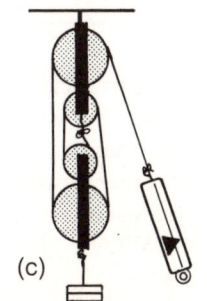

Two, three and four wheel pulley systems

10 What is the velocity ratio of each of the pulley machines pictured above? (Velocity ratio for a pulley = the number of ropes holding up the bottom wheels. Do not count the rope that goes to the spring balance.)

11 Copy and complete

	Pulley (a)	Pulley (b)	Pulley (c)
Load	24 N	24 N	24 N
Distance that the load is lifted	1 m	1 m	1 m
Effort	16 N	12 N	8 N
Distance that the effort has to move			
Mechanical advantage			
Efficiency			

12 Copy these pulley wheels and draw in the string. What is the velocity ratio of this machine?

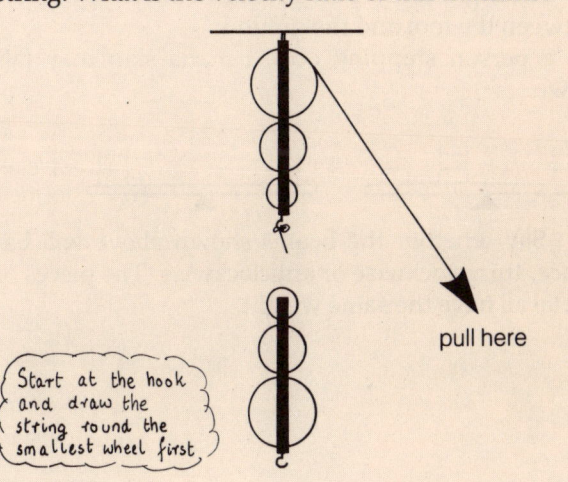

pull here

Start at the hook and draw the string round the smallest wheel first

Summary of force, work and machines

- The moment of a force (its turning effect) is .... the force × the perpendicular distance to the pivot.
- The work done by a force is .... the force × the distance moved in the direction of the force.
- Work and energy are both measured in .... joules.
- The power of a machine is .... the work it can do per second.
- Power is measured in .... watts.
- The mechanical advantage of a machine is .... the load ÷ effort.
- The velocity ratio of a machine is .... $\dfrac{\text{the distance moved by the effort}}{\text{the distance moved by the load}}$
- The efficiency of a machine is .... $\dfrac{\text{the work done on the load}}{\text{the work done by the effort}}$
- The place where the weight of an object seems to act is called its .... centre of gravity.

Further questions

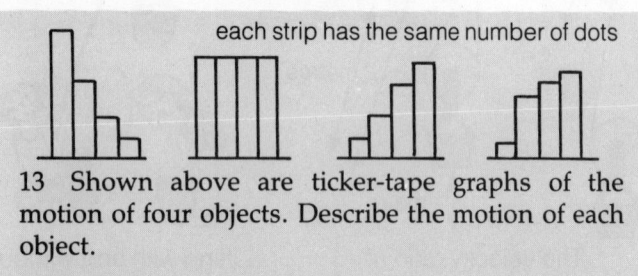

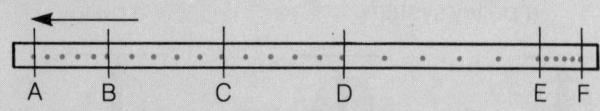

13 Shown above are ticker-tape graphs of the motion of four objects. Describe the motion of each object.

14 The ticker-tape above was obtained from a trolley that was running down a slope. The tape has been marked at equal time intervals.
(a) Over which section is the average speed the greatest?
(b) Which section shows an acceleration of the trolley?
(c) Which section shows a deceleration of the trolley?

15 With the aid of a simple diagram explain why:
(a) walking is only possible when there is friction between the foot and the ground;
(b) a person stepping on a banana skin may fall down.

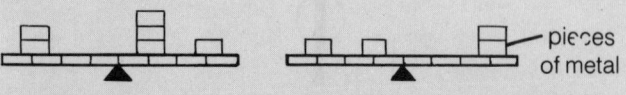

16 Say whether the beams shown above will balance, turn clockwise or anticlockwise. The pieces of metal all have the same weight.

17 Explain the following:
(a) a door handle is placed well away from the hinge.
(b) it is hard to steer a bicycle by gripping the handlebars near the centre.
(c) a mechanic would choose a long spanner to undo a tight nut.

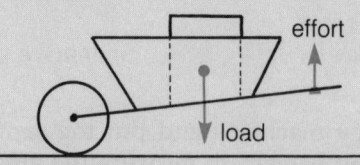

18 The diagram shows a load being lifted in a wheelbarrow by an effort.
(a) Will the effort be greater than the load? Give a reason for your answer.
(b) Where is the pivot of a wheelbarrow?
(c) State two ways of reducing the effort needed to lift the same load.
(d) The man does work lifting the handles. What form of energy does the load gain?

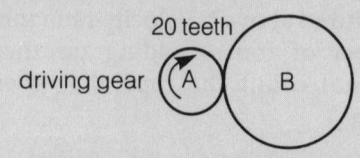

19 (a) If gear B is to be driven at half the speed of A, how many teeth should it have?
(b) Will B turn clockwise or anticlockwise?
(c) Copy the diagram and draw in a third wheel C which will rotate in the same direction as A but faster than A or B.

32 Pressure

You cannot push your thumb into a table but with the same force you can push a drawing pin into the wood. To explain how the same force can have such different effects we must consider the area on which the force presses. When the area is small, the force makes a large dent in soft substances. The force produces a large pressure if the area is small. Pressure is the force that acts on 1 cm² and is calculated by dividing force by area.

Pressure = force/area.

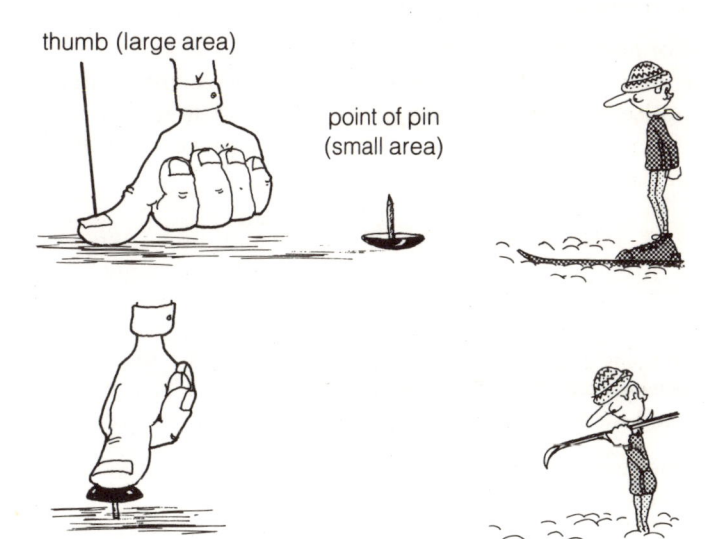

1 Copy the table and for each object say whether it has a 'large' or 'small' contact area and whether the pressure under it is 'large' or 'small' when it is being used.

Object	Area	Pressure
Nail		
Ice skates		
Hippo's feet		
Knife edge		
Caterpillar tracks		

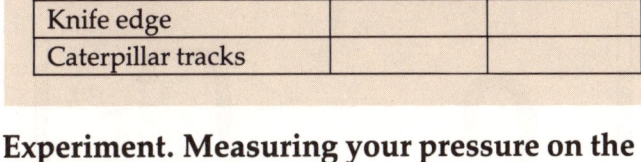

Experiment. Measuring your pressure on the ground

Find your weight (in newtons) from a balance or scales. Draw round your feet on squared paper. Find the area you stand on by counting the squares inside the outline of your shoes. Calculate your pressure on the floor (weight ÷ area).

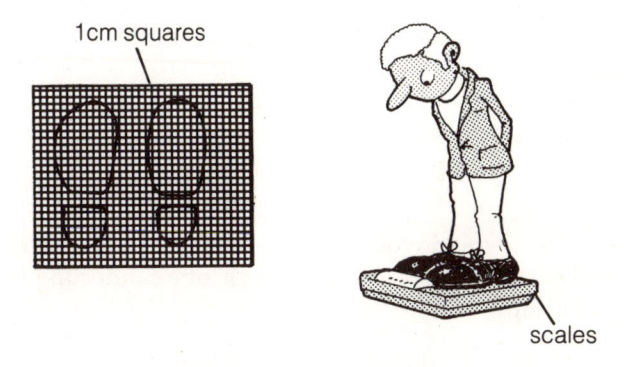

Example
A boy weights 500 N and the area of both his shoes came to 250 cm². His pressure on the floor = $\frac{500}{250}$ = 2 N/cm².

Sometimes the area used is 1 m². As there are 100 × 100 centimetre squares in a 1 metre square, the above pressure is 2 × 100 × 100 N/m² = 20 000 N/m² = 20 kN/m².

Measuring your pressure

2 Which of these people would probably cause the greatest pressure on the ground:
(a) a fat man with big feet
(b) a fat man with small feet
(c) a thin girl with big feet
(d) a thin girl with small feet.

3 Copy and complete this table.

Force	Area	Pressure
200 kN	2 m²	
50 kN		10 kN/m²
	4 m²	8 kN/m²

4 A person pushes his thumb onto a table with a force of 12 N. His thumb has a contact area with the table of 4 cm². He then pushes with the same force on a drawing pin that has a contact area of 1 mm² (= 1/100 cm²). Calculate the pressure exerted on the surface (a) by his thumb, (b) by the drawing pin.

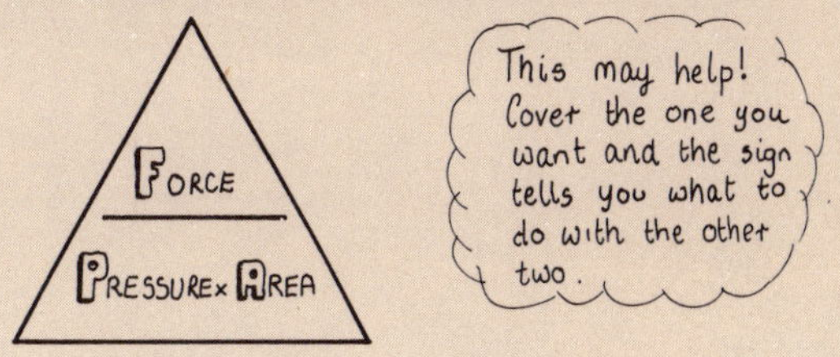

This may help! Cover the one you want and the sign tells you what to do with the other two.

$$\frac{\text{Force}}{\text{Pressure} \times \text{Area}}$$

■ pressure = force/area.

Manometers

Experiment

Can you lift 50 N by blowing? Fit a tube to a plastic bag and place the 50 N weight on a board on this bag. Blow in the tube until the pressure is enough to lift the weight. You will find it is quite easy.

Connect another tube from the bag to a glass U-tube containing a little mercury. Blow up the weight again and notice how the mercury levels change. The difference in the mercury levels is a measure of the pressure of the air in the bag.

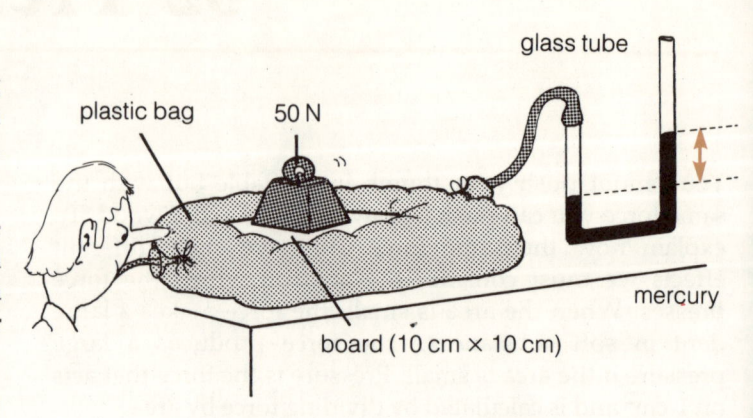

> 5 If the board in this experiment measures 10 cm × 10 cm, what is the pressure on the air in the bag?

A glass U-tube containing liquid and used to measure pressure is called a **manometer**. Mercury is the liquid used for high pressures and water for low pressures.

The pressure is measured as the distance between the levels in centimetres or metres.

Experiment. Using manometers

(a) Use a small water manometer to measure the pressure of the 'gas'.
(b) Use a manometer with unequal arms (e.g. a bottle and a tube) to measure the same gas pressure. Do you get the same difference in water levels? It does not matter if a manometer has unequal arms, the difference in levels is the same.
(c) Use a large water manometer to measure your lung pressure. (Do not blow too hard.)

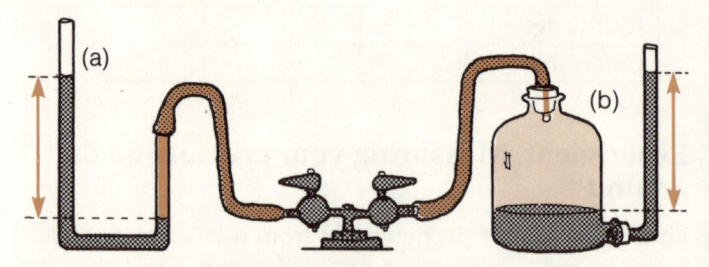

> 6 How would you use manometer (a) to tell if there was a gas leak in the rubber tube connecting it to the tap?
>
> 7 What will happen when the gas tap is turned on, if the gas pressure is 5 cm of water?

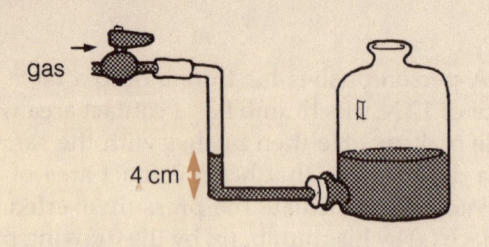

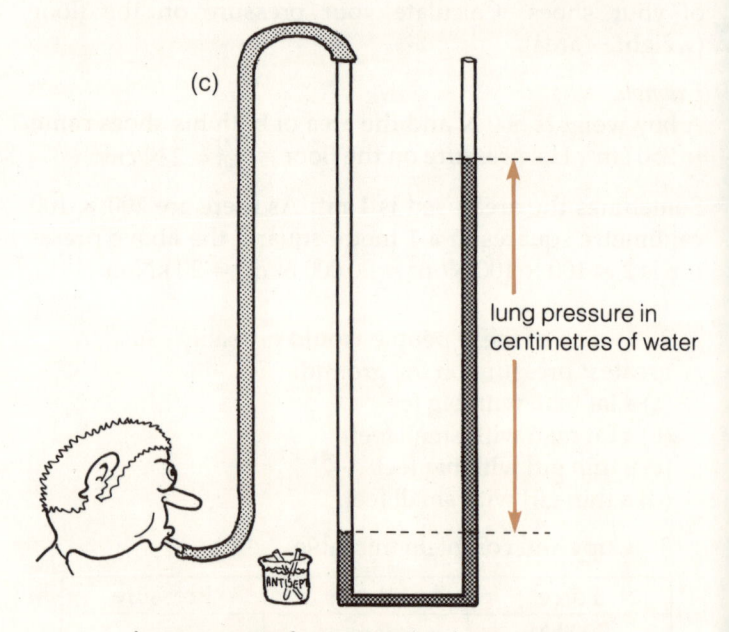

■ Manometers measure pressure in centimetres of liquids (e.g. water or mercury). The difference in levels does not depend on the width of the tube.

The pressure of the atmosphere

Experiment. Does the air around us exert a pressure on us?

Take an old metal can and fit it with a cork and tube. Connect the tube to a vacuum pump and remove the air from inside the can. You will see the can crumple under the great pressure of the outside air. Normally the air pressure inside balances the air pressure outside but by removing the air inside we see what the outside pressure can do.

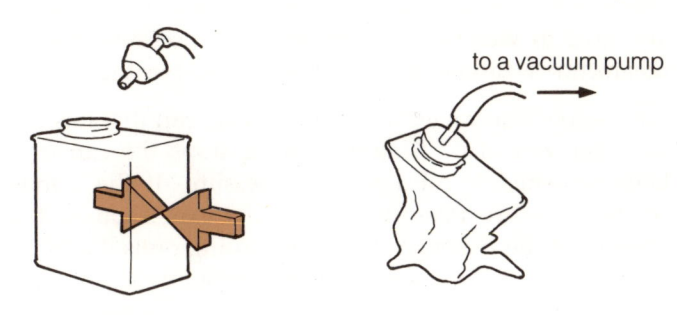

The crushing effect of air pressure

Experiment. How great is the pressure of the air around us?

Take a large mercury manometer and remove the air from one side by connecting it to a vacuum pump. You will see that the air on the other side has enough pressure to make the mercury rise about 76 cm (= 100 kN/m^2). This is a considerable pressure and is the pressure of the atmosphere.

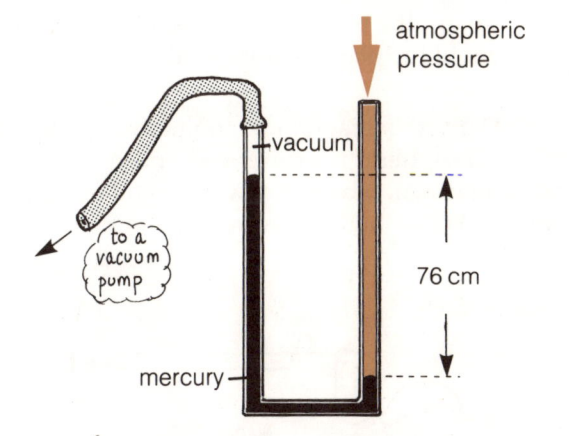

Measuring atmospheric pressure

Experiment. More evidence of the atmosphere's great pressure

Fit two metal hemispheres together and remove the air from the space inside. You will find it extremely difficult to pull the two halves apart unless you let the air back inside. It cannot be the vacuum that is 'sucking' the two halves together – a vacuum means nothing is there. It must be the pressure of the atmosphere outside that presses the two halves so tightly together.

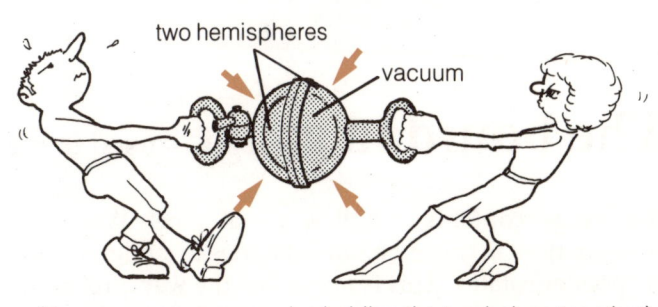

(there are no screws or glue holding the two halves together)

Pulling against atmospheric pressure

8 How does this experiment show that atmospheric pressure acts upwards and sideways as well as downwards?

9 Explain why liquid fills a syringe when the plunger is pulled out and the end is under the liquid.

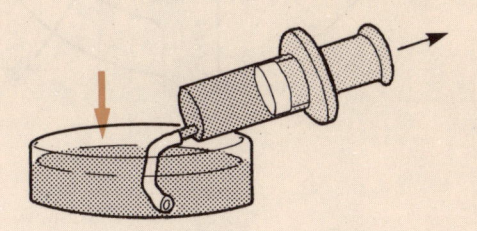

10 When you suck up liquid with a straw, it is atmospheric pressure that pushes liquid up the straw. Why is it impossible to suck liquids from the bottle on the right?

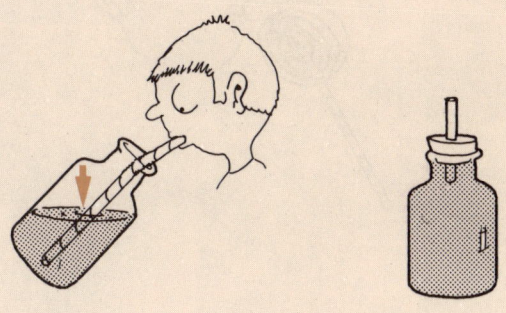

Aneroid barometer

A barometer measures atmospheric pressure. As atmospheric pressure changes with the weather, barometers are used in weather forecasting. High pressure usually means fine weather and low pressure bad weather.

An aneroid barometer uses a thin metal can that has had air taken out of it. A strong spring stops the can from being crushed by atmospheric pressure. If the atmospheric pressure rises, the lid of the can is pushed in slightly. If the pressure drops, the spring pulls the lid up a little. The small movement is magnified by a pointer or gears.

This sort of barometer can be fitted into an aeroplane and flown to high altitudes. Since atmospheric pressure drops as you go up, the barometer reading can be used to show the height of the plane. It is then called an altimeter.

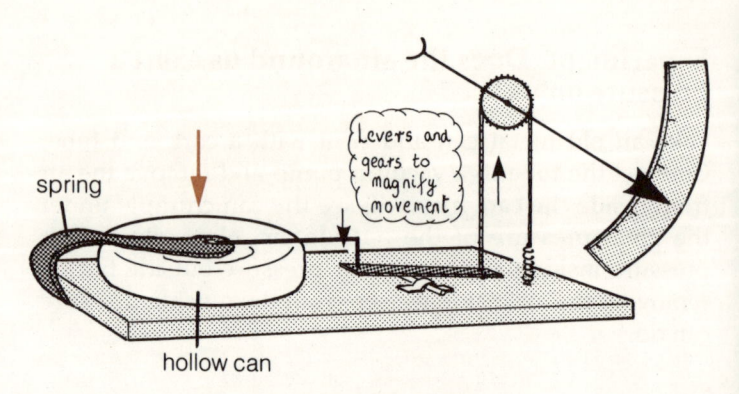

An aneroid barometer

11 Draw this diagram of an aneroid barometer. If the atmospheric pressure rises, pushing the lid of the can down, which way will the end of the pointer move? Write 'high pressure' and 'low pressure' on the scale.

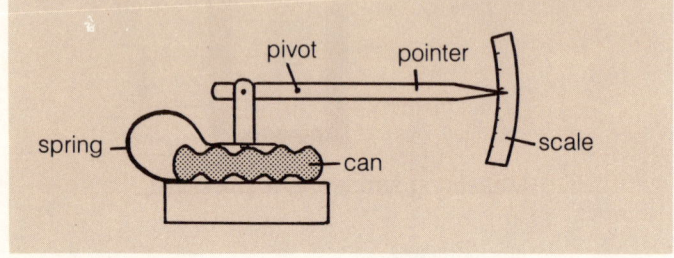

The bourdon gauge – used to measure gas pressure

The gauge contains a hollow metal tube. When the pressure rises in this tube, the tube tries to straighten and the pointer rotates. This is rather like the way a rolled up paper tube, containing a spring, straightens when you blow into it.

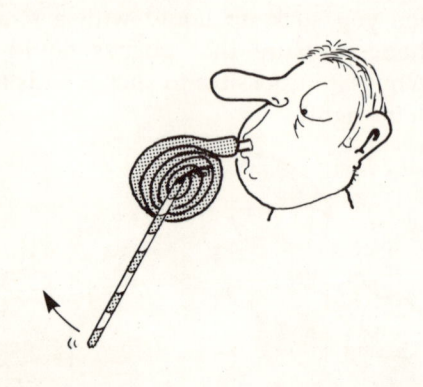

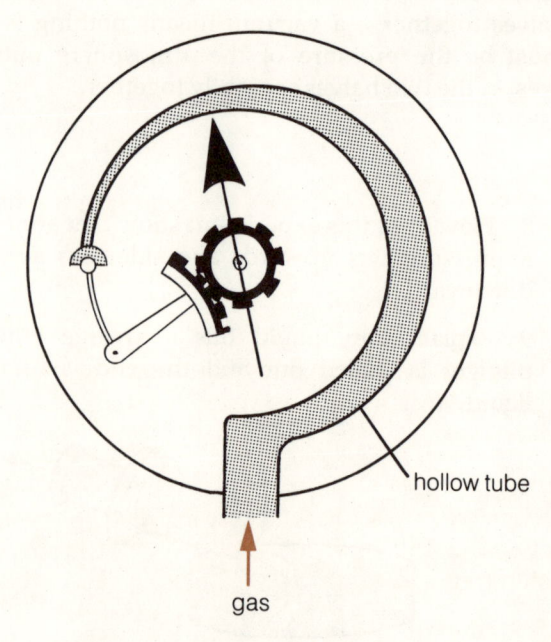

A Bourdon pressure gauge

Air pumps

We find it very useful to compress air and so increase its pressure.

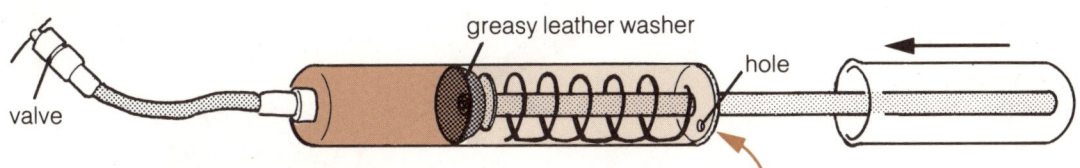

A cycle pump

Experiment with a cycle pump

Find the volume of air pushed out by a bicycle pump in one stroke. Do the same with a car foot pump if you have one. Find also the volume of air you breath out in one breath. Is this more or less than the volumes from the pumps?

12   This question is about the way these pumps work. They contain a strong flexible washer that plays an important part in compressing the air. The table describes what happens inside the pump as the handle is pushed in and pulled out. Copy it and put 'in' or 'out' instead of the question marks.

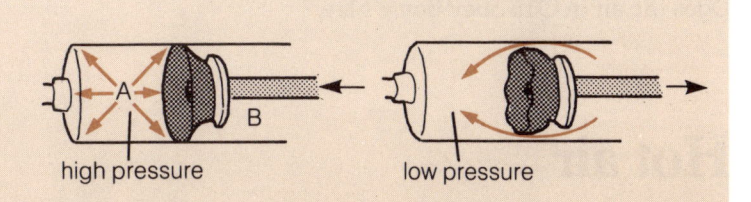

Pump handle moving ?	Pump handle moving ?
Air in A is compressed and forced out.	A partial vacuum forms in A.
The washer is pressed hard against the barrel of the pump.	Air squeezes past the edge of the washer from B to A.
Outside air goes through the hole into B.	

13   Why is the valve necessary? What would happen if it was not there?

14   How can you alter this pump to make it suck instead of blow?

Compressed air

Try squeezing the air in a bicycle pump. Notice how springy it is. Note how increasing the pressure forces the air into a smaller volume.

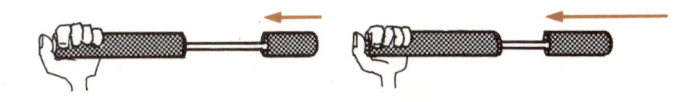

Experiment. How does the volume of some trapped air change as the pressure on it is increased?

Use this or similar apparatus to get readings of the volume of the air and the pressure on it. Notice how it gets more and more difficult to compress the air as its volume gets less.

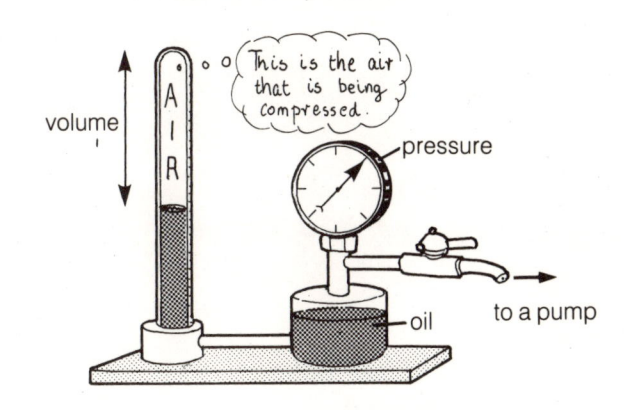

143

15 These readings are from such an experiment:

Pressure	1	2	3	4	5
Volume	1	½	⅓	¼	⅕
Pressure × volume					

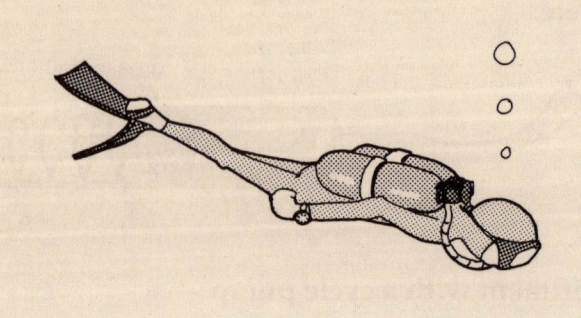

(a) Copy and complete. 'As the pressure increases, the volume ____.
(b) Work out pressure × volume for each reading. Copy the table and put your answers in the spaces.
(c) Plot a graph of pressure against volume.

Experiments have shown that for many gases:
the pressure of the gas × its volume = the same (constant) number . . .
. . . provided its temperature does not change. This law was discovered by Robert Boyle and is called Boyle's law. Does the air in Q15 obey Boyle's law?

Hot air

If the air in a tin is heated and it cannot expand, what will happen to it. The volume of the gas cannot change but what happens to its pressure?

Experiment. Heating and cooling air

Warm some air in a strong flask and then push in a bung fitted with a pressure gauge and thermometer. Allow the air to cool and measure the pressure and temperature as they drop.

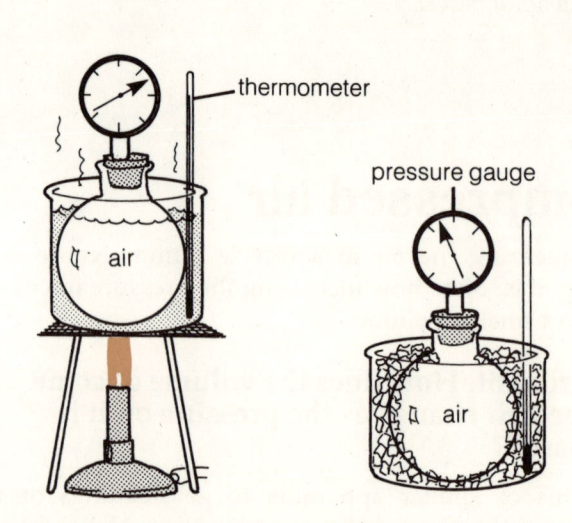

16 Here are some readings from such an experiment.

Pressure (kN/m²)	128	121	114	107	100	93	89
Temperature (°C)	100	80	60	40	20	0	−10

(a) Copy and complete. 'The pressure of a gas _____ as its temperature rises.'

(b) Plot these readings on a pressure/temperature graph. Use axes like those shown so that you can continue the line backwards. From the graph find out how cold you must make the gas to lower its pressure to zero*.

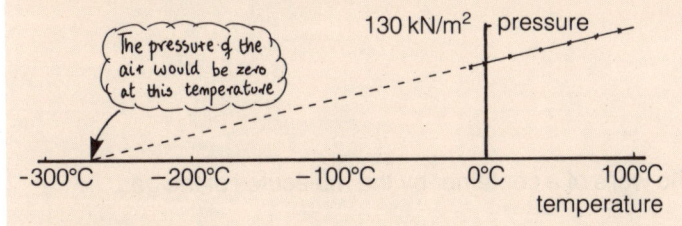

(c) What is likely to happen before the gas reaches this temperature?
(What happens to steam – which is a gas – when you cool it?)

17 One way of getting dents out of ping-pong balls is to put them in boiling water. Explain why the dents get pushed out.

*The temperature (in theory) is −273°C (273°C below zero). This is as cold as anything can be and is called the **absolute zero of temperature**.

Sometimes temperatures are measured on a scale that starts at the absolute zero. This is called the **Kelvin scale**. The ice point (0°C) would be 273 K on this scale; the steam point (100°C) would be 373 K. Temperatures on the Celsius scale can be converted to the Kelvin scale by adding 273.

■ The pressure of a gas can be raised by compressing it or heating it.

Gas pressure and the kinetic theory

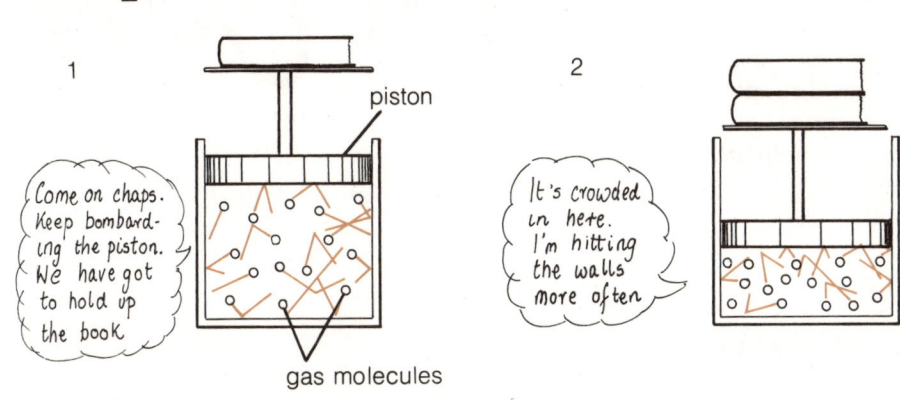

1. The molecules of a gas move quickly and there are millions of molecules present. So there is an enormous number of tiny collisions between the molecules and the container each second. This constant bombardment of the walls is why a gas exerts a pressure on the walls.

2. If the gas is compressed, the molecules have less volume to move in. They collide more often with the walls and the pressure of the gas rises.

3. If the gas is heated, the molecules move more quickly. So they collide more often with the walls and the pressure of the gas increases.

18 Copy the table and insert 'no change' or 'increases' into the boxes.

	Reducing the volume of the gas	Increasing the temperature of the gas
What happens to the speed of the molecules?		
What happens to the number of collisions per second?		
What happens to the pressure of the gas?		

If the gas is cooled down, the molecules slow down. At the absolute zero of temperature (p. 145), the molecules would have lost all their energy and the pressure of the gas would be zero.

■ Gas pressure is caused by the continuous bombardment of the walls of a container by the molecules of the gas.

Pressure through liquids

Draw some water into a bicycle pump and try to compress it. Is it springy like air? Can you squash water into a smaller volume?

Experiment. Liquids transmit pressure

Connect two syringes together as shown. If you push in both of the plungers you feel that the water is 'rigid' and not squashy. The pressure from one piston goes through the water and acts on the piston of the other syringe. You will notice that one piston needs more force to hold it than the other. Which one is this?

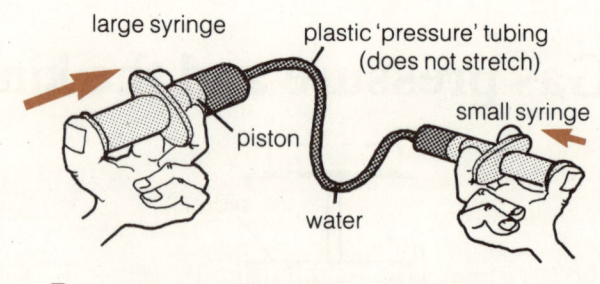

Transmitting pressure through a liquid

A simple hydraulic machine

Although the pressure is the same on both pistons, more force acts on the large piston than on the small one. A hydraulic press uses this idea to increase force. Two cylinders of different sizes are connected by a pipe full of liquid. A load is put on the large piston and the effort is pressed on the small piston. You will find that a small weight can lift a large weight with this machine.

Why does it work?

Pressure produced by the effort passes through the liquid to the load's piston. This piston has a large area and so the pressure presses on a large area. This produces a large force. If the load piston has 4 times the area of the effort piston, the force on it will be 4 times more.

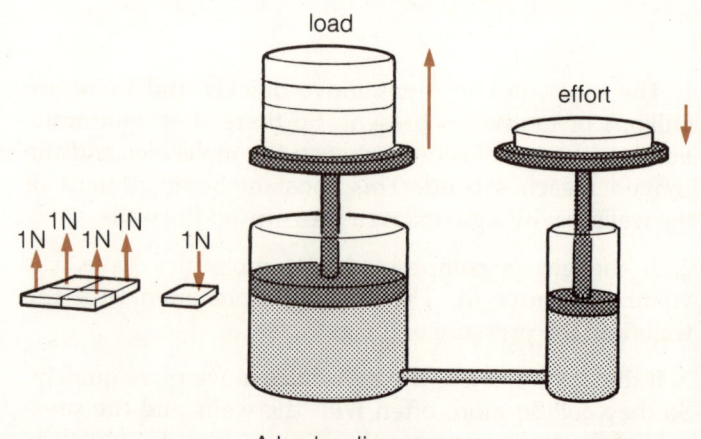

A hydraulic press

19 Copy this table and write large, small or same in the gaps.

	Effort	Load
Size of force		
Area of piston		
Pressure on piston		

20 If the effort's piston moves down, the load's piston moves up but not as far. Why does the large piston move less than the small piston?

21 This picture shows how all the brakes of a car are connected by pipes to a 'master' cylinder. The pipes and cylinders are full of light oil. When you press the foot brake, pressure passes through the oil to the brake cylinders. Pistons inside move, putting on all the brakes of the car together.
(a) Would the front brakes still work if the pipe got blocked at X?
(b) What difference would it make to the movement of a piston if one of the cylinders had air in it instead of oil (an air-lock)?
(c) The brake cylinders are larger than the master cylinder. Why is this an advantage to the driver?

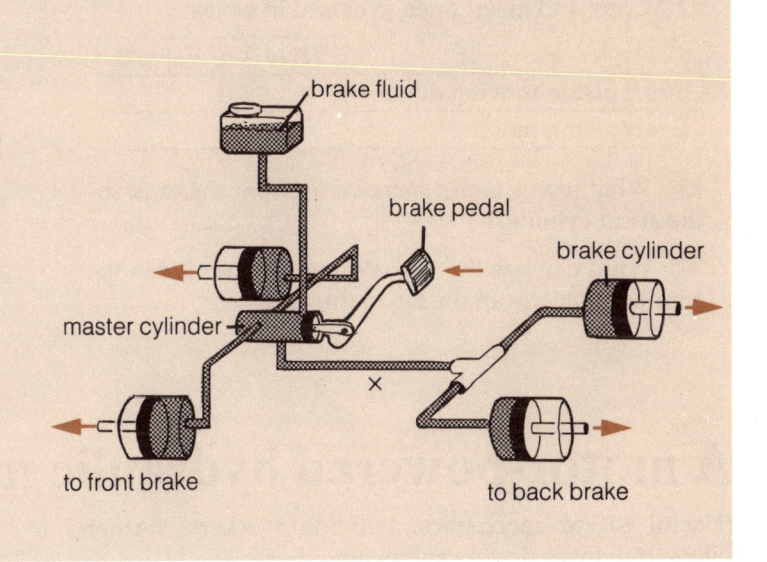

Car brakes

Car drum brakes have two curved brake shoes placed just inside the rotating wheel drum. These shoes can be moved outwards at the bottom by the piston in the brake cylinder. When the foot pedal is pushed, pressure passes through the liquid and moves that piston so that the brake shoes move onto the wheel drum. Friction then stops the wheel from going round. Note that water is not used as the liquid in hydraulic machines because it evaporates rather easily and can contain dissolved air. This air may form air bubbles or dangerous air-locks in the pipes.

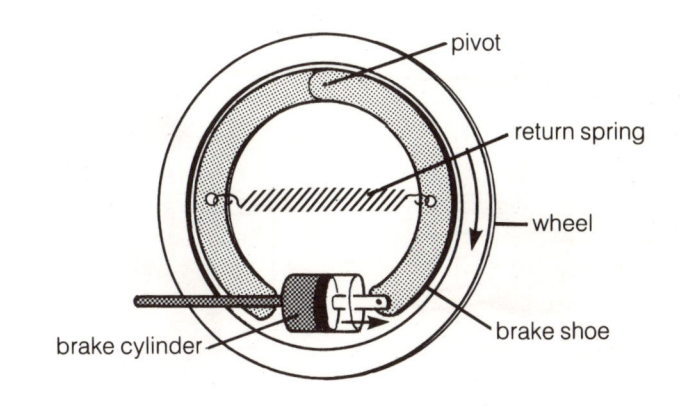

Disc brakes

To make a more effective brake, a thick disc of metal is bolted to the wheel. As the wheel goes round, this disc rotates between two brake pads. When the brake pedal is pushed, these pads are forced onto the disc from each side. Friction then acts on the disc in the opposite direction to its motion and stops the wheel. The pads can be made to pinch the disc with great force because they are connected to the pedal by a hydraulic system. The large surface area of the disc helps to keep the brakes cool by removing heat from the friction pads.

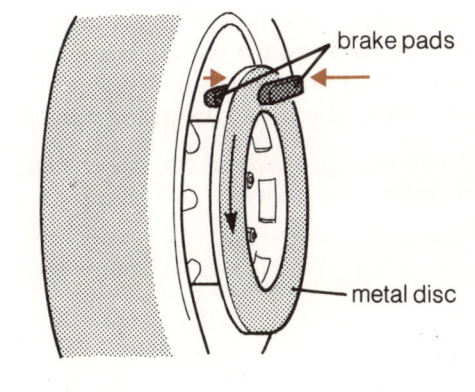

■ Liquids cannot be compressed and so they transmit pressure.

Other hydraulic machines

This (man-powered) hydraulic jack has two valves. When the effort piston moves down it forces liquid into the load cylinder. When the effort piston moves up, liquid refills the effort cylinder. This movement can then be repeated. The load is lifted in stages through a large distance.

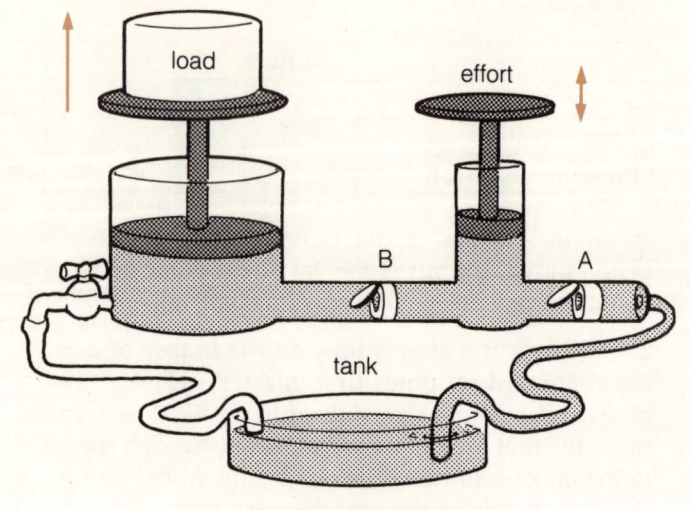

22 Copy and insert open or closed in boxes.

	Valve A	Valve B
Effort piston moving down		
Effort piston moving up		

23 What forces liquid to move up from the tank to the effort cylinder?

24 What use has the tap? Why is it a good idea to connect a pipe from the tap to the tank?

A hydraulic jack

A motor-powered hydraulic machine

(Useful to car mechanics, building workers, farmers, pilots, bulldozer drivers and many others)

A pump drives oil round a circuit ABCD. A control valve can then send liquid into either end of the working cylinder. The operator can thus move the piston in this cylinder to the right or left with immediate control and great force.

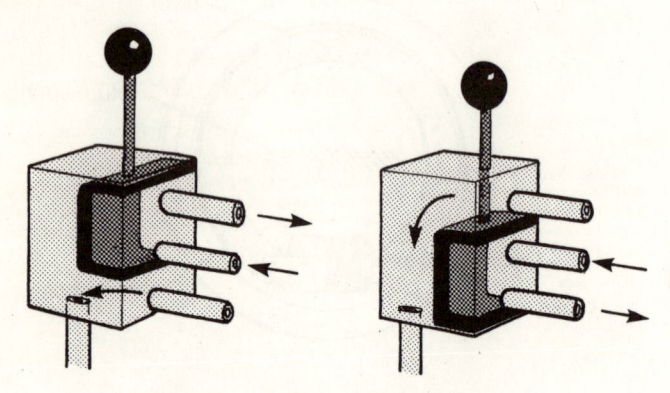

How the control valve works

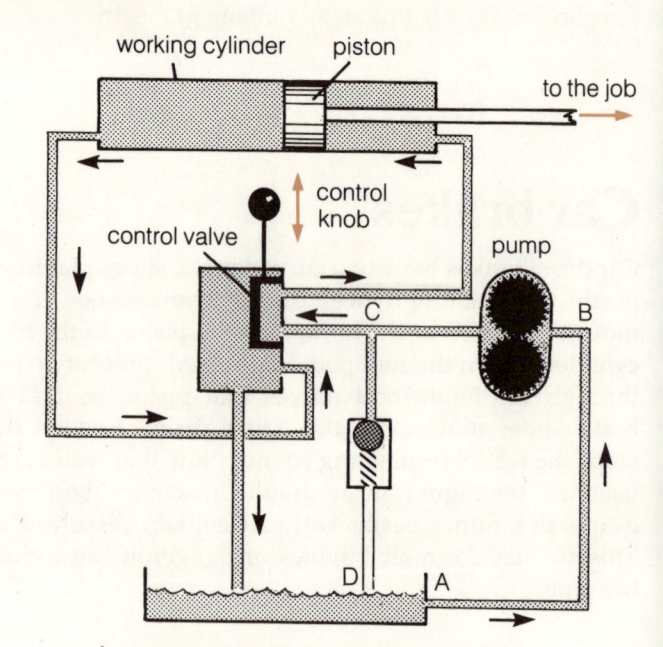

A motor powered hydraulic machine

25 Draw the simple picture of this machine with the control valve covering the bottom two pipes as shown. Draw arrows to show the flow of liquid into the cylinder. Which way would the piston move?

26 What two differences would it make if a larger working cylinder were used? (The pump is not changed.)

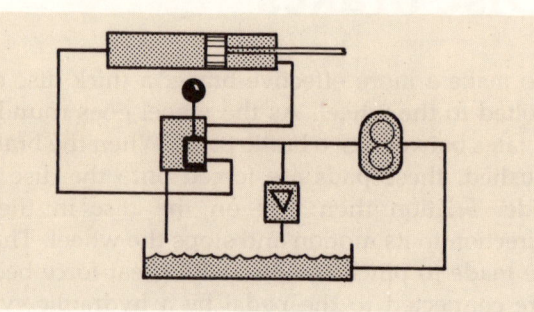

Summary of pressure

- Pressure is .... the force per square metre.
- The unit used to measure pressure is .... N/m^2.
- A glass U-tube that contains liquid and is used to measure pressure is called .... a manometer.
- The pressure of 'the air' is called... atmospheric pressure.
- An instrument that is used to measure atmospheric pressure is called .... a barometer.
- Boyle's law states that, for a fixed mass of gas at a constant temperature .... the pressure × the volume is constant.
- If a gas is heated but not allowed to expand, its pressure will .... increase.
- The lowest temperature possible (−273°C) is called... the absolute zero of temperature.

Further questions

27 (a) Make a list of the apparatus you would need to find how the pressure of a gas changes when it is heated or cooled.
(b) Draw a sketch of the apparatus properly assembled for the experiment.
(c) Describe how you would take readings of the temperature and pressure of the gas.

28 A gas is enclosed in a gas-tight cylinder by a piston. If the piston is fixed and the gas is heated what happens:
(a) to the pressure of the gas,
(b) to the molecules of the gas,
(c) if the piston is released and the gas is cooled?

29 A car weighs 12 kN and is equally supported on its four wheels.
(a) Calculate the load carried by each wheel.
(b) Calculate the area of each tyre in contact with the road if the pressure in the tyres is 150 kN/m^2.
(c) What is likely to happen to the pressure of the air in the tyres if the car goes on a long journey? Assume the tyres do not leak.

30 Explain how each of the following makes use of atmospheric pressure:
(a) an altimeter,
(b) a vacuum cleaner,
(c) a drinking straw,
(d) a syringe.

31 Explain the following:
(a) it hurts to hold a heavy parcel by the string,
(b) it is more comfortable to sit on a chair than on a fence,
(c) heavy lorries may have eight rear wheels,
(d) it is less painful to lie on a beach of pebbles than to stand on it.

32 In a hydraulic brake system, a force of 5000 N is applied to a piston of area 5 cm^2. (a) Calculate the pressure transmitted through the brake fluid. (b) Calculate the force on a piston of area 20 cm^2 connected to the system.

Electricity

33 Electric circuits

What do the things in the pictures have in common? They all need electrical energy to work them and they all use 'dry cells' to provide that energy. One common type of dry cell is illustrated here. It has two terminals. The cap at the top is the positive terminal and the case at the bottom is the negative terminal.

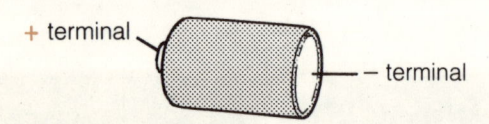

Experiment. Building an electric circuit

Take a dry cell, a lamp and two pieces of copper wire. Connect them together so that the lamp lights.

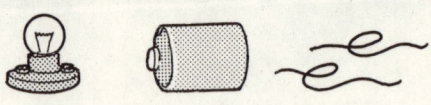

Build these parts into a circuit

1 Which of these arrangements would make the lamp light?

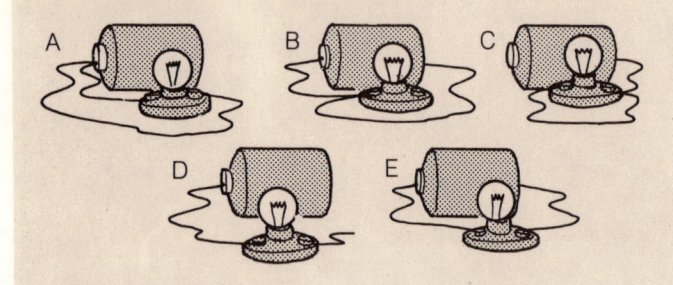

2 A student connected the lamp and cell as shown. The wires were connected properly but the lamp did not light. What could be wrong? (Two possibilities)

The experiment above shows that for the lamp to light: (a) the cell must have energy, (b) there must be a closed metal path between the terminals of the cell. This is called a circuit. An electric current will flow round any circuit that connects the terminals of a cell.

Circuit symbols

To make drawing circuits easier symbols are used for the lamp and the cell.

Circuit symbols for a cell and lamp

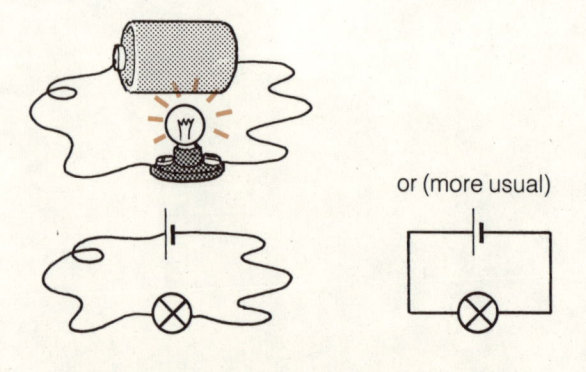

Drawing a circuit using circuit symbols

or (more usual)

■ A source of electrical energy and a closed circuit are needed before an electric current can flow.

Experiment. Circuits with more than one cell

Connect a lamp in a circuit with two dry cells. What difference does the extra cell make to the lamp? The two cells, properly connected, drive a larger current through the lamp. Cells in line like this are said to be in **series**.

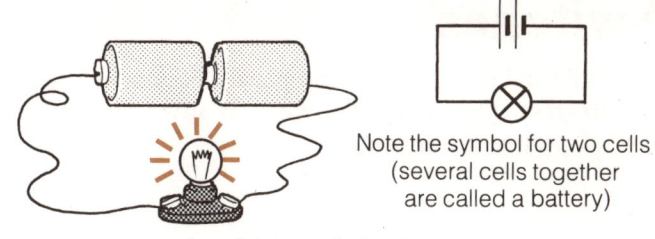

Note the symbol for two cells (several cells together are called a battery)

A two-cell circuit

3 In which circuit would the lamp be (a) brightest, (b) out.

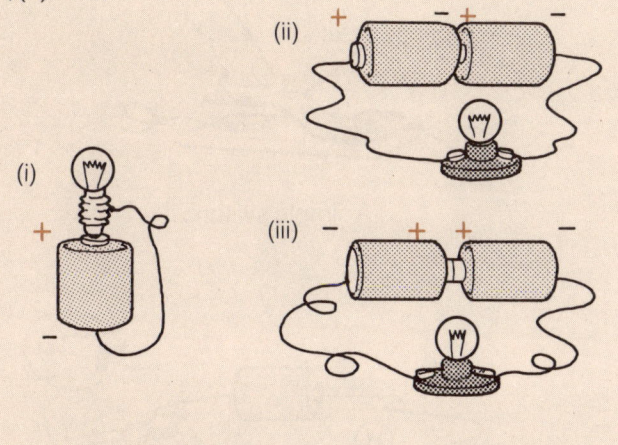

5 In which of these devices have the cells been put in wrongly?

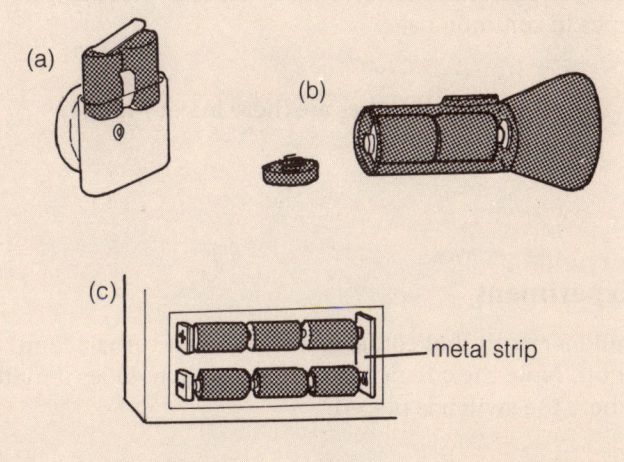

4 Should cells be connected + to − or + to +?

Experiment. Looking into batteries

Collect some of the different sorts of battery you use. A battery is made of two or more cells so open them up and find out how many cells there are inside. You will find there is a connection between the number of cells and the voltage of the battery.

Batteries and cells like these can only provide small electric currents and have to be thrown away when they are dead. For the larger currents needed by such things as cars and electric milk floats, batteries containing liquids are used. Lead/acid batteries are examples of these (p. 164). This sort of battery is expensive but can be recharged and used again and again.

6 Give two reasons why lead/acid cells are not used in torches.

A selection of batteries

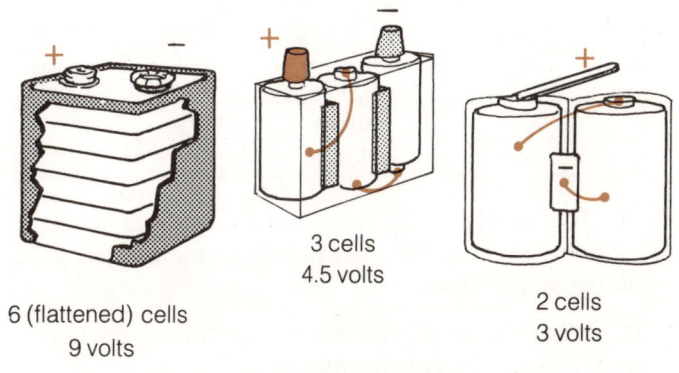

6 (flattened) cells
9 volts

3 cells
4.5 volts

2 cells
3 volts

The cells inside batteries

■ Cells are usually connected + to − to make a battery.
■ The more cells there are, the higher the voltage of this battery.

153

Switches

A circuit can be broken in many places. Four are shown in the diagram. Disconnect the wires at any point and the flow of electric current stops.

A switch is a more convenient way of breaking a circuit. Most electric circuits have a switch and there are many types in common use.

7 How many switches are there in your home?

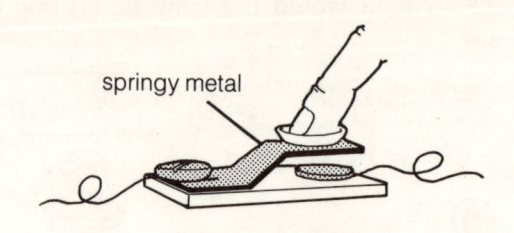

A simple switch

Experiment

Build a circuit that contains a switch that turns a lamp on or off. Note the circuit symbol for a switch. Does it matter where the switch is placed?

8 Draw the circuit A but with the switch in a different position and still able to operate the lamp.

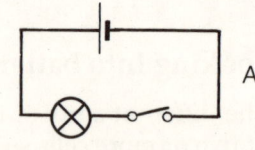

A circuit with a switch

Experiment

Connect up these circuits with two switches. They all have practical uses:
(a) A safety circuit.

9 Copy and insert on or off for the lamp.

Switch A	Switch B	Lamp
open	closed	
closed	open	
closed	closed	

10 Two switches like those in this circuit are used for safety reasons. Why is this arrangement easier to switch off than on?

11 What happens to the filament of the lamp when electric current flows through it?

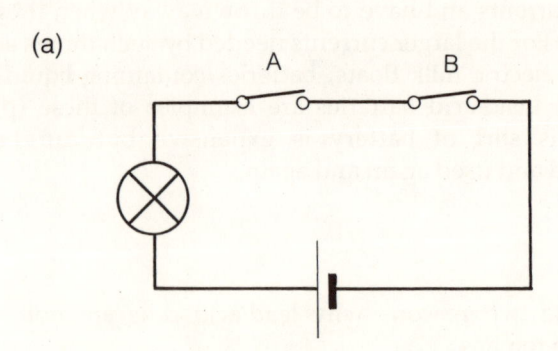

A circuit that is easier to switch off than to switch on

■ A break anywhere in a circuit will stop the current.

(b) Front door/back door.
The lamp in this circuit can be switched on and off from two different places.

> 12 Copy and put on or off for the lamp.
>
> | Switch A | Switch B | Lamp |
> |---|---|---|
> | open | closed | |
> | closed | open | |
> | closed | closed | |
>
> 13 If switch A is used to put the lamp on, can switch B be used to put the lamp off?

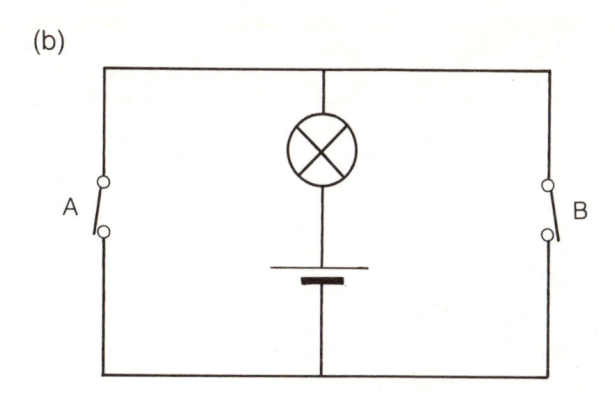

A circuit that can be switched on and off from two places

(c) Upstairs/downstairs.
The lamp in this circuit can be put on by one switch and off by another. The circuit uses a switch that can connect first to one wire and then to another. This type of switch is called a two-way switch.

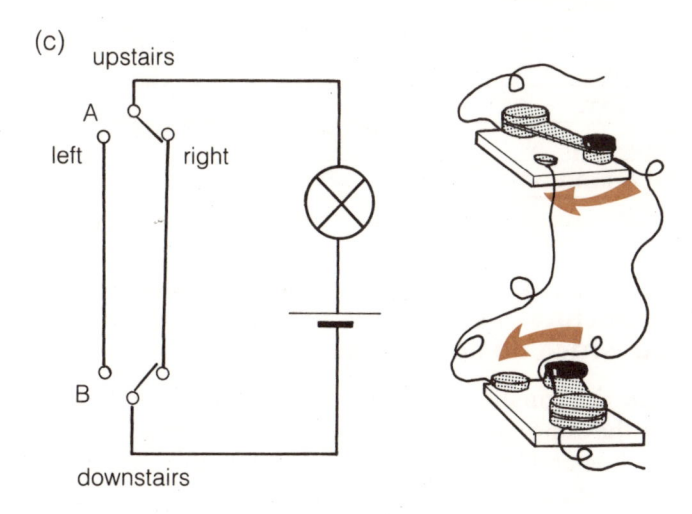

A circuit that can be switched on at one place and off at another

14 Copy and put on or off for the lamp.

Switch A	Switch B	Lamp
left	right	
right	right	
right	left	
left	left	

15 Explain the difference between the way the switches work in circuits (b) and (c).

16 Describe one common use for circuit (c).

17 How can a two-way switch be used as an on/off switch?

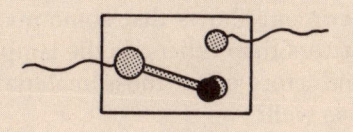

A two-way switch being used as a one-way switch

155

34 Conductors and insulators

We have seen that electric current can flow along copper wires and through the filament of a lamp. Materials like these, that allow electric current to pass easily, are called **conductors** and materials that do not allow current to pass are called **insulators**.

> 1 Copy and give an example of a conductor and insulator for each form of energy.
>
> | Energy | Conductor | Insulator |
> |---|---|---|
> | Electricity | | |
> | Heat | | |
> | Light | | |
> | Sound | | |

Experiment. Finding materials which are good conductors of electricity, which conduct a little and which do not conduct at all

Build this circuit and touch the clips together to check that the lamp lights. Connect different materials between the clips and use the lamp to show whether current can pass. Put your results into a table.

Results

Material		
Can current pass?		

Copy the table and insert 'yes', 'no' or 'a little'.

> 2 This experiment shows that some materials are better conductors than others. Is the lamp brightest for good conductors of for those materials that do not conduct so well?

Experiment. Can liquids conduct electricity?

Connect two carbon rods to a lamp and battery. Touch the rods together to check that the lamp lights. Dip the rods into clean water in a small beaker. Does the lamp light? Add a spoonful of salt to the water. Notice that when the salt has dissolved, the lamp lights. Add other substances to fresh water and try other liquids. (Wipe the rods between tests.)
Find out which liquids will conduct electricity and which will not.

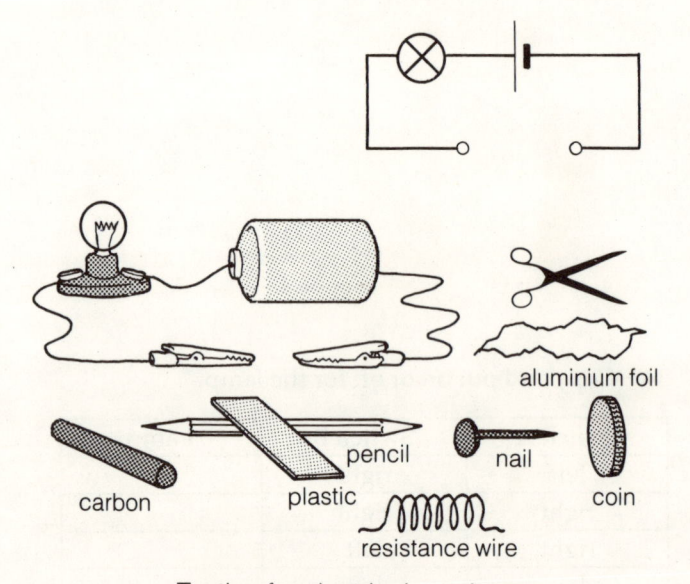

Testing for electrical conductors

Testing for liquids that conduct

Results

Liquid	Can current pass?	Does anything else happen?
Water	no	no
Water with salt	yes	bubbles of gas seen
Water with sugar	no	no
Water with copper sulphate	yes	one rod goes pink bubbles of gas seen
Water with dilute sulphuric acid	yes	bubbles of gas seen
Paraffin	no	no
Methylated spirits	no	no

You will notice that bubbles of gas are produced in those liquids that conduct electricity, and with copper sulphate one rod gets a pink copper coat. The current causes chemical changes as it passes through the liquid. This process is called **electrolysis** and the conducting liquids are called **electrolytes**.

> 3 Which of the liquids above are electrolytes?

Pure water does not conduct electricity well at these low voltages. Water that contains certain substances becomes a good conductor. At high voltages, such as mains voltage, water can conduct enough current to be dangerous. Water and electricity should be kept away from each other.

- Metals, carbon and some solutions are good conductors of electricity.
- Most materials, including pure water, are insulators at low voltages.

Measuring electric current

The brightness of a lamp is one way of measuring electric current. A better way is to use an **ammeter**. This instrument measures current in units called **amperes**. An ammeter has its terminals marked + and −. To give correct readings it must be connected the right way round. The + terminal of the cell should go to the + terminal of the ammeter.

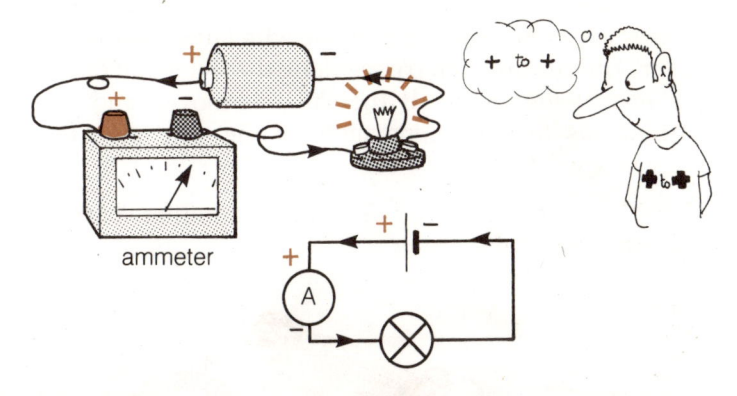

The direction of an electric current

The current, we say, flows from the (+) terminal of the cell through the ammeter and lamp to the (−) terminal of the cell. This is the 'conventional' direction of the current flow.

Connecting an ammeter to measure current in a circuit

> 4 An ammeter can be connected in two positions between the lamp and the cell. One position is shown. Draw a circuit diagram showing the ammeter in the other position. Do you think it will give the same reading?

Never connect an ammeter to a cell without a lamp or other component in the circuit

Experiment. What is resistance?

Connect a lamp, ammeter and cell together and complete the circuit with a length of 'resistance' wire. Use a short length of wire between the clips at first and the lamp should light. What happens when you move one clip so that there is a longer length of resistance wire in the circuit? You will find that less current passes and the lamp may even go out. The long length of wire has 'resisted' the flow of current and we say that the wire has **resistance**. The more resistance the wire has, the smaller the current will be.

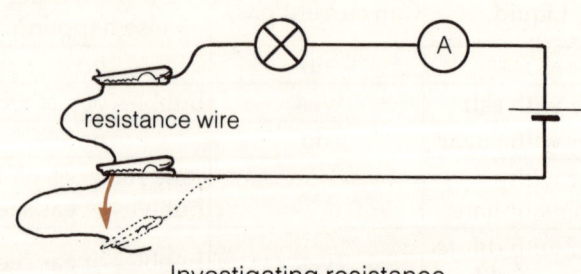

Investigating resistance

5   Is a lamp always able to tell us when a current is flowing in a circuit? Explain your answer.

- Electric current is measured by an ammeter in amperes.
- The electric current in a circuit gets less as the resistance of the circuit increases.

Resistors

Conductors that are used because they have resistance are called **resistors**. Resistors can be made of wire of special alloy, usually wound into a coil. They can also be made from powdered carbon mixed with a powder that does not conduct.

Variable resistors

These are resistors whose resistance can be changed. They can be used to change the current in a circuit. Variable resistors have a sliding contact that can be moved along a resistance wire or carbon track. The current goes round only part of the wire until it meets the slider. The current then passes along the slider and out to the rest of the circuit. If the slider is moved and the current has to pass along more of the wire then the resistance will be larger.

Variable resistors are used as volume and other controls in electronic circuits.

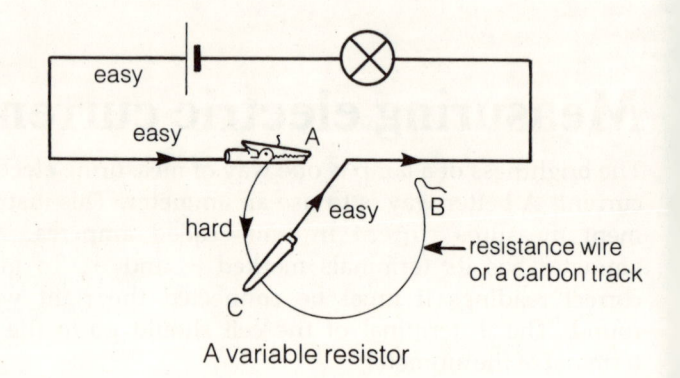

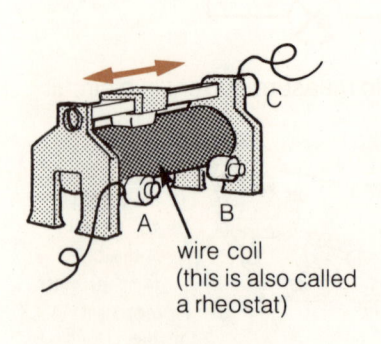

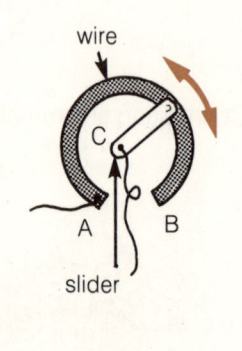

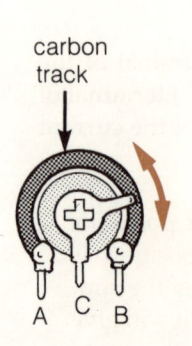

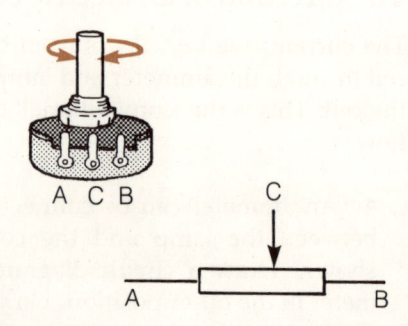

A variable resistor

Types of variable resistor

Experiment

Connect a lamp, a cell and a variable resistor so that you can control the brightness of the lamp. Variable resistors usually have three contacts. Only two are used in this circuit; one to the slider and one to the end of the resistance wire.

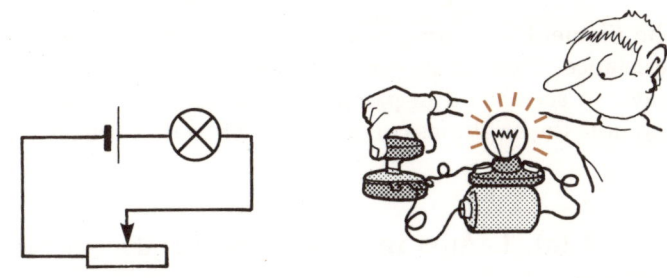

Using a variable resistor to control the current in a circuit

6 At which end of the resistance wire, A or B, should the slider be for: (a) greatest resistance; (b) smallest current; (c) smallest resistance; (d) greatest current?

7 If the connections were made to A and B, would the resistance be variable? Explain your answer.

Experiment. Investigating the resistance of pencil leads

Sharpen a pencil at both ends and pass a current through the lead. (Use the circuit shown in the diagram.) Measure the current that flows. Repeat using pencil leads of the same length and thickness but of different hardness. You might use 4H, HB and 3B. Which type of lead has the greatest resistance?

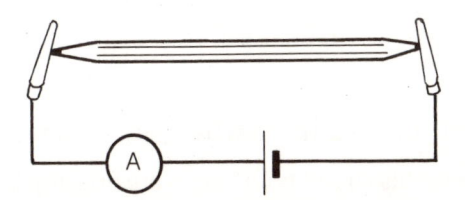

8 An experiment with pencil leads gave the following results:

Type of lead	Current
4H	0.03 A
HB	0.10 A
3B	0.70 A

(a) Which type of lead has the greatest resistance?
(b) Pencil leads contain carbon. Which type of pencil do you think contains the most carbon?

Experiment. Does the body conduct electricity?

Try to pass an electric current through your body using a dry cell. A lamp in the circuit will not light but a sensitive ammeter will show that a small current does flow. The body does conduct a little. Try when your skin is moist and also try the same path through other people. Is the current the same for everyone?

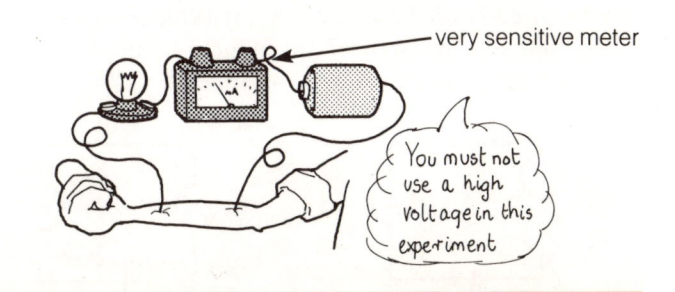

9 In an experiment like this, the skin was made wet and the current got larger. Does the skin have more or less resistance when wet?

10 One type of 'lie-detector' measures skin resistance. Lying is supposed to make you sweat. How do you think this lie-detector works?

- Electricity can pass through the body.
- Quite small currents can cause death (p. 209).

Two lamp circuits

The filament of a lamp is a coil of thin wire that has a resistance. Two lamps can be connected to a cell in two ways: in **series** and in **parallel**. Build the circuits below and note the brightness of the lamps when they are on.

Circuit (a). Lamps in series (one after the other in line)

Notice that the lamps are not as fully lit as when there is only one lamp in the circuit, and that the current is less with two lamps.

11 Does the switch work both lamps?

12 Why is the current less with two lamps (in series) than with one on its own?

13 What happens if you take one lamp out of its socket?

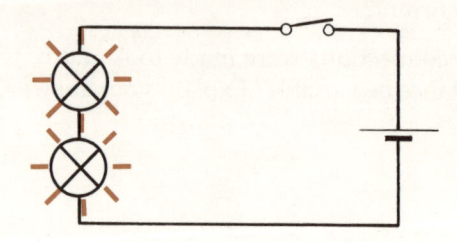

Circuit (b). Lamps in parallel (side by side)

Notice that in this circuit both lamps are brightly lit.

14 What happens if you take one lamp out of its socket in this circuit?

15 Give two reasons why lamps in parallel is a better arrangement for lighting lamps than lamps in series.

Lamps in series and in parallel

16 The numbers by the ammeters show the current in each of these circuits. (a) Which circuit has the smallest resistance? (b) Which circuit has the largest resistance?

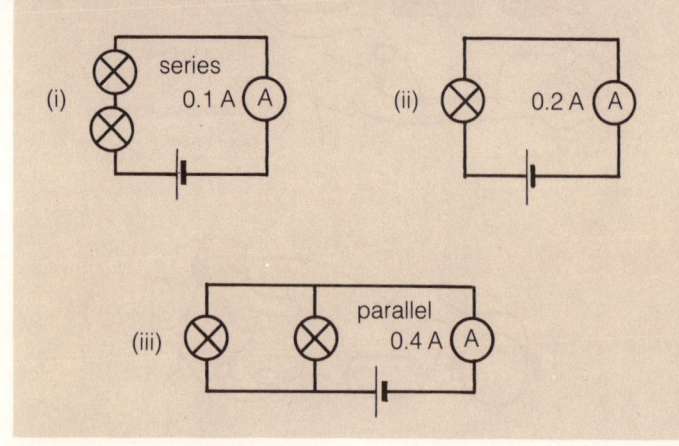

(i) series 0.1 A

(ii) 0.2 A

(iii) parallel 0.4 A

17 Copy and complete: 'When a lamp is added in series to another lamp, the resistance in the circuit ___*___. When a lamp is added in parallel to another lamp in a circuit, the resistance of the circuit ___**___'.

18 Explain why adding an identical lamp in parallel with another in a circuit doubles the current that flows from the cell.

19 Are these lamps in series or in parallel?

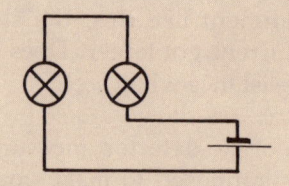

*increases **decreases.

- Lamps in parallel are brighter than lamps in series for the same voltage.
- Also if one lamp goes out, the others are not affected.

35 Electric heating

Experiment. Passing large currents through wires

Use a car battery (or a laboratory low voltage supply) for this experiment because large currents are needed. Connect the circuit shown and pass a current through a piece of thin copper wire. Increase the current by moving the rheostat slider and watch what happens to the wire. Replace the wire with a piece of plastic covered copper wire, the sort used for connecting circuits. What happens when a large current passes through this wire? Then use a length of tin wire (or solder). What happens to the tin when it gets hot?

Results

Material	Observations
Thin copper wire	The wire takes a large current before it gets red hot and breaks
Plastic covered wire	The plastic melts
Tin wire	The tin melts at a low temperature. Tin wire is soft and breaks easily

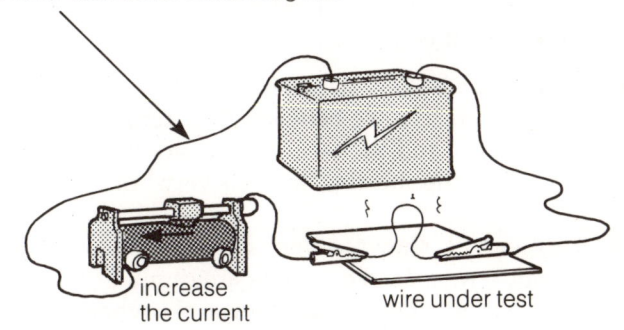

1 The following observations were made when heating wires with an electric current:

Material	Observations
iron . . .	. . .was able to stay red hot for a while but eventually burnt and broke
nichrome . . .	. . .could stay red hot for a long time without damage
a tungsten lamp filament	. . .could be made white hot without breaking

Using these observations and the results of the experiment above, try and answer these questions.

(a) Give one reason why the heating coils of electric fires, irons and kettles are made from nichrome wire? (Nichrome is a mixture of nickel and chromium.)

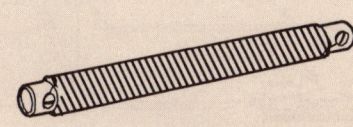

A nichrome heating coil

(b) Why is tungsten a good material to use for the filaments of lamps?

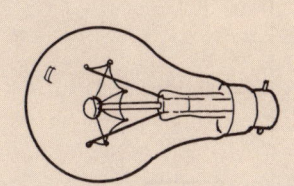

A lamp with a tungsten filament

(c) Why is most of the air in filament lamps replaced by a gas that does not support burning?

(d) Tin wire used to be used as fuse wire but has been replaced by copper wire (usually coated with tin). Give one reason why copper is better than tin for fuses.

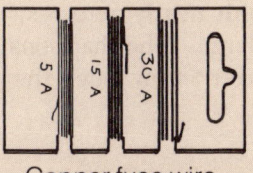

Copper fuse wire

2 A roll of plastic-covered connecting wire is labelled 5 A wire. What do you think this means? What would happen if a current of 10 A was passed through it?

Short circuits

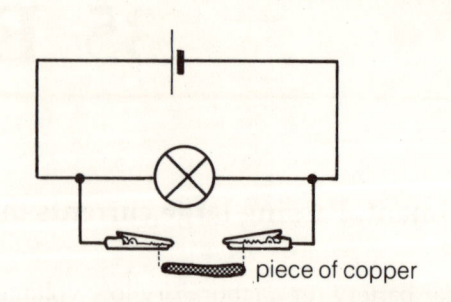

The circuit shows a cell driving a current through a lamp. What do you think will happen if a piece of copper is connected between the clips? Most of the current will take the easy route through the copper and the lamp will go out. A low resistance path like this that bypasses the lamp, is called a **short circuit**. (What would happen if an insulator was connected between the clips?)

Short circuits can be very damaging to cells and batteries. With nearly no resistance between their terminals, large currents will flow and they will quickly go 'flat'. There is also a fire risk as the shorting link gets very hot.

> 3 This circuit shows a foolish way to connect lamps and switches. The lamps are dimly lit when the switches are open. What will you see when:
> (a) Switch A is closed (two things);
> (b) Switch B is closed as well?
>
> 4 What is the danger of connecting a circuit like the one in Q3? 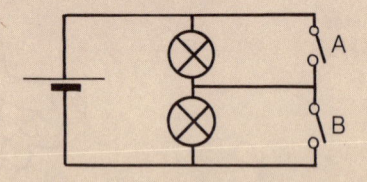

- Electric currents cause heating in wires with resistance.
- A short circuit is a low resistance link between the battery terminals.

Fuses

Experiment

Build a circuit with a battery and lamp and include a length of 'fuse wire'. After checking that the lamp lights, 'short out' the lamp by connecting a piece of wire between the points A and B. The current will no longer go through the lamp because it can pass through the piece of wire more easily. (The wire has a much lower resistance.) But with nearly zero resistance the current will become very large. What happens to the fuse wire? Why does no current flow after the fuse has melted ('blown')?

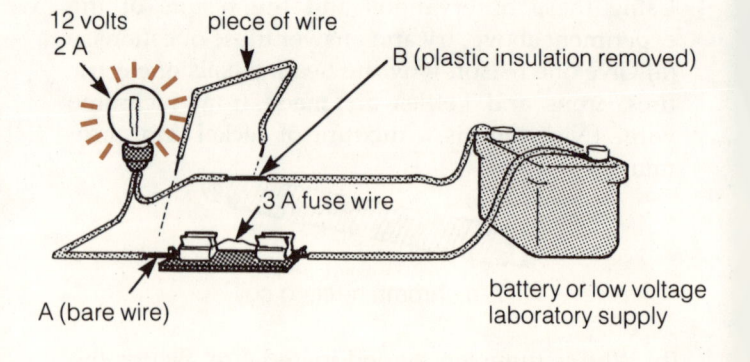

> 5 What is a 'short circuit'?
>
> 6 What is the advantage of putting a fuse in a circuit? What would happen to the connecting wires in this circuit if there was a short circuit and no fuse?
>
> 7 A current of 2 A passes through the lamp used above. Why is it important to use a fuse wire that melts when 3 A pass through it and not '1 A fuse wire'?

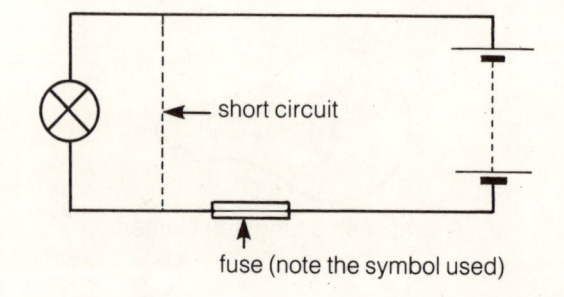

36 Cells and voltage

In a torch the cell supplies energy that changes into heat and radiation. The cell also makes current flow through the lamp. Without the cell there is no current. The chemicals inside the cell provide the (+) terminal with more electric potential energy than the (−) terminal. This energy difference is measured by the **voltage** between the terminals and can move electric current round a circuit. (Voltage is also known as **potential difference (p.d.)**.)

The voltage of a cell is measured by a **voltmeter** in **volts**. Note how to connect the terminals of a voltmeter to a cell.

Using a voltmeter to measure the voltage of a cell

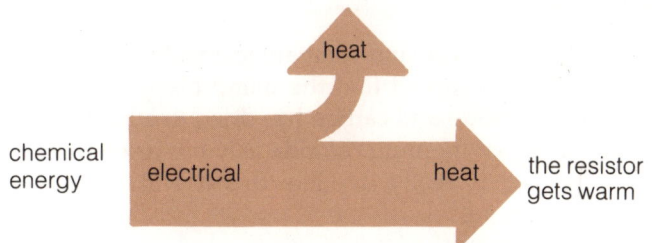

An electric current transfers chemical energy from the cell to heat energy in the resistor

Experiment. Connecting cells together

Measure the voltage of two cells separately and joined together in the three ways shown below.

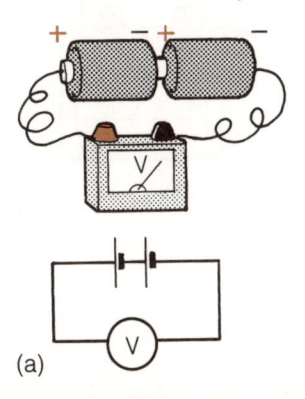

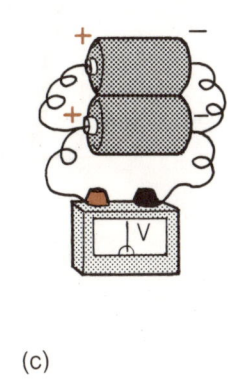

(a)   (c)   (b)

1 In an experiment like this the voltage of each cell was found to be 1.5 volts. When connected together, they gave voltage readings of 1.5 volts, 0 volts and 3 volts. Which arrangement would give which reading?

2 A boy put 6 new cells into his 9 V radio-cassette recorder but it did not work. Why not? Draw a diagram of how they should have been put in.

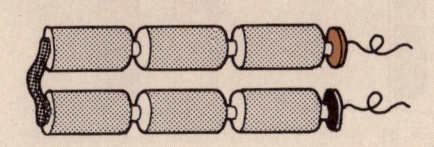

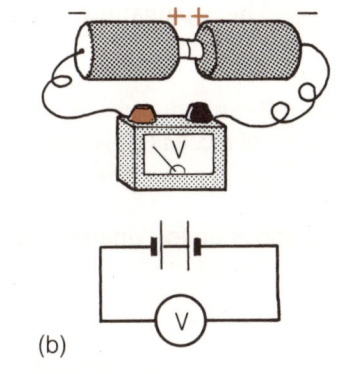

3 What would the voltmeter read in these circuits? (All cells have a voltage of 1.5 volts.)

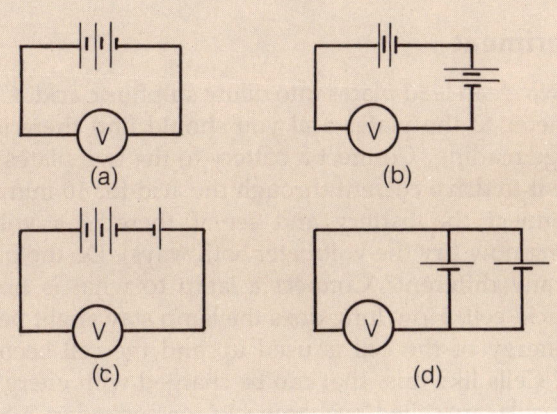

(a)   (b)   (c)   (d)

163

Inside a dry cell

There are different sorts of 'dry' cell but the most common is the zinc/carbon cell.

Experiment

Cut open a fresh dry cell and see if you can find the following parts:

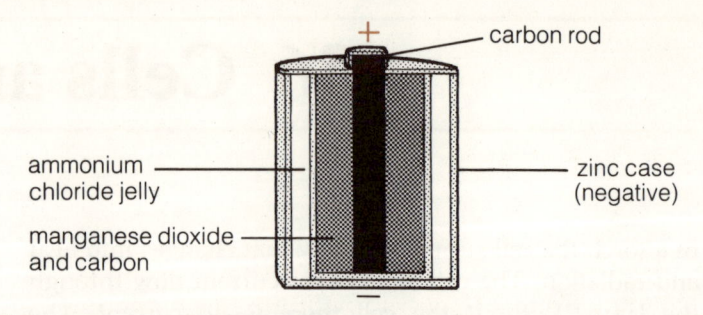

Part	Notes
Carbon rod	Electricity can pass through carbon. This is the (+) terminal of the cell
Zinc case	This is the (−) terminal
Ammonium chloride jelly	This sticky mixture is smeared on the inside of the zinc case
Manganese dioxide and carbon powder	This black mixture moves hydrogen from the cell. (Hydrogen is formed in the cell and reduces its voltage.) The mixture is called a depolarizer

Experiment

Cut open a 'dead' cell and compare its insides with those of a fresh cell. You will find the damp black mixture of manganese dioxide and carbon has dried to a hard solid, and the sticky ammonium chloride jelly has dried up too. When the cell is really dry like this it will no longer produce a voltage.

4 Is a 'dry' cell really dry? What happens if it does become dry?

Experiment. Making a wet dry cell

Place the carbon rod of your dry cell and a piece of its zinc case into a solution of ammonium chloride. Connect a voltmeter to your cell and notice that a voltage is produced that quickly drops. If you remove the carbon rod for a while and then replace it, the voltage rises but not for long. The manganese dioxide stops this drop in voltage in a 'dry' cell.

5 How can you use a voltmeter to find which terminal of a cell is (+) and which is (−)?

- Cells use chemical energy to produce a voltage.

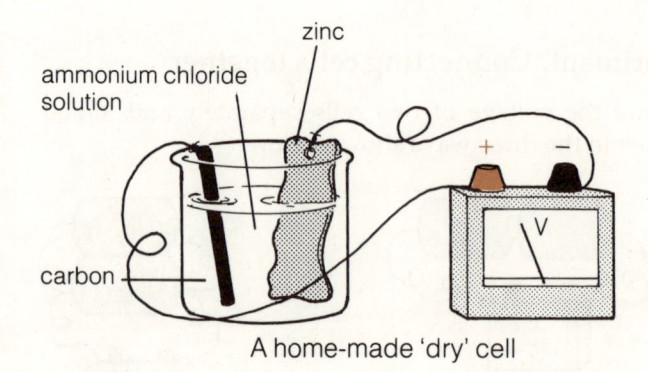

Lead-acid cells

Experiment

Put two clean lead plates into dilute sulphuric acid. Clip a voltmeter to the plates and you should find there is no voltage reading. Connect a battery to the two plates and allow it to drive current through the acid for 10 minutes. Disconnect the battery and see if there is a voltage reading now (try the voltmeter both ways). Do the plates look any different? Connect a lamp to what is now a lead/acid cell. How long does the lamp stay alight before the energy of the cell is used up and the cell becomes 'flat'? Cells like this, that can be charged with energy by other cells, are called 'rechargeable' (or 'secondary') cells.

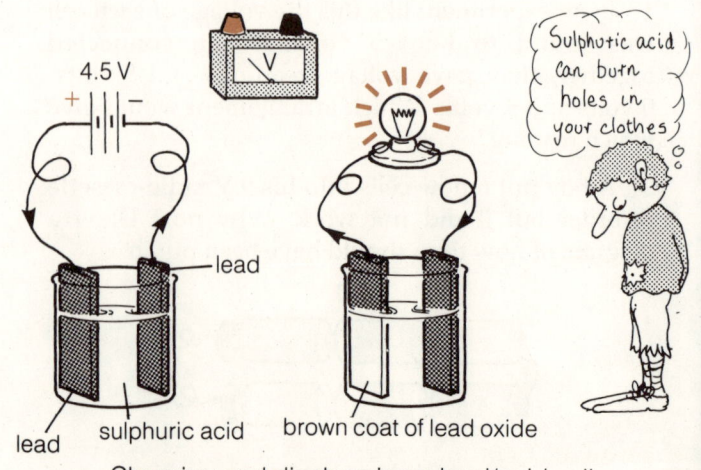

6 What can these 'rechargeable' devices store up? Copy and complete.

Spring	Fountain pen	Water pistol	Lead/acid cell	Storage radiators	Sponge

7 When a lead/acid cell is charged, chemicals are formed on its plates that store the energy of the cell. Which of these diagrams shows the energy changes that take place while the cell is being charged, and which shows the discharge energy changes? Copy the diagrams and label them 'charge' and 'discharge'.

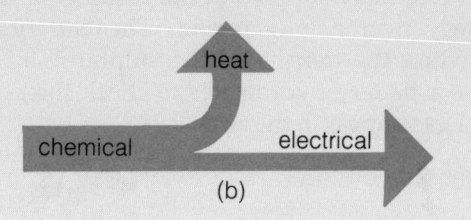

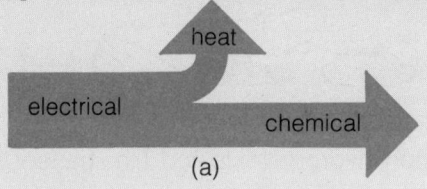

Car batteries

The lead/acid cell in the experiment above has a voltage of 2 volts when it is charged. Car batteries usually have 6 of these cells connected together to make a battery with a voltage of 12 volts.

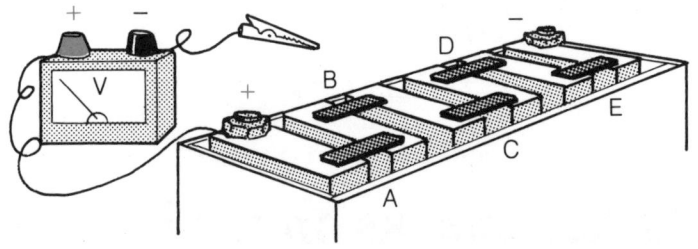

A battery of six lead/acid cells

8 Copy this diagram of 6 cells and draw in wires connecting them together to make a battery of 12 volts.

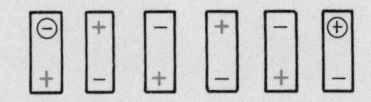

9 The metal strips connecting the cells in the diagram above are labelled A,B,C,D,E. What voltage reading would you get when you connect a voltmeter between the (+) terminal and each strip? Each cell has a voltage of 2 volts.

Strip	Voltage
A	
B	
C	
D	
E	

10 The proper use of ammeters and voltmeters.
(a) Which of these circuits show an ammeter and voltmeter properly connected?
(b) In which two circuits would the ammeter probably be damaged?
(c) Copy and complete these sentences:
_____ measure current and are connected in the circuit so that the current can pass through them.
_____ are connected across a cell and measure the voltage of the cell.

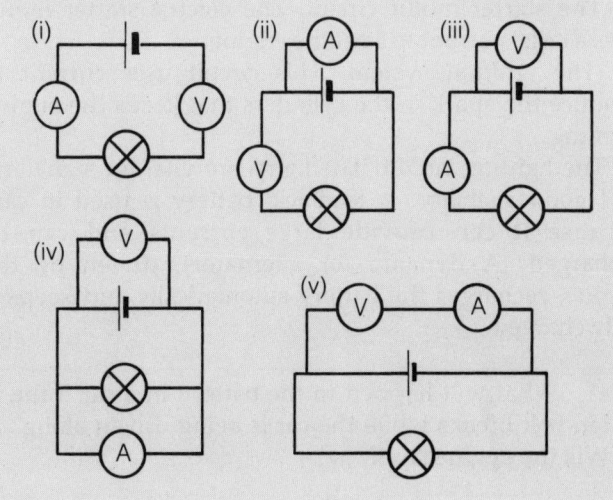

■ Two lead plates in sulphuric acid can be made into a 2 volt cell by passing an electric current between them.
■ Electrical energy is changed into chemical energy during this 'charging' process.

Recharging a lead/acid battery

Experiment. Using a battery charger

A battery charger has two leads marked (+) and (−). Connect these leads to the battery (+ to +, − to −) and adjust the charging current to about 3 A. If a larger current than this is used the plates of the battery may be damaged. A battery can be recharged with energy from the mains electricity supply but the recharging has to be done slowly over a long period. The battery is fully charged when the density of the sulphuric acid is 1.2 g/cm^3 (use a battery hydrometer to check this) or when bubbles of gas appear in the acid.

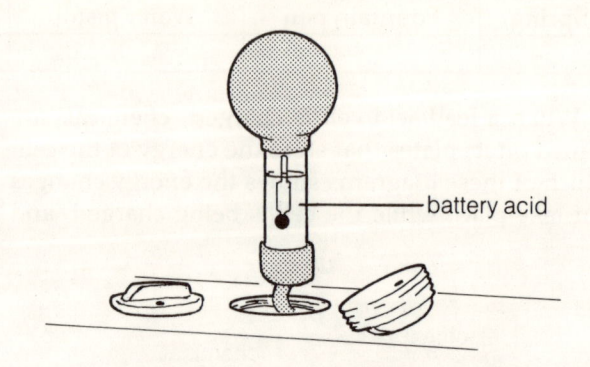

Using a battery hydrometer to find if the battery is charged

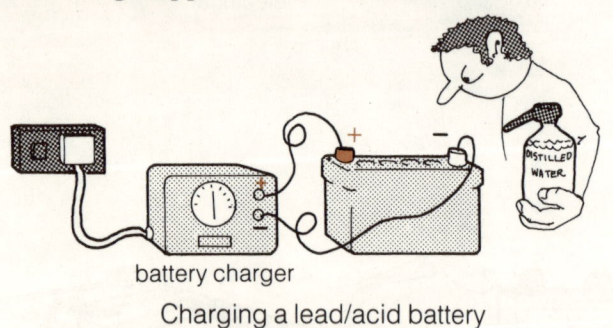

Charging a lead/acid battery

Other checks on the battery

While the battery is charging check the level of the acid in **each** cell. Use distilled (pure) water to 'top up' the acid level to just above the plates. Keep the terminals clean and lightly greased.

Why do cars need batteries?

Cars with petrol engines have a battery to work their many electrical parts. Current is needed by three circuits:
(a) The starter motor circuit. The electric starter motor uses a large current to start the engine.
(b) The ignition system. This circuit uses current to produce the spark in the cylinders that keeps the engine running.
(c) The lighting circuit. The lights are vital for signalling and good visibility. A lead/acid battery is used in cars because it can provide large currents and can be recharged. A dynamo (or alternator), driven by the engine, recharges the battery automatically and keeps it fully charged.

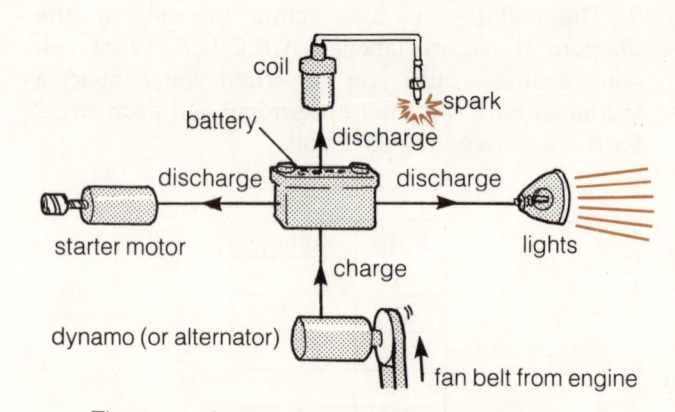

The way a battery is normally used in a car

11 What will happen to the battery in a car if the fan belt breaks while the car is being driven along? Will the engine stop?

- Lead acid batteries are especially useful because they can supply large currents and can be recharged.
- Unfortunately they are expensive and heavy.

37 Measuring resistance

Experiment

Use an ammeter to measure the current that passes through some common devices when they are connected to a 12 volt battery. Although the voltage is the same for each device the current that flows is different. This shows that each device has a different resistance.

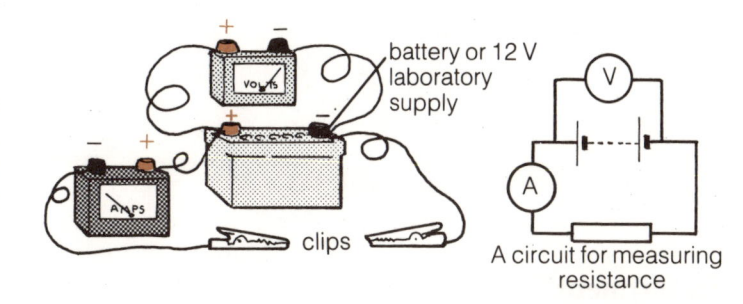

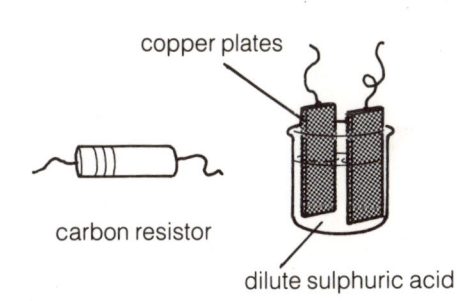

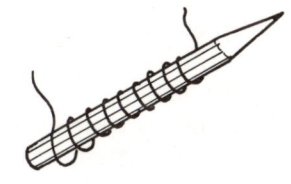

A circuit for measuring resistance

carbon resistor

copper plates / dilute sulphuric acid

electric motor

electric heater

torch bulb

1 metre of resistance wire

1   The current and voltage readings in the table below were taken from an experiment like this.

Device	Carbon resistor	Dilute sulphuric acid	Torch bulb	Motor	Heater	Resistance wire
Voltage	12 V	12 V	12 V	12 V	12 V	12 V
Current	¼ A	2 A	½ A	4 A	3 A	1 A
Voltage/current						
Forms of energy produced						

(a) Which device has (i) the greatest resistance, (ii) the smallest resistance?

(b) Copy the table and calculate voltage ÷ current for each device. (e.g. for the carbon resistor: 12 ÷ ¼ = 48)

You will notice that the value of voltage ÷ current is largest for the devices with the largest resistance (when the current is smallest). For this reason voltage ÷ current is called the **resistance** of the device.

$$\text{Resistance} = \frac{\text{Voltage}}{\text{Current}}.$$

3   Write down the devices in Q1 in order of their resistances, the one with the lowest resistance first.

Units If 1 volt drives a current of 1 A through a conductor, then that conductor has a resistance of 1 ohm (symbol Ω). The unit of resistance is the ohm.

2   Each device changes electrical energy into different forms. Write the forms of energy produced by each device in the last row of boxes in Q1.

The resistance may be different if we use a different voltage, Sir!

True, Albert. Why not change the voltage and see if it is.

- Resistance = voltage/current
- Resistance is measured in ohms.

167

Voltage and current

We have seen how the voltage of a cell moves current round a circuit. If this voltage is increased, will the current increase too?

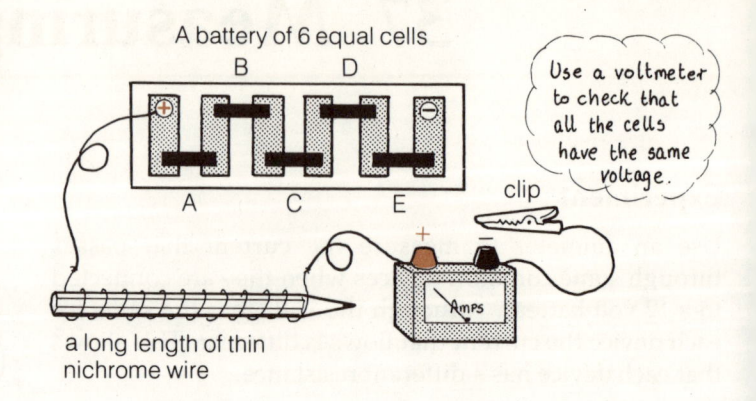

Experiment

Build the circuit shown and connect the clip to the first metal strip A. (This puts one cell into the circuit.) Measure the current that flows round the circuit. Next double the voltage by connecting the clip to strip B, putting two cells into the circuit. Measure the current again. Has it doubled too. Carry on until all six cells are in use. Put your readings into a table like the one in Q4. Do they show a link between voltage and current?

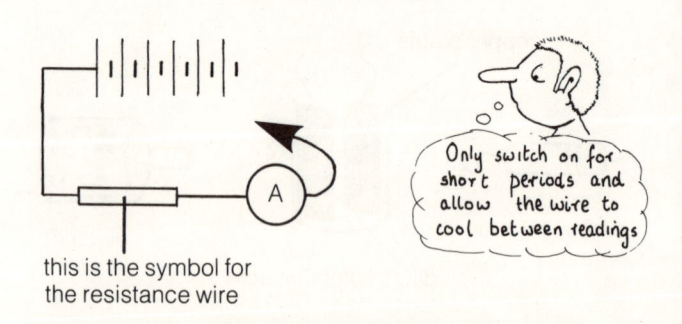

4 The readings below were obtained from an experiment like this. The voltage of each cell was 2 volts.

No. of cells in use	Voltage used	Current (A)	Voltage / Current
0		0.	
1		0.1	
2		0.2	
3		0.3	
4		0.4	
5		0.5	

Copy this table and work out the voltages used. Divide this by the current to get the numbers for the last column. Which of these sentences is correct according to these results?
(a) The current stays the same whatever voltage is used.
(b) The current goes down as the voltage goes up.
(c) The current rises as the voltage rises.
(d) Doubling the voltage, doubles the current.
(e) Voltage ÷ current always gives the same number (a constant).

Ohm's law

For the resistance wire in Q4, dividing the voltage by the current comes to 20 each time. Do your results show that voltage ÷ current comes to the same number each time? Careful experiments have found that for many conductors 'voltage ÷ current is constant, provided the temperature of the conductor does not change'.
This is known as Ohm's law.

Voltage ÷ current is resistance. So conductors that obey Ohm's Law have a resistance that does NOT change when the voltage changes

5 Describe how you would find out whether the material of a length of wire obeys Ohm's law.

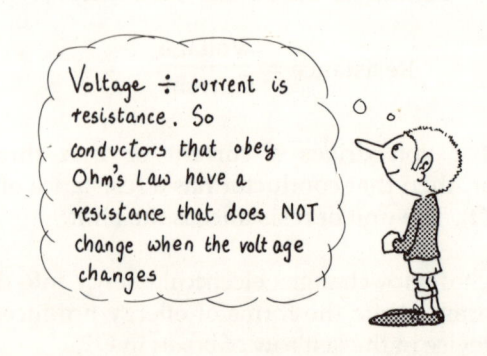

■ Ohm's law states that voltage ÷ current for a conductor is constant, provided the temperature of the conductor does not change.

The effect of temperature on resistance

Experiment. Measuring the resistance of lamp filaments

(a) A lamp with a metal (tungsten) filament. Use a 12 volt lamp and measure its resistance at two voltages, 2 volts and 12 volts. In each case find the current that flows through the lamp and calculate the resistance of the filament. Is this resistance the same in both cases?

These results were obtained from an experiment like this:

Voltage = 2 volts   Voltage = 12 volts
Current = 0.5 A   Current = 2 A
Resistance = 2/0.5   Resistance = 12/2
        = 4 ohms (cold)   = 6 ohms (hot)

The resistance of the metal is NOT constant, it increases as the metal gets hotter.

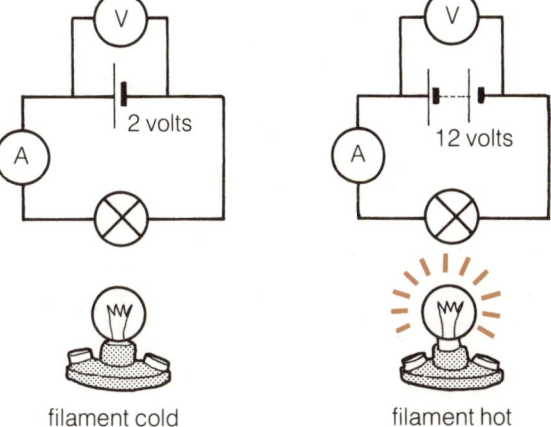

(b) A lamp with a carbon filament. The results below show readings taken of the resistance of a 'mains' carbon filament lamp, using low voltage (2 V). The lamp was 'out' and the filament cold. They also show readings taken at 240 V when the filament was white hot.

Results

Voltage = 2 volts   Voltage = 240 volts
Current = 0.004 A   Current = 0.5 A
Resistance = $\frac{2}{0.004}$ Resistance = $\frac{240}{0.5}$
         = 500 ohms   = 480 ohms

The resistance of carbon gets LESS as it gets hotter.

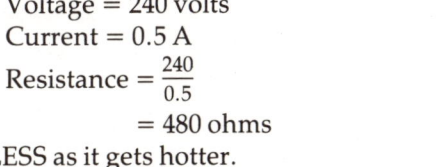

We cannot tell whether the lamp filaments obey Ohm's Law because their temperatures change.

---

6 Copy and complete these sentences:
As the temperature rises the resistance of tungsten _____ and the resistance of carbon _____ .

7 Would the ammeter show more or less current as the carbon rod gets hotter?
The carbon rod is replaced by a tungsten wire. Would the ammeter show more or less current as the tungsten gets hotter?

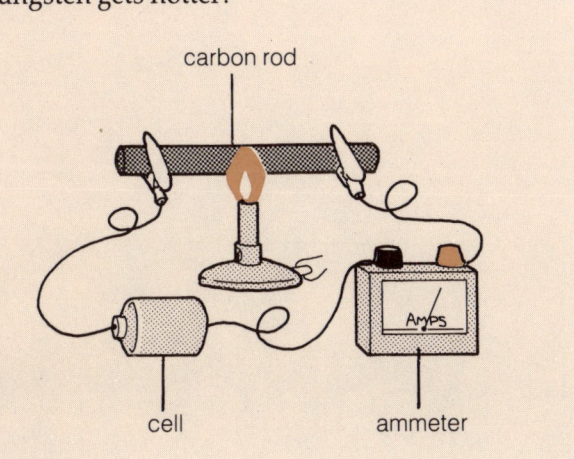

■ The resistances of most materials change when their temperatures change.

169

38 Measuring electrical energy

We have seen ways that electrical energy can be changed into light, heat, movement and sound. Electrical energy can be measured by a **joulemeter** (p. 101).

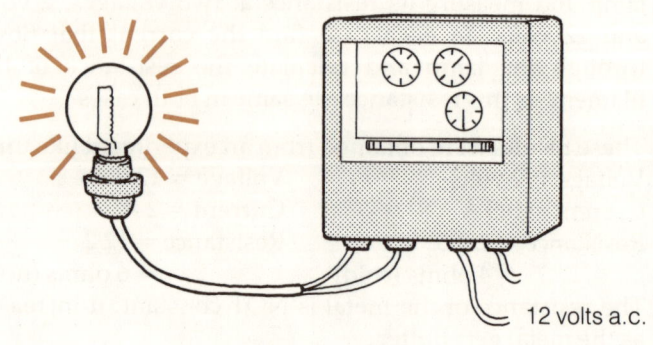

Experiment. Using a joulemeter

Connect a lamp to a joulemeter and a 12 volt supply as shown. Switch on and watch the dials of the joulemeter move round. It is measuring the electrical energy that the lamp is changing into heat and radiation. The electricity meters in our homes are high voltage versions of the joulemeter (p. 202).

1   To find how much electrical energy has changed, the joulemeter has to be read twice. Once before you switch on and then after you switch off.
What are the two readings shown and how much energy has changed?

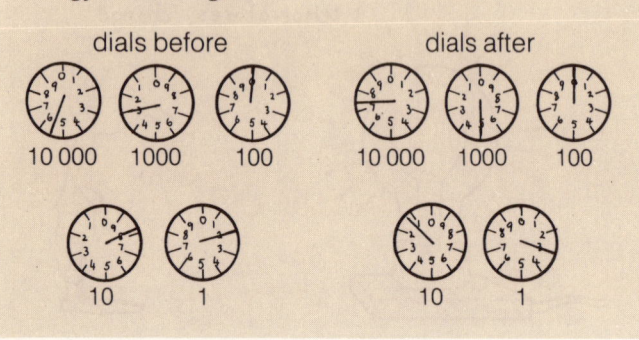

dials before   dials after

10 000   1000   100   10 000   1000   100

10   1   10   1

12 volts a.c.

Using a joulemeter

How to read the 'meter.
1. *First read the dial with the largest units, then the next smaller one and so on........*
2. *If the pointer lies between two numbers, always write the smaller one.*

Experiment. Measuring electrical energy

Use the apparatus above to find the electrical energy changed in one minute by the following items of equipment: a headlamp; torch lamp; electric motor; heater. (They must all work on 12 volts.)

Electrical power

You will find that some of the 'electrical energy converters' above change energy faster than others. For example, a headlamp uses energy more quickly than a torch lamp and produces more light as a result. The headlamp has more power than the torch lamp. Power is the energy changed per second by the device. It can be calculated from the equation

$$\text{power} = \frac{\text{energy changed}}{\text{time taken}}$$ (p. 129).

Units
Energy is measured in joules (J)
Time is measured in seconds (s)
Power is measured in watts (W)

170

2 This table gives the energy changed by each piece of equipment in 1 minute. Copy the table and fill in the power of each device.

	(bulb/fire)	(lamp)	motor	heater
Energy changed	1200 J	120 J	600 J	3000 J
Time taken for this	60 s	60 s	60 s	60 s
Power				
Forms of energy produced				

The power of a device tells us how quickly it changes energy from one form to others.

100 W

100 J of electrical energy/second into heat and radiation

100 W

100 J of chemical energy/second into gravitational energy and heat

100 W

100 J of chemical energy/second into heat

2 W   10 W   20 W

3 (a) How much energy will each of these energy converters change in one second?

(b) How long will it take each one to change the same energy as the more powerful version can in 1 second.

■ Power is energy changed per second and is measured in watts.

We have measured electrical power by using a joulemeter (to measure energy) and a clock to measure time. Electrical power can also be measured using an ammeter and a voltmeter. This is because electrical power can be calculated by multiplying voltage × current.

electrical power = voltage × current
  watts   volts   amperes

We have two ways of measuring the same thing.

Experiment. Measuring electrical power

Use an ammeter and a voltmeter to measure the power of an electric heater. Build the circuit shown so that you can measure the voltage of the supply and the current through the heater. Calculate the power of the heater using the equation above.

4 Draw the circuit diagram for this experiment. Use these symbols. (The heater is just a resistor.)

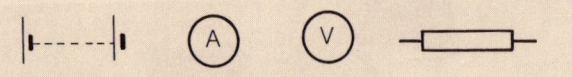

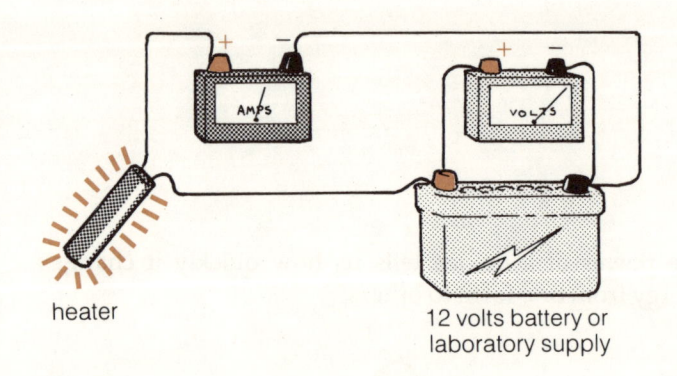

heater

12 volts battery or laboratory supply

5 Calculate the power of the following items. Copy the table and fill in the spaces.

	Tube light	Mains lamp	Electric kettle	One bar electric fire	Transistor radio
Voltage	240 V	240 V	240 V	240 V	9 V
Current	⅙ A	½ A	10 A	4 A	⅑ A
Power					

6 Voltage and current values can also be used to calculate resistance. Copy this table and work out the answers that go in the spaces.

	'Fridge	Iron	Television
Voltage	240 V	240 V	240 V
Current			1 A
Resistance		80 Ω	
Power	80 W		

7 You have calculated the power of 12 electrical devices on the last two pages. Write a list of them in order of the power they use.

Paying for electrical energy

Look at the dials of your electricity meter at home and you will see that it measures electrical energy in **kilowatt hour** (kWh). 1 kilowatt hour is the amount of energy used by a 1000 W appliance in 1 hour (1000 watts for 1 hour). Electrical energy is sold in these units of kilowatt hour. Electricity Boards call one kilowatt hour a 'unit'.

■ Power = voltage × current (watts = volts × amperes)

8 How many kilowatt hours of energy would a 3000 W heater use if it is turned on for 4 hours?

9 How long would it take a 200 W television set to use 1 kWh of energy? The television changes this energy into three other forms of energy. What are these?

The cost of 1 kWh of electrical energy varies. Find out what it costs by looking at your electricity bill.

172

Summary of current electricity

- Electric current is measured by an ammeter in.. amperes.
- The property of a material that limits the current that flows through it, is called its........ resistance.
- Resistance is calculated from .... voltage ÷ current
- Resistance is measured in... ohms.
- Voltage ÷ current is constant for materials (at a steady temperature) that obey .... Ohm's law.
- The power of an electrical device is .... the energy it changes per second.
- Power is measured in .... watts.
- A low resistance short-cut for current is called .... a short circuit.
- A weak link, especially built into a circuit is called a .... fuse.
- If cells are connected in series they are usually connected .... + to −.
- ohms = $\dfrac{\text{volts}}{\text{amperes}}$; watts = volts × amperes; joules = watts × seconds.

Further questions

10 The diagram shows how two lamps and two switches are connected to a battery in a doll's house. Draw a circuit diagram of the arrangement.

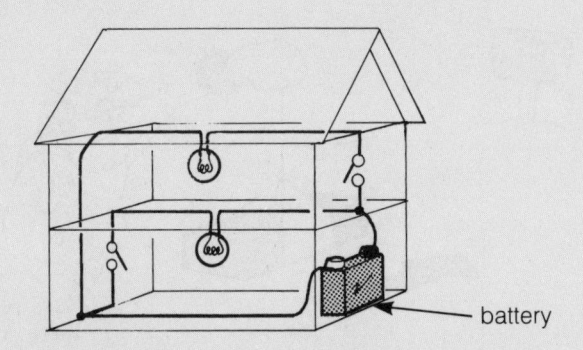

11 All the lamps in the circuit below are 24 W, 12 V.
(a) Which two lamps burn at full brightness?
(b) Which two ammeters have the same reading?
(c) Calculate the reading of ammeter A_2.
(E. Anglia).

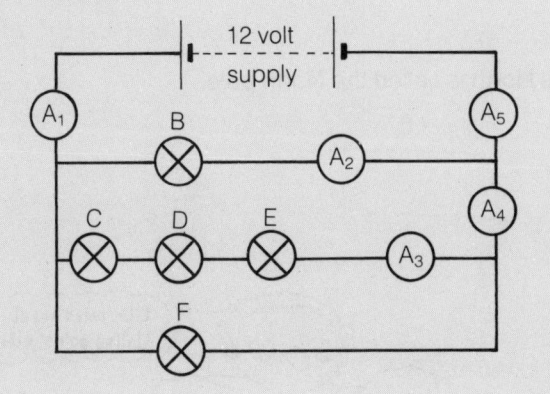

12 A 12 V battery is connected to a 6 ohm lamp.
(a) Calculate the current that flows through the lamp.
(b) What energy changes take place in the lamp?
(c) How much energy is changed in the lamp in 10 seconds?

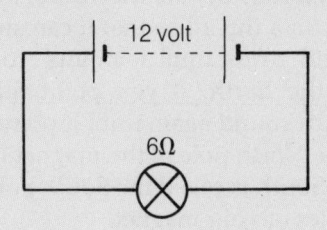

13 Redraw the diagram in Q9 to show an ammeter and voltmeter properly connected to read the current and voltage of the lamp.

14 Explain why:
(a) tungsten is used for lamp filaments;
(b) thin copper wire is used for fuses;
(c) nichrome is used for heating elements.

39 Magnets

Experiment. Finding the poles of a magnet

Roll a magnet in iron filings. You will find that the filings stick mostly round the ends of the magnet. These places, where the magnetism is strongest, are called the **poles** of the magnet. How many poles has your magnet got, and where are they?

The poles of a magnet

Experiment. Are both magnetic poles the same?

The two poles of a bar magnet are near its ends and they both attract iron filings but are they different in any way? Hang a magnet on a thread so that it can swing. You will see that one end turns until it points (roughly) to the North pole of the Earth. If you point this end to the South, it will turn round again until it points North. This pole is called the North pole of the magnet (N). The other end that points South is called the South pole (S). Write N and S on the poles of your magnet.

> 1 If you wanted to label the poles of a horse-shoe magnet, would you hang it on a thread like (a) or like (b)? Explain your answer.

Finding the N pole of a bar magnet

■ A magnet that can swing freely will set N and S. The pole that points North is called the North pole.

Forces between magnetic poles

Experiment

Place two magnets on some polystyrene beads (so they can slide easily) with N-poles together. Let go and the magnets fly apart. Each magnet pushes the other away (repels it) even when they do not touch. S-poles repel each other too but S and N poles attract.

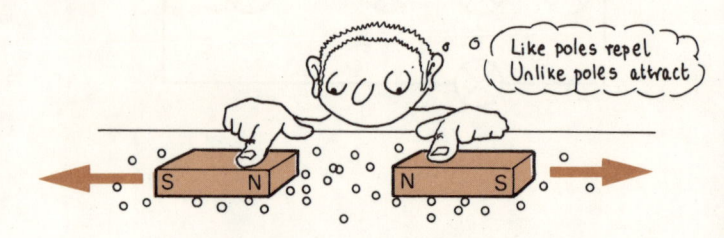

Magnets repelling each other

2 Copy this table and write 'repel' or 'attract' to say what happens when the poles meet.

	North	South
North		
South		

3 These two magnets repel when placed like (a). Will they attract or repel when placed like (b)?

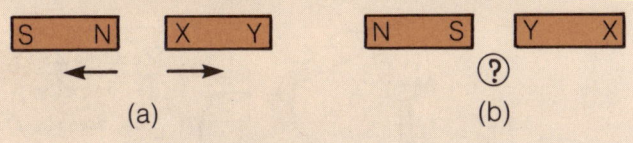

[S N] [X Y] (a)

[N S] [Y X] (b)

4 The needle of a compass is a magnet that can spin on a point. (a) Should the arrow of the needle be a N or S pole? (b) Sometimes the needle gets magnetized the wrong way round. How would you check which end of the compass needle was the N-pole?

The needle of a compass should point North.

5 The two compass needles set as shown when placed near the magnet. What type of poles are X and Y?

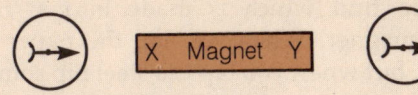

6 A student placed a compass under wire in an electric circuit. When the current was switched on, the compass needle no longer pointed North.
(a) What does this experiment suggest about electric currents?
(b) What could you do to make sure that light from the lamp is **not** causing the movement of the compass needle?

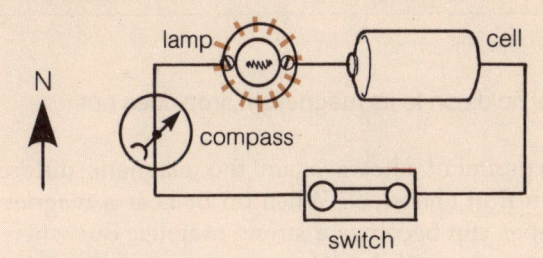

An electric current can move a compass needle

- Like poles repel (N and N; S and S).
- Unlike poles attract (N and S).
- A compass needle is a magnet.

The Earth is magnetized

The N-pole of a magnet that can swing freely will point to the Arctic. Since N-poles are attracted to S-poles, the Arctic must be like a S-pole and the Antarctic a N-pole. The Earth acts like a magnetized ball with its magnetic poles near the geographical poles.

My geographical North Pole is near my magnetic South Pole!

The magnetic and geographical poles of the Earth

A model of the Earth magnet

Experiment

Make a model of the 'Earth magnet' by burying a bar magnet in a ball of plasticine. Roll the ball in iron filings to show up the magnetic poles and use a small compass to show that compass needles point to the Arctic wherever they are.

Experiment. Making a steel magnet

Start with a piece of steel that is not magnetized (test it by dipping it in iron filings). Slide the N-pole of a strong magnet along the steel many times in the same direction. The steel should become a magnet. Check by dipping it again in iron filings. Does end X become a N or S-pole. Use a compass needle to find out*. (A S-pole will attract the point of the compass needle and repel its tail.)

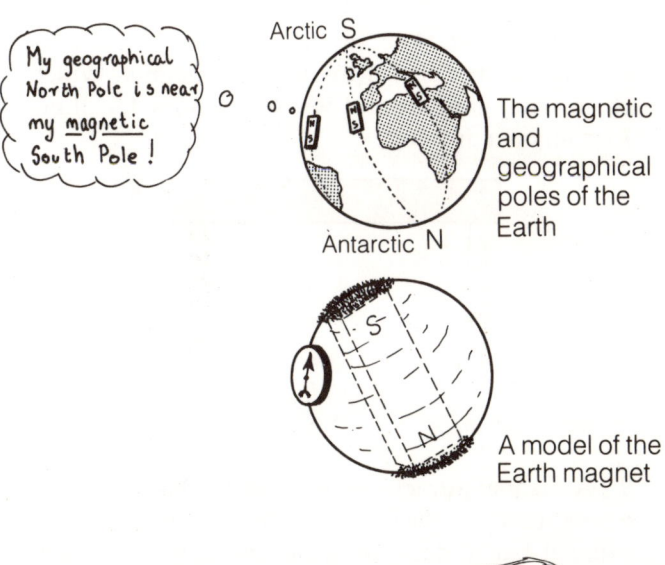

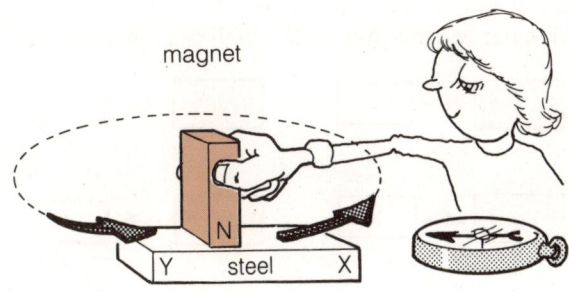

Magnetizing a piece of steel

*X becomes a S-pole.

Experiment. Can you make an iron magnet?

Use the method on p. 175 to try and magnetize a paper clip (iron) and a pen nib or screwdriver blade (steel). Use iron filings to find which is made into a 'full-time' (permanent) magnet. When you tap the paper clip the filings fall off, but when you tap the steel nib some filings stay on.

7 Copy this table and insert yes or no into the spaces.

Iron	Steel	
		Is it attracted to a magnet?
		Can it be made into a permanent magnet?

■ Steel holds on to its magnetism, iron does not.

This experiment shows again the magnetic difference between iron and steel. When on or near a magnet, an iron paper clip becomes a strong magnet. But when the magnet is removed the iron loses its magnetism. A steel nib or sewing needle on the other hand holds on to its magnetism after the magnet has been removed.

Iron... ...loses its magnetism

Steel... ...keeps its magnetism

8 The diagram shows paper clips and nibs hanging from a magnet. The two chains are removed by pulling the first clip away from the magnet. Which chain will fall apart and which will stick together? Explain your answer.

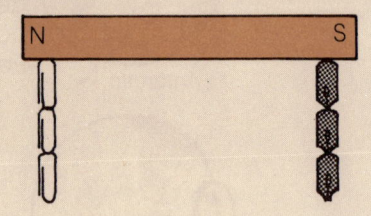

9 A magnet attracts a metal bar X whichever pole is used to do it. The same magnet attracts and repels a metal bar Y depending on which pole is used. Which bar is a magnet, and which is a piece of iron?

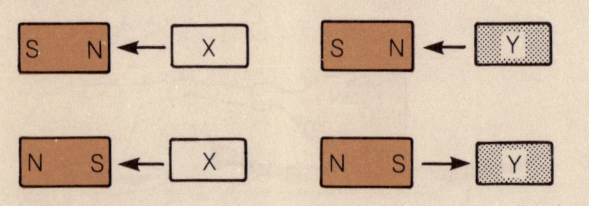

■ A sure test for a magnet is repulsion by another magnet.

10 Why is repulsion the only sure test that a metal bar is a magnet?

11 Explain why needles, hung from the ends of a bar magnet, lean towards each other as shown.

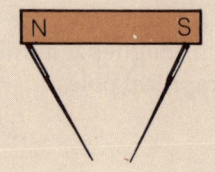

12 **Storing magnets**

Magnets keep their magnetism longer if they are stored in pairs with iron 'keepers' across their ends. Explain why magnets arranged like this are not very good at picking up iron filings.

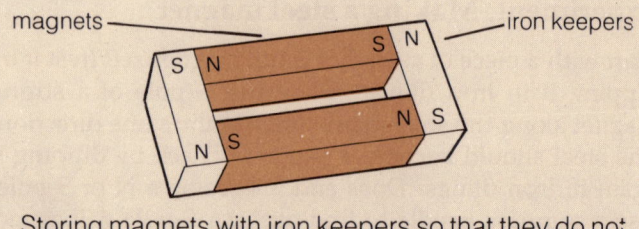

Storing magnets with iron keepers so that they do not lose their magnetism

40 Magnetic fields

The influence of a magnet can be detected in the space around it. A force acts on pieces of iron and steel in that space. A magnet is surrounded by an invisible **magnetic field**. Iron filings can be used to show up the shape of the magnetic field.

Experiment. Looking at magnetic field patterns

Sprinkle a fine even coat of iron filings on a sheet of paper that is covering a bar magnet. Tap the paper gently and the filings will move into a pattern that shows the shape of the magnetic field. Make a drawing of the magnetic field.

The iron filings can be fixed to the paper by spraying them gently with 'hair spray'.

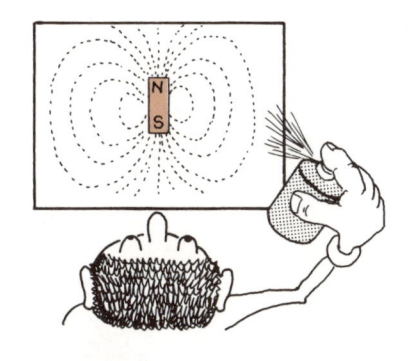

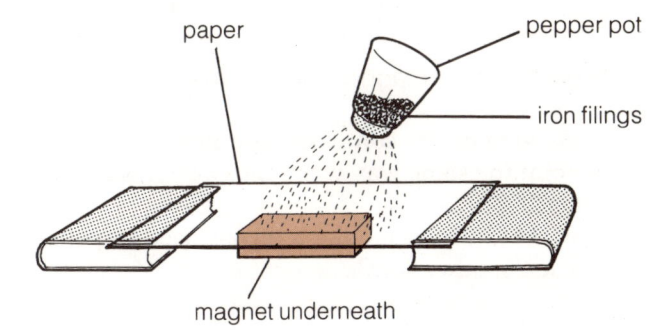

Using iron filings to show up a magnetic field

Problem experiment

You will have to do an experiment to answer this problem. Take two magnets with their poles marked and lay them end to end under paper. There should be a gap between their poles at least equal to their length. Sprinkle iron filings on the paper until the magnetic field pattern shows up. Does your pattern look like the drawing on the right or on the left of the diagram? From the poles on your magnets, work out what type of poles X and Y are*.

Next lay your magnets side by side. Compare your magnetic field patterns with those in the drawing on the right and work out again what type of poles X and Y must be*.

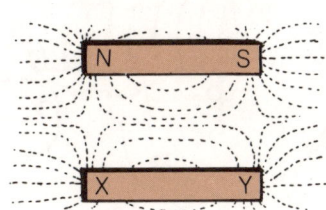

*X is N; Y is S.

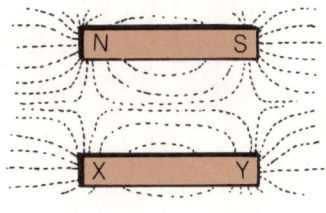

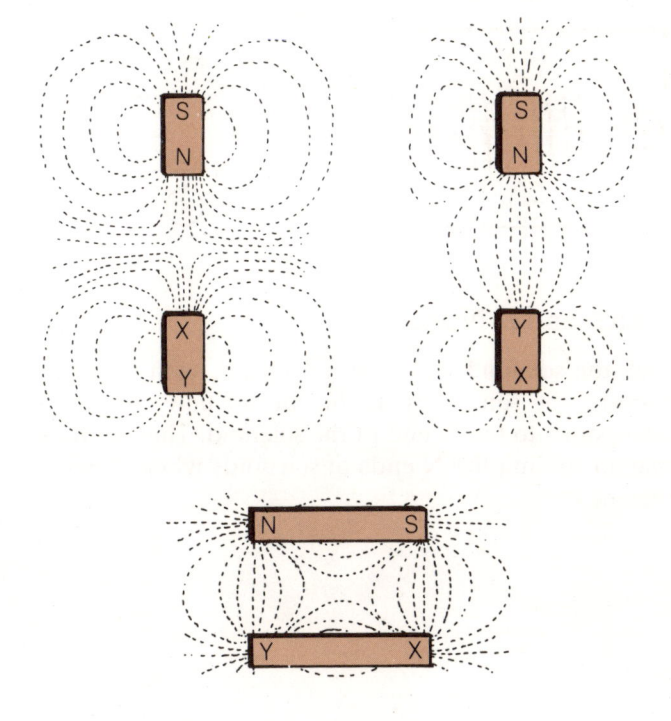

■ Magnetic fields can be shown up by iron filings.

An electric current and its magnetic field

Experiment

Pass an electric current along wires that go through the middle of a board. Sprinkle iron filings on the board and tap gently. The filings form into circles showing that a magnetic field is present when a current flows. Compass needles set in circles around the wire, each one pointing in a different direction.

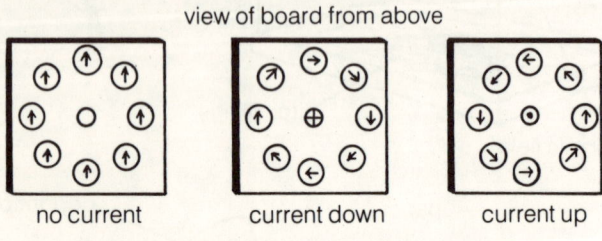

view of board from above

no current   current down   current up

Looking at the magnetic field of an electric current

wires carrying an electric current

low voltage

1   As long as the compasses are not too close they all point the same way when the current is off. Why is this?
How could you make the compass needles point in a circle the other way?

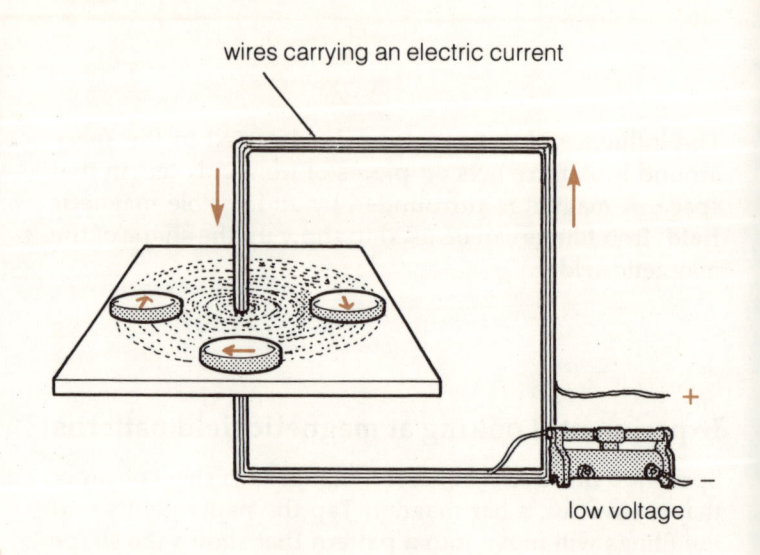

Experiment. The magnetic field of a current in a solenoid

A solenoid is a length of wire wound into a long coil. Iron filings on a board through its middle show a magnetic field is present when a current flows. The magnetic field has the same shape as the field of a bar magnet. A solenoid carrying a current has a strong magnetic field inside and its ends behave like N and S-poles.

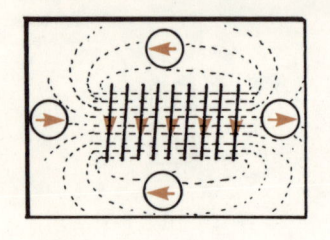

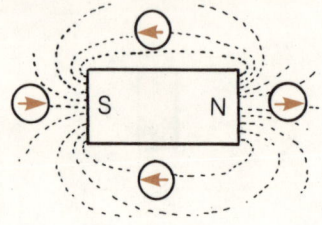

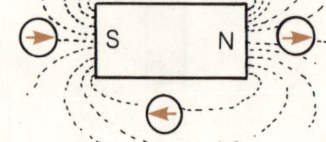

Which end is North?

Grab the solenoid with you right hand, with the fingers pointing the same way as the current flow. The thumb then points to the N end of the solenoid. This is a handy rule for finding the N ends of solenoids when they carry current.

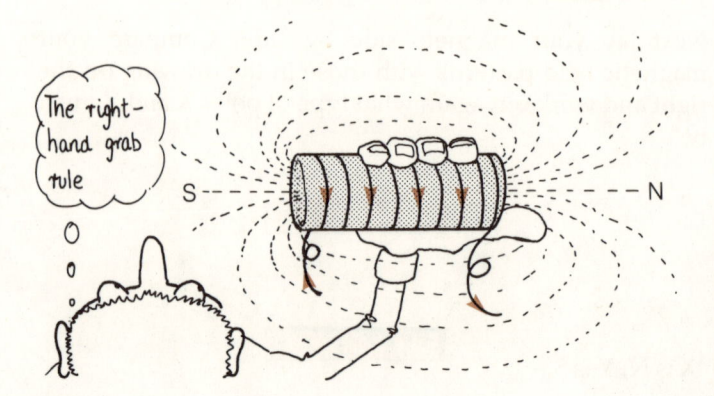

The right-hand grab rule

■ There is a magnetic field around wires carrying electric currents.

41 Uses of solenoids

Magnetizing

The strong magnetic field inside a solenoid carrying a current can be used to make steel into a magnet. The direction of the current determines which end of the steel becomes the N-pole.

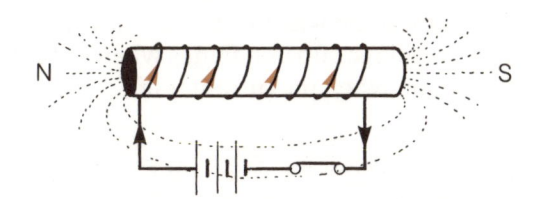

Using a solenoid and current to magnetize steel

1 Which end of the bar becomes a N-pole?

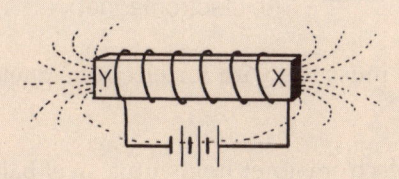

2 An alternating current (current that keeps changing direction rapidly) can be used to magnetize steel, but you can never tell which end will be a N-pole when you switch off. Can you explain this?

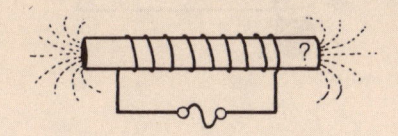

3 When the switch in this apparatus is pressed, the solenoid magnetizes and pulls the magnet down. If you press in rhythm with the bouncing magnet, large amplitude bounces build up.
(a) Should the top end of the solenoid become a N or S-pole for this to work? (b) Is the battery in the diagram connected correctly to do this? (c) Give another example of small regular forces being used to build up large amplitude vibrations.

Demagnetizing

An excellent way of getting rid of magnetism is to put the magnet in a solenoid carrying alternating current and then to pull it out until it is well clear. You will feel the vibrations as the tiny magnets in the metal are jumbled up by the magnetic field of the alternating current.

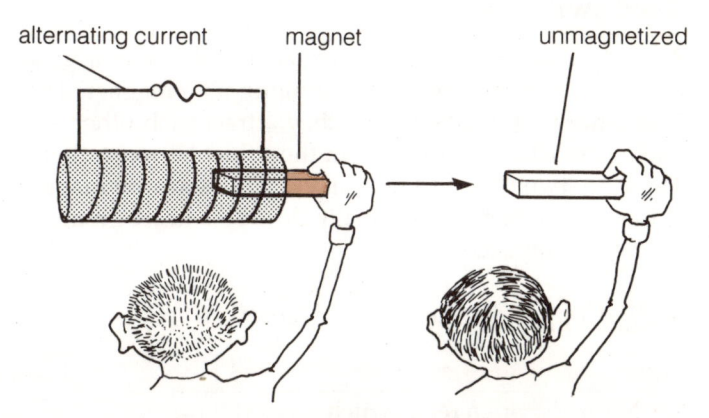

4 Pieces of iron and steel are wound with wire that is connected to a battery and switch. Both the iron and steel magnetize when the switch is closed. What will happen in each case when the switch is opened again?

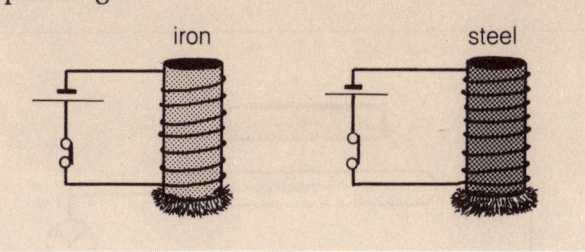

Using a solenoid and alternating current to demagnetize a magnet

5 Describe how you can use a solenoid
(a) to magnetize
(b) demagnetize a piece of steel.

■ A solenoid carrying a current can be used to magnetize iron and steel.

Electromagnets – magnets that can be switched on and off

Experiment. Making and testing an electromagnet

Wind about 2 metres of plastic-covered wire onto a piece of **iron** and connect the wire to a battery and switch. Your electromagnet will pick up iron filings when the current is on and drop them when the current is off.

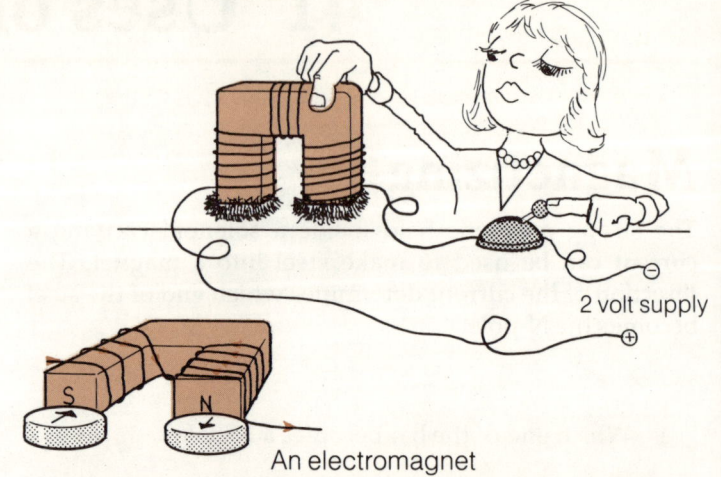

An electromagnet

6 Why is iron (and not steel) used for electromagnets?

7 Two electromagnets were made, one with an iron core and one with a steel core. What will happen when the current is switched on and off? Copy the table and put 'magnetized' or 'unmagnetized' in the boxes.

	Iron	Steel
Current on		
Current off		

8 Why must the wire for electromagnets be insulated?

9 An electromagnet holds up a steel ball. (a) Give two ways of making the electromagnet stronger. (b) The ball does **not** fall off when the magnet is switched off. Explain why not.

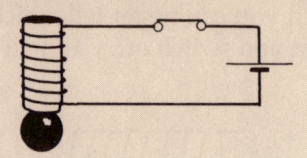

Uses of electromagnets

Reed switches

A reed switch has two iron reeds sealed inside a glass tube. The switch is closed by bringing up a magnet. This magnetizes the reeds so that they attract each other and make contact. The current can then flow between them. There are two types: (i) normally open – a nearby magnet closes the contacts; (ii) normally closed – a nearby magnet opens the contacts.

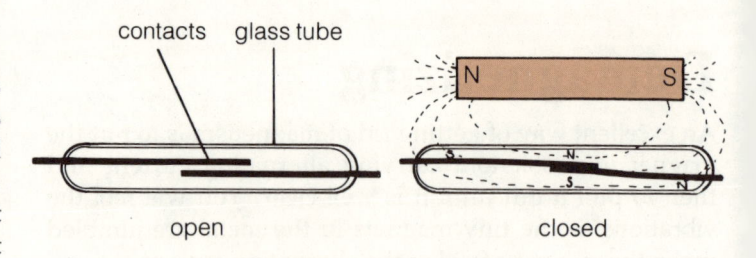

Normally open reed switch

10 Copy and write 'open' or 'closed' in spaces.

	Magnet near	Magnet nowhere near
Normally open reed switch		
Normally closed reed switch		

Experiment

Build this circuit and light the lamp by bringing up a magnet. Can you explain why it is best to hold the magnet parallel to the reed switch?

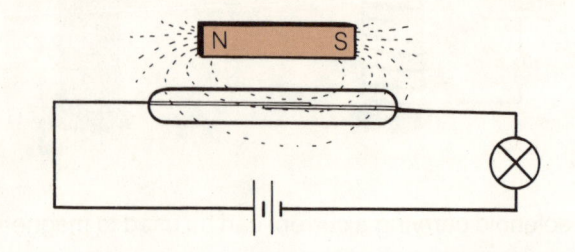

11 How to make an automatic door bell. Fix a magnet on the door and a reed switch to the door frame. Connect the reed switch to a bell and battery. When the door opens, the magnet moves away from the reed switch allowing it to close and ring the bell. (a) Is a normally open or normally closed reed switch needed for this? (b) Why is this arrangement not a very effective burglar alarm?

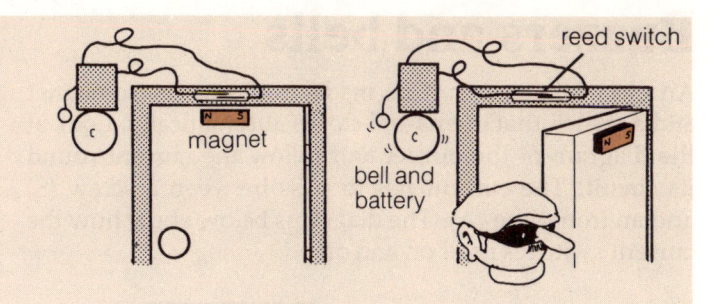

Reed relay

A current in a solenoid can be used instead of a magnet to switch on a reed switch. Closing the switch S produces a magnetic field in the solenoid. This closes the reed switch and switches on the lamp. Note there are two quite separate circuits. This arrangement is called a **relay.**

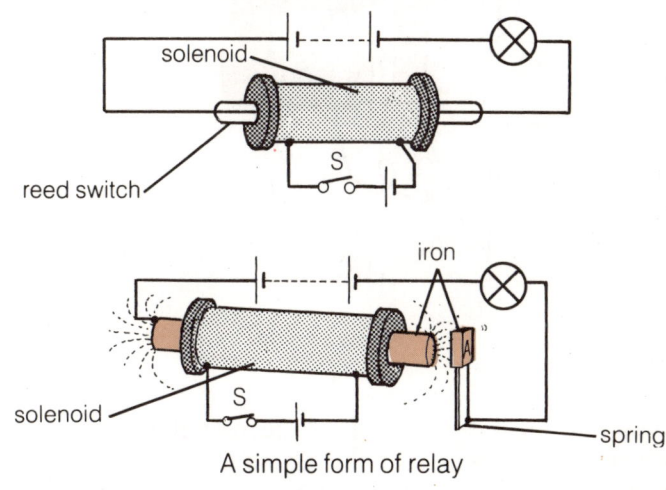

Electromagnetic relay

Closing switch S in this relay will magnetize the iron core. This core will then attract A, closing the lamp circuit and lighting the lamp. A small current in the solenoid can switch on a large current in the lamp circuit.

A simple form of relay

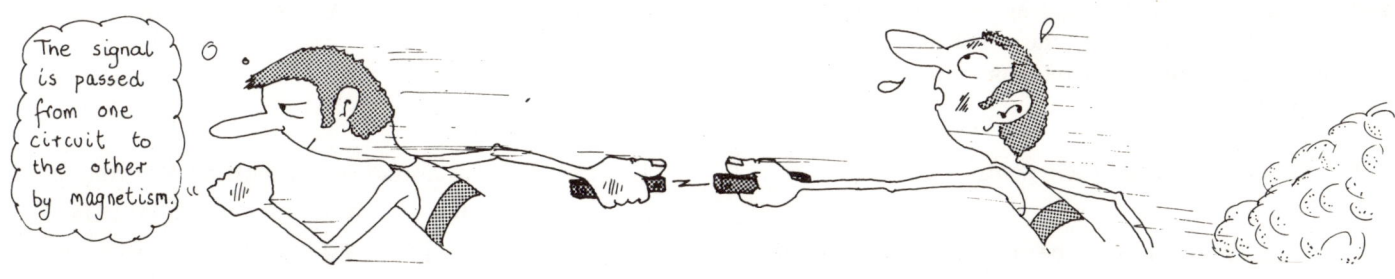

- A relay has two circuits.
- A small current in one circuit magnetically closes contacts in the other so that a large current can flow there.

The use of a relay in a car

The starter motor in a car uses a very large current (up to 100 amperes). A relay is used so that this large current can be switched on by a small current. The small current flows through the starter switch and into a solenoid. The solenoid magnetizes and pulls in a piece of iron, closing heavy duty contacts between the battery and starter motor.

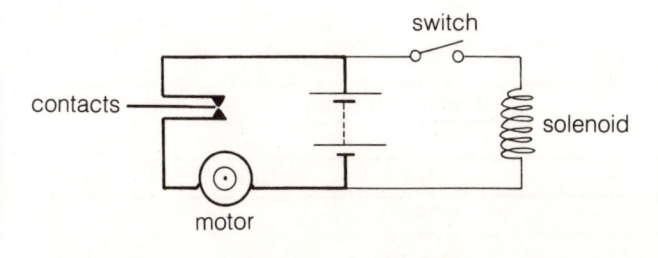

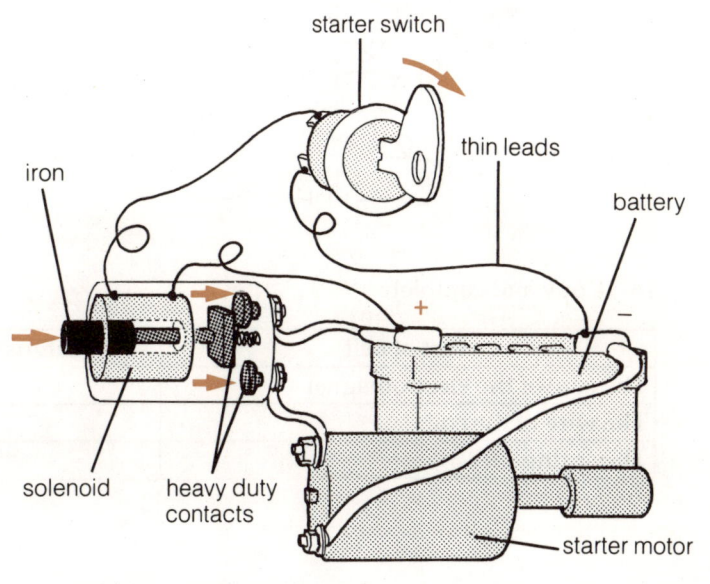

Using a relay to switch on a car starter motor

12 Explain why the leads to the starter motor are very thick and are kept as short as possible.

Buzzers and bells

An electric buzzer can be made from an electromagnet and a switch that opens and closes automatically. Look at the diagram of the buzzer and follow the current round its circuit. The current has to pass between a screw (S) and an iron piece (A). The diagrams below show how the current switches itself on and off.

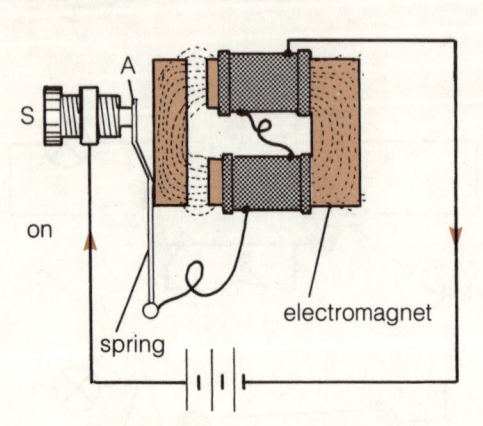

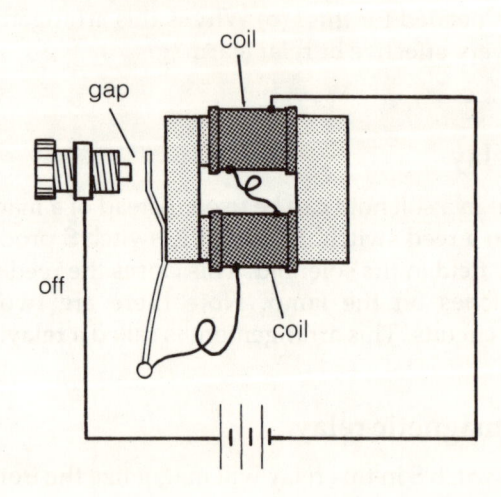

Start here
When A touches the screw a current flows, and the electromagnet switches on. A is attracted to the magnet and moves away from S. A gap appears between A and S. The current switches off, the electromagnet loses its magnetism and the spring returns A to the screw S. (Go back to 'start'.)

This to and fro motion happens very quickly (about 10 times a second) and makes a buzzing noise. In an electric bell a hammer attached to A hits a gong and makes it ring.

13 Describe in your own words how this buzzer works.

14 Why must piece A be made of iron and not steel? What would happen if it was made of steel?

15 Would the buzzer work with the wires connected as shown in this diagram? What happens when you switch on?

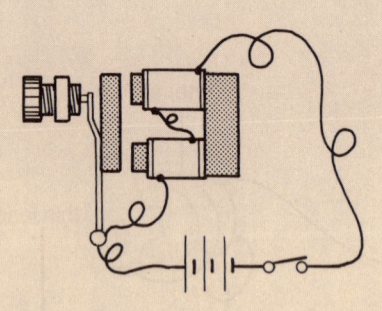

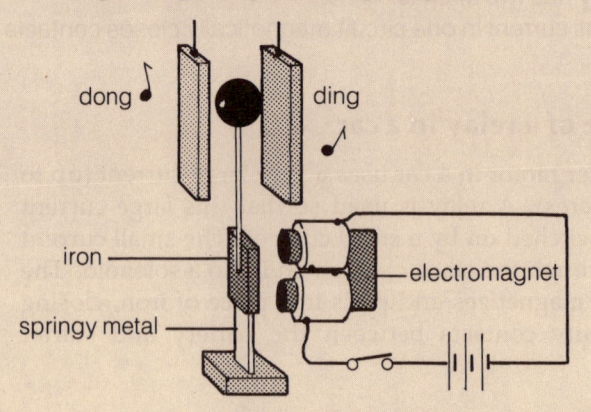

16 Copy and complete

Part of bell	Material used	Reason for using that material
The core of the electromagnet		
The wire of the coil		
The spring		

17 The diagram shows a bell with an electromagnet that can make a hammer hit two metal plates. When struck, the plates go 'ding' and 'dong'. The switch is closed and then opened again. Would the bell go 'ding-dong' or 'dong-ding'?

■ Buzzers and bells often contain electromagnets.

Summary of magnets and electromagnets

- Most magnets have two poles which are named .... North and South.
- Like poles .... repel.
- Unlike poles .... attract.
- An example of a material that can be made into a permanent magnet is .... steel.
- An example of a material that can be magnetized but that cannot hold its magnetism is .... iron.
- The Earth has a magnetic field. The arctic behaves like a magnetic .... S-pole.
- The magnetic field of an electric current in a straight wire is .... circular.
- The magnetic field of an electric current in a solenoid is similar to that of a .... bar magnet.
- A solenoid wound around an iron core is an .... electromagnet.
- Electromagnets are used in .... bells and relays.

Further questions

18 You are given three equal metal rods all painted the same colour. One rod is a magnet, one iron and one copper. Describe how you would find the material of each rod using only a compass needle.

19 Explain with the aid of a diagram how a piece of steel can be magnetized by a magnet. Label all the magnetic poles.

20 The diagram below shows the magnetic field between two parallel magnets. (a) One pole is marked. What are the poles A,B,C? (b) If the magnets were free to move, what would you expect to happen?

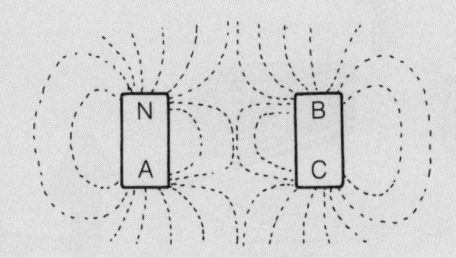

21 This diagram is of an electric bell.
(a) Name the parts A and B. (b) Name the materials used to make parts C,D and E. (c) Explain why the bell vibrates when the switch is closed.

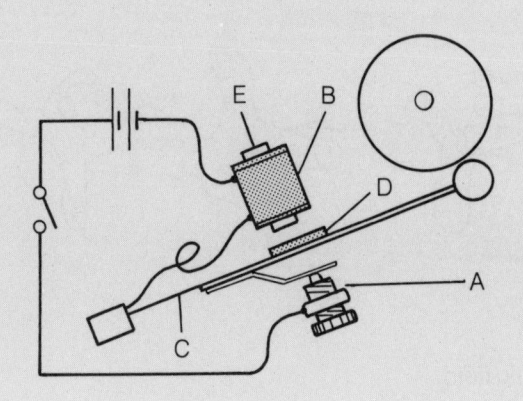

22 Shown below are iron filing patterns of magnetic fields. Which pattern is produced by:
(a) attracting magnets;
(b) repelling magnets;
(c) a solenoid carrying a current;
(d) a long straight wire carrying a current?

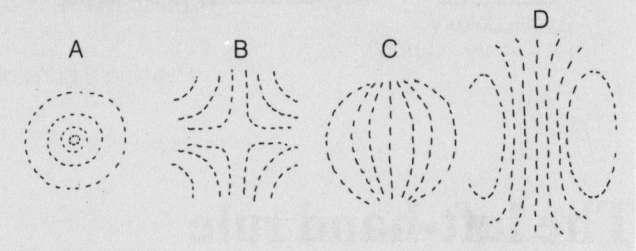

23 The diagram shows an electromagnet and two cells. Draw the magnet and cells connected so that the strength of the magnet is a maximum. (E.Anglia)

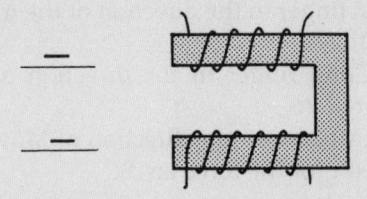

24 The diagram shows a simple electromagnet.
(a) What metal is used for the bar AB?
(b) Give two ways of making the magnet stronger.
(c) Sketch the magnetic field around the magnet.
(d) What is the effect, if any, of reversing the battery?
(e) Why is the copper wire of the coil insulated?

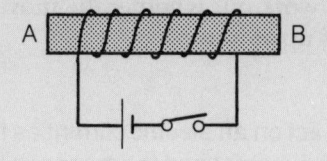

42 When an electric current crosses a magnetic field

Experiment

Fix a strip of aluminium foil between the poles of a strong magnet and clip wires from a battery and switch to each end of the foil. Switch on the current and you will see the foil jump. A force acts on the electric current as it passes along the foil through the magnetic field. Make the current flow the other way by changing the leads at the battery and note that the foil moves the other way. Reversing the magnet has the same effect.

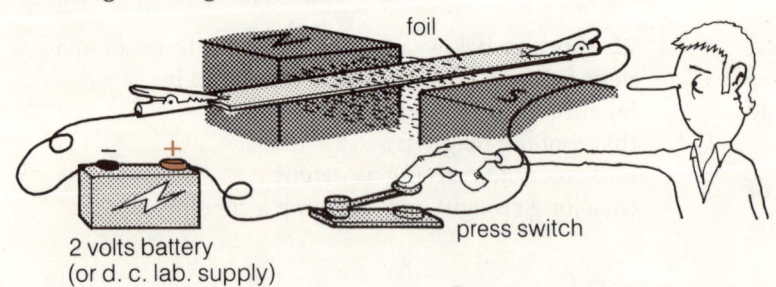

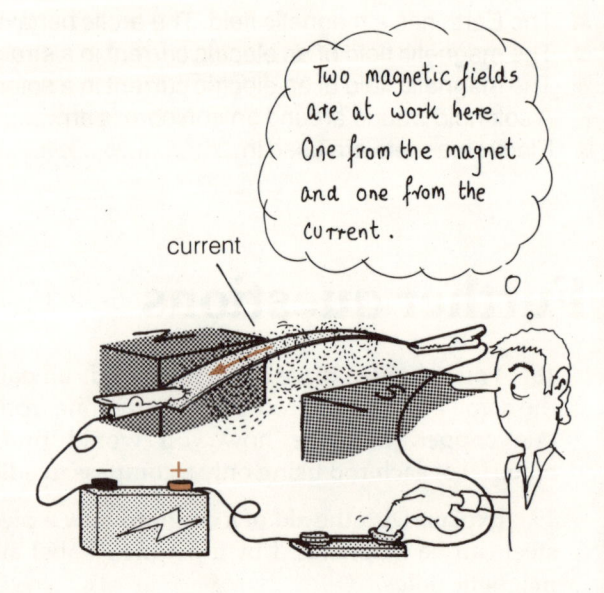

Two magnetic fields are at work here. One from the magnet and one from the current.

Passing a current through a magnetic field

The left-hand rule

The movement, the electric current and the magnetic field are all in different directions. You can use your left hand to work out which way the foil (or a wire carrying a current) will move.

Point the First finger in the direction of the magnetic Field (N to S)
    the seCond finger in the direction of the electric Current (+ to −)
    the thuMb shows the direction of Movement of the conductor (or the force on it).

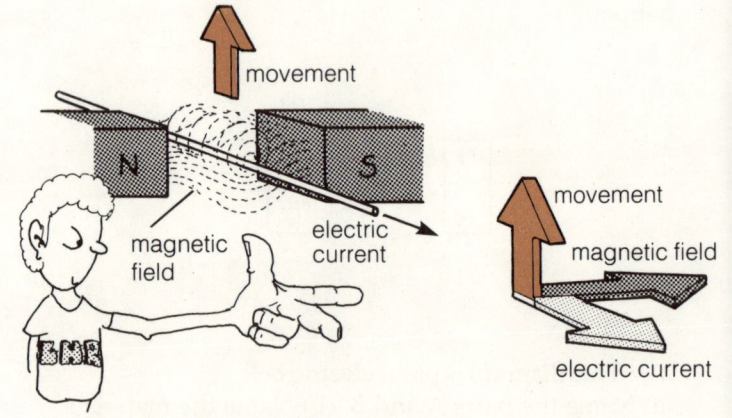

The direction of the force on an electric current in a magnetic field

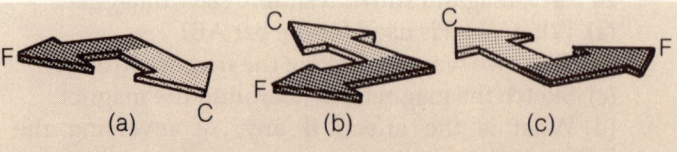

1 If the magnetic field (F) and electric current (C) are in the directions shown by the arrows, use your left hand to work out whether the movement of the conductor is up or down.

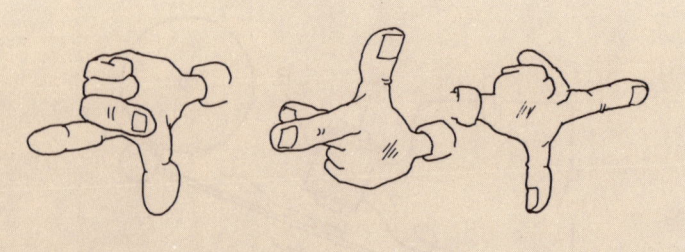

■ A force can act on an electric current as it passes through a magnetic field.
■ The force, the current and the magnetic field are all in different directions.

The electric motor

If an electric current flows through two copper wires that are between the poles of a magnet, an upward force will move one wire up and a downward force will move the other wire down. If a loop of wire is made, that can spin on an axle, the two forces will turn the loop. It will not go far though because the wires from the battery will get twisted and after half a turn the forces will flick the loop back.

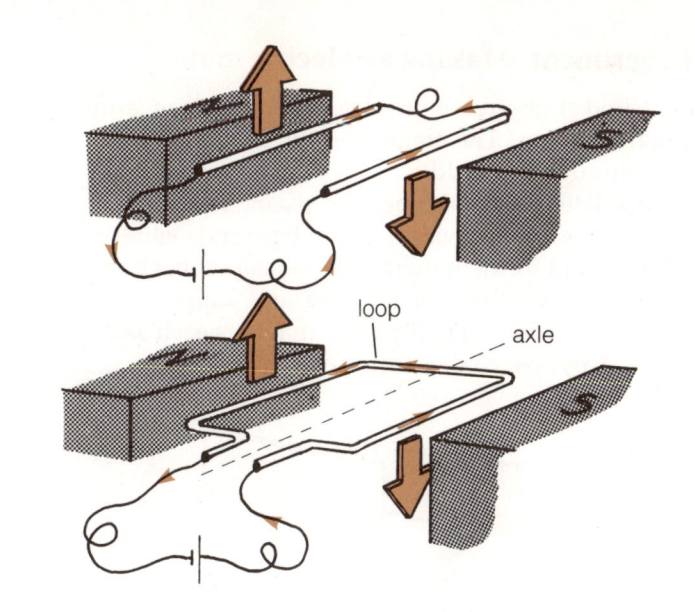

How the loop can be made to go round and round

The loop can be made to spin by fixing a half circle of copper to each end of the loop. (These copper strips are called a **commutator**.) Current is passed into and out of the loop by 'brushes' that press onto the strips. (Brushes are usually made from carbon or copper.) The brushes do not go round so the wires do not get twisted. This arrangement also makes sure that the current always passes down on the right and back on the left (in this case) so that the rotation continues. This is how a simple electric motor is made.

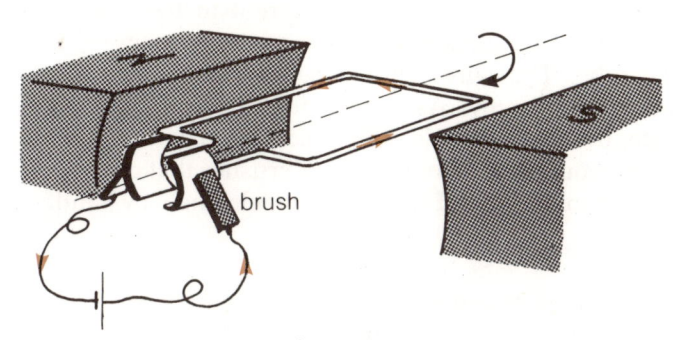

A simple electric motor

How to make the motor more powerful

(a) Take a long piece of wire and wind a loop of many turns. 10 turns increases the turning force 10 times (for the same current).
(b) Put a second loop on the same axle. This is like having two motors on the same axle giving more force and more even running.
(c) Wind the loops on an iron core. This increases the strength of the magnetic field through which the current passes.

> 2 Why is the number of strips on the commutator equal to twice the number of loops on the armature?

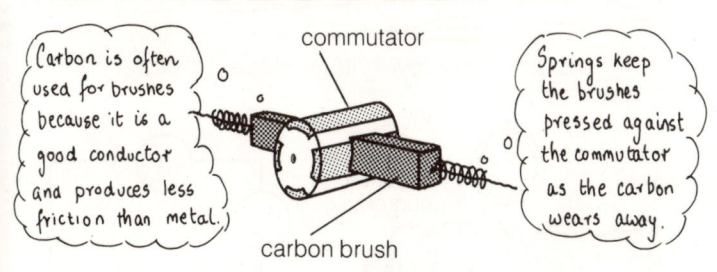

Carbon is often used for brushes because it is a good conductor and produces less friction than metal.

Springs keep the brushes pressed against the commutator as the carbon wears away.

The brushes of an electric motor

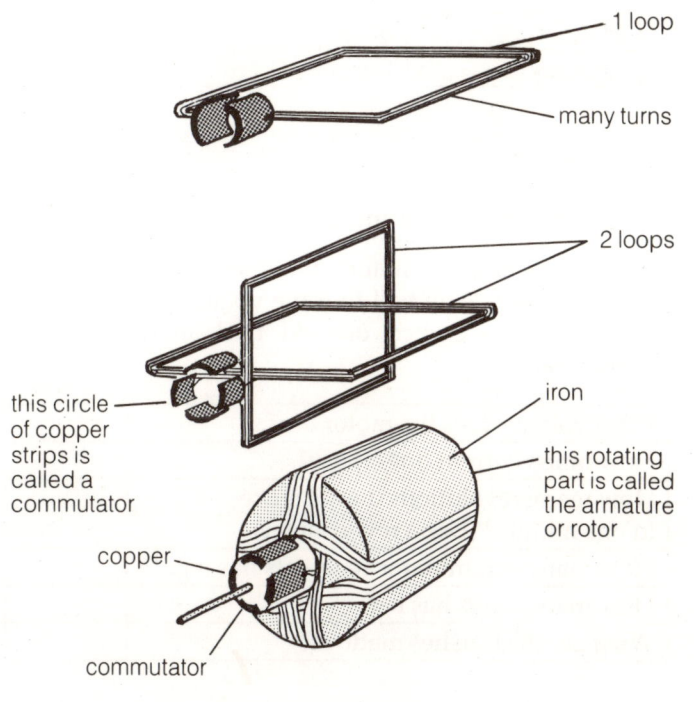

Improving the rotor to make a more powerful motor

■ A simple electric motor can be made from a loop of wire, a magnet, a commutator and two brushes.

185

Experiment. Making an electric motor

(a) Wind 1 metre of insulated copper wire around a wooden frame. The frame should have a hollow metal tube through the middle.

(b) Insulate the metal tube with plastic tape and bare the ends of the copper wire. Lay the bare ends either side of the tube and fix them there with a small rubber band.

(c) Put an axle through the tube and support it at each end by a split-pin. Finally place magnets each side of the coil with opposite poles facing each other.

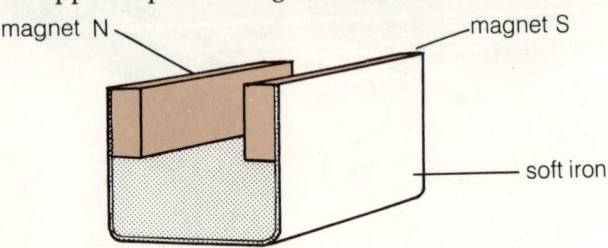

An iron yoke is an effective way of holding the magnets

The simplest way of feeding current to the loop is to touch the bare ends of connecting wire on either side of the tube. The wires should be connected to a 2 volt laboratory supply. As current flows round the loop of wire, the motor should spin rapidly (it may need a flick). When your motor works, design brushes that can supply current to the loop of wire without being held by hand.

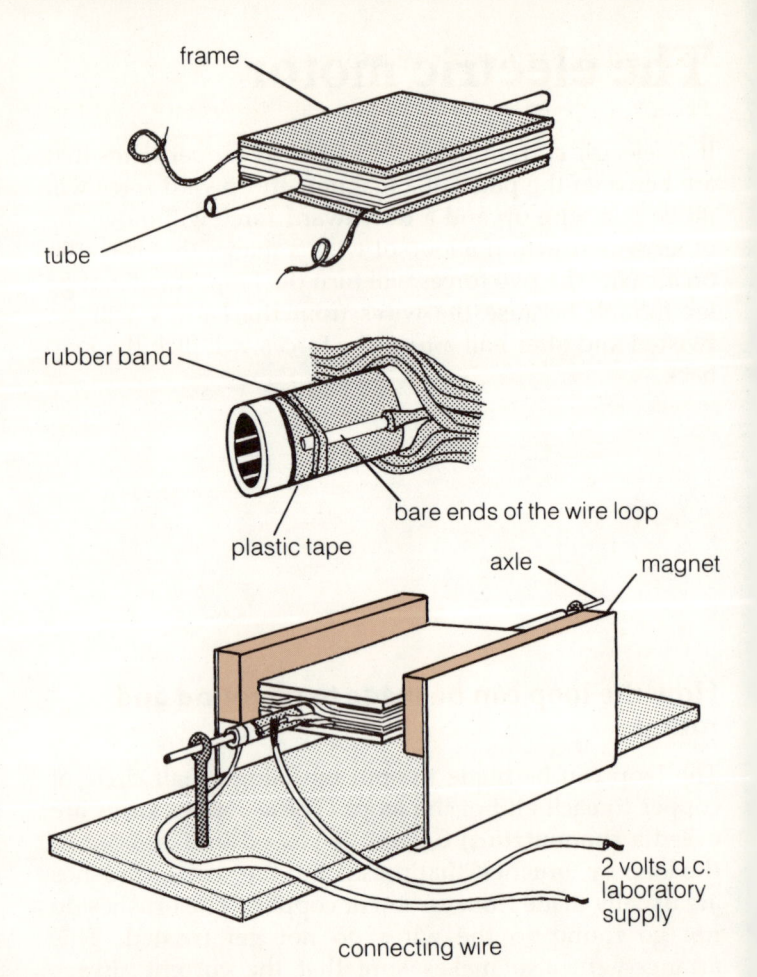

3 An electric motor has the following parts made from the materials shown. Copy the table and put reasons for choosing these materials.

Part	Materials used	Reason for using these materials
Coil of wire	Copper metal coated with enamel	
Magnet	Steel	
Brushes	Carbon	

Experiments with a motor

Connect an electric motor, ammeter and switch to a voltage supply. (You will find the voltage to use written on the motor.) Switch on and find answers to this questionnaire.

What voltage does the motor use?	
How much current does it use?	
How many revolutions does it make in one minute? (Use a rev. counter)	
How many commutator segments has it got?	
How many loops has it got?	
What are the brushes made of?	

Examining a low voltage electric motor

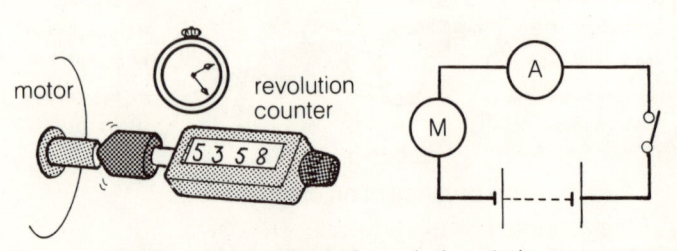

Finding the number of revolutions/minute

A speed control for the motor

Include a rheostat in the circuit with the motor and the ammeter. Moving the rheostat slider will change the current going to the motor and its speed. Use a revolution counter to measure the speed of the motor (in revs/minute) for different current values. Note there are different types of electric motor that have other ways of controlling their speed.

Controlling the speed of a low-voltage motor

4 Draw a circuit diagram for the circuit with the rheostat.

5 Make a list of 10 machines that have an electric motor in them. Put a * by those that have a speed control for the motor.

6 Which loop in these diagrams will turn clockwise and which will turn anticlockwise?

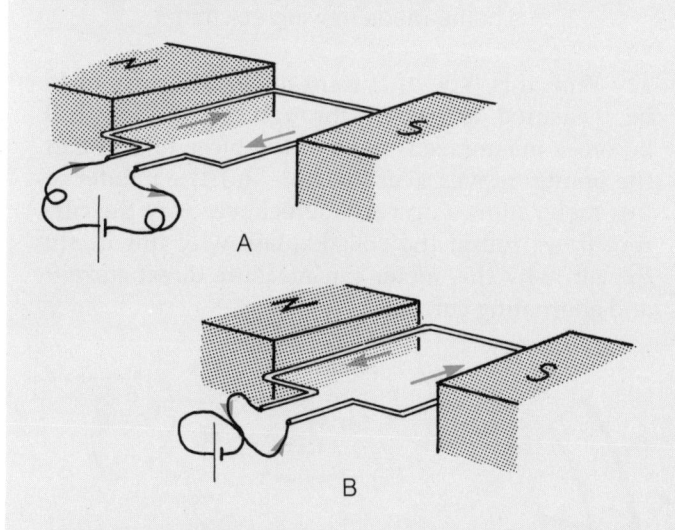

7 Which way will the forces act on each side of the loop when it is in this position?

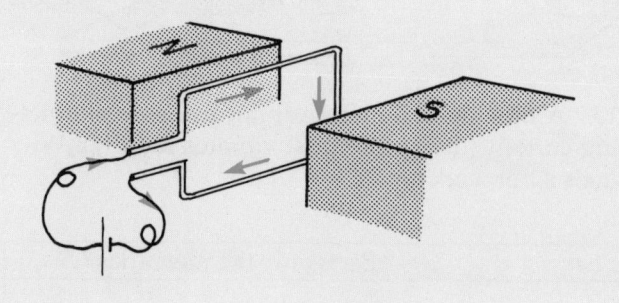

8 Make a list of the steps you have to take to start up a steam engine. Name three advantages that an electric motor has got over a steam engine.

9 This diagram shows how electrical energy is changed into other forms by a motor fitted with a propeller. (a) Describe the energy changes in your own words. (b) What do you think will happen eventually to the kinetic energy of the air?

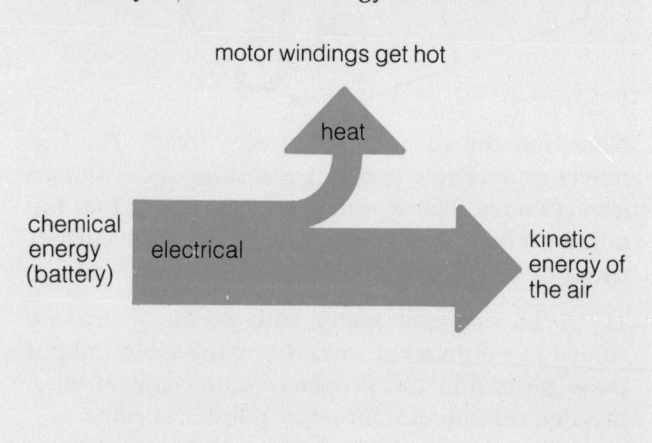

- Electric motors start at the press of a switch.
- Their speed can be easily controlled; they are powerful for their size and do not waste much energy.

Moving coil meters

The force that turns an electric motor is used in **moving coil** meters to move a pointer. The movement is used to measure electric current. Moving coil meters can be altered to measure voltage as well.

Experiment. Making and testing a moving coil current meter

Wind insulated wire round a frame, leaving two long ends. Turn the ends round a pencil to make weak springs and support the frame on an axle between the poles of a magnet. Fix a straw to the frame to act as a pointer. Connect a battery to the ends of the wire and notice how the pointer flicks to one side when the current flows.

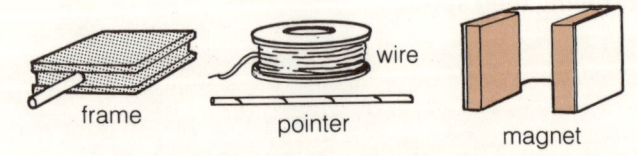

Parts needed to make a moving coil meter

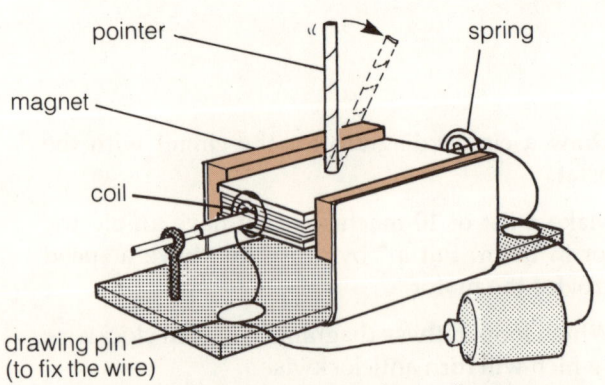

A home-made moving coil meter

How it works

Two forces act on the frame as current passes round the coil. These turn the frame. As it turns, the springs tighten until they balance the turning force on the frame. The movement then stops. The bigger the current, the bigger the movement or deflection will be.

10 This diagram shows the insides of a moving coil meter. Which letter shows each of the following parts: the moving coil; the permanent magnet; the control springs; the pointer?

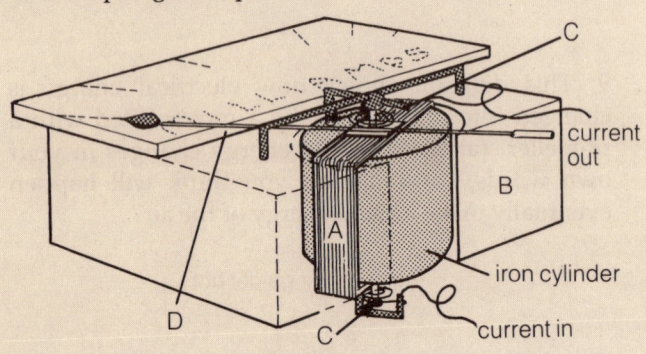

Note that the magnet poles are curved. The coil moves in a narrow gap between these poles and an iron cylinder. This arrangement is used so that the pointer moves evenly over the scale as the current rises.

11 A moving coil meter and electric motor are similar in a number of ways. Copy this table and put these parts into the proper columns: coil of wire; magnet; commutator; brushes; pointer; springs.

12 With this type of current meter, the current to be measured is passed through a coil. The coil becomes magnetized, pulls in the piece of iron and the pointer moves over the scale. (a) The pointer of this meter moves upwards whichever way the current flows round the coil. Explain why this is. (b) Explain why this meter can measure direct current and alternating current.

13 A moving coil meter cannot measure alternating current (the pointer just vibrates rapidly). Why does it not work for a.c.?

Parts they both have	Parts only the motor has	Parts only the meter has

■ A moving coil meter uses the force on a current in a magnetic field to measure that current.

Loudspeakers

Loudspeakers bring speech and music into our homes. They produce much of the music we hear and copy our voices when we speak on the telephone.

14 Make a list of the things you have at home that contain loudspeakers.

15 Which of the following do not use loudspeakers to make music: radio; record player; pipe organ; piano; electronic organ; violin?

Experiment. Making a simple loudspeaker

Make a tube and cone and stick them together as shown. Wind fine copper wire tightly round the tube and connect its ends to a battery radio in place of its own loudspeaker. Hold a magnet just inside the tube and you will feel the magnet and cone vibrating. Can you hear any speech or music?

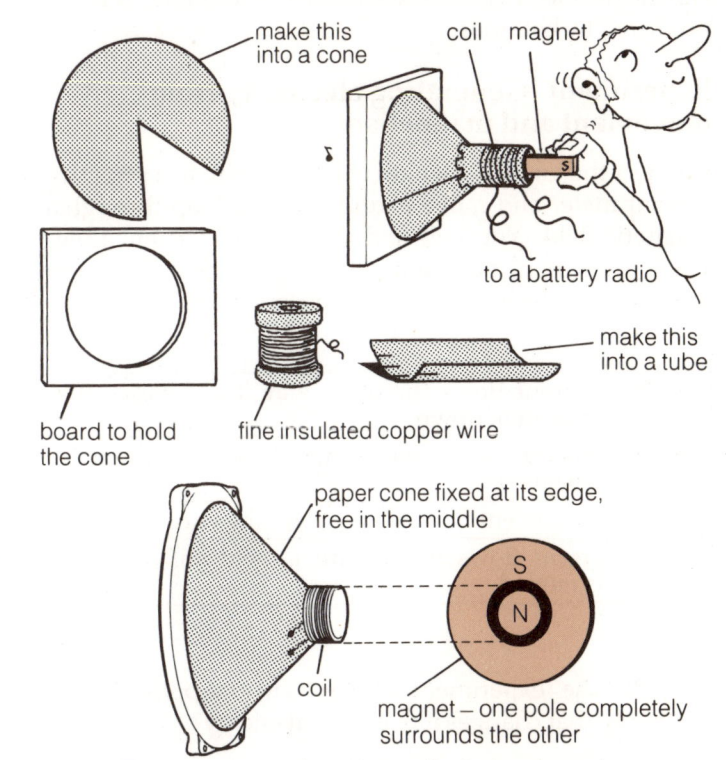

Real loudspeakers

The magnet of a moving coil loudspeaker has a narrow circular gap between its poles. A coil, fixed at the point of the cone fits into this gap without touching the sides.

The magnet and moving coil of a loudspeaker

How does it work

If you connect a battery to an old loudspeaker, you will see the centre of the cone jump out or in. As current passes through the coil in the magnetic field, a force acts on the coil. This force moves the coil in or out of the magnet gap depending on the direction of the current. The current from a radio amplifier changes direction rapidly. So as it passes through the coil of the loudspeaker, the coil moves rapidly in and out of the magnet. The cardboard cone is made to vibrate in step with the current and sends out sound waves into the air.

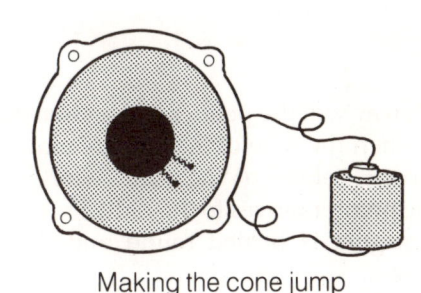

Making the cone jump

16 A loudspeaker makes energy change form. This diagram shows those changes. Describe them in your own words.

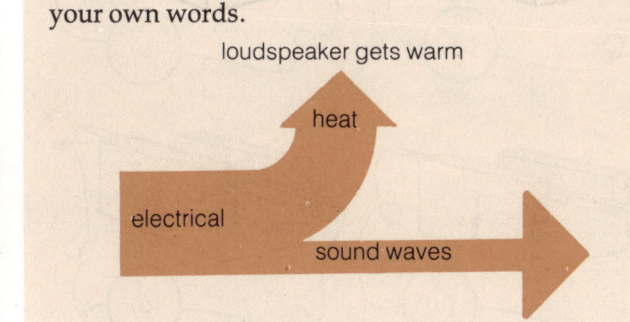

17 If the current and the magnetic field of a loudspeaker are in the direction shown in this diagram, will the coil move to the right or the left?

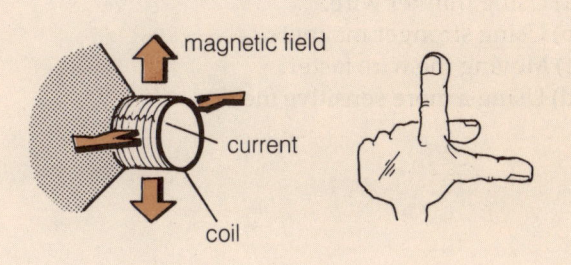

■ The force on a changing current in a magnetic field is used to vibrate the cone of a loudspeaker.

43 Making electricity

How is the electricity made that we use at home? It is not produced by batteries.

Experiment. Generating electricity from movement and magnetism

Connect the ends of a length of copper wire to a sensitive current meter and move part of the wire loop through a magnetic field. You will find that a small current flows while the wire is moving in the magnetic field. Use your apparatus to check the following observations.

| (a) The current flows the other way if you move the wire up instead of down. |
| (b) There is no current when there is no movement or no magnetic field. |
| (c) A larger current flows if you move the wire faster. |
| (d) A current flows if the wire is held still and the magnet is moved. |

A current flows and there is no battery in the circuit

Generating electricity from movement and magnetism

1 In the experiment above, what supplies the energy that changes into electrical energy?

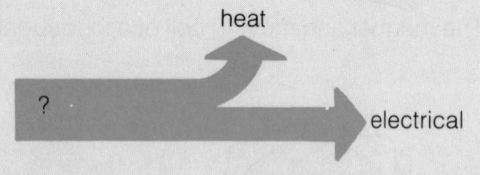

? → electrical / heat

2 Which way will the pointer of the ammeter move (if at all) when the wire or magnet are moved in the ways shown below? (When the wire is moved down, the pointer moves to the right.)
(a) The magnet is turned round and the wire is moved down.
(b) The magnet is moved up.
(c) The magnet is moved down.
(d) The wire is moved sideways from one magnet to the other.

3 Which two of these changes will probably make the current larger?
(a) Using thinner wire.
(b) Using stronger magnets.
(c) Moving the wire faster.
(d) Using a more sensitive meter.

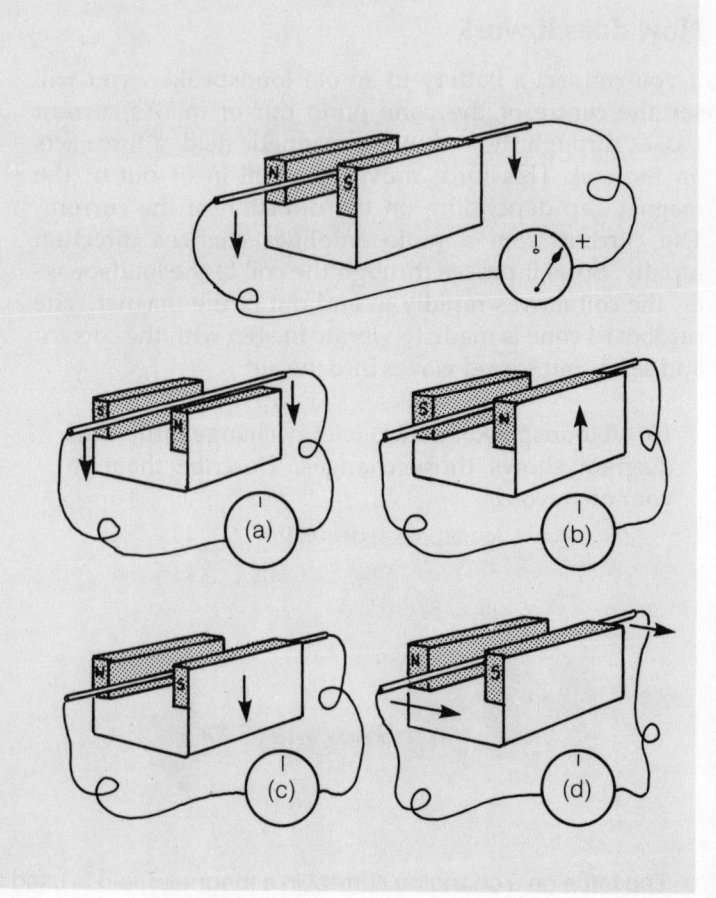

The right-hand rule

The fingers of the right hand can be used to find the direction of the current produced by the movement and the magnetism. The fingers are used in the same way as the left-hand rule (p. 184).

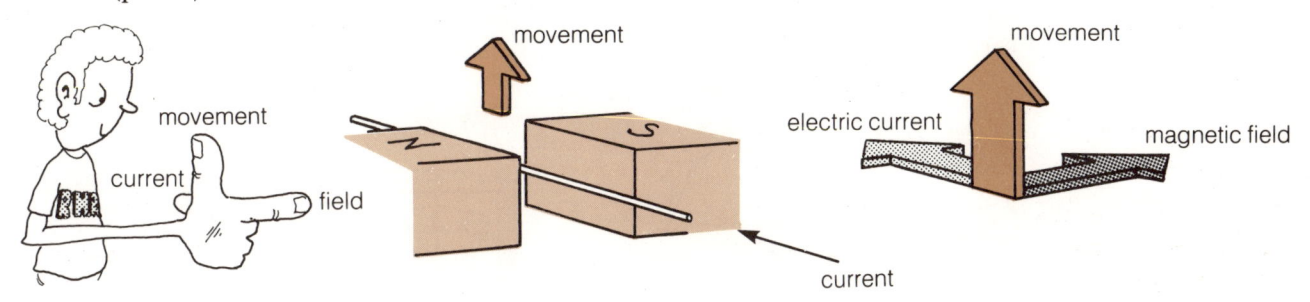

Finding the direction of the generated current

Dynamos – direct current generators

To make a current that flows all the time, the wire is bent into a loop and rotated in a magnetic field. Current is generated by the movement and passes out through brushes to an outside circuit. This arrangement is a simple dynamo.

4 Is there any difference between the construction of a dynamo and an electric motor (see p. 185)?

5 Which diagram shows the energy changes in (a) an electric motor, (b) a dynamo?

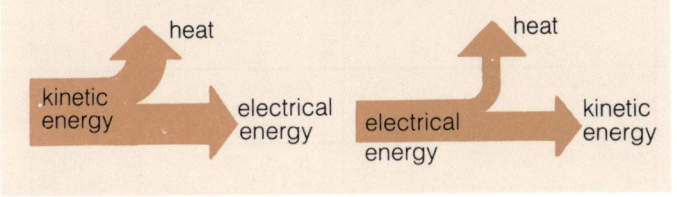

A d.c. dynamo

- A current will flow in a loop of wire if part of the loop is moved across a magnetic field.
- The current, the movement and the magnetic field are all in different directions.

Experiment. Looking at the current from a dynamo

Connect a dynamo to an ammeter that has zero in the centre of its scale. Turn the dynamo and you will see the pointer move out and back on one side of the zero. The current flows one way round the circuit and rises and falls in value. (The current from a cell flows one way and has a steady value.) This is called **direct current**.

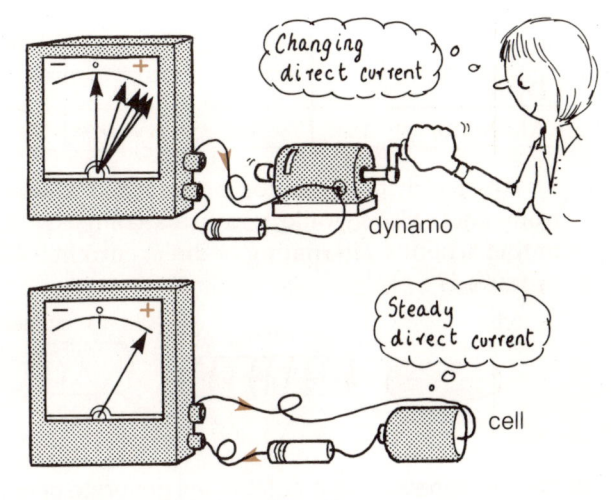

Steady and changing direct current

Alternators – alternating current generators

If two circular 'slip rings' are used in a dynamo instead of two half rings, the current it generates will flow first one way through the circuit then the other. This is called **alternating current** (a.c.). It lights a lamp almost as well as direct current but makes the pointer of an ammeter swing from + to − to + each turn of the loop.

slip rings
brushes
An a.c. alternator
Alternating current 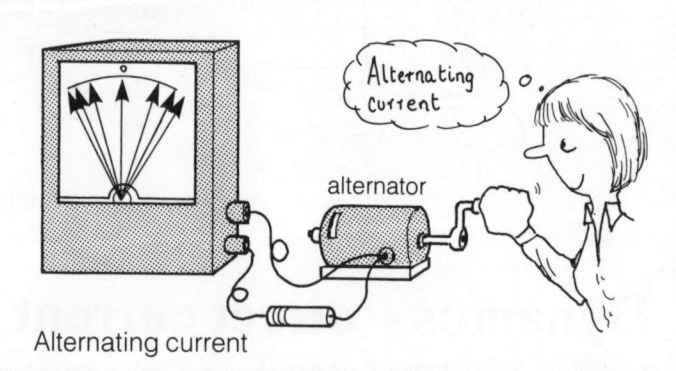
alternator

6 Copy this table that describes the current produced by dynamo, alternator and cell. Draw these graphs alongside the description that it fits.

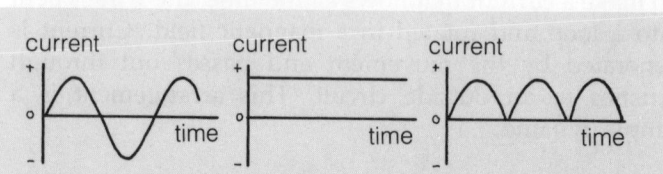

Description of the current	Graph of the current against time	What produces current like this?
The current gets larger then smaller until it dies away altogether. The current then continues to rise and fall in size, always flowing one way through the wires		
The current stays the same size and flows the same way all the time		
The current gets larger then smaller until it dies away altogether. It then begins to flow the opposite way, getting larger and smaller in the other direction		

7 Copy and complete.

Source of current	Is the current steady?	Does it flow one way only?	Does it flow both ways?	Is the current changing in size all the time?	a.c. or d.c.?
Cell					
Dynamo					
Alternator					

8 An electricity generator is connected to an electromagnet. How would you use a compass needle to find whether alternating or direct current is being produced?

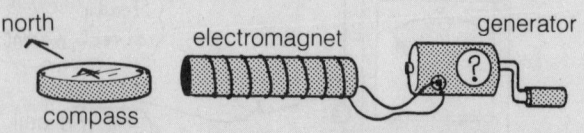

north
compass
electromagnet
generator

9 Suggest one way of making a dynamo generate more electric current.

10 What type of current is 'mains current', alternating or direct current?

- Dynamos have a commutator and generate direct current.
- Alternators have slip rings and generate alternating current.

Practical generators of electricity

Alternator

The current produced by an alternator can be increased by winding a loop of many turns of wire onto an iron core and curving the poles of the magnet. Sometimes electromagnets are used instead of permanent magnets. Electromagnets can be stronger but need a supply of direct current to work them. Alternators are found in some car and lorry engines.

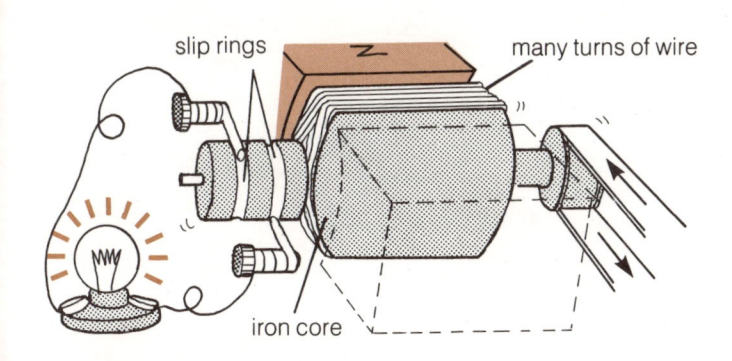

Cycle alternator

We have seen that current is generated if the magnet is moved instead of the wire (p. 190). Sometimes it is more convenient to move the magnet. Brushes and slip rings are not needed if the coil does not move. The cycle alternator shown here has a circular magnet that is made to spin inside an iron core. Alternating current is generated in a coil wound on this core.

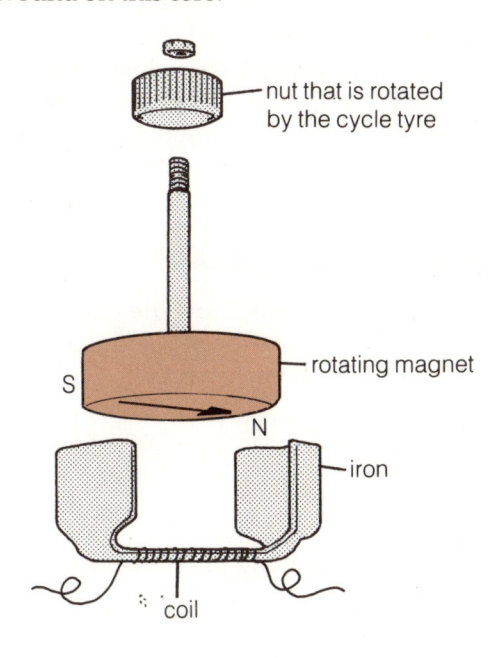

Mains alternator

The alternators that produce 'mains' electricity also have a rotating magnet inside stationary coils. The rotating magnet is an electromagnet that is supplied with direct current from a dynamo on the same drive shaft. The electromagnet and dynamo are kept spinning at exactly 50 revolutions/second by a steam turbine (p. 67). Alternating current is generating in the stationary coils and can be led to our homes without brushes or slip rings.

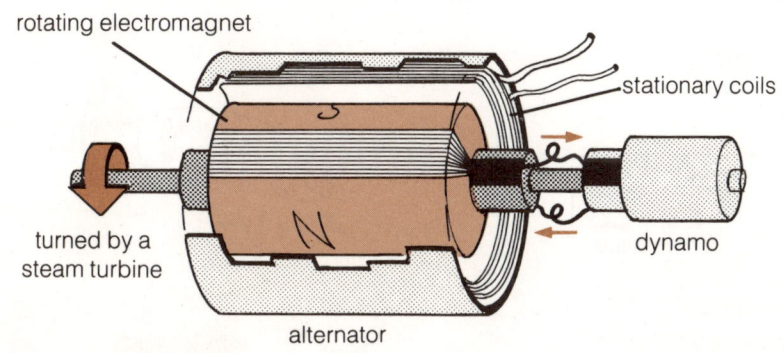

■ If the magnet is rotated in an alternator, instead of the coil, slip rings are not needed to take out the current.

The moving coil microphone – a generator of small electric currents

Microphones are widely used in broadcasting (radio and television) and recording of sound. Microphones change sound energy into electrical energy. You probably have more than one microphone at home in a telephone or tape recorder. Loudspeakers are designed to change electrical energy into sound but they will work in reverse as microphones.

Experiment

Connect two loudspeakers together with two long wires. Speak into one loudspeaker while a friend listens to the other. Can you generate enough electric current in your loudspeaker to work the loudspeaker at the other end? Can your friend speak to you through the wires?

11 Which loudspeaker in the diagram above is being used as a microphone?

12 These diagrams show the energy changes that take place in a loudspeaker and microphone. Copy them and label them correctly.

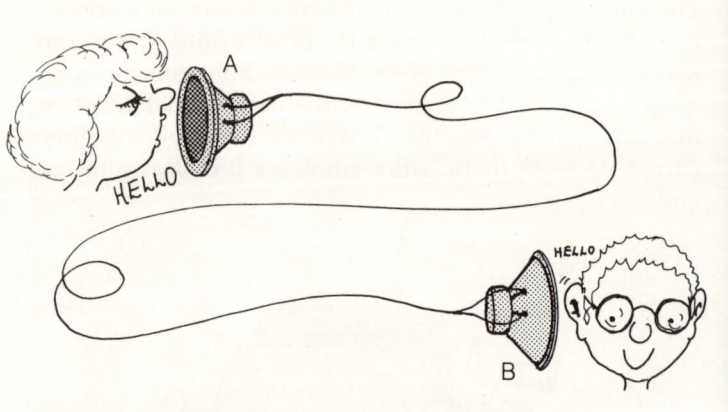

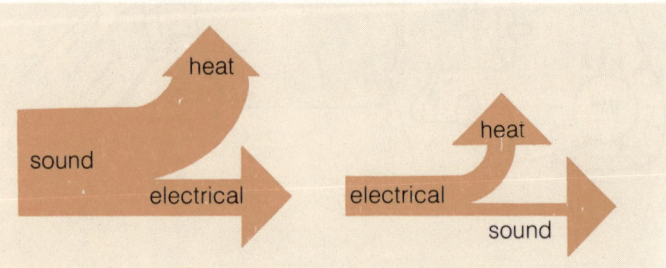

How does a moving coil microphone work?

This type of microphone has a light coil that is held in a circular slot between the poles of a magnet (very much like a loudspeaker coil, p.189). Sound waves make the coil vibrate in and out of the slot. This movement induces an electric current in the coil; a current that changes in step with the vibrations. This current can be changed back into sound by passing it through a loudspeaker. Because of energy losses this sound will not be very loud.

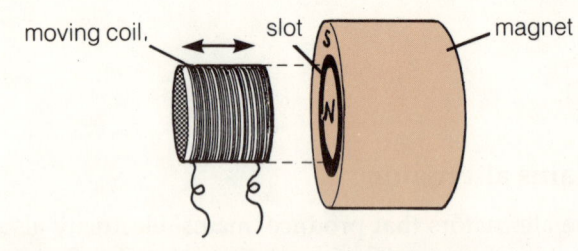

The moving coil and magnet of a microphone

Experiment. Using an amplifier

Connect an amplifier between the two loudspeakers. Now what happens when you speak to your friend? Can he speak to you now?

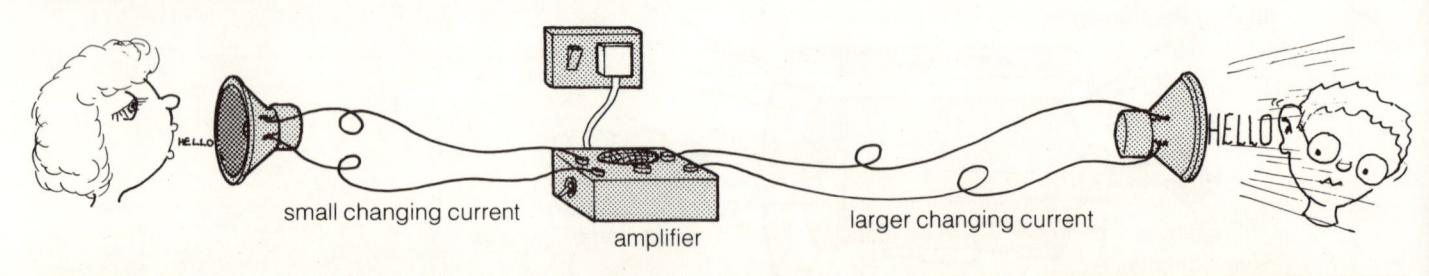

13 What does the amplifier do in this experiment? Why is a microphone nearly always connected to an amplifier?

14 This diagram shows the energy changes that take place in the amplifier experiment. Can you explain these changes?

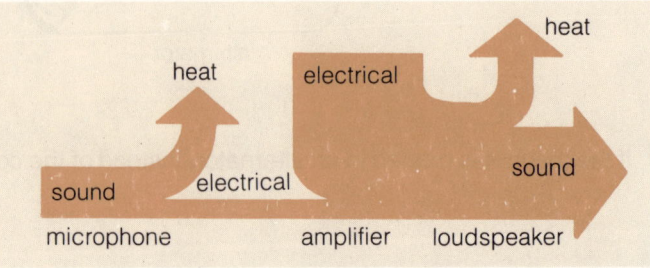

Changing a.c. to d.c.

Most electronic devices use direct current so it is useful to change the alternating current of the 'mains' to direct current.

Experiment. What can a diode do?

A diode is a small electronic component that has a useful property. Build a diode, a lamp, a cell and an ammeter into a circuit. Connect the diode first pointing one way then the other. You will see that current can only pass through this diode in one direction. Current trying to pass the other way is blocked. The diode is an electronic 'valve'.

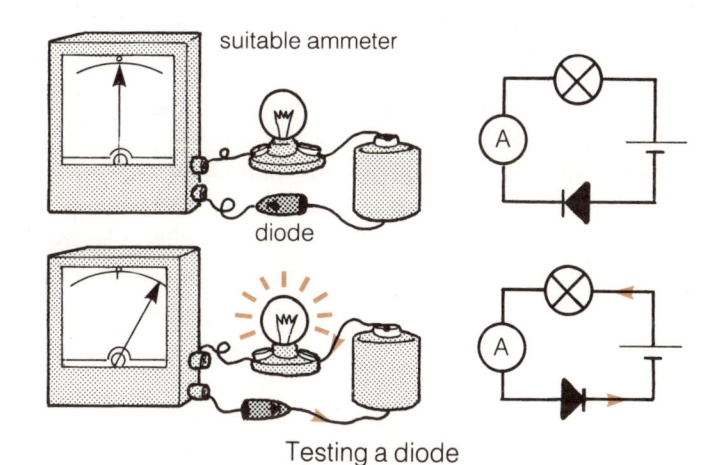

Testing a diode

15 Here are some one-way devices. Copy the table and write what it is that can flow one way but not the other.

Turnstile	
Tyre valve	
Heart valve	
Diode	

16 Draw these circuits and put -☼- on the lamps that light.

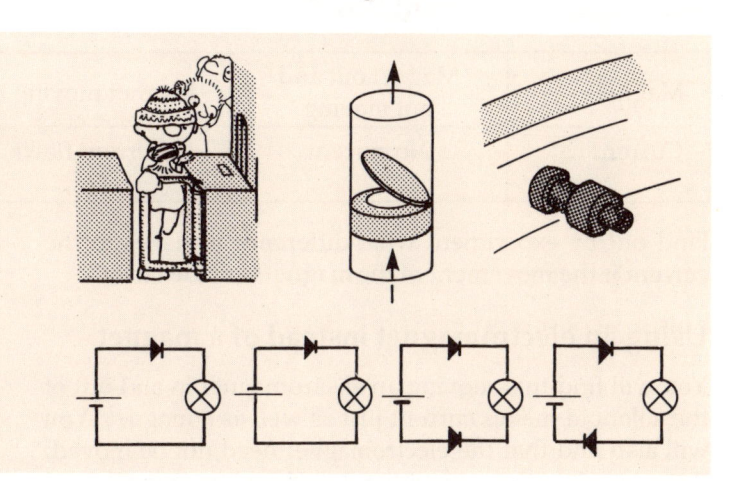

Experiment

Connect an alternator (or a supply of slow alternating current) to a diode, lamp and centre-reading ammeter. Turn the alternator and watch the ammeter.

A current flows for half of each turn but when the alternator tries to drive the current the other way, none flows. The diode blocks the reverse flow and makes sure the current flow is one way only. A diode changes alternating current into direct current. This process is called **rectification**.

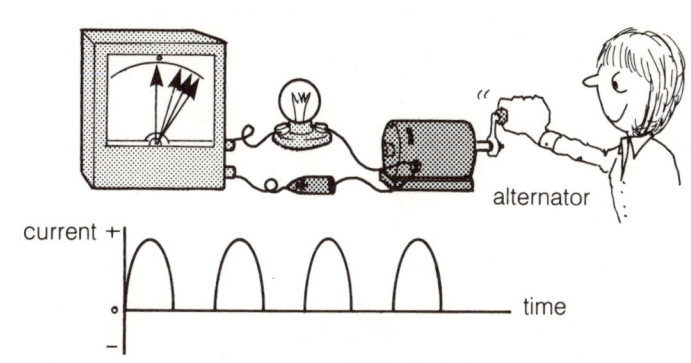

A diode being used to change a.c. to d.c.

A one-way circuit

- A diode will only allow a current to pass one way.
- Changing a.c. to d.c. is called rectification.
- A diode can be used as a rectifier.

195

44 Making electricity again

Experiment

Connect a solenoid with a large number of turns of wire to a sensitive current meter. Move a magnet in and out of the solenoid and you will see the pointer of the meter move. You have made an electric current by moving a magnet passed wires in a circuit. This is called **electro-magnetic induction**.

Generating electricity by moving a magnet into a coil

When does the current flow?

Magnet	Magnet out and not moving	Magnet moving in	Magnet in and not moving	Magnet moving out
Current	No current	Current flows	No current	Current flows the other way

Find out by experiment what difference it makes to the current if the movement of the magnet is made faster*.

Using an electromagnet instead of a magnet

You will find that moving an electromagnet in and out of the solenoid makes current just as well as a magnet. You will also find that the electromagnet need not be moved. It can be left in the solenoid and switched on and off.

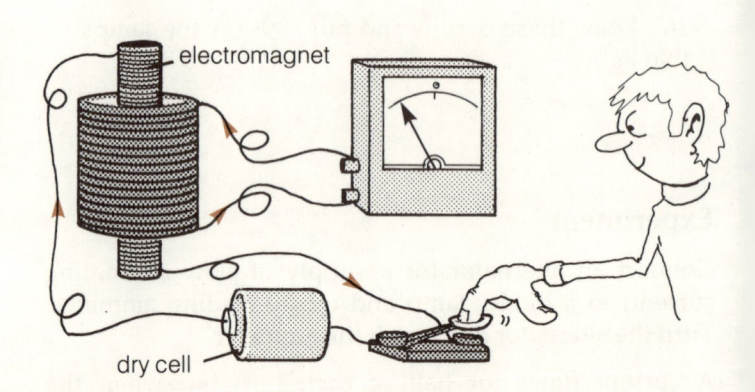

1 Copy and complete.

When the electromagnet is . . .	switching on	on	switching off	off
Is there a current flowing through the meter?				

2 A magnet on a spring bounces in and out of a solenoid.
(a) Describe the movement of the pointer of the meter.
(b) The magnet stops bouncing sooner when it is going in and out of the solenoid than when it bounces freely on the spring. Why is this? What is happening to the kinetic energy of the magnet?

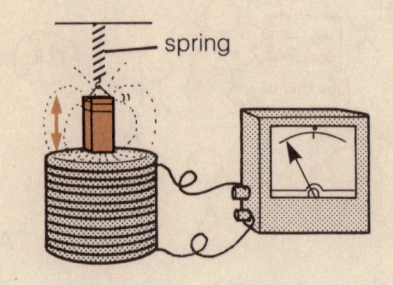

*The current is larger but does not last for so long.

The induction coil

A high voltage generator

The induction coil has an inner electromagnet and a separate outer coil of many turns of wire. An automatic switch (like the switch of an electric bell) is used to turn the electromagnet on and off. As it does so, a voltage is generated (induced) in the outer coil. If this coil has a large number of turns, the induced voltage is very large; much larger than the voltage of the electromagnet. The following changes would increase the voltage from the outer coil:

(a) increasing its number of turns;
(b) increasing the voltage to the electromagnet;
(c) switching on and off more rapidly.

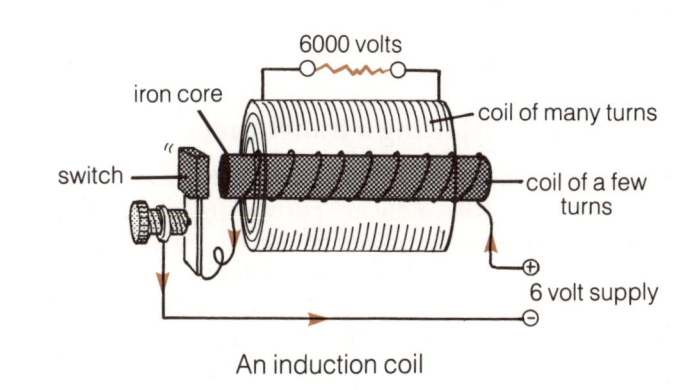

An induction coil

3 In the diagram above how many times has the voltage been 'stepped-up'?

The induction coil in a petrol engine

The spark plug of a petrol engine needs about 15 000 volts to make it spark. An induction coil is used to 'step-up' the 12 volts of the battery to this high voltage. The induction coil has inner and outer coils, the inner one having many turns of fine wire. The current to the smaller outer coil is switched on and off by contact points. These are opened and closed by a rotating cam. The cam is driven by the engine and must open the points at the exact moment the spark is needed.

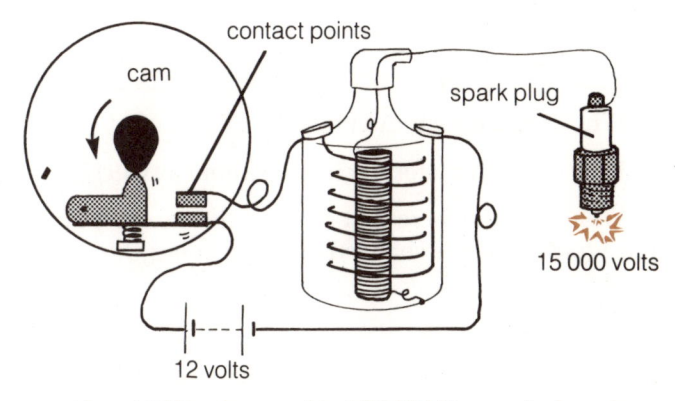

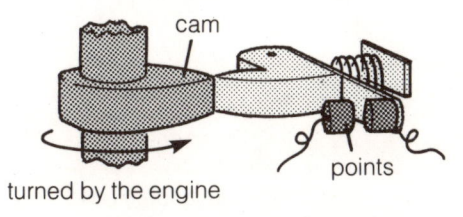

A view of the cam and points

How 12 V is changed to 15 000 V in a petrol engine

4 A petrol engine with one spark plug (a single cylinder engine) has a cam shaped like (A). A petrol engine with four spark plugs (a four cylinder engine) has a cam shaped like (B). (a) Can you explain why the 4-cylinder cam is shaped like it is? (b) What would the cam from a 6-cylinder engine look like? Try and draw it.

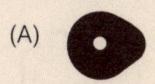

(A)   (B)

5 How many times does the car induction coil shown above step up the voltage?

Some electronic flash units use an induction coil to get a high voltage from a low voltage

High voltage from a low voltage! It could be an induction coil

- An induction coil can step-up voltage.
- It uses direct current and has an automatic switch.

The transformer

A transformer, like an induction coil, can be used to change voltage. It has two coils wound on an iron core but no switch.

Experiment. Making a transformer

Wind two coils onto iron ⊏-cores and fit them together into a closed loop. Pass a steady current (from a 2 volt d.c. supply) through one coil and connect a lamp to the other. The cores magnetize and attract each other but the lamp does not light. Change the voltage to 2 volts a.c. and the lamp will light. Only a changing current produces the changing magnetism in the core that is needed to produce a voltage across the secondary coil.

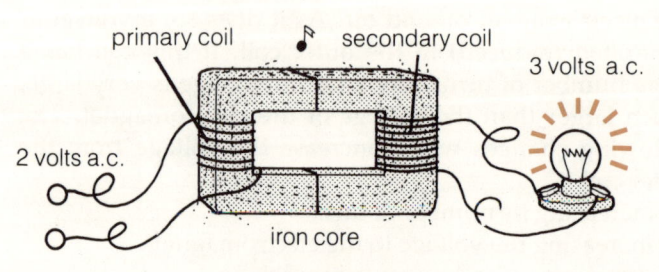

A simple transformer

6 Copy the table and write yes or no in the boxes.

	Direct current in the primary coil	Alternating current in the primary coil
Does the core magnetize?		
Does the magnetism change?		
Does the lamp light?		

7 Why does a transformer hum?

8 Why does a transformer work without a switch?

9 What proof is there that some of the energy put into a transformer is changed into heat energy?

10 This diagram shows the energy changes that take place in a transformer. Copy it and write in these missing forms of energy: magnetic energy; heat into the coils; heat into the core.

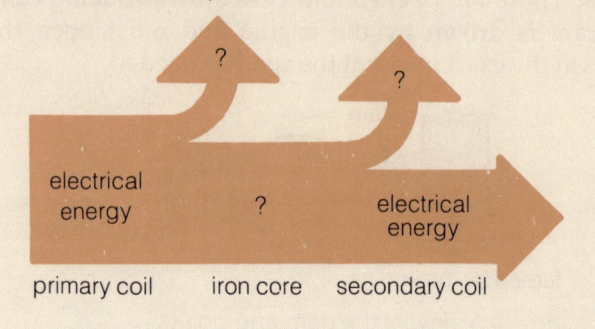

Experiment. Does the secondary voltage change when the number of secondary turns is changed?

Wind more turns on to the secondary coil and reconnect the lamp. Does the brightness of your lamp tell you that the secondary voltage has increased? Find out if reducing the number of secondary turns reduces the voltage to the lamp.

11 The transformer shown at the top of the page is called a step-up transformer, why? What would you do to change it into a step-down transformer?

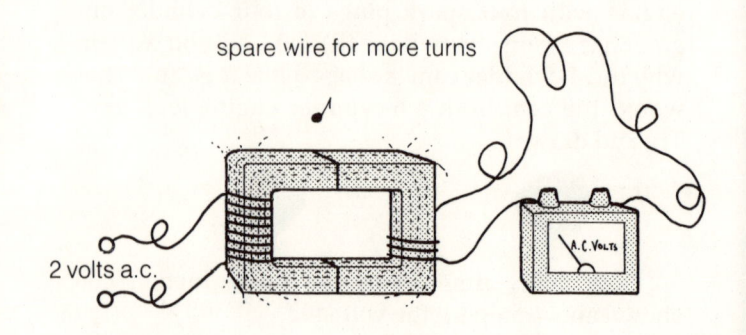

■ A transformer can change voltage.
■ As it uses alternating current, a switch is not needed.

The power 'wasted' by a transformer

A transformer can be used to step down voltage. This is useful if you want to light a 12 volt lamp from a 240 volt 'mains' socket. To reduce the voltage like this, the secondary coil must have less turns than the primary coil (about 20 times less in this case). The diagram shows meters connected to a transformer so that the currents and voltages of each coil can be measured.

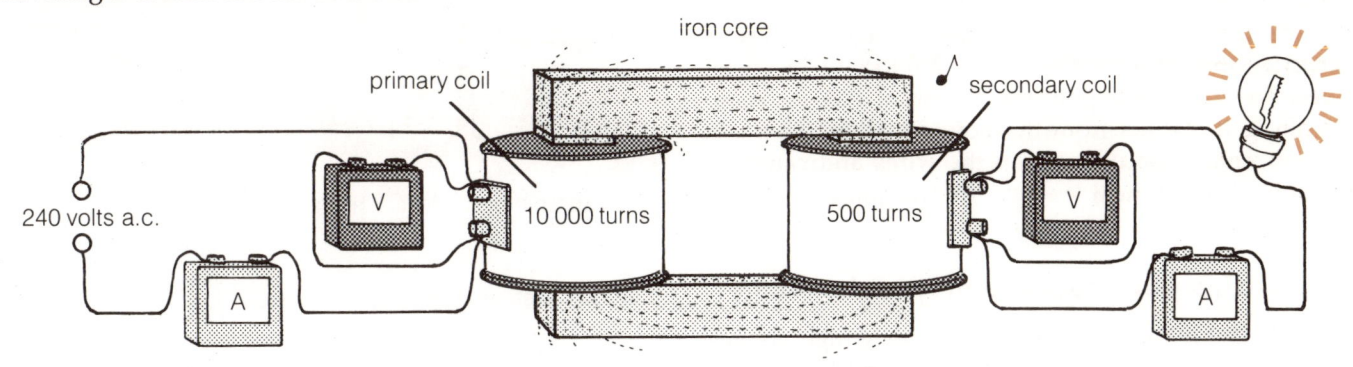

Measuring the power wasted by a transformer

Results

A very good transformer, connected as above, gave the following results:

Primary coil			Secondary coil		
Voltage	Current	Power	Voltage	Current	Power
240 V	1/10 A	24 W	12 V	2 A	24 W

These results show that, although the voltage is reduced on the secondary side, the current is increased. The results also allow us to calculate the power on each side. For a perfect transformer, the power of each coil would be the same. This shows that no energy is wasted when the voltage is stepped down. A real transformer would 'waste' energy and the coils and core would get hot.

Power = Voltage × Current

12 These readings were obtained from not such a good transformer.

Primary coil			Secondary coil		
Voltage	Current	Power	Voltage	Current	Power
200 V	1 A		1000 V	1/10 A	

(a) Does it step the voltage up or down?
(b) Calculate the power of each coil.
(c) How much power is 'wasted' by the transformer?
(d) What happens to this wasted power?

13 Copy and complete:
'The diagram above shows a step-____ transformer. The secondary voltage is 20 times smaller than the primary voltage, but the secondary current is ____ times larger than the primary current.'

Transformers are used in power packs, battery chargers, voltage controllers for model trains and cars, radios, television sets and many other electronic devices. The circuit symbol for a transformer is

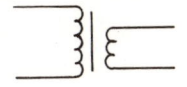

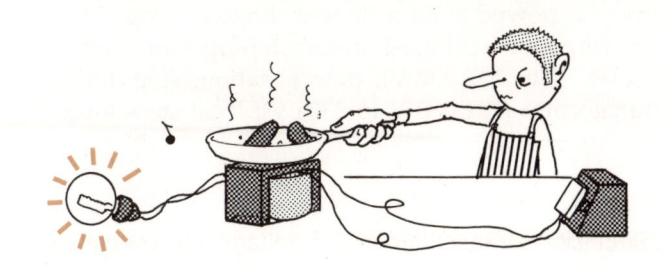

199

How electricity reaches our homes

Power stations are not usually built in towns and so the electricity they produce has to pass along wires to our homes and factories. It is best to move electricity about at extremely high voltages. Consider this example.

Transmitting power at high voltage

A small village has 'mains' electricity supplied at 200 volts. At peak times, when people are using a lot of electricity, the whole village uses 200 kW of electrical power. To supply this power a current of 1000 A has to pass along the wires from the power station. This is a huge current. It would heat up the wires and cause an enormous loss of heat energy on the journey to the village.

Transmitting power at extremely high voltage

To supply 200 kW of power at an extremely high voltage (e.g. 100 000 V) requires only a small current (2 A in this case). A small current like this would not generate much heat in thick wires and the heat loss on the journey to the village would be much less for the same power. Such high voltages would be extremely dangerous in our homes, so step-down transformers are used to reduce the voltage at the end of the journey.

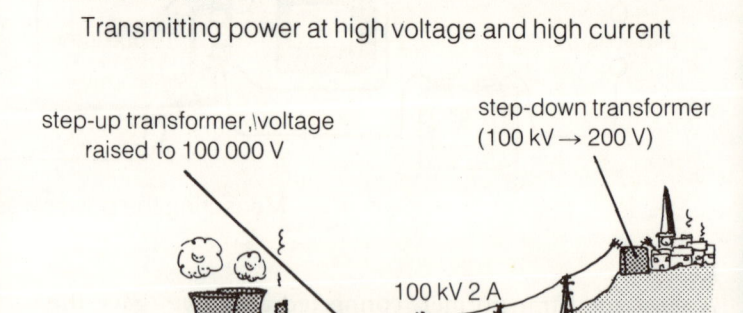

Transmitting power at high voltage and high current

Transmitting the same power at extremely high voltage and low current

The National Grid

Electricity is carried about the Country at extremely high voltages, by a network of wires (the National Grid). The Grid is supplied with electricity by a number of large power stations. When electricity is needed it is drawn from the National Grid by transformers that reduce the voltage to a level that is safe to use. Transformers play a vital part in this supply network.

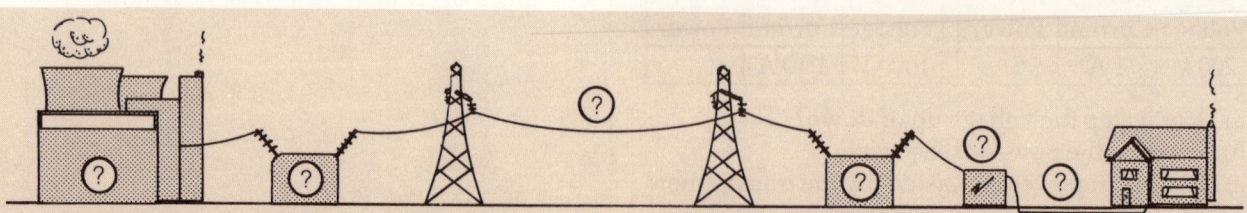

14 This diagram shows how electricity is carried from a power station to our homes. Copy the drawing and label these items: step-up transformer (11 000 V to 132 000 V); power station; step-down transformer (132 000 V to 3300 V); local step-down transformer (3300 V to 240 V); overhead high voltage transmission lines; underground mains voltage cables.

15 Why is electrical power transmitted at extremely high voltages?

■ Electricity is transmitted at high voltage and low current to reduce heating losses.

Summary of electromagnetism

- A force can act on an electric current as it passes through a magnetic field.
- The force, the current and the magnetic field must all be in .... different directions.
- Electric motors use this force to produce .... motion.
- Moving coil meters use this force to measure... current.
- Loudspeakers use this force to produce .... vibration and sound.
- The rule to work out the direction of this 'motor' force is the .... left-hand rule.
- Current can be generated by moving a wire across a magnetic field or by changing the magnetic field around a coil. Making electricity this way is called........................... electromagnetic induction.
- The rule used to work out the direction of the current is the .... right-hand rule.
- Current that only flows one way round a circuit is called .... direct current (d.c.).
- Current that flows first one way then the other is called .... alternating current (a.c.).
- An electronic device that only lets current pass through it one way is the .... diode.
- Changing a.c. to d.c. is called .... rectification.
- Direct voltage can be stepped-up by an .... induction coil.
- Alternating voltage can be stepped up and down by a... transformer.
- Electrical power is transmitted at high voltage and low current to reduce .... heating losses.

Further questions

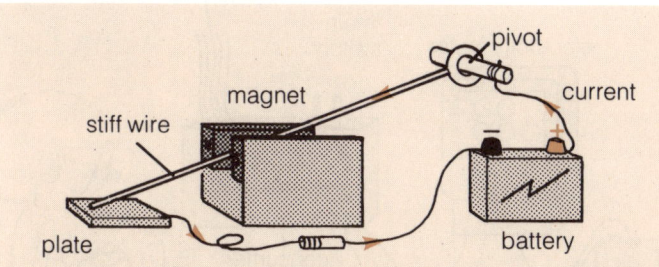

16 The diagram above shows a stiff wire that is pivoted at one end. The other end rests on a metal plate. The wire passes between the poles of a strong magnet. A current is passed along the wire as shown. Explain why the wire jumps up and down on the plate.

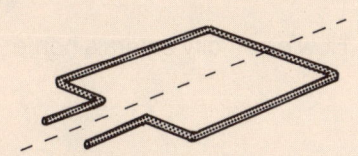

17 The diagram shows part of a simple generator that is to supply alternating current. Copy the diagram and complete it by adding: (a) two magnet poles, (b) two slips rings, (c) two brushes. Draw a labelled diagram of a commutator suitable for getting direct current from this generator.

18 This circuit can be used to change the voltage of the 'mains' to a voltage suitable for recharging a lead/acid battery.
(a) Give two reasons why a battery cannot be recharged by plugging it straight into the mains.
(b) Name the component X. What is its job in the circuit?
(c) Name the component Y. What is its job in the circuit?
(d) Would you connect the positive terminal of the battery to A or B?

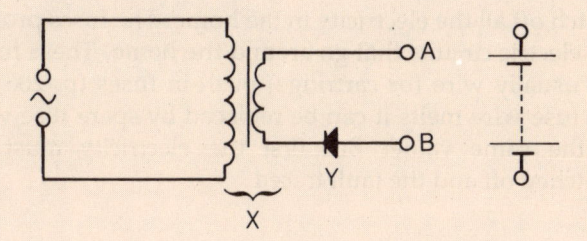

45 Electricity in the home

Electricity is supplied to your home at a high voltage. To touch any bare wire or metal connected to the mains electricity supply will drive a current through your body that could kill you. Never experiment with the 'mains'. It is highly dangerous for a person without proper training to touch household circuits. Two wires bring the electricity into your home. One wire (live) is at a high voltage and the other (neutral) is at 0 volts. Appliances are connected to the live and neutral wires and the voltage drives current through them.

The electricity meter

The live and neutral wires first pass through the electricity meter. This meter measures the amount of electrical energy used in the home. If the meter has dials, they are read in the same way as the dials on a joulemeter (p. 170).

The consumer unit

The live and neutral wires then pass into the **consumer unit.** This unit contains a switch and a number of fuses. You should know where this switch is because it can switch off all the electricity in the home. The fuses protect the electric circuits that go around the home. These fuses are usually wire (or cartridge) push-in fuses (p. 206). If the fuse wire melts it can be replaced by spare fuse wire of the same value. But first the electricity must be switched off and the fault traced.

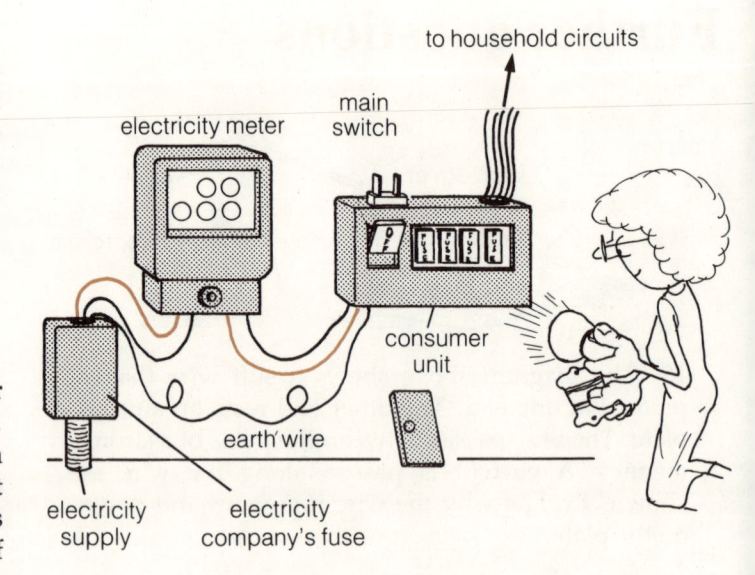

How electricity enters a home

The earth wire

A third wire connects the consumer unit to a plate or pipe in the ground. This is called the earth wire. Its use will become clear later.

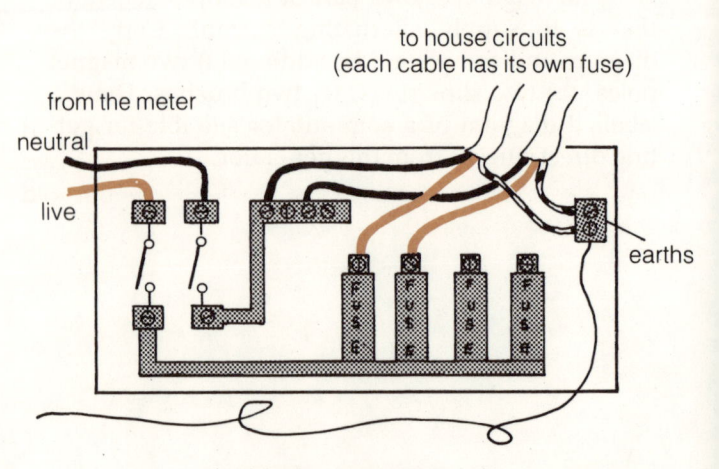

Inside the consumer unit

Electric cables with three wires inside leave the consumer unit and carry the electricity around the house. These cables are usually under the floor or buried in the walls. There are three main types of circuit.

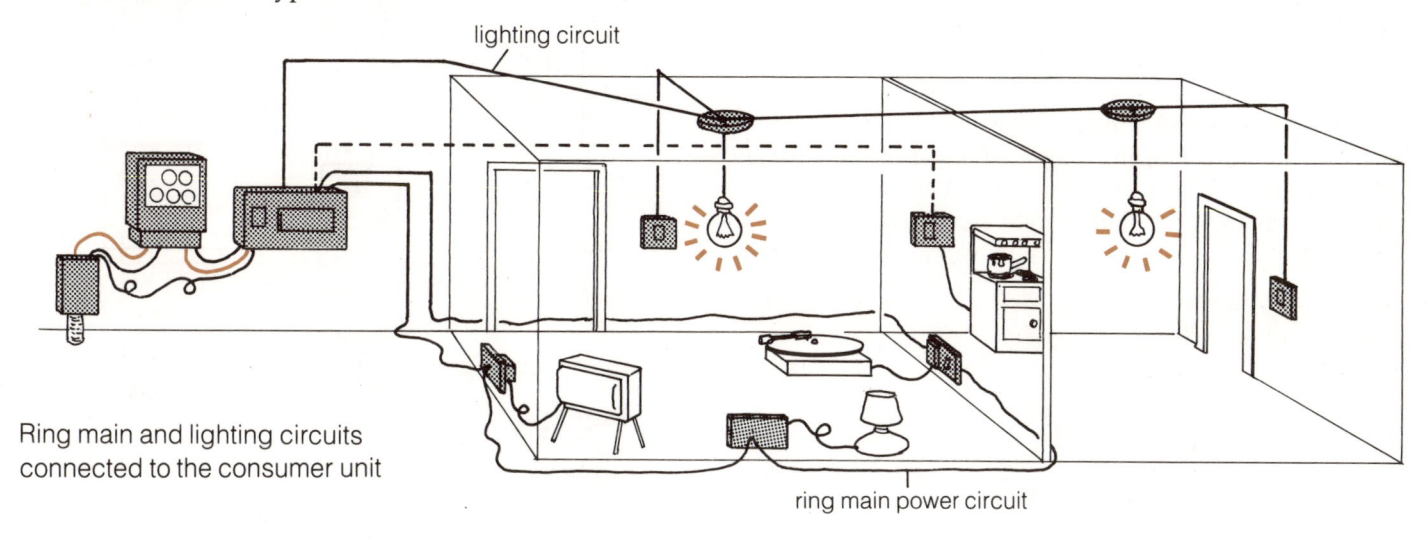

Ring main and lighting circuits connected to the consumer unit

The lighting circuit

The lights in a house are always connected in parallel (p. 160). (What would happen if the lamps were in series and one lamp went out?) The **live** wire to each lamp passes through a switch. This makes sure the lamp socket is not live when the switch is off. One terminal of the **switch** however is always live (unless the **main** switch is off).

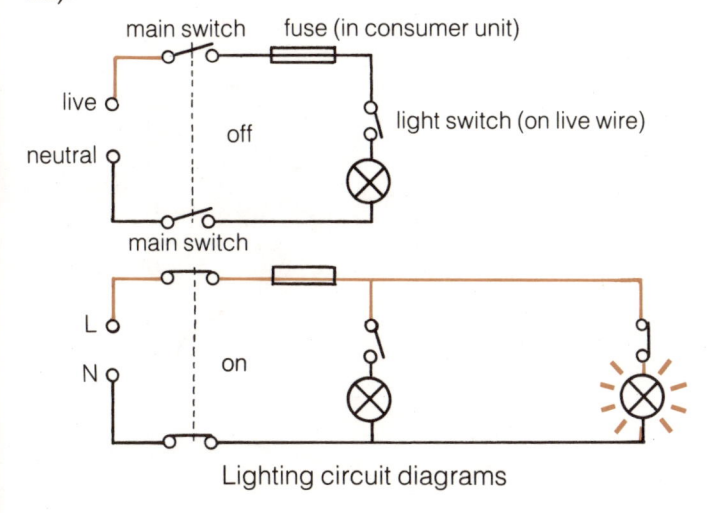

Lighting circuit diagrams

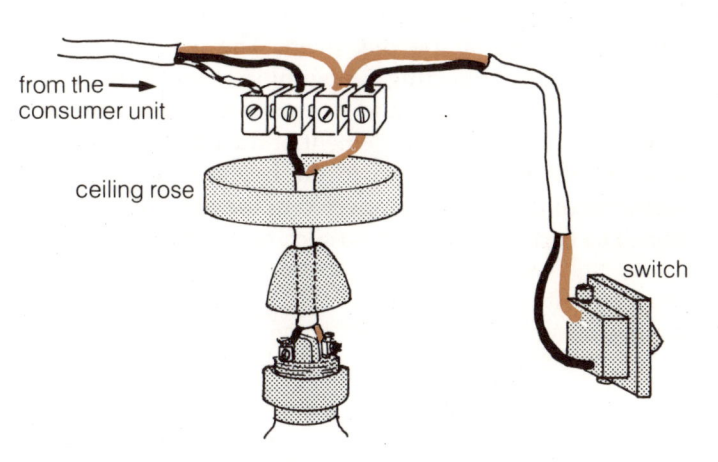

How a lamp and switch are wired up

Experiment

Use two-core cable to connect a lamp and household switch to a battery or low voltage electricity supply. Follow the diagram. If you have not got a household switch use a simple laboratory switch.

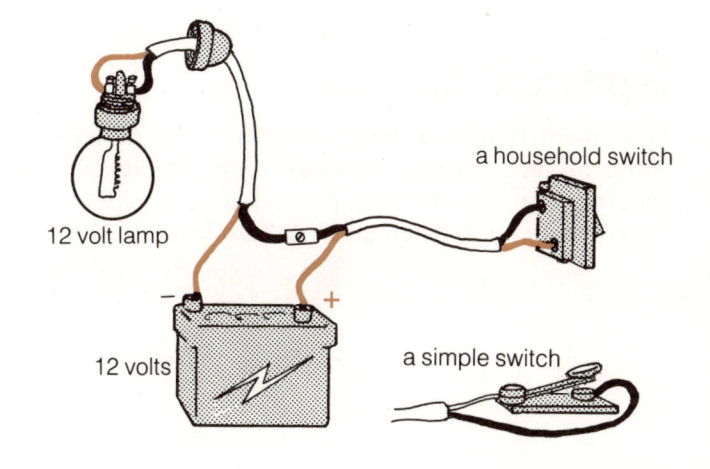

The ring main power circuit

This circuit uses cable with three wires, live, neutral and earth, and connects sockets to the consumer unit. The live and neutral wires are connected to the bottom two holes of each socket. These holes are the ones through which the current enters and leaves. The earth wire is connected to the larger hole at the top. Note that each wire forms a 'ring' starting and finishing at the consumer unit. It takes a little more cable to join the sockets in a ring. The advantage is that current can reach a socket by two routes and each wire has to carry only half the current.

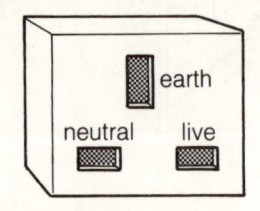

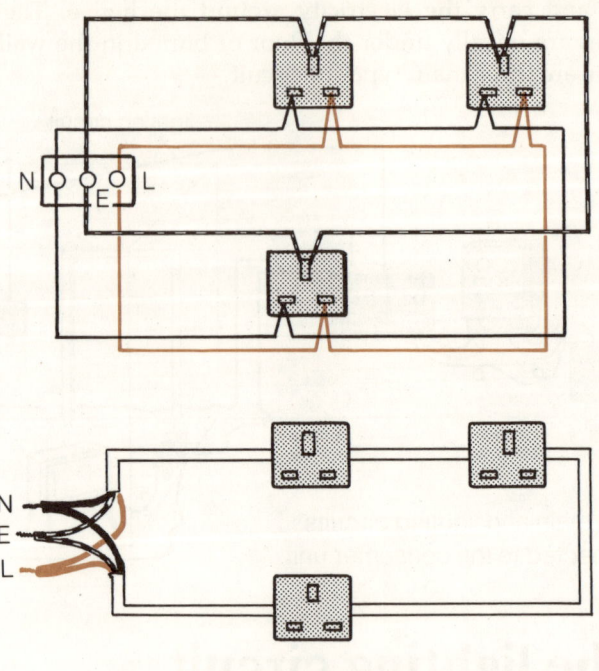

A ring main circuit

Plugging into the ring main

Three-pin plugs are used to connect electrical equipment into the sockets of the ring main. The diagram shows three-core flex connecting a 3-pin plug to an electric iron. The wires from the live and neutral pins of the plug are connected to the heating element of the iron. The current flows through these wires to the heating element. The earth pin of the plug is connected to the metal case of the iron. The earth wire carries no current in normal use.

Special circuits

Equipment that uses large currents – electric cookers, water heaters, 'instant' showers – are not plugged into the ring main. The device is connected by its own cable to the consumer unit where it has its own fuse.

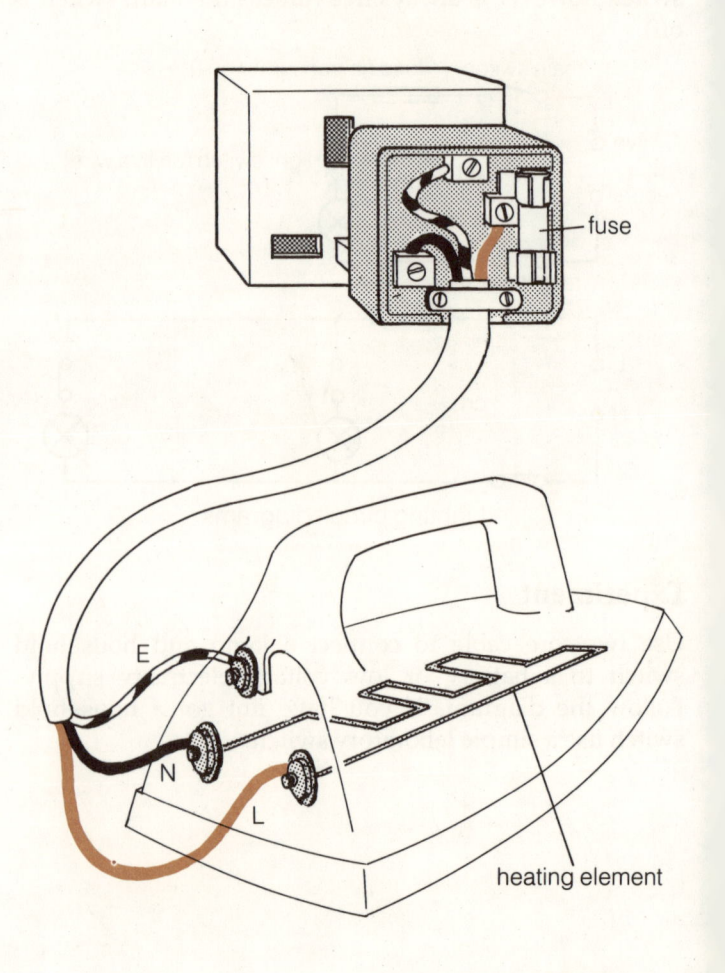

Earthing

What are the earth pin and earth wire for?

Look at the iron in the picture. It is not earthed. If a loose live wire touches the case, it would be raised to 240 V. If you touched the case, this voltage could drive enough current through your body to kill you. If the case is properly earthed contact with live wire would cause a large current to pass along the earth wire into the ground. The fuse in the plug would melt, cutting off the electricity supply. It is best to earth electrical equipment that is meant to be handled.

Equipment such as electric kettles, irons, guitars, cookers, desk lamps, washing machines, vacuum cleaners, refrigerators, and electric heaters should be securely connected to the earth. Some equipment that carries the label ▢ is double insulated. This need not be earthed.

1   What would happen if you connected the earth wire from an electric iron to the live pin of a three-pin plug? (This is very dangerous. Never get the wires of a plug mixed up like this.)

2   Why would it be especially dangerous to touch an iron with a live case if you have wet hands?

3   Why are battery radios and cassette recorders not earthed?

4   Describe the route connecting the case of an earthed appliance to the plate in the ground.

Electric jobs you can do for yourself

Fixing a plug to a flexible cable (flex)

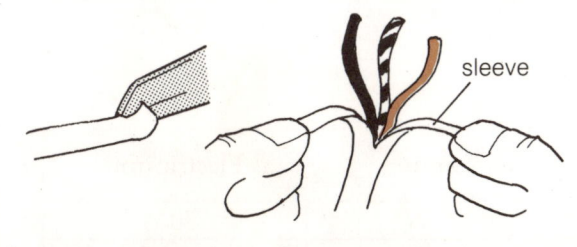

Snip the sleeve of the cable in two places. Pull back and trim off 5 cm of sleeve revealing the three wires inside.

Push the flex under the flex grip and screw it down. Cut each wire just long enough to reach its pin and strip off the last centimetre of plastic insulation. Fix each wire to its proper pin (brown to live; blue to neutral; yellow/green to earth).

Turn the wire clockwise round the screw (or push it right into the hole of the connecting block). No bare wire should be visible when the screw has been tightened up.

Replace the back of the plug.

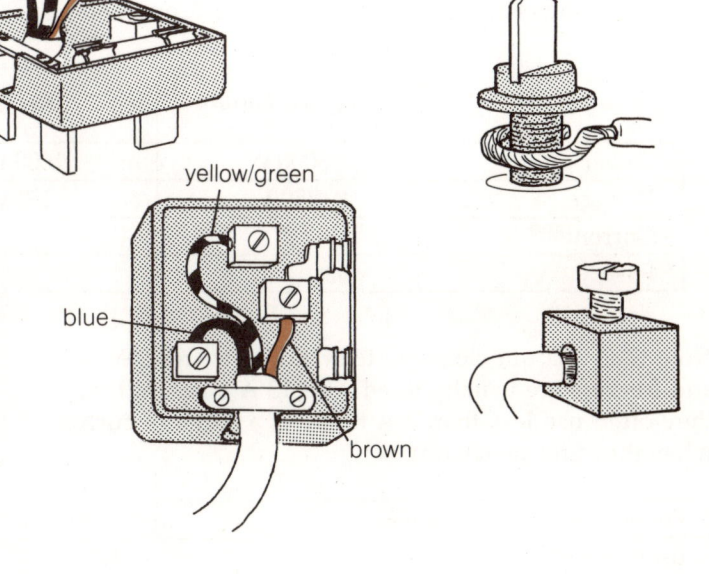

Changing a fuse in a plug

Simply take the back off the plug (having removed it from the socket), lift out the fuse and replace it with one with the correct value (p. 207).

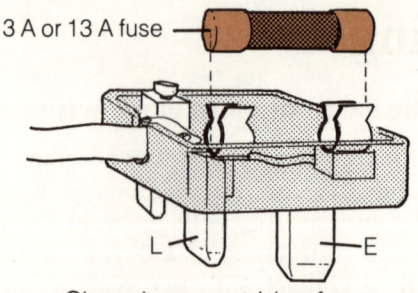

Changing a cartridge fuse

Mending a wire fuse

Have a torch and screwdriver handy, then switch off the main **switch**. Pull out the fuses and find the one with the broken wire. Take out the broken pieces, clean up any burn marks and fit a new piece of fuse wire of the correct value (usually 30 A, 15 A or 5 A).

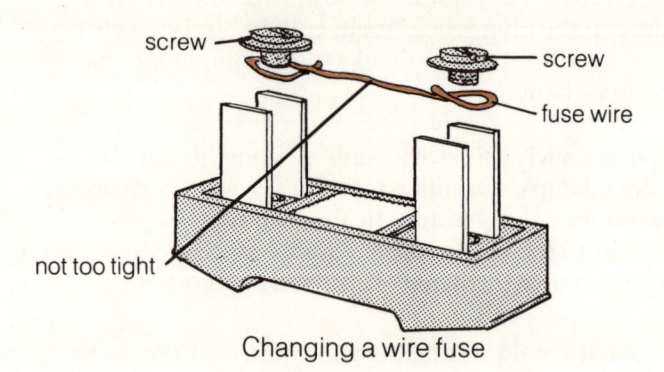

Changing a wire fuse

How to choose a fuse

Fuses sometimes break because they are old but usually a broken fuse means that there is a fault somewhere in the circuit. The fault should be found and put right. Then the fuse must be replaced with one of the correct value.

How to work out which fuse to use

All electrical equipment should have written on it the power and voltage it uses. An electric kettle for example may be marked 3000 W, 250 V. This information can be used to calculate the current used and the fuse needed. The electric kettle will use a current of 3000/250 = 12 A. A 13 A fuse will allow a 12 A to pass without melting, but will melt if a fault causes the current to rise to 13 A or more. A 13 A fuse is suitable for this kettle.

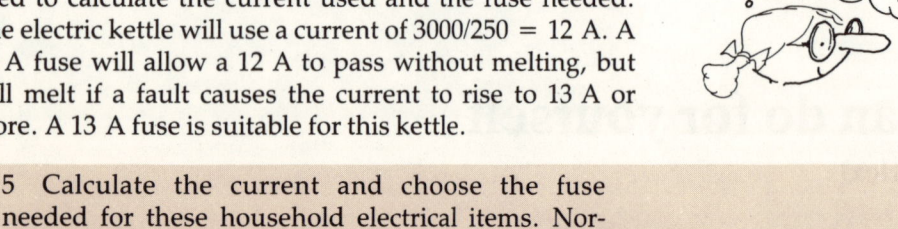

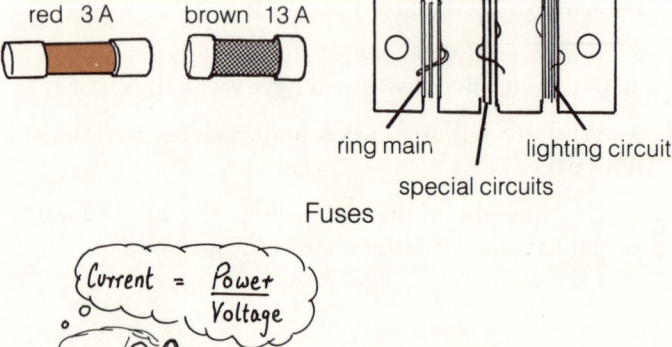

Fuses

$$Current = \frac{Power}{Voltage}$$

5 Calculate the current and choose the fuse needed for these household electrical items. Normally only 13 A or 3 A fuses are used in plugs. Choose one of these fuses for each item. Copy and complete.

	Electric kettle	1 bar fire	Lamp	Electric iron
Power	3000 W	1000 W	125 W	750 W
Voltage	250 V	250 V	250 V	250 V
Current				
Fuse				

Note that vacuum cleaners, television sets, refrigerators and freezers are usually fitted with 13 A fuses, although they often use less than 3 A (there is a surge of current when they first switch on).

6 Make a list of all the electrical equipment you have at home. Against each item write the power it uses and the value of the fuse it should have.

For equipment with power . . .	up to 720 W	720–3000 W	more than 3000 W
use fuses of . . .	3 A	13 A	Do not plug into a socket

Appliances

		Fuse needed	The time it takes to use 1 kWh of electricity
POWER			
	Cooker	30 A (in consumer unit)	15 minutes
3000 W	Electric water heater	15 A (in consumer unit)	20 minutes
	Electric kettle	13 A	
	Washing machine	13 A	
2000 W	Fan heater	13 A	30 minutes
	Electric radiators	13 A	
1000 W	Radiant heaters	13 A	1 hour
	One bar electric fires	13 A	
	Hair drier	13 A	1¼ hours
	Electric iron	13 A	

↑ 13 A fuse
↓ 3 A fuse

500 W	Vacuum cleaner	13 A*	2 hours
400 W	Colour television	13 A*	3 hours
300 W	Black/white television	13 A*	5 hours
200 W	Lamp	3 A	10 hours
	Record player	3 A	
	Music centre	3 A	
100 W	Refrigerator	13 A*	20 hours
	Fluorescent tube light	3 A	
0 W	Cassette recorder/Radio	3 A	100 hours

*For technical reasons 13 A fuses are used although the current may be less than 3 A.

Safety

Electricity brings many benefits into our homes but it can bring danger too. Apart from fires, electricity can cause serious injury. It is best to be very careful when using electricity at home. Here are some common sense rules to prevent injury to you and your family.

1) Do not plug anything into light sockets except light bulbs.

2) Make sure leads are not worn, frayed, cut or show bare wire at any point. Do not join on extra wire to make leads longer. Fit a completely new longer lead (or use a proper extension lead).

3) Do not overload sockets. Double sockets and multi-socket blocks are better and safer.

4) Do not run extension leads into the bathroom or use plug-in electrical equipment in the bathroom (except electric shavers in shaver sockets).

5) Do not trust sockets. Switches can go wrong and 'off' may still be 'on'. Pull out the plug before changing fuses or filling an electric kettle.

6) Do not poke anything into sockets or electrical equipment.

7 Reasons for the safety rules are given below. Work out which reason goes with which rule.

(a) The weight of two or three plugs on an adapter can pull it partly out of a socket, exposing live metal prongs and making a bad connection. Too many high power appliances in one socket will cause it to overheat or blow a fuse in the consumer unit.

(b) The effect of an electric shock on the body can vary greatly:
The skin is often wet in the bathroom and there should be no sockets or wall-mounted light switches in that room. An electric shock there could be fatal.

(c) Heating elements in toasters and electric fires are not insulated and are at a high voltage. Metal wires and knives used to poke the element will connect you to the mains. Ring main sockets are protected when not in use but small children should not be allowed to touch mains sockets at all.

(d) The lighting circuit is only designed for lamps. Other appliances, especially those that have heaters, may draw too much current through the cables. This will blow a fuse in the consumer unit, or over-heat the cable. The appliance will not be earthed.

(e) Constant use may cause bare wire to show through the insulation of a length of flex. The bare wire may be live and could shock you or start a fire. Exposed live and neutral wires may touch (blowing a fuse) or break (cutting off the electricity). Keep leads short and safe.

(f) You must be especially careful when handling electrical appliances with wet hands (something often done in the kitchen). The low resistance of the body when wet makes electric shocks particularly dangerous.

1(d); 2(e); 3(a); 4(b); 5(f); 6(c).

Body condition	Body resistance	Typical current	Effect of a shock
With dry skin and thick insulation under foot	High 240 kΩ	small (1 mA)	The shock will give you a nasty jolt
With sweaty skin and with part of the body earthed	Low 8 kΩ	large (30 mA)	The heart will fail and you could die

46 Electric charge

Do these experiments.
Rub a piece of polythene energetically on a jumper or cloth. Place the end you rubbed close to the following: a feather, small piece of paper, a compass and a thin stream of water.
Rub a balloon against a woolly jumper and drop pieces of fluff, paper, bubbles or feathers past the places you have rubbed. Can you make a balloon stick to your clothes, and pieces of paper dance under a perspex sheet? The pieces of plastic you have rubbed can make light objects move. They are said to be **charged** with electricity.

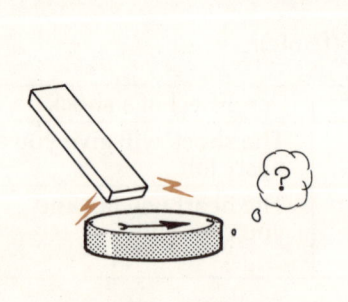

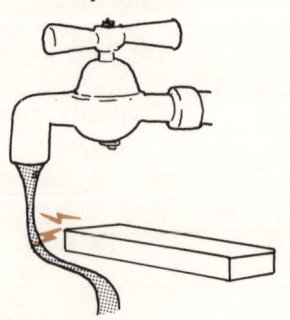

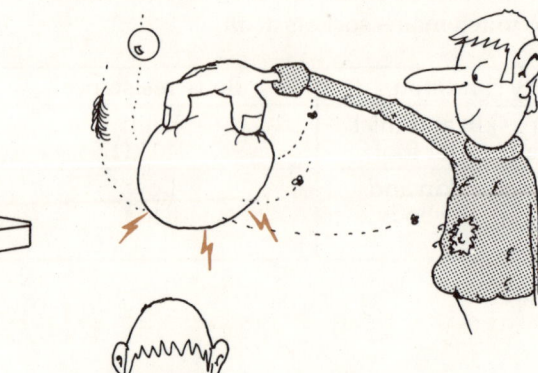

1 Can this type of electricity act as a source of energy?
How do you know?
2 This diagram shows the energy changes that take place when a material is charged by rubbing. Copy it and fill in the forms of energy given.

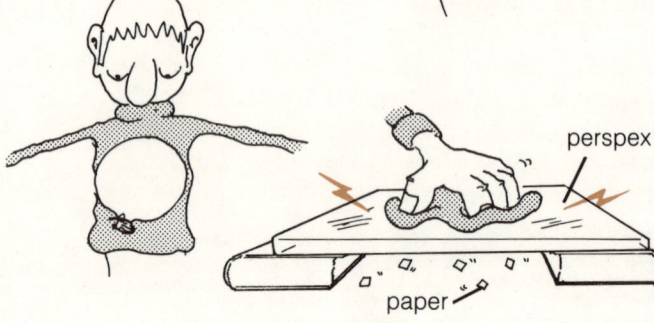

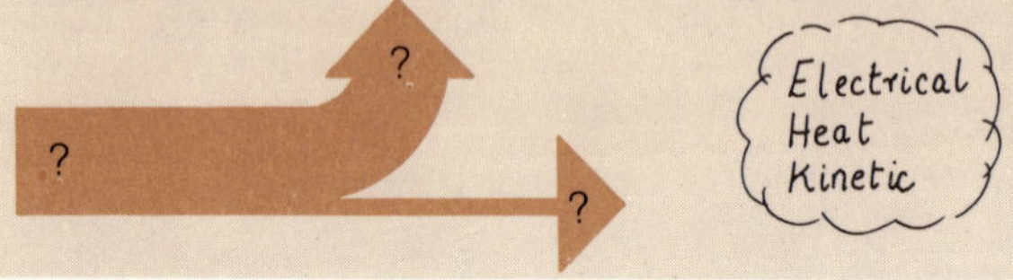

Experiments with electric charge

Experiment. Getting a shock from electric charge

Press a lump of plasticine onto a large metal tray. Using the plasticine as a handle, rub the tray over a sheet of plastic (a plastic rubbish sack will do). Lift the tray and bring it near to your body. You will see sparks. If you have a small neon lamp, hold one of its wires and touch the other on the tray. The lamp will flash as electric charge passes through it to your hand.

Lighting a lamp with electric charge

3 Write down three things that electric charge can do.

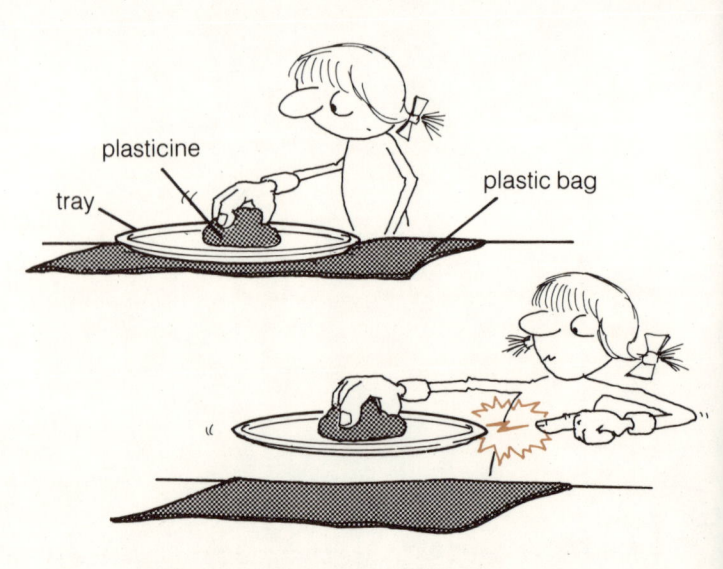

Getting a shock from electric charge

More about electric charge

Experiment. To show that when two materials are rubbed together they both become charged

Use the tray and plastic bag of the experiment on page 210. Charge up the tray and test it with a neon lamp (the lamp will flash). Then test the part of the plastic bag that was underneath the tray. Touch the wire of the neon lamp on the plastic. You will see it glimmer with light as you move it from place to place. When you charge up the tray you also charge up the plastic bag.

> 4 In this experiment the charged tray and the charged plastic bag both have energy (they both make the lamp light). Where does this energy come from?
>
> 5 Touching the tray with the neon lamp gives one big flash of light. Touching the plastic bag in different places gives lots of little flashes. Can you explain why the tray (metal) and plastic bag behave differently?

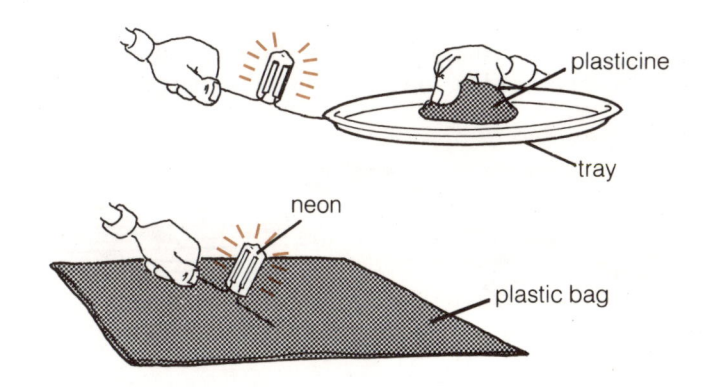

The bag and the tray are both charged

There are two types of electric charge

An electrometer is an instrument that measures electric charge. Rub a polythene rod and touch it on the cap of an electrometer, you will notice that the pointer of the meter deflects. If you then rub a piece of cellulose acetate (the type of plastic used to make film) and place that on the cap, the meter deflects the other way. Clearly the charges on the rods are not the same. There are two types of electric charge. Both types can pick up light objects and cause sparks. They are called **positive** and **negative**. (No one has yet discovered a third type of electric charge!)

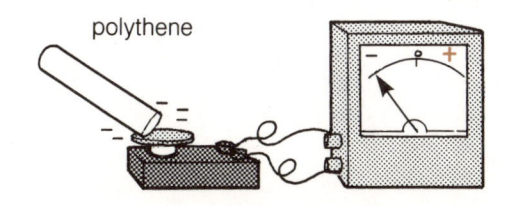

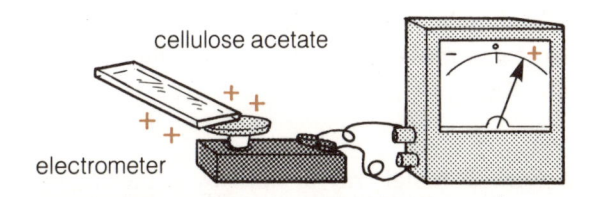

Using an electrometer to show there are two types of charge

> 6 When the charged rods are removed from the electrometer the pointer does not go back to zero. Can you explain why the pointer stays where it is?

- When one material becomes charged by rubbing it against another, the other becomes charged too.
- There are two types of electric charge. They are called positive and negative.

Forces between charges

Experiment

Charge up polythene and acetate rods and balance them on watchglasses so that they can spin freely.

Bring up other charged rods as shown, and watch for movement caused by forces between the charges.

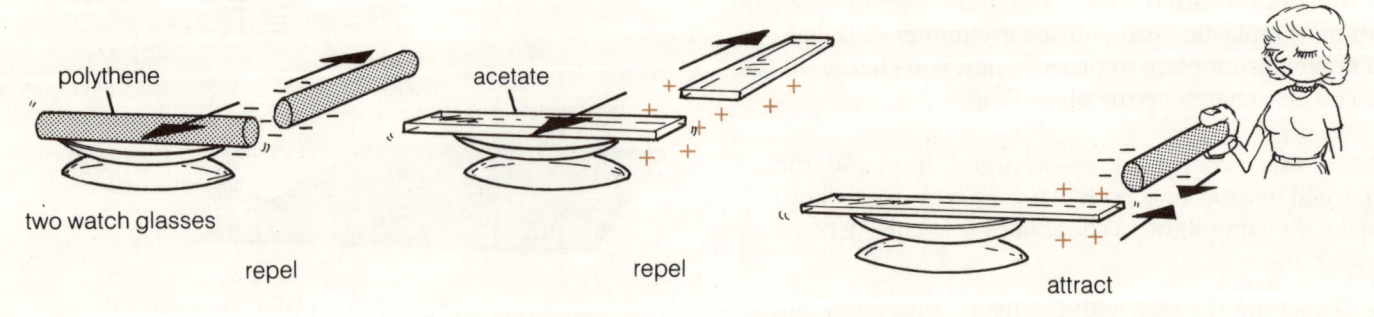

Testing the forces between charges

7 Copy and say whether these charges attract or repel when they meet.

	Negative charge	Positive charge
Positive charge		
Negative charge		

8 Copy and complete
Like charges _____
Unlike charges _____

Insulators

The charges on the plastic rods stay in place. They do not move along. Plastic and other materials that do not allow electric charge to move are called **insulators**. Electricity that does not move is called **static electricity**.

Conductors

There are materials, such as metals, through which electric charge can move freely. These are called conductors of electricity.

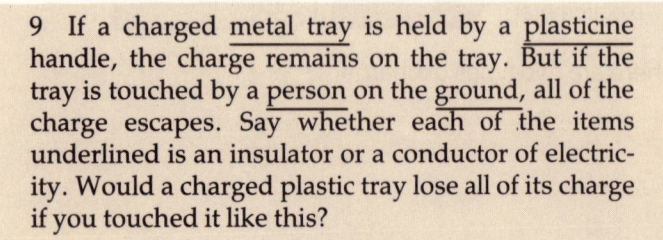

9 If a charged metal tray is held by a plasticine handle, the charge remains on the tray. But if the tray is touched by a person on the ground, all of the charge escapes. Say whether each of the items underlined is an insulator or a conductor of electricity. Would a charged plastic tray lose all of its charge if you touched it like this?

- Like charges (+ and +, − and −) repel.
- Unlike charges (+ and −) attract.
- Electric charge can move through conductors but not through insulators.

Using very large charges

A Van de Graaff generator is a machine that can produce large charges and very high voltages. A rubber belt carries negative charge up to a large metal dome. The dome is supported on an insulating column so that the charge on it cannot escape. If you charge the dome and place an 'earthed' ball nearby, large sparks, like miniature lightning, strike across the gap. There is so much negative charge on the dome that the air (normally an insulator) becomes a conductor for a moment. There is a spark and the charge escapes to the 'earthed' ball (or to you if you get too close).

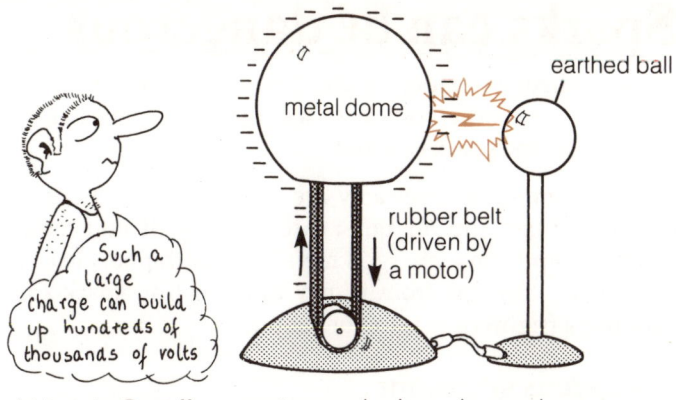

A Van de Graaff generator producing a large charge

10   What energy changes take place in a spark? Copy and complete the energy change diagram.

Other electrostatic happenings

Can you explain them? Use a Van de Graaff machine to perform these electrostatic tricks.

Hair standing on end

The hairs of a wig placed on the dome stand upright and away from each other (hair is a conductor at these voltages).

Jumping pith balls

The light metal-coated balls rise up, hit the 'earthed' lid and fall again.

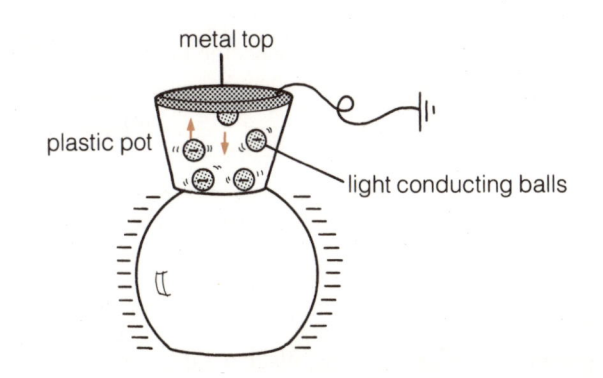

Vibrating ping-pong balls

Wrap a ping-pong ball in aluminium foil and hang it between two metal plates. Earth one plate and connect the other to the dome of the generator. Charge the dome and the ball will swing backwards and forwards between the plates.

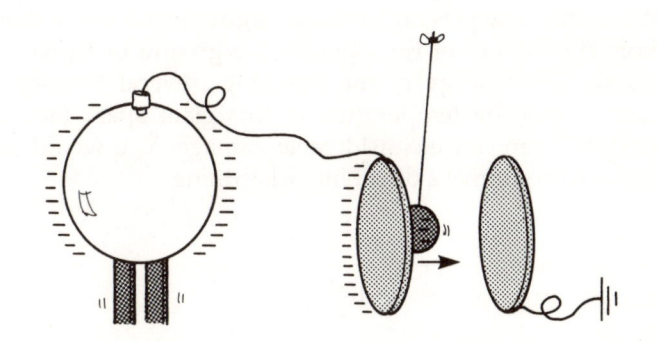

11   Use the facts that negative charges repel and that 'earthing' allows charge to escape, to explain these three happenings.

Sparks can be dangerous

Place a sheet of paper in the path of sparks from an induction coil and you may see the paper burst into flames. Electric sparks are hot.

Sparks from static electricity are hot enough to make a mixture of gas and air burst into a flame. If you make sparks jump from a charged metal tray to the nozzle of a gas burner, the gas from it may light. A tiny spark can produce a frightening burst of flame.

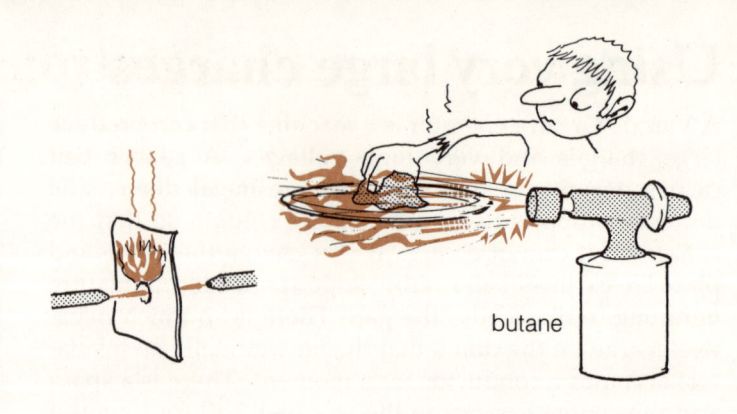

Dangerous situations

The flame from a gas burner burns steadily but some mixtures of gas and air do not burn. They explode violently. Examples of these explosive mixtures are petrol vapour and air and some anaesthetics. A small spark can trigger off a large explosion of these mixtures.

(a) Petrol and oil tankers.
The movement of petrol and oil as it is being transported in tankers can build up an electric charge. A spark from this charge could make petrol vapour explode. An escape route for the charge has to be provided to prevent any possibility of sparking. A chain to the ground, or tyres made from special conducting rubber, are used to allow the charge to escape to 'earth'.

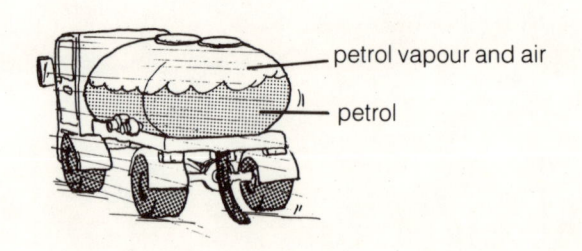

(b) The operating theatre.
Sudden movement of blankets, apparatus or clothes in operating theatres can cause sparks to fly. Careful precautions are taken to make conducting paths to the ground so that static charges do not build up. Sparks are especially dangerous because of the flammable gases used to anaesthetize the patient and the large amount of oxygen present in the air of the theatre.

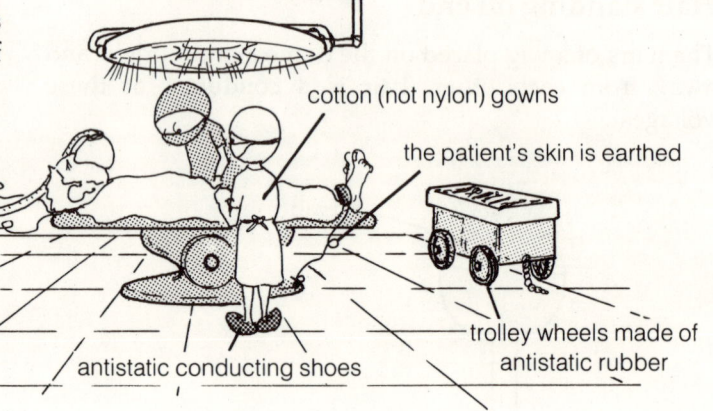

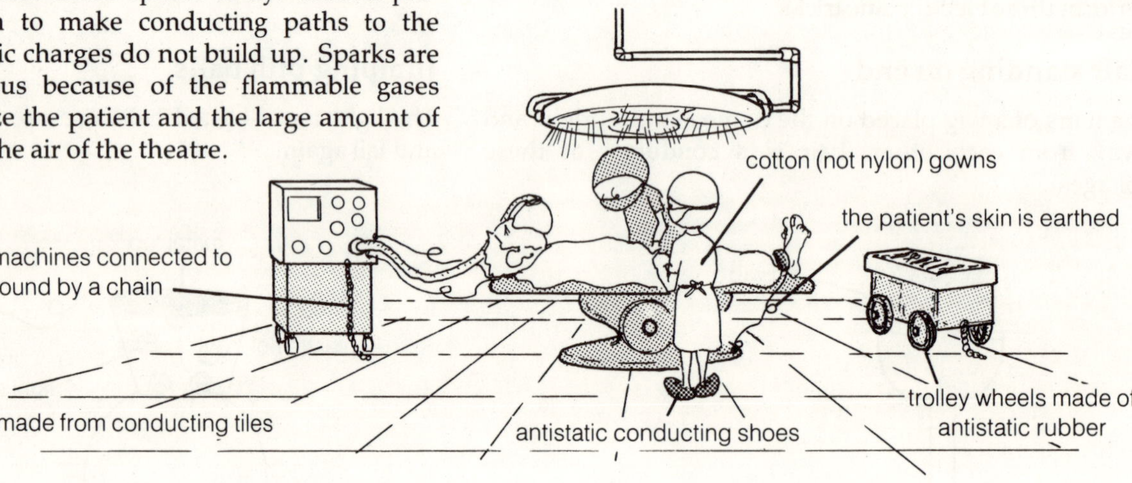

(c) Lightning.
Thunderclouds are natural electrostatic generators. Violent activity inside the cloud separates electric charge making the top of the cloud (+) and the bottom (−). When the voltage is high enough, lightning strikes, either from the bottom of the cloud to the ground or between clouds. The energy of the lightning (several thousand 'units') and the temperature of this giant spark (about 10 000°C) can cause considerable damage. You would be unlikely to survive a direct hit by lightning.

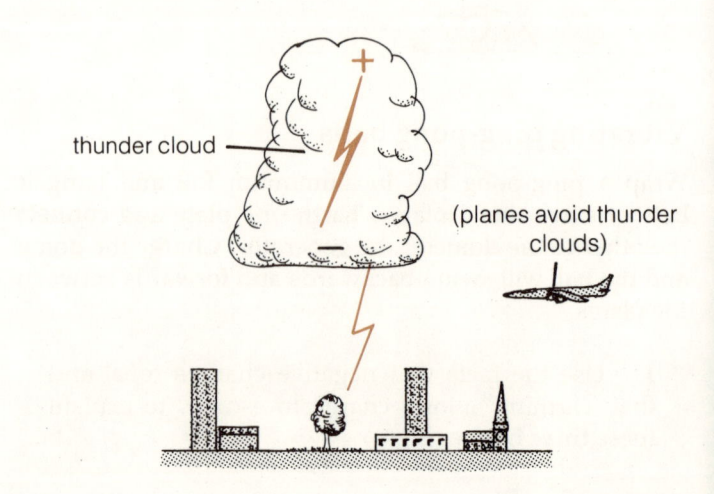

Charges, atoms and electrons

We are familiar with the idea that all matter is made of atoms and these atoms are extremely small. For many years it was thought that atoms were the smallest particles in existence. However, in 1897 an even smaller particle was discovered. This particle had a negative charge and much less mass than an atom. Atoms are small but this particle was two thousand times smaller than the lightest atom. It is now thought to be one of the particles found inside an atom. Its name is the **electron**. Work with radioactive substances (p. 230) led to the discovery that atoms have a very small, dense **nucleus** at the centre with a positive charge. An atom is made from a nucleus and electrons. Although the nucleus is much heavier than the electrons it has the same amount of electric charge. The atom as a whole is not charged because the (+) charge on the nucleus and the (−) charge on the electrons cancel out. (An atom can sometimes lose an electron, in which case the atom will have a net (+) charge.)

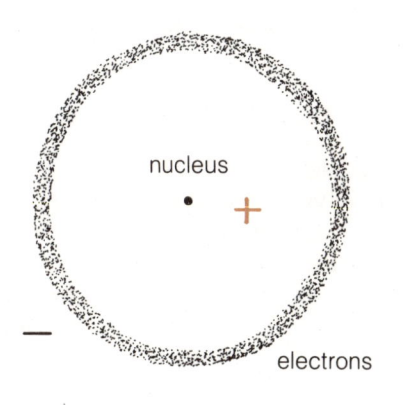

A picture of an atom

The electron theory of electric charge

When polythene is charged by rubbing it with fur, electrons move from the fur to the polythene. Since electrons are charged negative, the polythene gets a negative charge and the cloth is left with a positive charge.

12 When fur charges polythene one of the materials gets slightly heavier. Which one is this?

13 Copy and complete.

Materials that are rubbed together	Type of charge it gets	Has it lost or gained electrons?
Polythene		
Fur		
Cellulose acetate	positive	
Cloth		

■ When materials become charged they lose or gain electrons.
■ A negative charge is due to extra electrons.
■ A positive charge is due to loss of electrons.

215

Electric charge and electric current

We have met two sorts of electricity: static electricity produced by friction and electric current produced by batteries and generators. How are the two sorts of electricity linked?

Experiment. Travelling electrons

Connect a thread from the dome of a Van de Graaff generator to a very sensitive ammeter. Complete the circuit with a wire from the meter to the base of the generator. Turn the belt and charge up the dome of the generator. A negative charge on the dome means it has a large number of extra electrons. The thread is an escape route for these electrons; they travel down it and through the meter. The meter deflects just as if electric current from a battery is flowing through. This experiment suggests that an electric current is the movement of electrons.

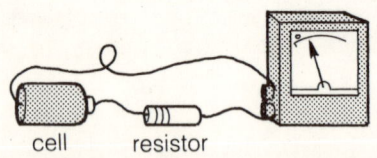

Lamps without filaments also show that electron flow is the same as electric current

Fluorescent tube lights and the brightly coloured 'neon' signs used by advertisers are lamps that have no filament. The electricity passes through a gas inside a tube. Small neon lamps are examples of these gas discharge lamps. They glow with red light when the voltage is high enough (about 50 volts) to pass current through the neon gas inside the lamp. If electrons from a Van de Graaff dome pass through such lamps they also glow with light. Electric current and moving electrons have the same effect when they pass through the neon gas.

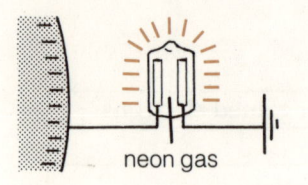

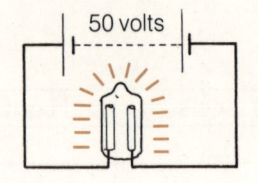

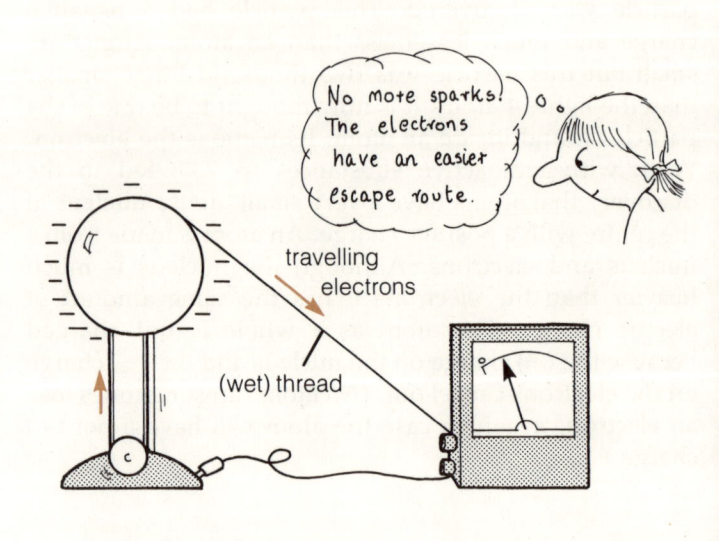

Electric current in wires

A copper wire contains many millions of electrons. If the ends of the wire are made positive and negative (by connecting to a battery for example) some of the electrons begin to drift to the end that is positive. This movement of electrons is an electric current.

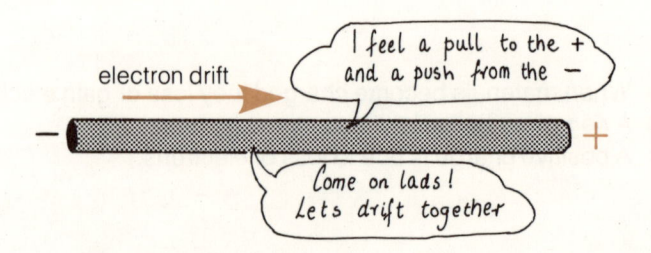

■ An electric current is the movement of electrons through a conductor.

Capacitors

Capacitors are electronic components that are used to store charge or separate a.c. from d.c. One common type is made from two thin aluminium plates separated by an insulator such as waxy paper. This sandwich is rolled into a small cylinder.

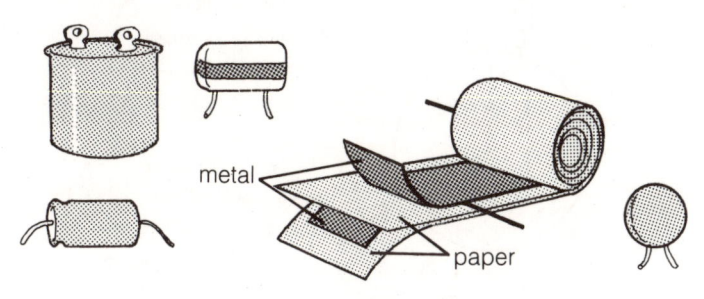

Inside one type of capacitor

Experiment. Capacitors can store electric charge

Connect a battery to a capacitor. Current flows for a moment as the plates become charged — one positive, the other negative. Take away the battery and connect the charged capacitor to a lamp. The lamp lights for a moment as charge from the capacitor flows through it.

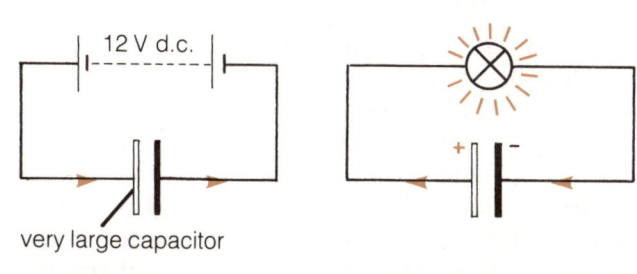

Charging a capacitor — Discharging a capacitor

14 What energy changes take place in circuit (b) when the capacitor discharges?

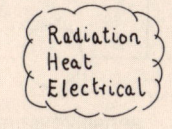

15 Does the 'discharge current' (in circuit (b)) flow the same way as the charging current or the opposite way?

16 What can be 'stored' in the following items: sponge; a purse; storage heaters; a toilet cistern; a record; a capacitor?

Experiment: Can an electric current flow in a circuit with a capacitor?

Build these two circuits. Use the lamps to show if there is a current.

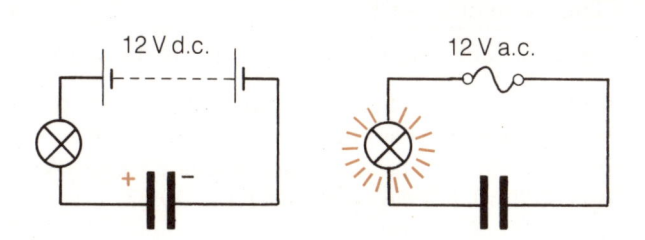

17 Copy and complete this sentence.

This experiment shows that alternating current _____ flow in a circuit with a capacitor, direct current _____.

- Capacitors can store electric charge.
- Steady direct current cannot flow in a circuit with a capacitor, alternating current can.

47 Electrons in space

Metal wires contain millions of electrons. Can these electrons be got out of the wire?

Simply heating a wire gives some electrons enough energy to escape from the metal. Electrons are released when the filament of a lamp is heated for example. But the electrons get mixed up with the gas inside the lamp and nearly all of them return to the filament.

Experiment. Releasing electrons and catching them on a plate

A rather special tube is needed to make use of electrons that have been released from hot wires. It contains a filament, a catching plate and has no air inside to obstruct the electrons. Connect a low voltage supply to the wire filament and a high positive voltage to the catching plate. You will notice that the ammeter shows a current is flowing around the circuit. The filament gets hot and releases electrons, then the positive plate attracts them. Most of the electrons that hit the plate go back into the metal and continue round the wires of the circuit.

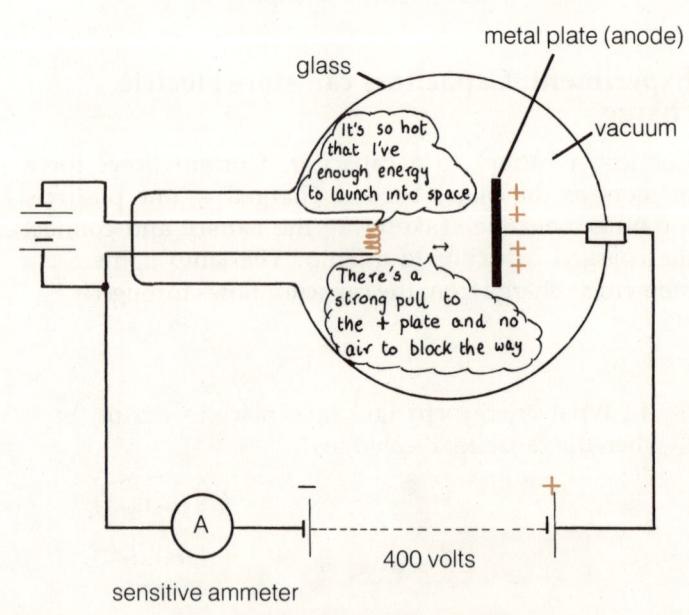

Making electrons cross a gap

1 How can we tell that electrons are crossing the gap, when electrons are invisible?

2 Explain how it is possible to make an electric current flow round a circuit that has a gap in it.

3 Will electrons flow when:

	The plate is (+)	The plate is (−)
The filament is cold		
The filament is hot		

Copy the table and insert 'yes' or 'no' in the spaces.

4 (a) In which circuit will current flow? Explain why current does not flow in the other circuit.
(b) This vacuum tube is called a **diode valve**. Why do you think it is called a valve (cf. p. 195)?

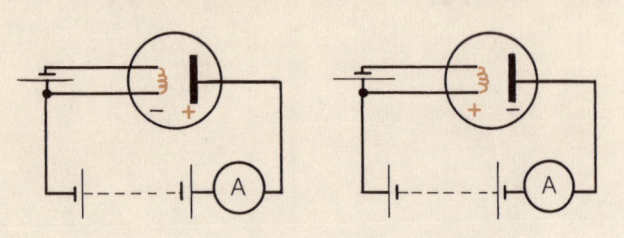

■ Electrons can be released from a metal wire by heating it.
■ Electrons can be made to cross empty space.

Electron beams — electric currents without wires

Electron beams in vacuum tubes are essential parts of television sets, oscilloscopes and radar equipment.
This diagram shows a vacuum tube that produces a fine beam of electrons. A metal cylinder with a hole in the centre is placed in the neck of the tube.

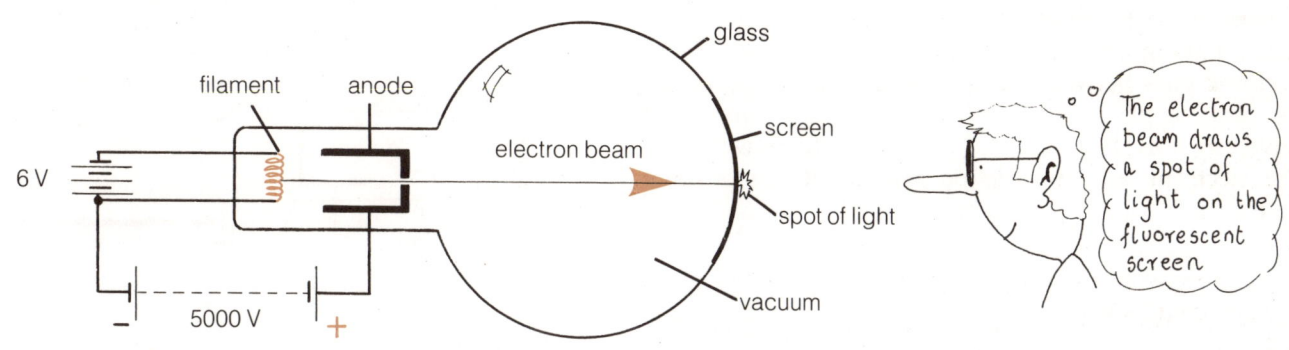

Producing an electron beam

The electron beam draws a spot of light on the fluorescent screen

The cylinder, called the anode, is given a high positive voltage. This attracts electrons released by the filament and accelerates them to enormous speeds. Some electrons pass through the hole and into the vacuum space – a fine, high-speed beam of negative particles. The tube has a screen painted on the inside of the glass. Where electrons hit this screen, a spot of light is seen.

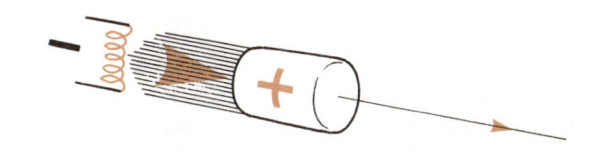

5   How are the electrons got out of the filament and into the vacuum tube?

6   How are the electrons got moving and formed into a fine beam?

7   Why must there be a high vacuum inside the tube?

8   When the electrons smash into the glass, why do they not break it?

9   The paint that is used to make the screen contains a chemical that 'fluoresces'. What do you think this means?

10   What energy changes take place when the electrons hit the fluorescent screen?

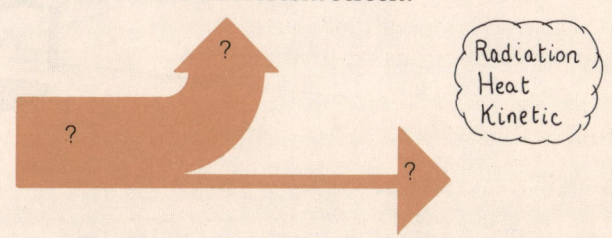

Radiation Heat Kinetic

11   If the filament is 'boiling off' electrons all the time, why does it not boil dry? Why does it not run out of electrons?

The positive anode really got me going. I was lucky to get through the hole

It was hot in that filament. The energy got me out

There are plenty more of us in the battery

My momentum is too small to smash the glass

My energy has made this fluorescent paint glow with light.

■ Electrons can be formed into thin, high-speed beams.

The control of electron beams

We must be able to deflect electron beams to make use of them. There are two ways of deflecting the beam.

1. Electrostatic deflection

A vacuum tube is needed with two metal plates inside as shown. A high voltage battery is connected to these plates making one positive and the other negative. As electrons pass between the plates they are attracted by the positive plate and repelled by the negative. They move down as they pass and the spot shifts downwards (the electrons are moving too fast to hit the positive plate).

> 12   How would you use the same plates to deflect the beam upwards?
>
> 13   What would you see happening to the beam if an alternating voltage was put on the plates?

Horizontal plates, like those that deflect the beam up and down are called Y-plates. Some tubes have two vertical plates called X-plates fitted as well. Voltages on these plates will deflect the beam sideways. Oscilloscope tubes have X and Y-plates.

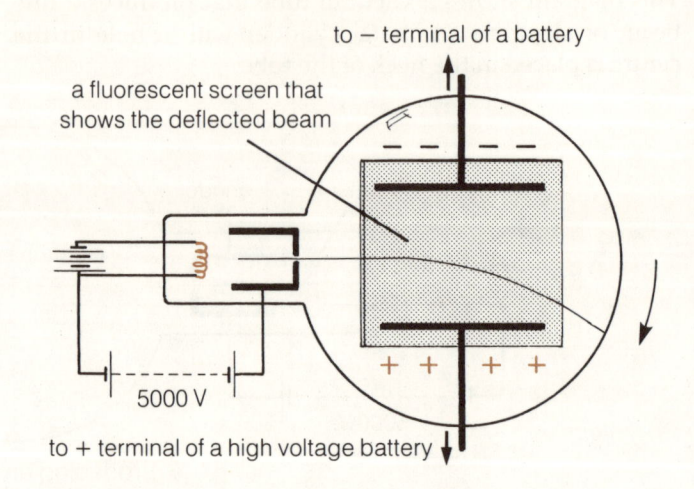

Electrostatic deflection of an electron beam

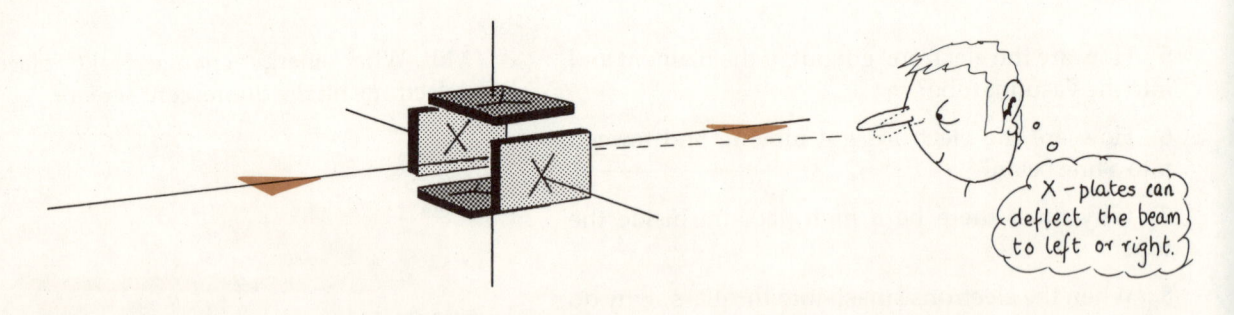

> 14   Copy the table and insert the charge on each plate that will produce the required movement. Use +, − or 0 for no charge.
>
> | Movement of the spot | X_{left} | X_{right} | Y_{top} | Y_{bottom} |
> |---|---|---|---|---|
> | to the left | + | − | 0 | 0 |
> | to the right | | | | |
> | up | | | | |
> | down | | | | |
> | to the top left hand corner | | | | |

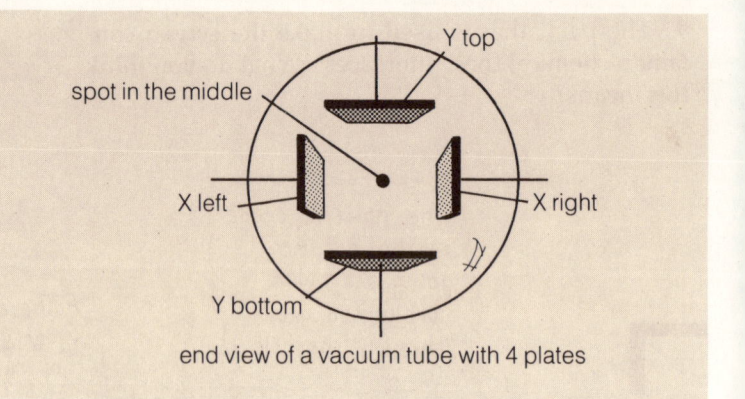

end view of a vacuum tube with 4 plates

2. Magnetic deflection

Place a magnet near the neck of the vacuum tube and you will see the electron beam deflect. The magnetic field, the electrons' movement and the deflection are all in different directions.

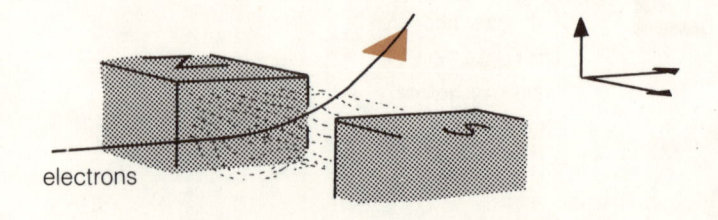

Magnetic deflection of travelling electrons

The oscilloscope

The oscilloscope is a useful instrument for giving a 'picture' of voltage, especially voltage that changes quickly. It has a vacuum tube with a filament and anode to produce an electron beam, and two sets of deflecting plates (X and Y).

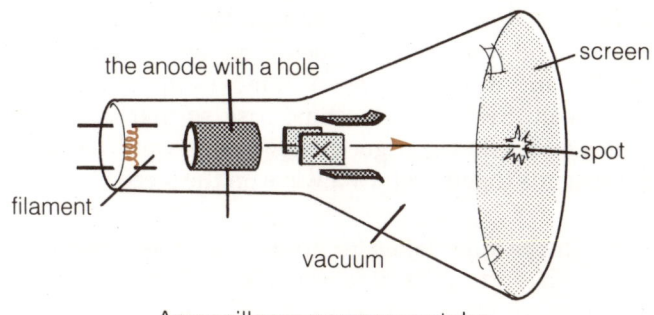

An oscilloscope vacuum tube

Experiment. Using the Y-plates

Switch on an oscilloscope and adjust it until you have a spot in the centre of the screen. The Y-plates are usually connected to the two terminals of the oscilloscope.
(a) Connect a dry cell to the two terminals. What happens to the spot? What happens to the spot if the cell is connected the other way round? Can you explain why the spot jumps up and down?
(b) Connect an alternating voltage to the Y-plates (e.g. from a transformer or an alternator). You will see a vertical line appear on the screen. The spot travels up and down tracing out a line of light. The spot moves so fast that the light has not time to die away before a fresh line is drawn.

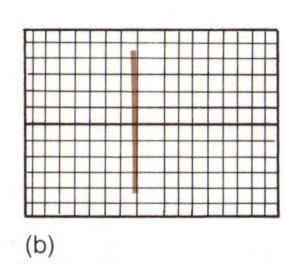

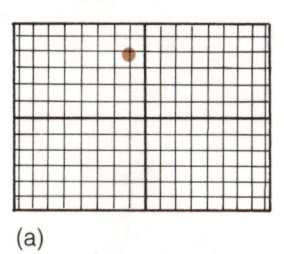

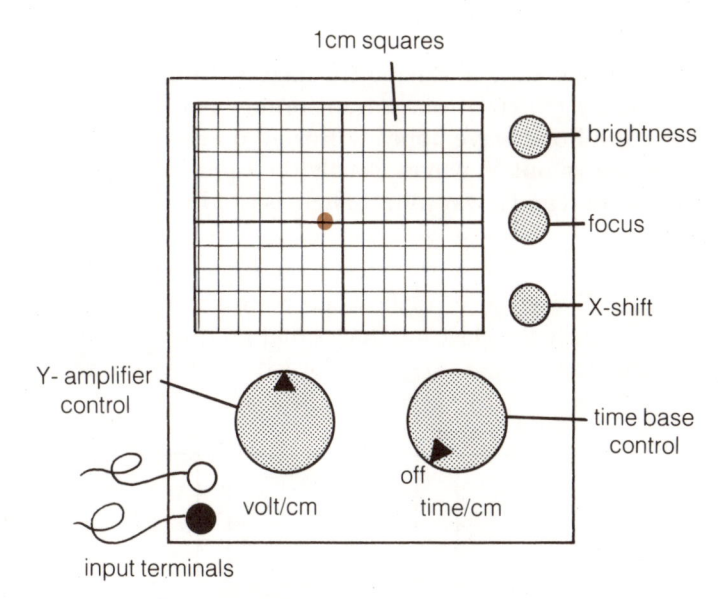

The control knobs of an oscilloscope

The Y-amplifier

The oscilloscope has an amplifier connected to the Y-plates that can magnify the size of the voltage that is being examined. This is especially useful if the voltage is small (like the voltage from a microphone). The Y-amplifier control knob shows how many volts are needed for a deflection of 1 cm.

Experiment. Using the X-plates

The X-plates of an oscilloscope are usually connected to an electronic circuit that pulls the spot steadily across the screen from left to right. When the spot reaches the end of the screen it flicks back quickly and starts again. This circuit is called the **time base** circuit. The time base control knob can change the time the spot takes to cross the screen. Turn on the time base and watch the spot cross the screen (the fly-back is too fast to be seen). Notice that when the spot moves quickly it draws a steady line of light.

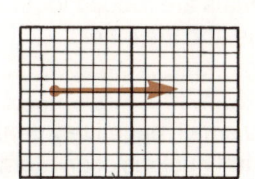

Experiment. Using the X-plates and Y-plates at the same time

Connect a slow alternating voltage to the Y-plates of an oscilloscope (an alternator being turned once a second will do) and watch the spot as it moves up and down on the screen. Switch on the time base so that as the spot goes up and down, it goes sideways as well. These two movements together draw a wave on the screen.

> 15 If the time taken to go up and down and the time taken to go across are both one second, then one wave is drawn. How many waves would be drawn if the time to cross was changed to 2 seconds?

Replace the slow alternating voltage with one of mains frequency (50 Hz) from a transformer. Adjust the time base until one wave appears 'frozen' on the screen. The spot draws out 50 waves exactly on top of each other in one second and a wavy line of light is produced.

> 16 Which electrical device would give which picture? Draw these oscilloscope pictures and beside each write the electrical device that produces it. (The time-base is set to 'freeze' each picture on the screen.)

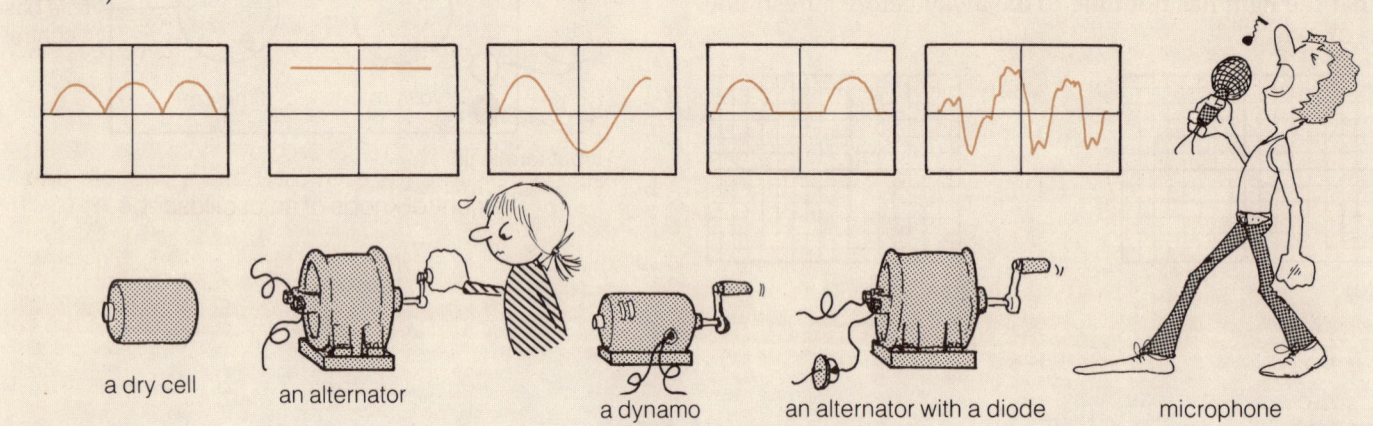

a dry cell   an alternator   a dynamo   an alternator with a diode   microphone

■ An oscilloscope can show the size and shape of a changing voltage.

Summary of electric charge

- There are two types of electric charge. They are called .... positive and negative.
- When two materials are rubbed together and become charged, one will get a positive charge and the other .... a negative charge.
- Like charges .... repel.
- Unlike charges .... attract.
- Atoms contain a small, negatively charged particle called the .... electron.
- The heavy, central nucleus of an atom is charged .... positive.
- An electric current is the movement of electrons through .... a conductor.
- Electrons can be released from a metal by .... heating it.
- Electron beams are attracted to a positive plate and repelled by a .... negative plate.
- Electron beams can also be deflected by a .... magnetic field.
- Oscilloscopes deflect electron beams with .... charged metal plates.

Further questions

17 Two metal plates A and B are electrically charged as shown. C is a small conducting ball suspended between the plates on a silk thread.
(a) If C is given a positive charge, which way will it move at first?
(b) What will happen to the charge on C when it touches B?
(c) Why would C then move to A?
(d) What will happen when C touches A?

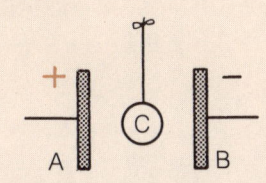

18 When a polythene rod is rubbed with a woollen cloth, the polythene becomes negatively charged and the cloth positively charged.
(a) What are the particles that carry the charge from one to the other?
(b) In which direction are they transferred?
(c) Where do these particles come from?

19 Explain the following:
(a) When pumping petrol from a tanker, the connecting pipe and the tanker are always firmly connected to the ground.
(b) The wearing of nylon underwear is often forbidden in operating theatres.
(c) Operating theatre staff wear boots that are made of rubber which contains a large amount of graphite.

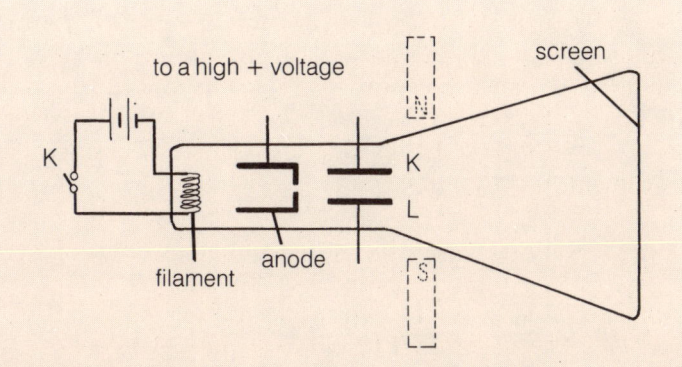

20 This diagram shows a section through an oscilloscope.
(a) What happens at the filament when switch K is closed?
State the energy changes that take place then.
(b) How does the high voltage on the anode help to produce the electron beam?
(c) Explain why the tube must be evacuated.
(d) Explain what will happen to the electron beam if plate K is given a positive charge and plate L a negative charge.
(e) What would happen to the beam if a pair of magnets were placed in the position shown?
(f) Draw a sketch of the oscilloscope screen showing:
(i) an alternating voltage waveform.
(ii) a half-wave rectified voltage waveform.
You may assume for each case that a suitable time base is operating.

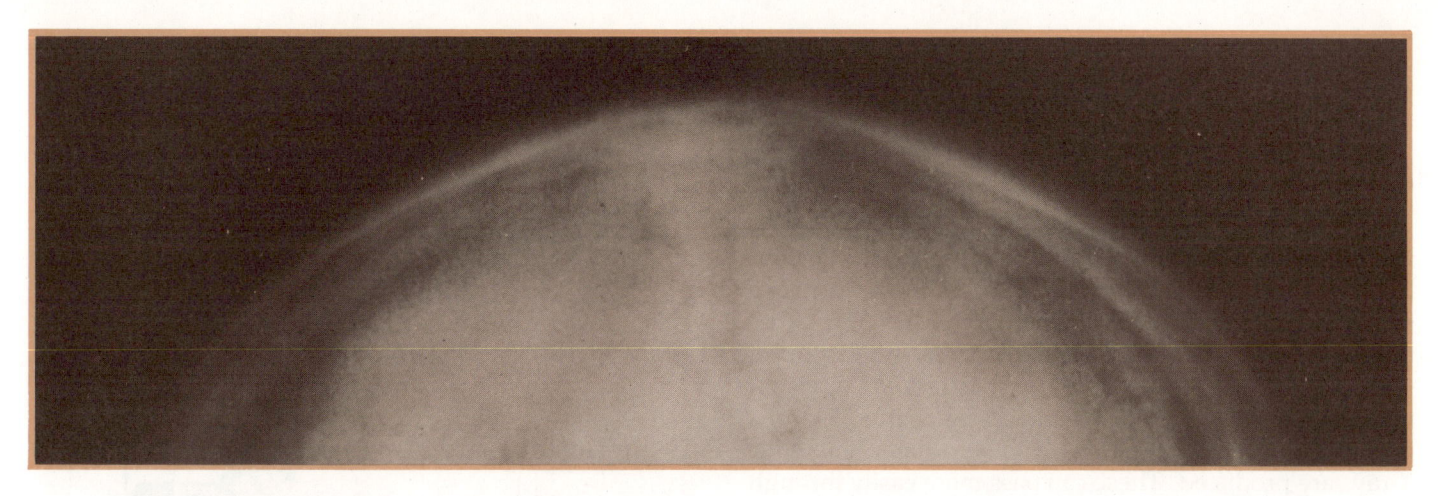

Invisible radiations and electronics

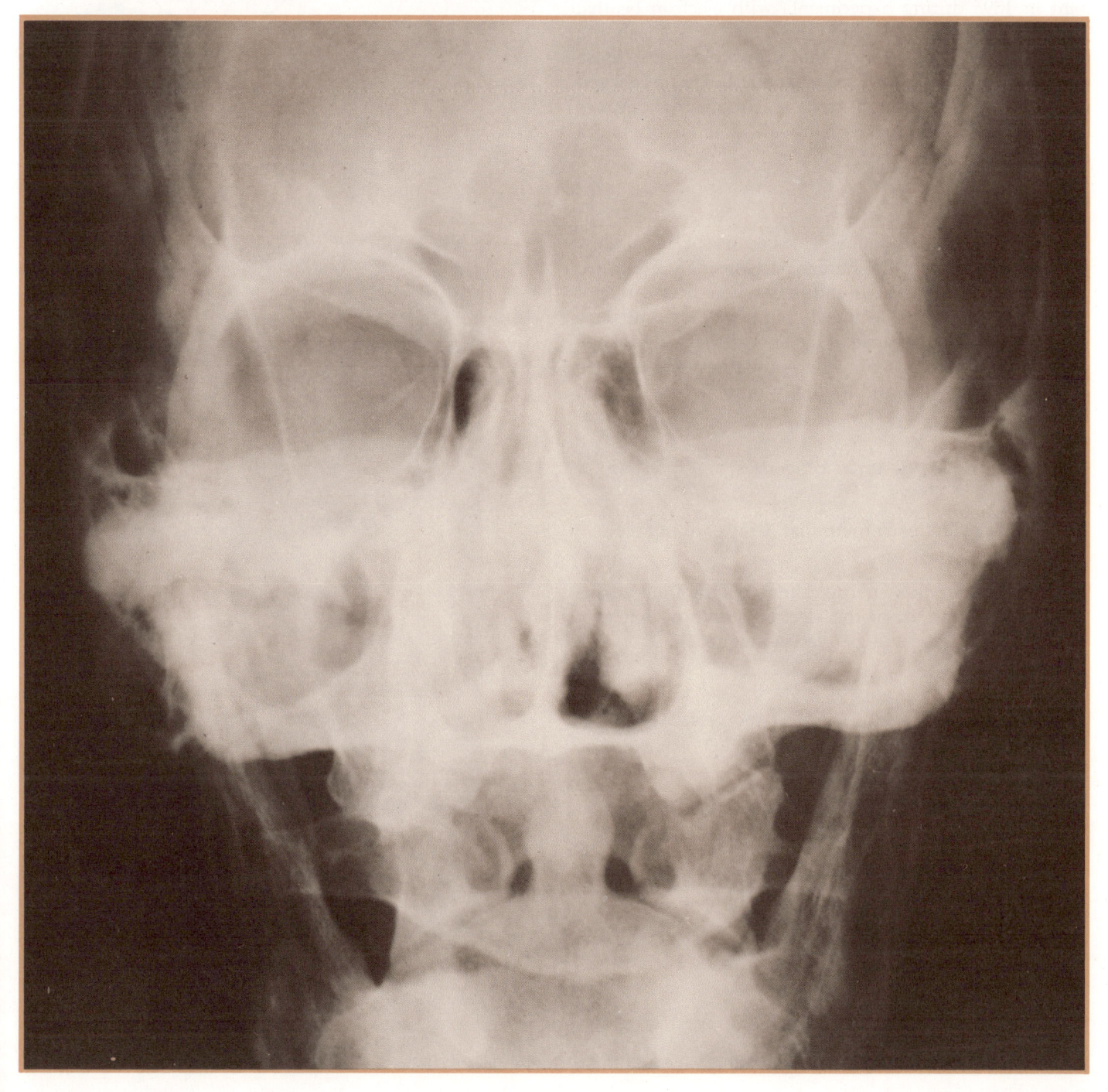

48 X-rays

Television and oscilloscopes use voltages up to about 25 000 V to accelerate electrons. When these electrons stop suddenly, some of their energy changes into radiation. Part of this radiation we see as light, but produced with the light is an invisible radiation called X-rays. If very high voltages are used to accelerate the electrons (100 kV) and metal targets used to stop them, energetic X-rays are produced. These can pass more easily through flesh than through bone and can make a fluorescent screen glow with light. X-rays were discovered by accident in 1895 during experiments with electron beams. They are produced when high speed electrons smash into metal targets. It was found that unlike electrons, these rays cannot be deflected by magnetic fields or charged plates. X-rays are thought to be electro-magnetic waves (like radio and light waves) but with more energy and a shorter wavelength.

A simple X-ray tube

Uses

X-rays find many uses in medicine because of the shadow pictures they give of the harder parts inside our bodies. They have a similar use in industry where they can spot cracks and faults inside metal castings. X-rays must be used with caution because of the energy they carry. They can damage the cells of your body (they are used to destroy cancer cells) and the body must not be X-rayed too often.

1 Write down (i) three properties of X-rays, (ii) three uses of X-rays.

2 What evidence is there that X-rays are not electron beams?

3 What does this energy change diagram tell you about the amount of the electron's energy that is turned into X-ray energy (electro-magnetic)?

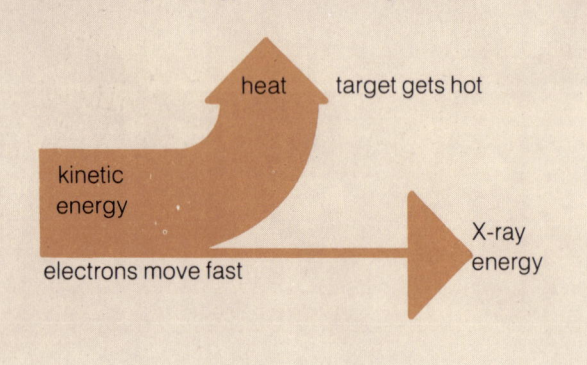

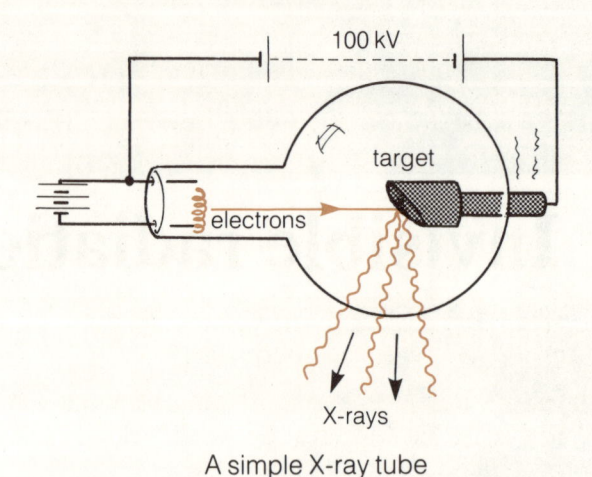

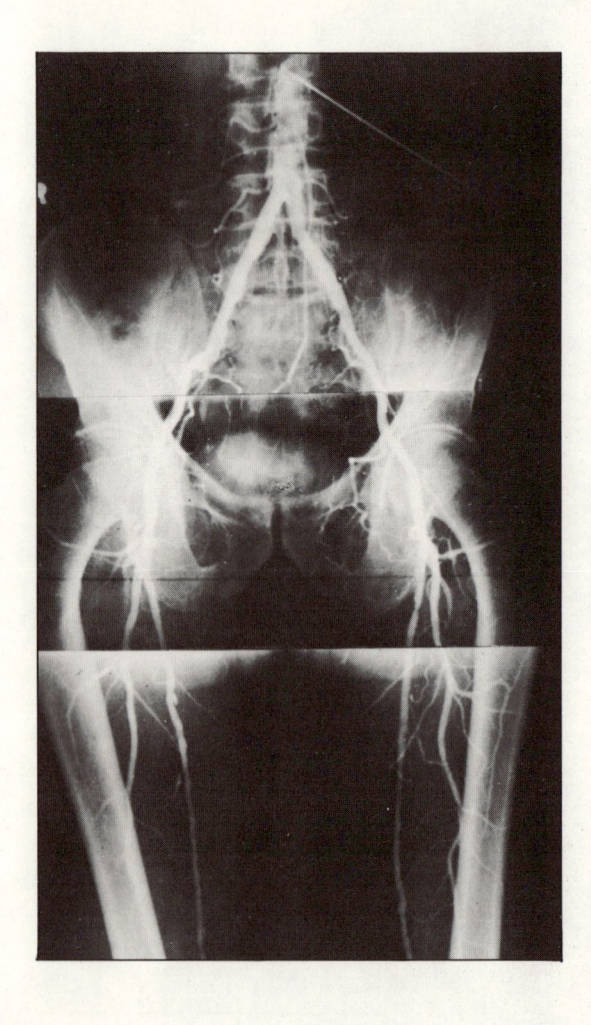

■ X-rays are electromagnetic waves with a wavelength shorter than light.

49 Radioactivity

Radioactivity was discovered in 1896 by a scientist named Becquerel. He was looking for X-rays from uranium and found a new type of radiation. The uranium atoms were radioactive. He found that rays from uranium could expose photographic plates even in the dark. Uranium was the first element that was found to be radioactive but a new more active element (radium) was discovered soon after by the Curies.

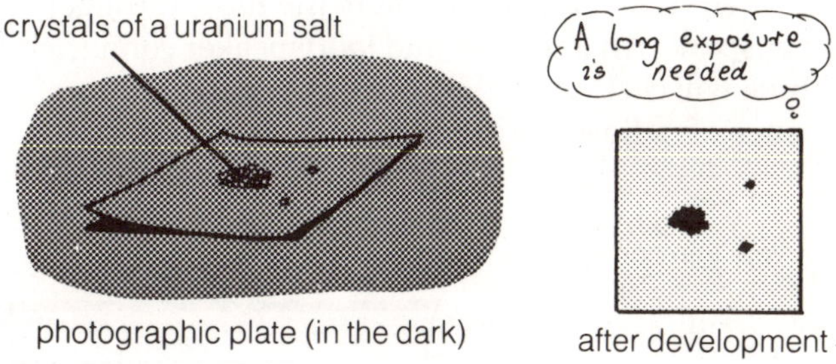

Radioactive radiation can expose photographic paper

Demonstration experiment. Detecting radioactivity with a spark counter

Make a spark counter by placing a stiff wire a millimetre or two away from a wire gauze. Connect the gauze to the negative and earth of a high voltage machine (up to 5000 volts) and the wire to the positive terminal. Turn up the voltage until sparks begin to flash between the wire and the gauze. Then turn the voltage down a little until the sparking just stops. Bring up a radium source, watch and listen. Use your apparatus to check the following observations.

(a) When the radium is close enough (2 or 3 cm), sparks can be seen and heard.
(b) The sparking is haphazard (random).
(c) A sheet of thick paper between the radium and the gauze cuts down the sparking.
(d) A few centimetres of air between the radium and the gauze also stops the sparking.

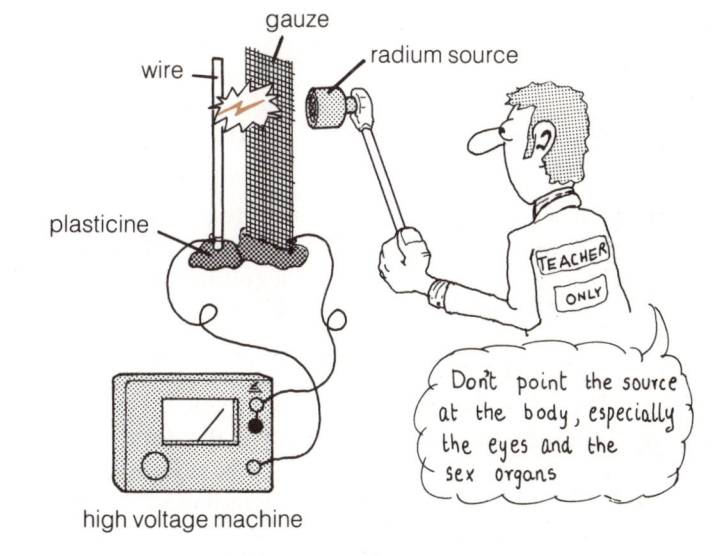

Using a spark counter

1 It appears that the sparks are triggered off by rays coming from the radium. Name two ways of stopping these rays.

2 Give two examples of haphazard happenings you have met in everyday life.

3 Radioactivity is rather like sparks and fireballs shooting out of a firework in fits and starts. Name one difference between getting a firework and getting a radioactive material to give out its 'radiation'. Give one difference between the 'radiations'.

4 Copy and insert X-rays or Radioactivity.

Need a high voltage to be produced		Can be switched off
Are produced naturally without any apparatus		Cannot be switched off

■ Radioactive materials send out high speed radiation that cannot be switched off.

The Geiger-Müller tube

This tube can be used to detect radioactivity. The tube contains a wire at a high voltage (about 450 volts) inside a metal case that is earthed. The voltage of the wire is made just too low to cause a spark between the wire and the case. Then, when radiation enters the tube, it triggers off a quiet spark. An amplifier and loudspeaker connected to the tube will click every time there is a spark, showing the presence of radioactivity.

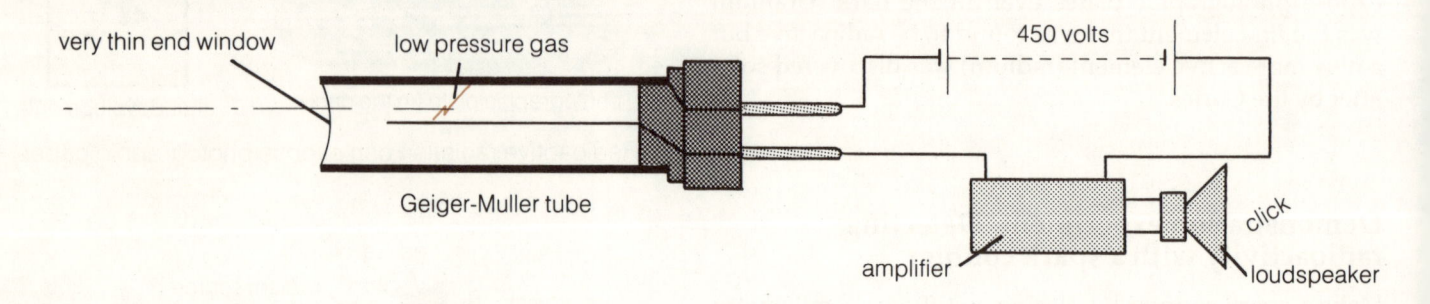

Demonstration experiment. Radioactivity is all around us

Switch on a G-M tube that is connected to a scaler. (A scaler is an instrument that usually contains an amplifier, a voltage supply for the tube and a counter.) Adjust the voltage to the tube and check that it is working by pointing the tube at a radioactive source. The scaler will count and click. Then remove the source to another room. The scaler will continue to count slowly as radiation is picked up by the tube. Move the tube around (carefully) to try and find out where this radiation comes from. Is there anywhere free from the radiation? What are your conclusions?

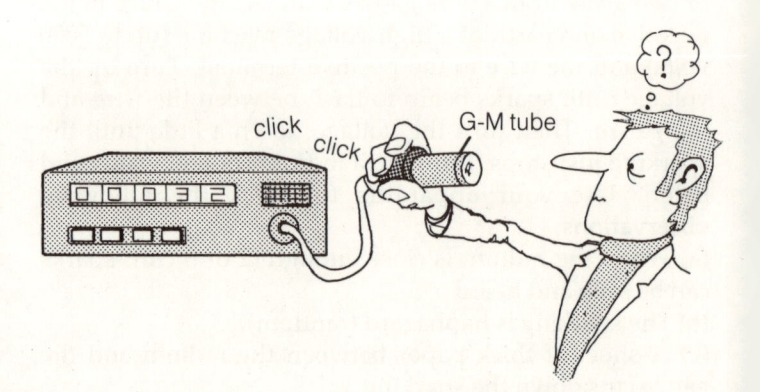

Detecting 'background radiation'

Background count

Use a clock with the apparatus to measure the number of counts this 'background radiation' gives in one minute. Is it always the same number each minute?

---

5   A student took readings of the background count for times of one minute. Here are his results:

| Counts/minute | 27 19 25 28 15 23 16 20 26 11 |

He had not altered his apparatus in any way, but his results were all different. Did he make a mistake or can you explain why his results are like this? Find the average background count rate.

6   Our world is radioactive and has been for a very long time. Some rocks on the Earth are radioactive, radioactive rays shower down on us from space, and man has added a little to Nature's radioactivity. Which of these statements contains the most truth:
(a) Background radioactivity will kill us.
(b) Background radioactivity does cause injury but so few people are affected that we accept it as normal.
(c) Radioactivity is completely harmless to our bodies (p. 232).

■ 'Background radiation' varies in strength a little but is always around us.

Is there more than one sort of radioactive radiation?

The early atomic scientists found that three different sorts of radiation came from radioactive materials. Each had a different penetrating power. They called the radiation alpha (α), beta (β) and gamma (γ) rays.

Demonstration experiment. Finding what materials are needed to stop alpha, beta and gamma rays

Line up a plutonium source with a G-M tube and scaler. (Plutonium gives out alpha rays.) Place a sheet of paper between the source and the tube to see if alpha rays can pass through paper. The scaler counts much slower, showing that very little radiation can get through. Replace the plutonium with strontium 90 (this gives out beta rays) and then cobalt 60 (this gives out gamma rays). Use thicker and thicker plates of aluminium and then lead to find what it takes to stop each radiation. You should find the following:

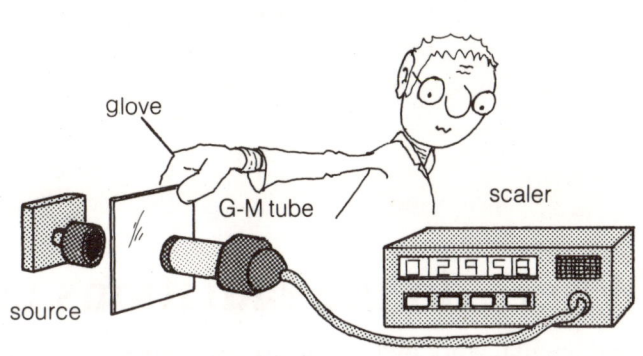

Testing for alpha, beta or gamma rays

Type of radiation	Material needed to stop it
Alpha	A sheet of paper (or 3 cm of air)
Beta	3 mm of aluminium
Gamma	3 cm of lead

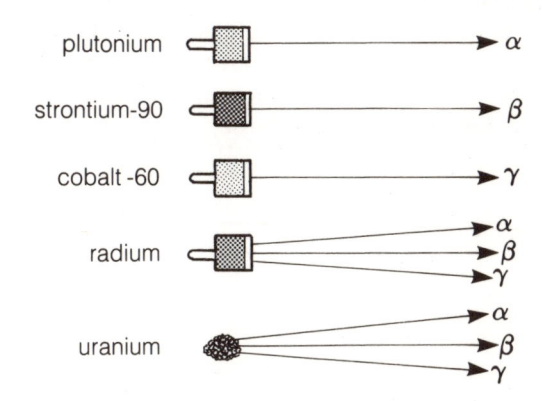

Note that some radioactive materials give out all three types of radiation.

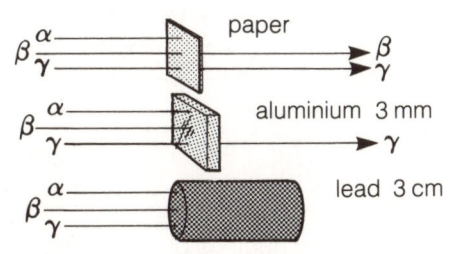

What is needed to stop each type of radiation

7 Which radiation:
(a) gets rids of its energy quickest?
(b) could not get through skin very easily?
(c) could go furthest through the air?

9 Radiation from some elements contains more than one type. Work out which types of radiation are present from the following readings (all corrected for background count).

8

Type	Paper	3 mm aluminium	3 cm lead
Alpha			
Beta			
Gamma			

Copy the table, put a ✓ in the square if the radiation can get through; an X if it cannot.

Element	Count/minute with nothing between source and counter	Count with paper in the way	Count with 3 mm of aluminium in the way	Count with 3 cm lead in the way	Types of radiation present
A	3500	2000	2000	0	
B	3500	3500	2000	0	
C	3500	2000	20	0	

■ There are three types of radioactive radiation, each with a different penetrating power.

What are the radiations made of?

Careful experiments by the early atomic scientists found that the radioactive radiations had the following properties:

Type	Effect of a magnetic field	What the radiation is made from
Alpha	Deflected like a 'heavy' positive particle	The nucleus of a helium atom with two positive charges
Beta	Deflected like an electron	A high speed electron
Gamma	Not deflected at all	Electromagnetic radiation with even more energy than X-rays

Where do the radiations come from?

Experimental work by Rutherford and Soddy in the early 1900's helped them to discover the origin of these radiations. They showed that the radiation came from inside the atom; from its tiny central **nucleus**. The nucleus of a radioactive atom is unstable and can suddenly break up, throwing out high-speed particles and radiation. The radiation we detect is a result of these nuclear events.

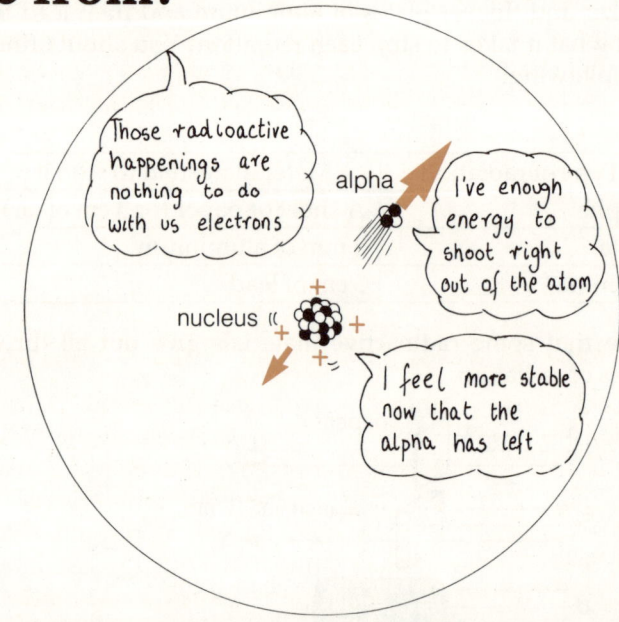

An alpha particle leaves the nucleus of a decaying atom

Ideas about the atom

Date	What the atom was thought to be like
Up to 1895	Just a very small particle
1911	Two parts. A small positive nucleus and negative electrons
1932	Many parts. Two new particles were found, the **proton** that has a positive charge, and the **neutron** that has no charge. The nucleus was thought to be made of protons and neutrons, each simple substance having a different number of these particles

You will notice how scientific discovery has led to a more and more detailed picture of the atom. The story of the atom is still unfolding.

■ Radioactivity comes from the nuclei of radioactive atoms.

Chance happenings

Experiment

Warm a little cooking oil in a frying pan and drop in a seed of 'popping corn'. Take cover and try to guess when the corn is going to explode. Throw in a handful of corn and watch. Do all the seeds explode together and can you tell which one will explode first? We know that all the seeds will explode eventually but we cannot tell when a particular seed is going to change.

> 10 Explain why the 'activity' of the corn is fast at first but gets less as time goes on.

Uranium atoms are unstable and we know they will break up sooner or later. But they do not all break up (decay) at once. We cannot tell which atoms are about to decay, nor can we force an atom to decay. Radioactive decay is a game of chance that Nature plays, completely outside of our control. When uranium decays it changes into a different substance with different properties. So the number of uranium atoms in the world gets less and less as time goes by.

Producing heat from radioactivity — nuclear fission

A special form of uranium can be used in atomic power stations to produce heat and turn water into steam. The heat is produced when the atoms of uranium split in two — a process that is called nuclear fission. Normally uranium atoms decay by sending out alpha and beta particles. These are small compared with the uranium nucleus. A different thing happens if a **neutron** enters the nucleus. A nucleus breaks up into two nearly equal parts and three more neutrons. Energy is released when this happens.

Atomic bomb

If these three neutrons enter three other nuclei, these would split and produce nine fresh neutrons to continue their work. A run-away 'chain reaction' would set in and the uranium would explode. This process is what happens in an atomic bomb.

Nuclear power

In nuclear power stations 2 of the 3 neutrons released are carefully absorbed, leaving 1 to carry on and split up the next uranium nucleus. The fission process then ticks over steadily, producing heat in a controlled way. A few kilograms of uranium can produce as much heat as hundreds of tonnes of coal in this way.

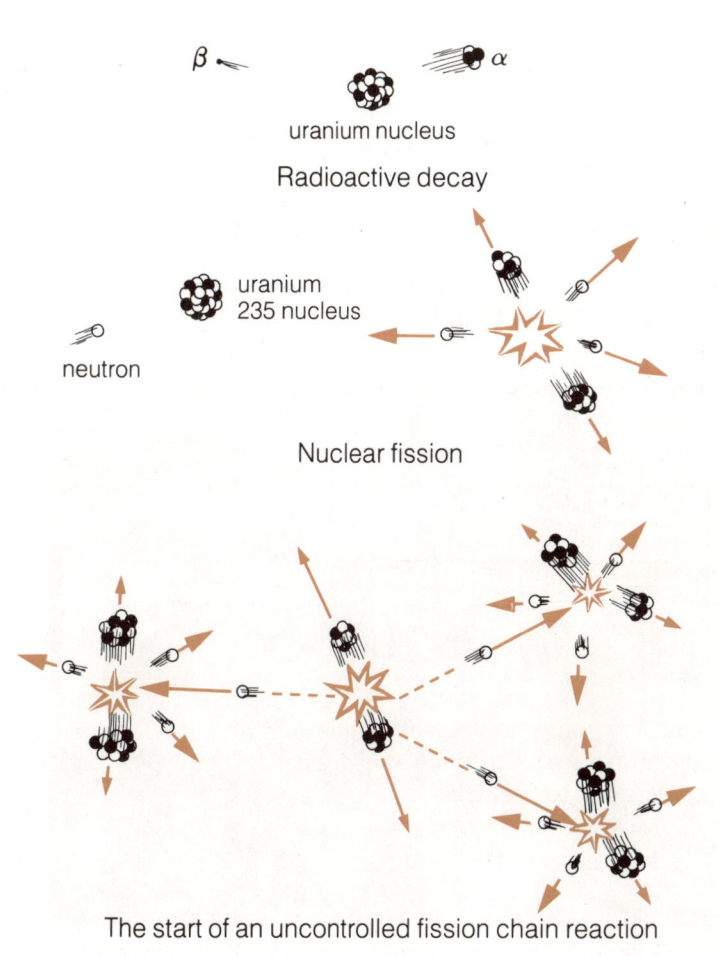

Radioactive decay

Nuclear fission

The start of an uncontrolled fission chain reaction

What radioactivity can do to our bodies

Very intense radiation

The effect of very intense radiation was seen soon after atomic bombs were exploded over Hiroshima and Nagasaki in 1945. Many people died immediately from the blast. Others did not feel the effect of the radiation until two or three days after the raids. These people began to be sick, they developed diarrhoea and a high fever — radiation sickness — from which many died. Some survived the fever only to find they had no resistance to normal infection. They died from mild diseases like tonsilitis. Others found that wounds and burns caused by the radiation would not heal because the healing properties of the blood had been destroyed. These injuries were triggered off by the radiation soon after the explosions. Radiation can also do damage to the body that does not show itself until years after the event.

Radiation hits us all

Radiation strikes our bodies even without nuclear explosions. Background radiation (p. 228) comes from space, rocks in the Earth and from man's use of radioactive materials. It passes into our bodies all the time. Radioactive materials are taken into our bodies as we eat and breathe. Some of these materials stay and collect in the bones and organs, gradually getting more concentrated. Radiation then strikes us from inside as well.

Long-term effects

Long exposure to even these low doses of radiation can produce disease. Leukaemia (cancer of the blood), cataract (causes blindness) and sterility are examples of these diseases.

Fast-growing cells

Cells that are multiplying quickly are more likely to be damaged by radiation than normal cells. A fast-growing baby in the womb of its mother is especially at risk. Radiation and X-rays could kill the baby or deform it in some way. Cancer cells also grow rapidly and radiation is widely used to kill cancerous growths. Doses of radiation (usually gamma rays) are aimed at the growth until it is destroyed.

Genetic effects

Radiation can kill body cells but it can also have a more sinister effect. It can affect the nucleus of cells. The nucleus contains the cell's instructions for making new life. Radiation can interfere with these instructions so that children are born with strange mutations. Hands with two thumbs or five fingers, cattle with five legs, dwarfs and giants are some of the effects of faulty instructions. These effects were a total surprise when they first happened. Radioactivity is not the only cause of mutations like these, but the more radioactivity there is around, the more common these abnormalities will become. Even gentle doses of radiation can spark off changes that are handed down from parents to children. These risks have to be balanced against the good that radioactivity can do.

Safety

Radioactive materials must be handled with great care. You should not touch them or point them at the body, especially the eyes and the sex organs. They should be held at arm's length and stored in a lead-lined box, in an out-of-the-way place. Do not take any risk with this invisible radiation. Damage it causes may not show up for several years, or until you have children.

---

11   Make a list of 10 of the effects of radiation mentioned above.

12   Rewrite your list under two headings: long-term effects; short-term effects.

13   Put a * by any good effects.

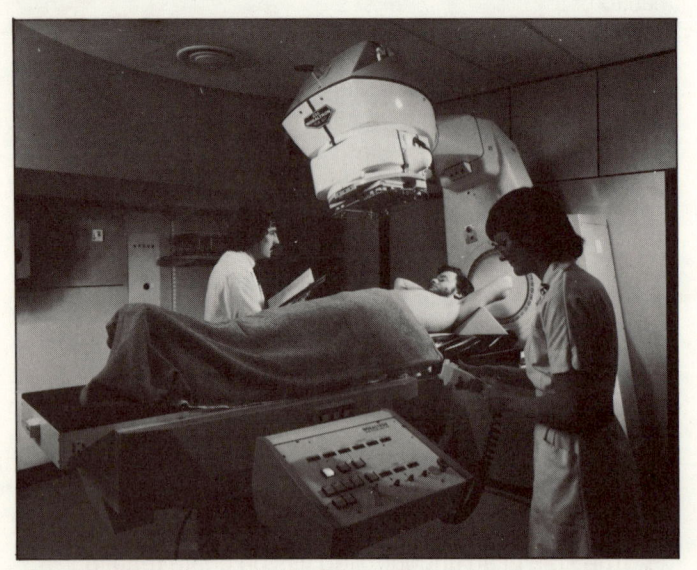

Gamma radiation unit used to destroy cancerous growths

50 The electromagnetic spectrum

Radio waves, infra-red radiation, light, ultra-violet radiation, X-rays and gamma rays are all wavelike radiations that can pass through the vacuum of space (see also p. 52). They all travel at the same speed in a vacuum — 300 million metres/second — and are electric and magnetic in nature. They form the electromagnetic family of waves. Each type of radiation is produced and detected in its own special way. The wavelengths of these waves vary over a wide range. The diagram shows these radiations spread out according to wavelength into an electromagnetic spectrum.

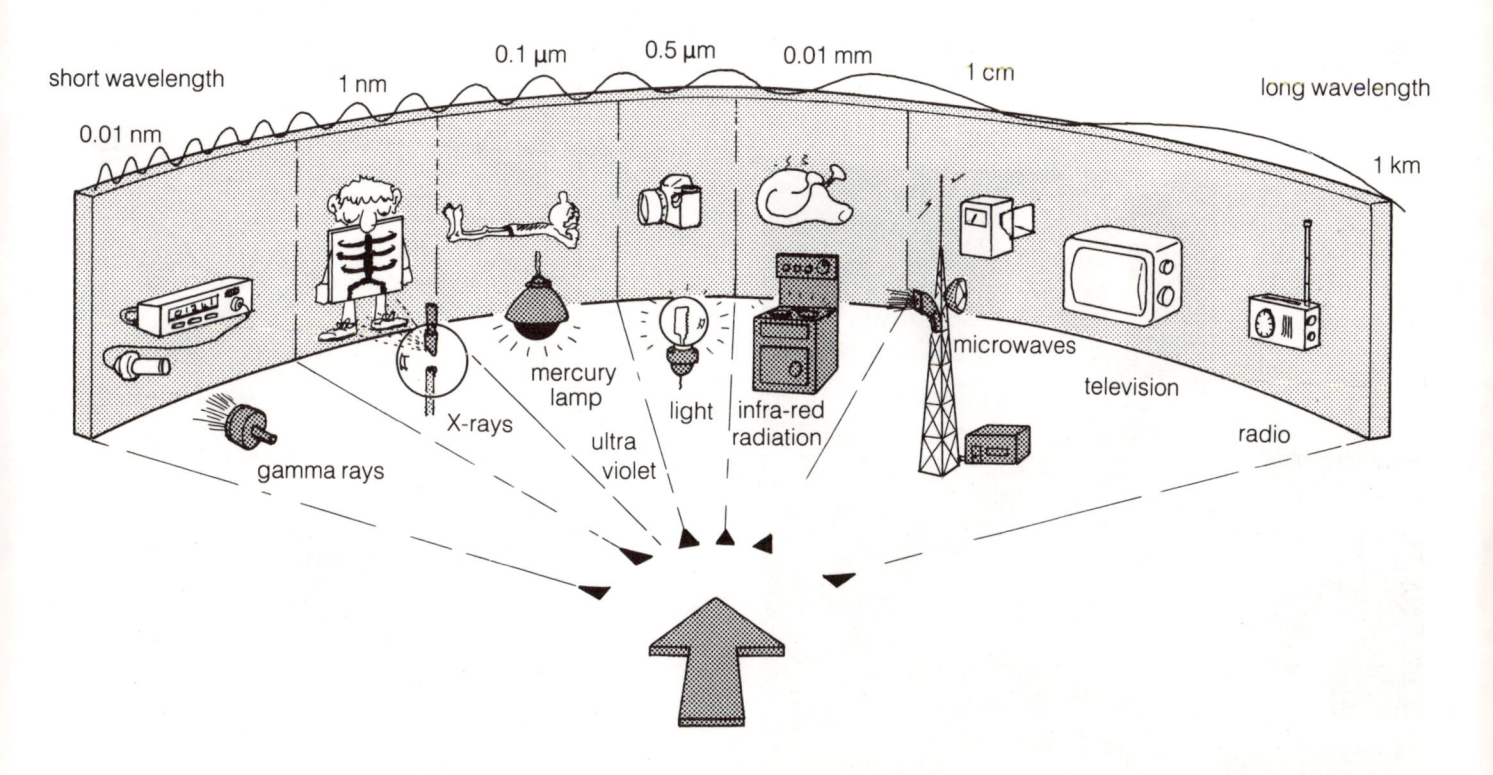

short wavelength 0.01 nm 1 nm 0.1 µm 0.5 µm 0.01 mm 1 cm long wavelength 1 km

gamma rays — X-rays — mercury lamp / ultra violet — light — infra-red radiation — microwaves — television — radio

1 Name two waves that cannot pass through a vacuum.

2 Make a list of each type of radiation and what is used to detect it. What does this detector produce when it receives its radiation?

3 Which of these radiations can we detect with our senses?

4 Which type of radiation cannot be switched off?

5 Write down one use that man has found for each type of radiation.

6 Name one type of radiation that (a) can pass through a thin sheet of lead, (b) causes a sun-tan, (c) can be used to take photographs, (d) is used for remote control.

- Electromagnetic waves carry energy at the speed of light.
- The waves have many properties that depend on the wavelength of the radiation.
- Each band of wavelength has its own special means of production and detection.

51 Radio waves

Electromagnetic waves with wavelengths between a few millimetres and several kilometres can be called radio waves. Radio waves are widely used to carry messages and television pictures around the world. They can also carry speech and instructions to people and equipment in space. They do this silently at the speed of light.

Radio waves are grouped into bands, each band having a special set of uses. Your radio set may be able to 'pick up' from the long, medium and very short wave bands; some receivers can also pick up short wave transmissions from distant countries. Special equipment is needed to transmit and receive radio waves from other bands.

1 Write an essay on 'the use of radio waves'.

A home radio station

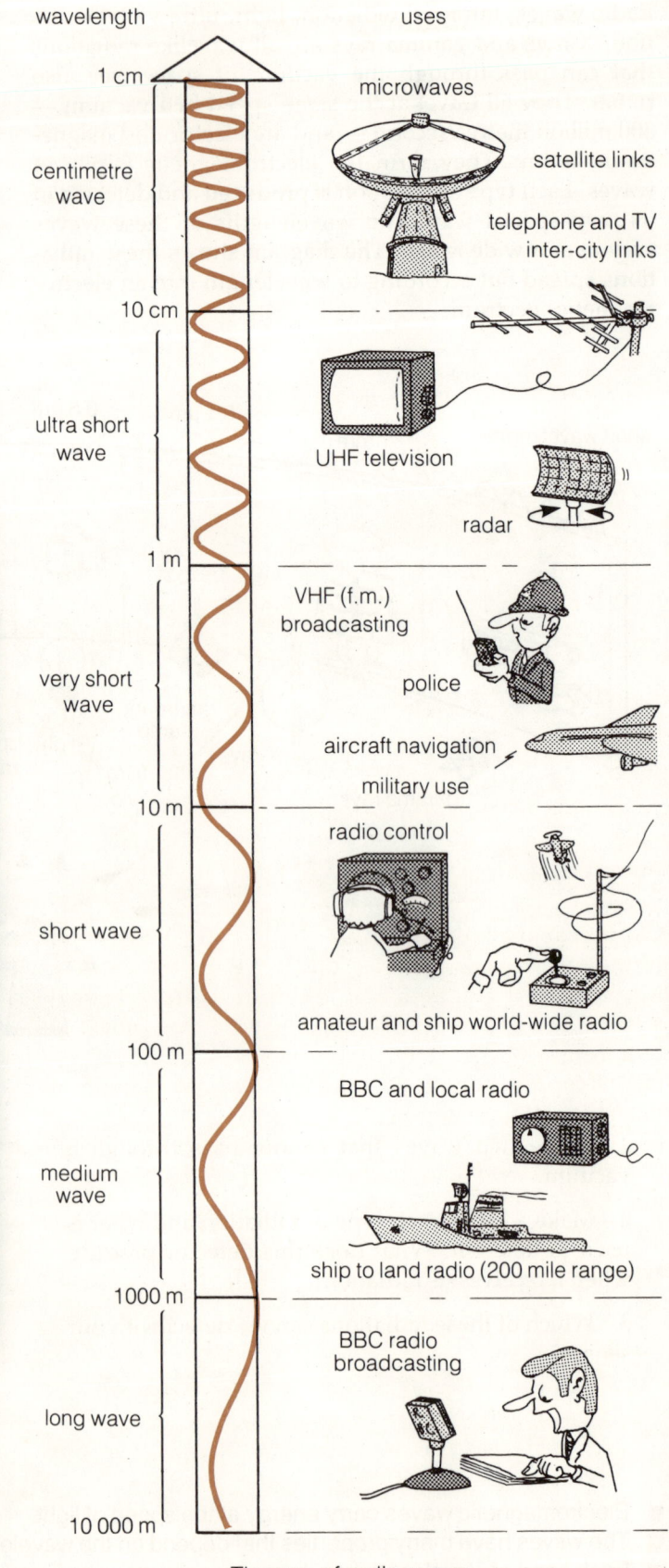

wavelength		uses
1 cm	centimetre wave	microwaves, satellite links, telephone and TV inter-city links
10 cm	ultra short wave	UHF television, radar
1 m	very short wave	VHF (f.m.) broadcasting, police, aircraft navigation, military use
10 m	short wave	radio control, amateur and ship world-wide radio
100 m	medium wave	BBC and local radio, ship to land radio (200 mile range)
1000 m	long wave	BBC radio broadcasting
10 000 m		

The use of radio waves

■ Radio waves are electromagnetic waves.

enlarger 36
evaporation 78-9
exams 243
expansion
   and convection 87-90
   of liquids 87
   of solids 83-6
   problems caused by 84
eye 37

floating and sinking 109-10
focal length 29
focus 29
force(s) 116-21
   and acceleration 123
   and motion 122-6
   turning effects of 131-3
freezing, boiling and 76-82
frequency 55
   natural 62
friction 119-21
   reducing 120
fuses 162, 202, 206

gamma rays 52, 229, 233
gas(es) 73
   pressure and kinetic theory 145
gauge, Bourdon 142
gears and pulleys 136
Geiger-Müller tube 228
generators
   a.c. 192-3
   d.c. 191
   high voltage 197
gravitational energy 4
gravity 117
   acceleration due to 124
   centre of 132

hearing, frequency and 55
heat
   and temperature 100-104
   and the change of state 71-5
   at work 66-70
   conduction of 91-2
   equation 102
heat energy 5, 66-104
   measuring 101
hertz 55
Hooke's law 118
hydraulic machines 146, 148
hydrometers 110

images
   formed by a lens 27-8
   mirror 16-18
   real 14, 30
   virtual 16, 31

induction coil 197
inertia 125
infra-red radiation 52, 93, 233
insulation, heat 95
insulators
   electrical 156, 212
   heat 92

jet engine 68
joule 127, 101, 170
joulemeter 101, 170

Kelvin scale 145
kilowatt hour 172
kinetic
   energy 5
   theory 74
   gas pressure and the 145

lamps
   in parallel 160
   in series 160
latent heat 76
   measuring 102
left-hand rule 184
lens(es)
   and rays 29-32
   camera 33
   concave 29
   convex 27, 28
   image formed by a 27-8
levers 134
light
   and shadows 12-13
   levers 18
   rays 12
   reflection of 17
   refraction of 22-6
light energy 5, 12-47
live wire 203
longitudinal waves 56
long sight 38
loudness of sound 60
loudspeaker 189
   resonating 62

machines 134-8
magnetic
   deflection 220
   poles, forces between 174
magnetic field(s) 177-8
   when an electric current crosses a 184-9
magnetism, earth's 175
magnets 174-6
   demagnetizing 179
   electro- 180
   making 175, 179

magnifying
   glass 28
   power 41
manometer 140
mass 106
matter, particles of 72
measuring
   electrical energy 170-3
   matter 106-12
   motion 113-15
   resistance 167-9
mechanical advantage 134
melting 81
meter
   moving coil 188
   moving iron 188
microphone, moving coil 194
microscope 42
microwaves 52
   uses of 53
mirror(s)
   concave 19
   convex 20
   curved 19-21
   images 16-18
molecules 72
moments 131
   balanced 131
momentum 125
motion, force and 122-6
motors, electric 6, 185-7

National Grid 200
natural frequency 62
neutron 230
newton 116
noise 60
   insulation 61
normal 17
nuclear
   fission 231
   power 231
nucleus 215

ohm 167
Ohm's law 168
optical
   illusions 40
   instruments 33-42
oscilloscope 221-2

paints 45
parallel circuits 160
particles of matter 72
penumbra 13
periscope 26
persistence of vision 40

Index

Absolute zero   145
acceleration   115
   due to gravity   124
   force and   123
air
   compressed   143
   hot   144
alpha rays   229
alternating current   192
alternators   192-3
ammeter   157
ampere   157
amplitude   59
angle
   of incidence   17
   of reflection   17
animation   40
appliances, electrical   207
atomic bomb   231
atoms   72, 215, 230

barometer, aneroid   142
base current   237
battery   153
   car   165
beta rays   229
bimetal strip   85
binoculars   26
binocular vision   39
boiling   76
   and freezing   76-82
boiling point
   and impurities   78
   and pressure   77
   changing the   77
Boyle's law   144
brakes
   disc   147
   drum   147
brightness and vision   40
Brownian motion   73
buzzers and bells   182

camera
   lens   33
   pinhole   14-15
capacitors   217
catapult   6
cells
   and voltage   163-6
   dry   152
   lead/acid   164
   recharging   166

   zinc/carbon   164
centre of gravity   132
charge(s), electric   210-17
   and electric current   216
   forces between   212
chemical energy   4
circuit
   lighting   203
   ring main power   204
   symbols   152
   time base   221
   tuning   235
clouds   79
collector current   237
collisions and blows   125
colour(s)   43-7
   filters   43
   primary   43
   secondary   44
   of the spectrum   43
commutator   185
concave
   lens   29
   mirror   19
condensation   79
conduction of heat   91-2
conductors and insulators of
   electricity   156-60, 212
conservation of energy   9
consumer unit   202
convection   88
   currents   87
   of air   89
convex
   lens   27, 28
   mirror   20
cooling fins   96
critical angle   24
crystals   72
current
   alternating   192
   direct   191
   voltage and   168
curved mirrors   19-21

dart, throwing a   6
decibels   60
density   107-9
   of air   109
depth of field   35
dew   80
diffraction of water waves   51
diode   195

direct current   191
dynamos   191

earthing   205
earth wire   202
eclipses   13
efficiency of machines   135
electrical energy   5
   measuring   170-3
   paying for   172
electric circuits   152-5
electric current
   and its magnetic field   178
   measuring   157-8
electric heating   161-2
electricity
   in the home   202-9
   making   190-201
   safety with   208
electricity meter   202
electric motor   6
electrolysis   157
electrolytes   157
electromagnetic
   induction   196
   spectrum   233
   waves   12, 52, 233, 234
electromagnets   180-1, 196
electrons(s)
   beams   219
   in space   218-23
   theory of electric charge   215
electronics   237-42
electrostatic deflection   220
energy   4-9
   and work   128
   chains   9
   chemical   4
   conservation of   9
   electrical   5
   forms of   4
   gravitational   4
   heat   5, 66-104
   kinetic   5
   light   5, 12-47
   potential   4
   sound   5, 50-64
   strain   4
   where it comes from   8
engines
   hot gas   67
   jet   68
   petrol   69-70
   rocket   68

Answers

8 Lenses and rays (pp. 29-32)
2 distances 5.3, 6.0, 7.5 cm; heights 1.5, 2.0, 3.0 cm
3 distances 6.0, 1.5 cm; heights 3.0, 1.5 cm

9 Optical instruments (pp. 33-42)
23 40 s, 80 s

12 Vibrations we can hear (pp. 54-5)
9 200 Hz

13 Sound waves (pp. 56-61)
7 100 m
8 2000 s
15 715 m
23 about 79 dB
25 ¼

14 Resonance (pp. 62-4)
5 4 s
7 3.4 km
9 1280 Hz,

17 Boiling and freezing (pp. 76-82)
1 (b) 100°C, 78°C

18 The expansion of solids (pp. 83-6)
8 4 minutes, 79%

23 Heat and temperature (pp. 100-4)
3 380 J
11 1700 kJ
12 17 kJ
15 1000 s
16 240 kJ
22 (a) 55°C; (b) 2.5°C; (c) 4200 J/kg/°C
23 (a) 250 000 J; (b) 2500 kJ

24 Measuring matter (pp. 106-12)
4 1 million
7 (a) 30; (b) 9 g
8 8 g/cm^3, 1 g/cm^3, 10 cm^3, 100 g
10 1.2 kg
11 (a) 60 m; (b) 72 kg
21 (a) 0.8
22 8 cm^3, 56 g
25 2 g/cm^3

25 Measuring motion (pp. 113-15)
3 0.1 s, 0.26 s, 0.04 s
7 3 cm/s, 25 cm/s, 100 cm/s

26 Forces (pp. 116-21)
4 10 N
9 60 N

28 Work (pp. 127-8)
1 (a) 1000 J; (b) 0.01 J; (c) 600 J
2 40 J, 800 J
3 25 kJ

29 Power (pp. 129-30)
1 2 J, 0.5 W; 600 J, 60 W; 6 kJ, 1 kW
2 200 W

31 Machines (pp. 134-8)
2 (a) 4, 5, 0.2
3 velocity ratios 5, 3, 20; mechanical advantages 4.5, 2.5, 18
4 work done by effort 10 J, 1.2 J, 0.5 J; work done on load 9 J, 1 J, 0.45 J; efficiencies 0.9, 0.8, 0.9

32 Pressure (pp. 139-49)
3 100 kN/m^2, 5 m^2, 32 kN
4 3 N/cm^2, 1200 N/cm^2
5 0.5 N/cm^2
29 (a) 3 kN; (b) 0.02 m^2
32 (a) 1000 N/cm^2; (b) 20 kN

37 Measuring resistance (pp. 167-9)
1 48, 6, 24, 3, 4, 12 ohms

38 Measuring electrical energy (pp. 170-3)
1 53 082 J, 75 013 J, 21 931 J
2 20 W, 2 W, 10 W, 50 W
3 2 J, 10 J, 20 J; 50 s, 10 s, 5 s
5 40 W, 120 W, 2400 W, 960 W, 1 W
8 12 kWh
9 5 hours
11 2 A
12 (a) 2 A; (c) 240 J

44 Making electricity again (pp. 196-201)
12 (b) 200 W, 100 W; (c) 100 W

45 Electricity in the home (pp. 202-9)
5 12 A, 4 A, 0.5 A, 3 A

49 Radioactivity (pp. 227-32)
5 21 counts/minute

Exams

If you are properly prepared you can even enjoy taking exams. Proper preparation will also ensure that you do your best and will show the examiners how good you really are. Here are some points to bear in mind as exams draw near.

Well before

(a) Start revision some months before the exams. Make brief notes from your notebooks and textbooks (see p. 1). Go over the work until you can remember it.

(b) Try questions from past papers. Practise all the different types of question that are asked. Work out how many minutes you have to answer each question and write out answers in that time. Learn to answer exactly what is asked. Putting ideas into words is difficult so take every opportunity to practise writing. Use drawings to help whenever you can.

Just before

Double-check the dates and times of the examinations. Arrive fresh and in good time to avoid last minute panic. Have two pens, a pencil, rubber, a watch, a calculator, a ruler and drawing instruments if they are needed.

During

Read the instructions carefully and ask if you do not understand them. If there is a choice, choose quickly but carefully, doing your best question first. Keep an eye on the clock so there is time to answer the right number of questions. At the end check your arithmetic, spelling and look for careless slips.

Good luck!

After . . .

Summary

- X-rays are electromagnetic waves with a wavelength shorter than light by longer than .... gamma waves.
- X-rays can be made by making high speed electrons .... stop suddenly.
- The three types of radioactive radiation are called .... alpha, beta, gamma.
- The radioactive radiation that surrounds us all of the time is called .... background radiation.
- Alpha and beta radiations are made up of high speed particles, but gamma rays are made up of .... electromagnetic waves.
- All radioactivity comes from the .... nucleus of atoms.
- Gamma, X-rays, ultra-violet, light, infra-red, microwaves and radio waves are all .... electromagnetic waves.
- A transistor has three leads called .... collector, base, emitter.
- The two currents that pass through a transistor are .... the collector and base currents.
- The smaller of these two currents (the one that controls the other) is the .... base current.
- A transistor can be used to .... amplify small changing voltages
    and as a .... fast acting switch.

Further questions

3 Before switching on an X-ray machine, the operator goes behind a safety screen.
(a) What material is this screen likely to contain?
(b) Is there any risk to the patient from the X-rays he receives?
(c) Name a radiation that is more penetrating than X-rays.

4 The three types of radioactive radiation are alpha, beta and gamma rays. Which of these radiations:
(a) most resembles light?
(b) carries positive charge?
(c) cannot penetrate paper?
(d) carries a negative charge?
(e) can pass through thick lead?

5 Radioactivity is sometimes used in the treatment of cancer.
(a) Which type of radiation is used?
(b) What effect does it have?
(c) Name one other danger of using this radiation.

6 This diagram shows a simple use of radioactivity to check if the powder inside a packet is up to a certain level.
(a) How would the detector reading show if the powder has passed its level?
(b) Which type of radioactive radiation could not be used for this job?

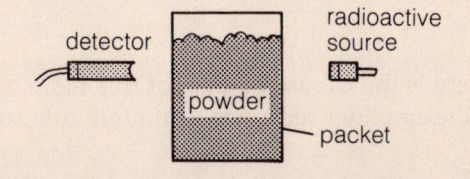

7 This diagram shows a simple amplifier.
(a) Name the leads X, Y, Z of the transistor.
(b) Which part is the microphone and which part is the loudspeaker?

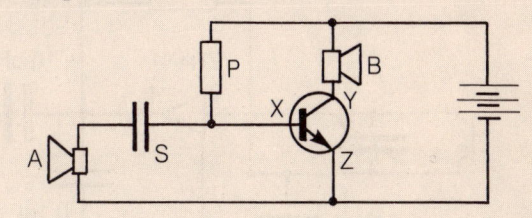

What to do

1) Lay your matrix board over the receiver diagram. Draw in the black lines and mark the positions of the circles.

2) Press pins into the holes marked with circles.

3) Connect thin copper wires from pin to pin along the black lines.

4) Put in the resistors and the capacitors. Twist each lead two or three times round its pin.
330 Ω   (orange, orange, brown)
470 kΩ (yellow, violet, yellow)
100 kΩ (brown, black, yellow)
10 kΩ   (brown, black, orange)
4.7 kΩ (yellow, violet, red)

5) Put in the transistors and the ZN414. Check the leads carefully and bind each one tight to its pin.

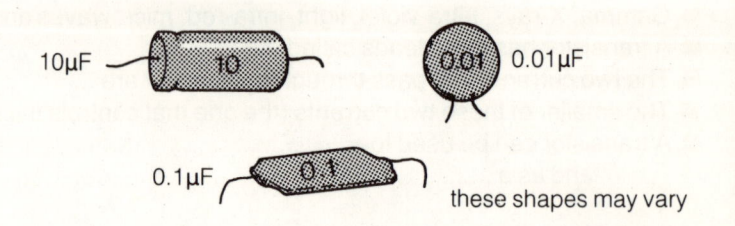

10μF 0.01μF 0.1μF

these shapes may vary

Final connections

Connect the tuning circuit to T and T.
Connect the loudspeaker to (+) and C.
Check that no leads are touching under the board, then connect a 4.5 volt battery to (+) and (−). Tune in a station and turn the board until the sound is loudest.

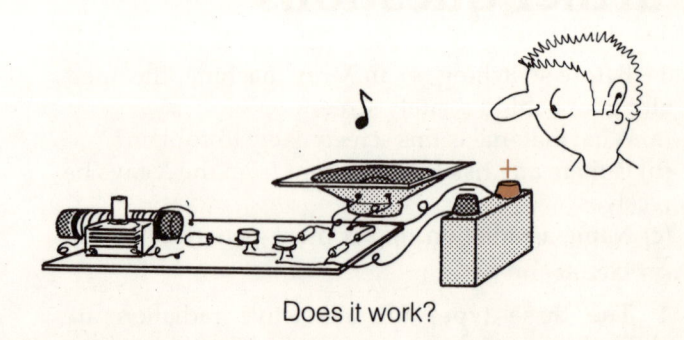

Does it work?

2. Here is the circuit diagram of this radio. Copy it and draw the amplifier section in a different colour to the rest.

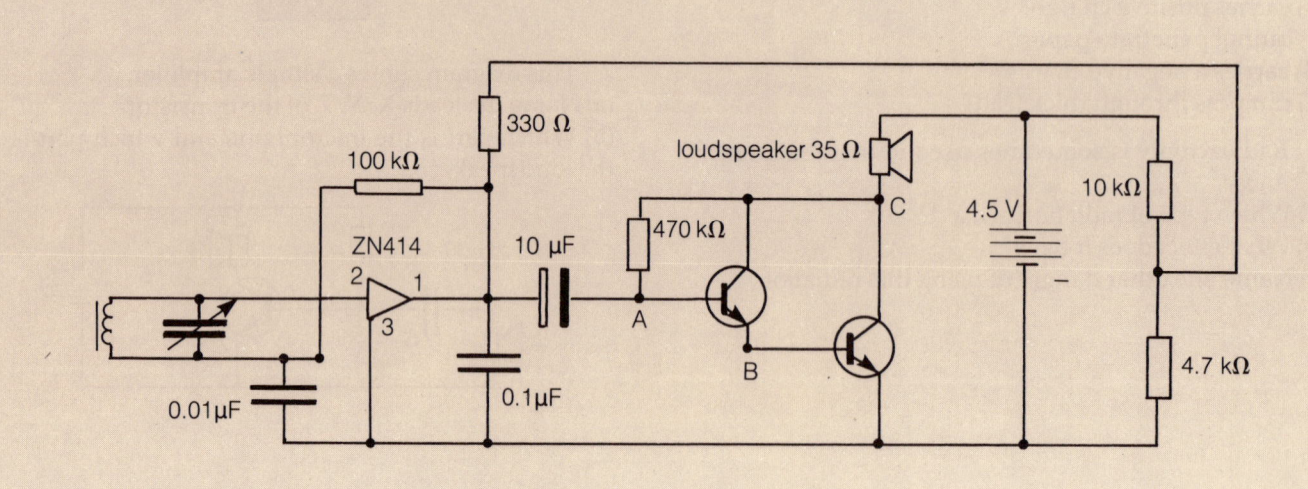

Experiment. Following the signal through a radio

Connect the earth terminal of an oscilloscope to the (−) pin and the other terminal first to the pin A, then pin B, and then pin C. The pictures you get on the screen show how the amplifier increases the size of the signal stage by stage.

241

The lamp should come on when you take the circuit into a dark place and go off when light falls on it.

The circuit below is also a twilight switch but contains two transistors. These make the circuit much more sensitive. See if you can build it on matrix board.

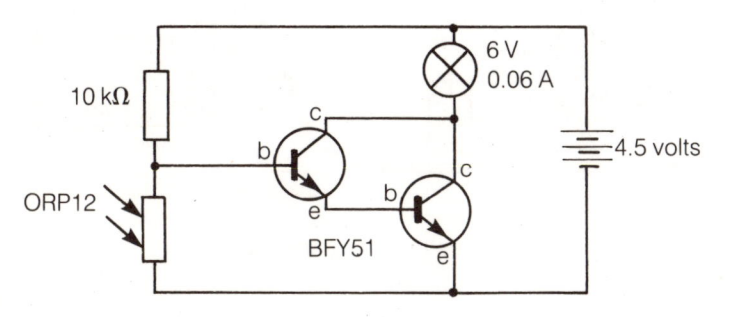

The light level falls .... the resistance of ORP12 rises .... the base current increases .... the collector current increases ... the lamp goes on.

■ A transistor can be used as a fast-acting switch with no moving parts.

A radio project

This radio will* work without an aerial and is powerful enough to drive a loudspeaker. It uses the same transistors and tuning circuit as before, but includes an 'integrated circuit' (ZN414). This device amplifies the radio signal and then does the job of the diode before passing the signal on to the amplifier. It is placed between the tuning circuit and the amplifier.

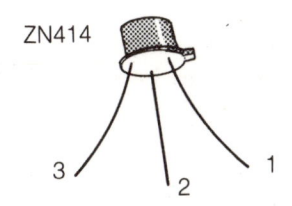

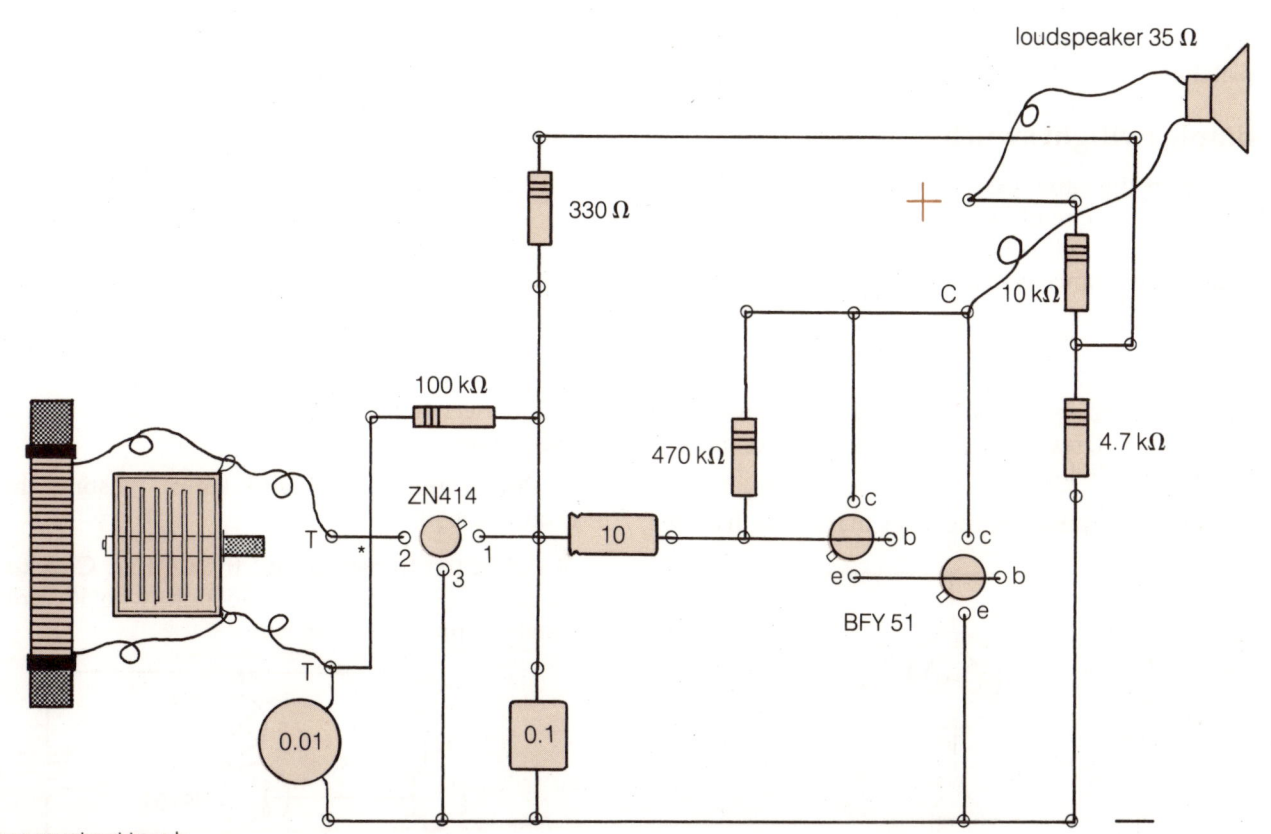

*these wires must not touch

*An aerial may be needed in areas of poor reception.

Does it work?

Use the small signal from a radio tuning circuit and diode (or a microphone or signal generator) as the test voltage. Connect this signal to IN. Then connect an oscilloscope to OUT to view the amplified voltage, and a 4.5 volt battery to (+) and (−) to provide the power. Tune in a radio station and the very small voltage that leaves the diode should appear amplified on the screen. It may just be possible to hear the sound in a **crystal** earphone connected in place of the oscilloscope.

This is the circuit diagram of the amplifier. Compare it with the drawing on your board. If a small changing voltage is connected to IN, a large version of that voltage will appear at OUT.

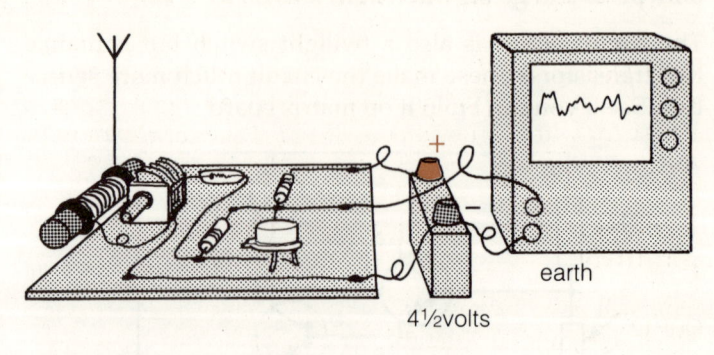

Testing the amplifier

■ A transistor can be used to amplify a small changing voltage.

Using a transistor as a switch

We have used a transistor to amplify the small signal in a radio. A transistor amplifies because a small change in the base current causes a large change in the collector current.

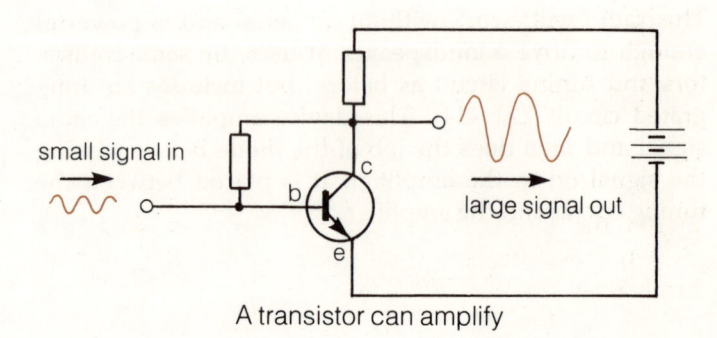

Transistors can also be used as fast electronic switches that have no moving parts. When the base current is switched on and off, the collector current switches on and off too. Here are examples of circuits that use transistors as switches.

A transistor can amplify

A simple twilight switch

The lamp in this circuit comes on automatically when it gets dark. The circuit uses a photocell (ORP12). The resistance of this cell gets less when light shines on it. In the dark its resistance is high.

What to do

1) Lay the matrix board on this diagram of the twilight switch circuit. Draw in the black lines and mark the position of the circles.

2) Press terminal pins into the holes marked with circles.

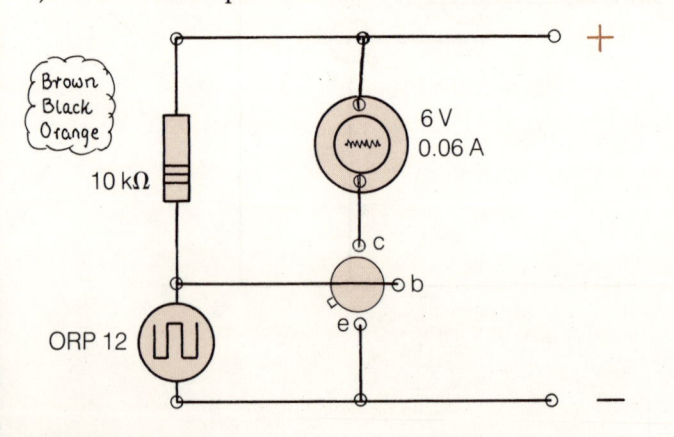

3) Connect thin copper wire from pin to pin along the black lines.

4) Put in the resistor and lamp, twisting their leads around the pins.

5) Put in the transistor and the ORP12. Check the leads carefully and bind each one tightly to its proper pin. Finally connect the battery.

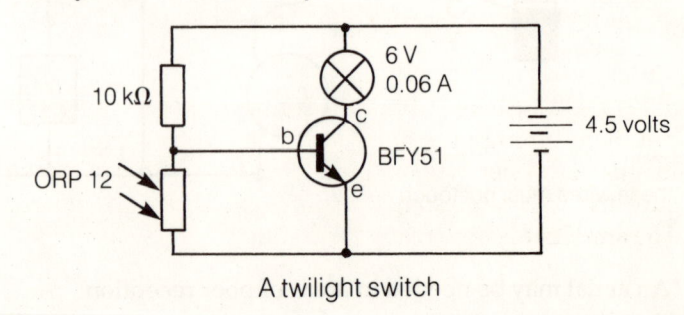

A twilight switch

Using a transistor to amplify

A transistor can be used to amplify small, changing, voltage signals. The amplifier described below uses a transistor with the number of BFY51. Take care to identify the three leads correctly.

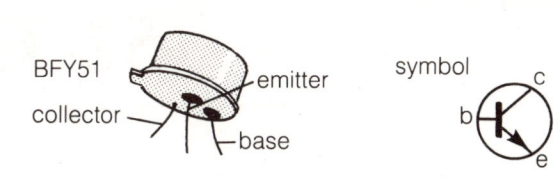

The leads of a typical transistor

Experiment. Building a 'one transistor' amplifier

You will need two resistors, 1 kΩ (colour coded brown, black, red) and 100 kΩ (brown, black, yellow), a transistor (BFY51) and a piece of matrix board. This is an insulating board covered with holes (10 per inch). The leads of components are pushed through the holes and wired to special terminal pins.

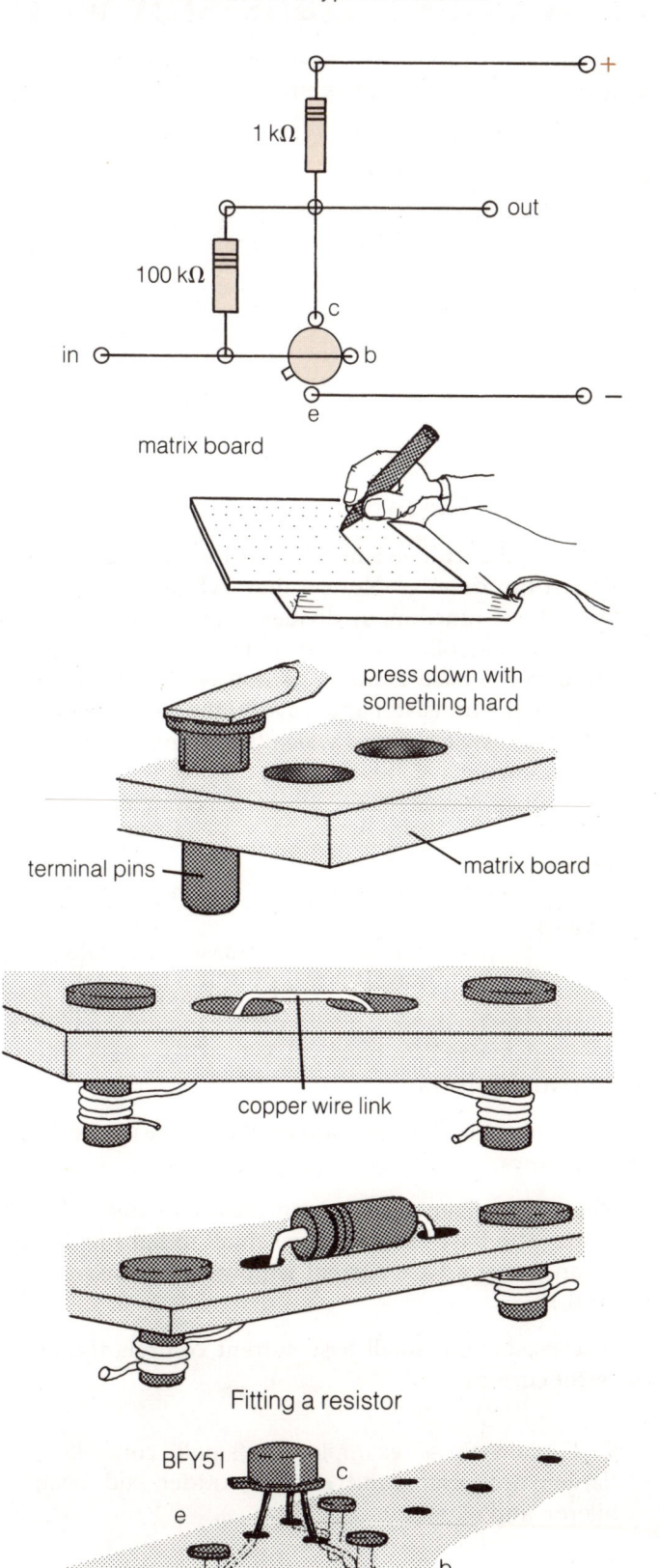

Construction

1) Lay your board over the diagram so that you can see the black lines through the holes. Draw the black lines on your board and mark the position of the circles.

2) Put the terminal pins into the holes marked with circles. Press the pins right down so that they become firmly fixed.

3) The black lines on your board are wire links. Use thin bare copper wire (about 32 gauge) to link from one pin to the next. Twist the wire four or five times round each pin to make a good connection. It is best to bring the wire to the top of the board in between pins so that you can see if you have missed any links. Snip off the loose ends with scissors.

4) Put in the resistors. Twist their leads round the pins two or three times.

5) Fix the transistor. Check the leads of the transistor and put them through the holes next to the correct pin. Use a length of copper wire to bind each leg to its pin. Make sure the transistor stands about 1 cm above the board. The amplifier is now ready for testing.

52 Electronics

How does a transistor work?

There are many types of transistor but they all have three working leads. The circuit symbols show this. The three leads are named:

collector (entrance)
base (entrance)
emitter (exit)

Current flows into a transistor through two entrances and out by one exit.

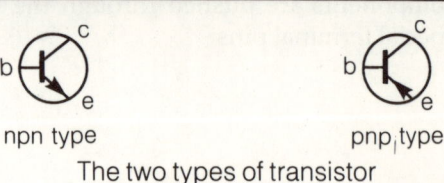

npn type   pnp type
The two types of transistor

Experiment. The two currents in a transistor

Build this test circuit on a matrix board — see page 238 for construction details. Notice that when the current reaches the T-junction, it divides. Most of the current passes into the collector entrance, but a small part goes round into the base entrance. These two currents combine inside the transistor and leave by the base exit. Open and close the switch X and watch the lamps. You should see the following:

Switch	Lamp A	Lamp B
X open	off (no collector current)	off (no base current)
X closed	on (collector current flows)	off (base current flows but is too small to light the lamp)

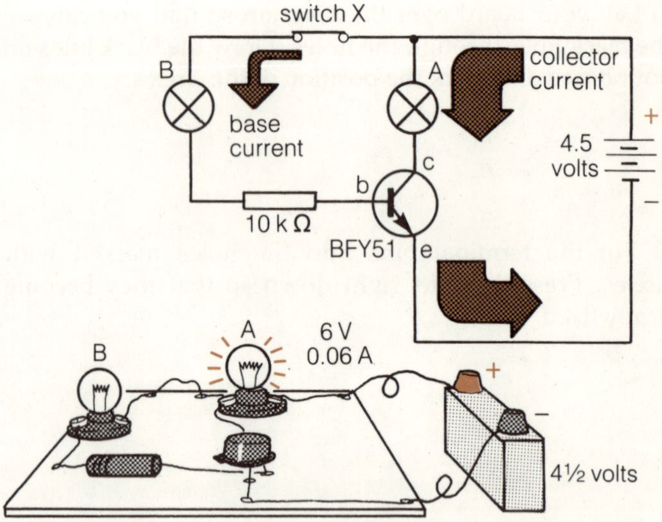

Two conclusions

1) The collector current cannot flow unless the base current flows.

2) The base current is much smaller than the collector current. (The base current is too small to light its lamp. You can prove a base current is flowing by unscrewing lamp B.)

In a transistor the small base current controls the large collector current.

> 1 Explain these examples of 'small' controlling 'large': accelerator and engine; rudder and boat; aileron and plane.

A circuit to show how the base current controls the collector current

A few controlling the many

■ Two currents flow through a transistor: the collector current and the (much smaller) base current.

Experiment. To show that a radio must include a diode

Connect the leads from a tuning circuit to a diode (OA91), an amplifier and a loudspeaker. Switch on and you will find that this apparatus is a radio receiver able to tune in several radio stations. Replace the diode by a piece of wire. Does the radio still work? The diode makes a vital change to the radio signal as it passes from the tuning circuit to the amplifier. Connect an oscilloscope to the circuit just after the diode. The signal will be small but you should see that it has a flat bottom and moving peaks on one side only. The diode has removed half of the radio signal. This change is necessary because the top and bottom sound waves would otherwise cancel out.

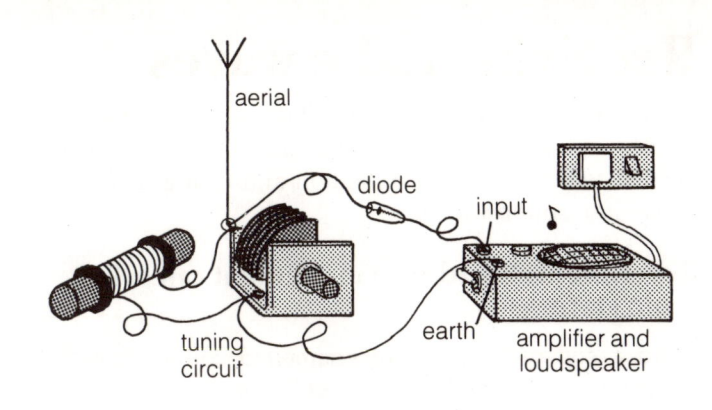

A basic radio receiver

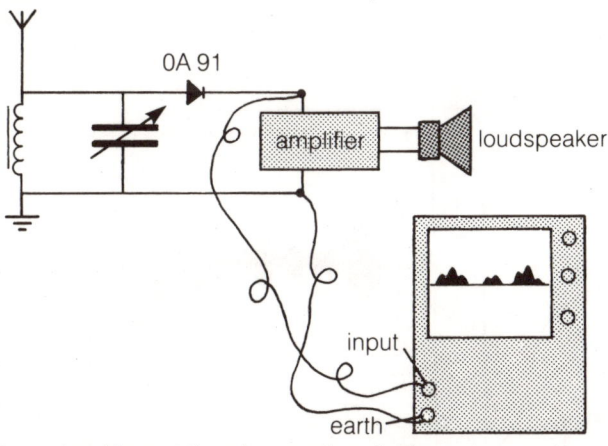

Looking at the change the diode makes

4 Why is a diode able to change a signal like (a) to a signal like (b)?

(a)   (b)

5 This diagram shows the energy changes that take place in a radio receiver. Copy it and write in these energy forms: electrical; sound; electromagnetic; heat.

6 Copy and complete this table. It is about the main parts of a radio receiver.

Name of the part	The job it does in the radio
Tuning circuit	
Diode	
Amplifier	
Loudspeaker	

■ A simple radio can be made from a tuning circuit, a diode and an amplifier with a loudspeaker.

Receiving radio waves

The air is full of radio waves. Luckily we cannot hear the jumble of radiation that fills our rooms. A radio receiver is needed to pick out a radio station and change the radio waves into sound waves.

Experiment. Building a circuit that can select radio stations

Wind a coil of 50 turns of enamelled copper wire (24 gauge) onto a ferrite rod. Connect the ends of the coil to a variable capacitor. This capacitor has a set of semicircular plates that can be moved between fixed plates. Different radio stations can be selected by turning the movable plates. The coil and the variable capacitor make up a **tuning circuit.**

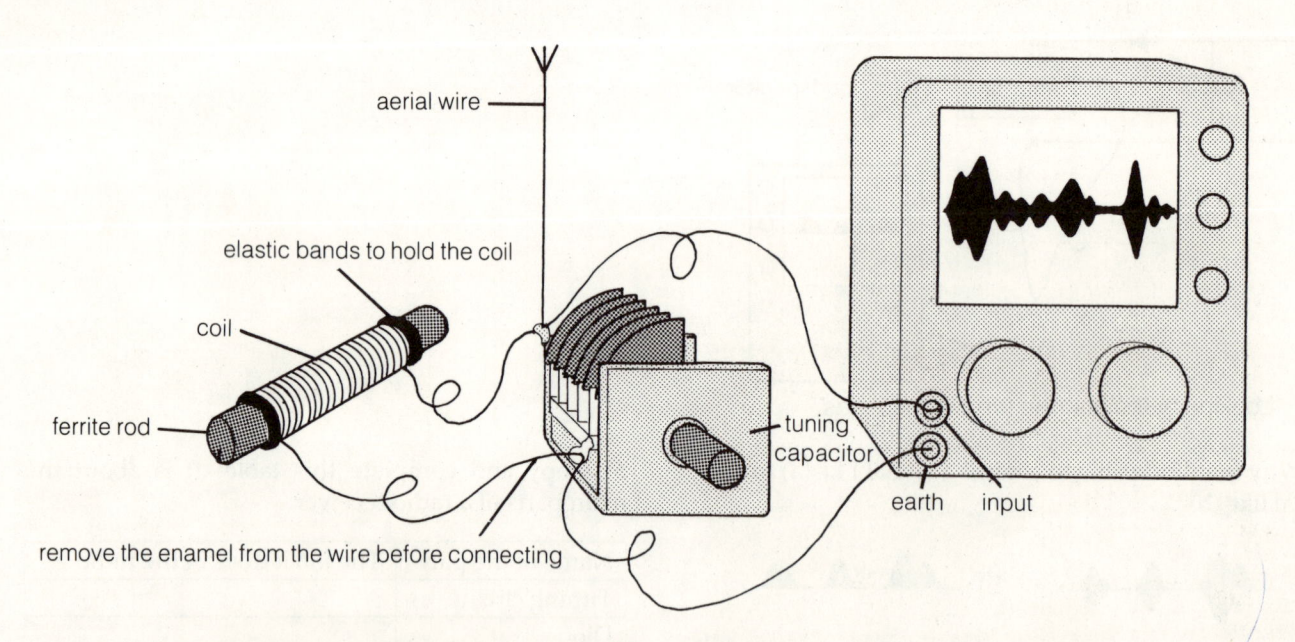

Connect an oscilloscope to this tuning circuit and carefully tune in a radio station. (You may need to connect a long aerial wire to the circuit to receive a strong enough signal.) Watch the oscilloscope picture and note the following:
(a) The top and bottom of the picture move as sound from the radio station changes.
(b) The top and bottom of the picture are the same shape.
(c) The picture on the screen grows bigger as the station is tuned in.
(d) The radio signal is very weak.

2 The tuning circuit produces a picture on the screen without a battery. Where does it get its energy from?

3 Describe the construction of a simple medium wave tuning circuit. What can this circuit do?

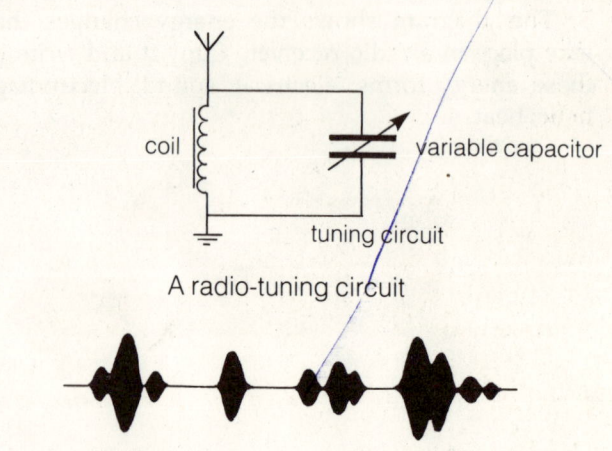

A radio-tuning circuit

An oscilloscope picture of a tuned-in radio signal

■ The first job of a radio receiver is to pick out just one radio wavelength from the many that fill the air.

235